MANAGING MARITIME RISK IN EARLY MODERN EUROPE

MANAGING MARITIME RISK IN EARLY MODERN EUROPE

GENERAL AVERAGE IN LAW AND PRACTICE IN SEVENTEENTH-CENTURY TUSCANY

Jake Dyble

THE BOYDELL PRESS

© Jake Dyble 2025

Some rights reserved. Without limiting the rights under copyright reserved above, any part of this book may be reproduced, stored in or introduced into a retrieval system, or transmitted, in any form or by any means (electronic, mechanical, photocopying, recording or otherwise)

The right of Jake Dyble to be identified as
the author of this work has been asserted in accordance with
sections 77 and 78 of the Copyright, Designs and Patents Act 1988

First published 2025
The Boydell Press, Woodbridge

ISBN 978 1 83765 155 9 (hardback)
ISBN 978 1 83765 282 2 (paperback)

This title is available under the Open Access licence CC BY-NC-ND
Jacob Arthur Dyble's work is funded by the European Union – NextGenerationEU and by the University of Padua under the 2023 STARS Grants@Unipd programme *AvCOL - Avania: Commerce, Orientalism, and Law in Early Modern Europe*

The Boydell Press is an imprint of Boydell & Brewer Ltd
PO Box 9, Woodbridge, Suffolk IP12 3DF, UK
and of Boydell & Brewer Inc.
668 Mt Hope Avenue, Rochester, NY 14620-2731, USA
website: www.boydellandbrewer.com

Our Authorised Representative for product safety in the EU is Easy Access System Europe – Mustamäe tee 50, 10621 Tallinn, Estonia, gpsr.requests@easproject.com

A CIP catalogue record for this book is available
from the British Library

The publisher has no responsibility for the continued existence or accuracy of URLs for external or third-party internet websites referred to in this book, and does not guarantee that any content on such websites is, or will remain, accurate or appropriate

The research for the book was conducted thanks to funding from the European Research Council (ERC) under the European Union's Horizon 2020 research and Innovation Programme ERC Grant agreement No. 724544: AveTransRisk-Average-Transaction Costs and Risk Management during the First Globalization (Sixteenth-Eighteenth Centuries)

For my parents

CONTENTS

Illustrations	viii
Acknowledgments	x
Abbreviations	xii
Note on Dates, Currencies, and Terminology	xiv
Introduction	1
1 The Free Port of Livorno and its Pisan Court	20
2 Defining Average in Early Modern Italy and Europe	45
3 Average in Practice: The Evidence from the Pisan Archive	77
4 Commercial Justice and Political Economy: Stephen Dring's Tale	120
5 How Early Modern Shipping Managed Risk	153
Conclusion	184
Appendix	193
Bibliography	199
Index	229

ILLUSTRATIONS

Figures

1. The relationship between the size of the case and expenses, 1600–1700 (arithmetic scale) — 115
2. The relationship between the size of the case and expenses, 1600–1700 (logarithmic scale) — 115
3. The relationship between the size of the case and expenses excluding the largest cases, 1600–1700 — 116
4. Breakdown of damages awarded in the case of the *Alice and Francis* (pieces of eight) — 133
5. Breakdown of the GA costs in the case of the *Cavallo Marino* — 175
6. A hypothetical partition of GA costs in the case of the *Cavallo Marino* with ship and freight contributing their full value — 176
7. The actual distribution of GA costs in the case of the *Cavallo Marino* following Tuscan customs — 177

Tables

1. Typology of maritime averages outlined in Carlo Targa's *Ponderationi sopra la contrattazione marittima* (1692) — 70
2. Typology of maritime averages outlined in Giuseppe Casaregi's *Discursus legales de commercio* (1707) — 76
3. Breakdown of expenses for two GAs in 1600 in Tuscan golden scudi — 113
4. Quaratesi and Beccuto's underwriting activity, 1671–8 (pieces of eight) — 165
5. Beccuto's underwriting activity, 1691–5 (pieces of eight) — 166

Cover Image

Extract from Pinturicchio, *Allegoria del Colle della Sapienza* (Allegory of the Hill of Wisdom) (1505), Siena Cathedral, Tuscany. The mosaic represents a group of pilgrims who have arrived at the 'hill of wisdom' by boat. Dominating this first part of the scene is the figure of *Fortuna*. The cornucopia she holds in one hand represents wealth, but she is deeply unstable, with her right foot resting on a sphere and her left in the ship with a broken mast. The sail in her other hand completes her association with that riskiest of environments: the sea. The mosaic is thus a near-contemporary representation of maritime risk: needless to say, the wisdom-seeking pilgrim is advised to leave such temptations behind. Reproduction authorised by the *Opera della Metropolitana Aut. N. 293/2024.*

ACKNOWLEDGMENTS

First of all, I would like to thank the residents of Europe, who have enabled this research to be carried out through their tax contributions. I hope that those of them who read this book will find it interesting, and that it will prove useful and illuminating to society as a whole in its own very modest way. I hope it will represent the first in a series of dividends rather than a final return on investment. The research for the book was conducted thanks to funding from the European Research Council (ERC) under the European Union's Horizon 2020 research and Innovation Programme ERC Grant agreement No. 724544: AveTransRisk-Average-Transaction Costs and Risk Management during the First Globalization (Sixteenth-Eighteenth Centuries), and funding from the European Union – NextGenerationEU and the University of Padua under the 2023 STARS Grants@Unipd programme (AvCOL - Avania: Commerce, Orientalism, and Law in Early Modern Europe).

I am in a position to carry out this work thanks to the efforts of many teachers and supervisors over the years. Paul Ponder, David Woodman, and William O' Reilly are just three of many I could mention. I would like to thank all the members of the ERC research project *AveTransRisk* for their comments and guidance during our workshops and conferences, especially Sabine Go and Guido Rossi for their advice, and Ian Wellaway for his patience and skill in constructing the *AveTransRisk* database. I would like to thank Gijs Dreijer, Lewis Wade, and Antonio Iodice for their solidarity, help, and comradeship, and all our friends in the Exeter Digital Humanities Lab for many conversations that had nothing to do with maritime law. I would also like to acknowledge the team behind the ERC project *MICOLL*, especially Stefania Gialdroni. Francesca Trivellato, Roberto Zaugg, Henry French, and Marcella Aglietti offered thought-provoking and helpful comments on earlier versions of this study, as did several anonymous reviewers. Above all, I would like to acknowledge Professor Maria Fusaro and Professor Andrea Addobbati for all their help and guidance.

It has been a pleasure to work with Peter Sowden, Henry Lafferty and the rest of the team at Boydell & Brewer. Thanks to Joshua Hey for careful copyediting, and to Frances Harty who proofread an earlier draft of the work. Thanks must also go to Massimo Sanacore, the director of the Pisan archive, Sara Caputo and Tom Drury for reading drafts and for continual encouragement, Martina Scattolin, my Italian teacher, and Alice Zanghi, my first Italian teacher. I would like to thank Mirela Balasoiu for her friendship. A big thank you goes to my sister, Lily; you are above average in every way.

My greatest debt of gratitude is owed to my parents – Karen Drury and Mark Dyble – to whom this work is dedicated.

ABBREVIATIONS

The documents pertaining to cases heard by the *Consoli del Mare di Pisa* (Consuls of the Sea in Pisa) are bound in numbered registers housed in the Pisan State Archive. Within each register, the cases are numbered and generally arranged in chronological order. Each case (except in the early part of the century when the registers are less well-organised) is bound within a title page, giving the names of the litigants and the date of the judgement. Some registers have a contemporary index, but there is no modern overarching index of cases, and I have included the date of the judgement in brackets when referencing each case in order that it might be securely identified.

All documents pertaining to the case were nested inside one another before being folded and bound into the register. In order to make reference to specific documents within a given case, I have appended a brief descriptive name of the document to each archival reference where appropriate.

The archival references thus follow the format: archive – archival series – subseries – register number – case number – (date of judgement) – name of document.

Abbreviations pertaining to archival references are as follows:

ASP, CM, AC	Archivio di Stato di Pisa, Consoli del Mare, Atti Civili
ASP, CM, S	Archivio di Stato di Pisa, Consoli del Mare, Suppliche
ASP, MM	Archivio di Stato di Pisa, Miscellanea di Manoscritti
ASF	Archivio di Stato di Firenze
ASF, MM	Archivio di Stato di Firenze, Miscellanea Medicea
TNA	The National Archives, UK

Other abbreviations used

cf.	*confronta* [compare]
D.	*Digest* of Justinian
ed./eds	editor/editors
edn	edition
f./ff.	folio/folios

GA	General Average
NIE	New Institutional Economics
p./pp.	page/pages
PA	Particular Average
r	*recto*
trans.	translated (by)
v	*verso*
vol./vols	volume/volumes
YAR	York-Antwerp Rules

NOTE ON DATES, CURRENCIES, AND TERMINOLOGY

Dates

Various calendars were in use in seventeenth-century Europe. Though the Gregorian calendar was used in Tuscany, the new year began on 25 March – three months after our own. This was the style known as *ab incarnatione* (from the incarnation). Only once did I encounter a date taken from the old Pisan calendar which began the new year on 25 March nine months before our own (thus making the Pisan calendar an entire year ahead of the Florentine). For the sake of clarity, all dates here have been given according to our modern calendar, that is the Gregorian calendar beginning on 1 January. The exception to this is dates in footnotes which refer to archival sources, where I have kept the date as it appears on the documentation itself in order that the sources can be securely identified. The sample years examined correspond to our modern calendar years i.e. January–December. I hope that the occasional discordance between the year given in the main text and the year shown in the footnote will not present a problem to the reader.

Currencies

The two principal currencies found in GA calculations in Tuscany are Tuscan golden *scudi*, which are generally used in calculations from the first half of the century, and silver pieces of eight (*pezze da otto reali*), which is the exclusive currency for GA calculations in the latter half of the century. 'Pieces of eight' was often shortened to 'pieces' (*pezze*). This latter coin was equivalent to the Spanish *real* or dollar and became widely used in international trade. Both the *scudo* and the *pezza* were subdivided into *soldi* (of which there were 20 to a piece) and *denari* (of which there were 12 to a *soldo*), thus analogous with the shillings and pence of the pre-decimal pound sterling. Prices are expressed in the sources using a colon to separate each unit of value, for instance, 57:2:9. In this work, however, I have used decimalised forms of each currency to lend clarity to tables and graphs. Each value is rounded to two decimal places.

Personal Names

There was no standardised spelling in the seventeenth century and certainly no one way to write personal names. The secretaries and notaries who wrote the vast majority of the documents examined here tended to 'translate' foreign names of both people and ships into Tuscan. Thomas Smith, for instance, becomes 'Tommaso Smit', while the ship *Alice and Francis* becomes *Alice Francesca*. Often the original can be guessed fairly securely, but not always. Giacomo Ardisson could plausibly have been translated from 'James Addison' or similar, but the source in fact records him as Genoese.

I have therefore stuck with the name given by the sources throughout, though I have made an exception for a single case – that of the aforementioned *Alice and Francis* – which is examined in considerable detail. Here, the ship's real name can be securely ascertained from various English sources. Where spelling varies, I use a single name for a single person: the variation is never so great that individual actors cannot be securely identified. I have opted for the version which appears most often in the sources or, failing that, the version which appears first in the plaintiff's libel, the *testimoniale e domanda*.

Titles and Roles

The terminology surrounding roles on board a ship is vexed because these terms were not used consistently by contemporaries. At the beginning of the seventeenth century, the word 'captain' and its cognates in other European languages were reserved for the commander of a military vessel, while a man in charge of a merchant vessel was known as a shipmaster. Over the course of the century, however, the commanders of large merchant vessels slowly became known as 'captains' in French and Dutch contexts. In Italy, the two words *capitano* and *padrone* roughly reflect this military and commercial division. In Venice, a captain was always a military commander, while *padron* was used for a man who was both the owner and master of the ship. In Genoa, *padrone* technically referred to the owner of vessel. In practice, the terms were used less precisely, and it's clear in both contexts that *padrone* could refer to the master *or* owner of the ship or someone who was both. More details on these divisions can be found in the table of roles compiled by the ERC project, *Sailing into Modernity*.[1]

In seventeenth-century Tuscany, as far as can be gleaned from the sources, the term *capitano* was used for military commanders, including the commanders of corsairing vessels. It was also clearly used for the commander of large commercial vessels. *Padroni* often owned a share of the vessel, as many of

---

[1] 'Sailing into Modernity: Table of Roles', <https://humanities.exeter.ac.uk/history/research/centres/maritime/resources/sailingintomodernity/roles> [1 February 2024].

the sources make clear, but it is impossible to be sure that this was always the case. For both *capitano* and *padrone*, therefore, I have used 'shipmaster' or 'master' if the man was commanding a commercial vessel, only using 'captain' when the man was clearly in charge of a military or corsairing vessel.

Place Names

With regards to places, I have always adopted that name which will be most familiar to a non-specialist Anglophone reader. I have thus used the common English names of major Italian cities (Venice, Naples, Florence, and so on) rather than their Italian names, as well as names such as Aleppo for the Syrian city of Halep. I have used Izmir rather than Smyrna for the same reason. I have used Livorno rather than Leghorn: certain older names are no longer as familiar to the generalist Anglophone reader.

Translation

The early modern English legal system was not the exclusive domain of the English common law. Several important courts – principally the ecclesiastical courts and the High Court of the Admiralty – used civil law procedures. There is therefore an existing vocabulary of technical terms available to translate much of the terminology employed by the court of the *Consoli del Mare*.[2] However, I have used the common law term 'attorney' instead of 'proctor' to translate *procuratore*, as this term is far better known.

One recurring term is *consolato*: this was the report submitted by a shipmaster after an accident to a recognised authority – often a consul, hence the name – which could then be presented as evidence in a court of law. In Pisan GA cases there also existed the *testimoniale e domanda*, which was the original complaint (libel) lodged before the *Consoli del Mare di Pisa* by a master who wished to declare GA. These documents integrate the report in the *consolato* (occasionally with some modification) with an official request for the declaration of Average, and the name reflects this dual function. In English, the *consolati* were known as 'sea protests', and I have sometimes used this term to refer to these narrative documents generally. This is explained more fully in the main text.[3] Finally, since 'sentence' in English means the punishment assigned to a defendant who is found guilty of a crime, I have rendered the *sentenza* pronounced by the *Consoli* as 'judgement' throughout.

---

[2] See also the glossary for the High Court of the Admiralty on the website of The National Archives: 'Research Guide: The High Court of the Admiralty', <www.nationalarchives.gov.uk/help-with-your-research/research-guides/high-court-admiralty-records/> [2 Feburary 2024].

[3] p. 80.

I have kept the names of magistracies in their original Tuscan. This is to avoid a proliferation of different translations being adopted in Anglophone scholarship on Tuscany. I have referred to the *Consoli del Mare di Pisa* (Consuls of the Sea in Pisa) as *Consoli* rather than consuls, both to distinguish them from the many 'national' consuls resident in port cities (representatives of national states and/or foreign merchant communities, depending on the place and time) and to avoid confusion with the Catalan collection of maritime customs known as the *Llibre del Consolat de Mar* (*Libro del Consolato del Mare* in Italian) and the aforementioned '*consolati*'. I have capitalised the adjective 'Consular' when referring to the *Consoli del Mare*.

Livorno was home to a significant number of foreign merchants who were often members of officially recognised ethno-religious communities which had been given special status by the Tuscan authorities: the *nazioni* or 'nations'. A not dissimilar practice was employed in other port cities, as well as in universities. In a university context, the Latin term *nationes* was used. For maximum clarity, I will adopt the Latin term *natio* when referring to these formally recognised communities. The English word 'nation' is admittedly unlikely to trouble a specialist, but the use of a separate term avoids any hint of confusion with the modern sense of the term.

All translations are my own unless otherwise stated.

The Language of Average

Averages represent a technical and rather arcane branch of maritime law which even many modern maritime lawyers view with trepidation. Today, Averages are dealt with by specialist 'Average adjusters', who serve a long apprenticeship and must pass a series of examinations before they are recognised as associates or fellows of the Association of Average Adjusters. I here provide a short explanation of the language used to talk about Averages.

Once it had been decided that an incident had taken place which warranted the use of an Average procedure, an Average was 'declared'. For heuristic reasons, I sometimes refer to a shipmaster 'declaring' Average on his arrival in port, but a shipmaster could not do this unilaterally. This was done in conjunction with the receiving merchants or by a recognised authority with jurisdiction over Average. With a Particular Average (PA), the 'declaration' could be as simple as recognising that the shipmaster was not responsible for the damage in question and that the owner of the affected property had to bear the cost; with a General Average (GA), this meant recognising that the damages had to be made good by all interested parties. 'Adjustment' refers to the process through which it was decided which Average was appropriate, which damages were eligible for the Average, establishing who needed to contribute, and how much they owed.

For a GA, a 'contribution rate' had to be determined: this was the percentage of the total overall value of the venture which had been lost, and thus the rate at which each interested party had to contribute to make good the loss. For example, if a jettison of cargo had been made worth 5 per cent of the overall value of the voyage, then all interested parties had to contribute 5 per cent of the value of their investment. This contribution rate was arrived at by means of a simple division: those damages which were deemed eligible for GA were divided by the total value of the voyage minus the value of any property which was not deemed eligible to contribute. The question of which things should be deemed eligible has been central to almost all disagreement surrounding GA. The eligible damages in a GA are sometimes referred to as the 'active mass'; the sum decided upon as the eligible value of the voyage is referred to as the 'passive mass'.[4] The contribution rate is thus the active mass divided by the passive mass, usually expressed as a percentage. Property included in the passive mass is said to 'contribute' to the GA. Both inanimate property, and the owners of that property, can be said to 'contribute' to an Average.

Finally, I have capitalised the words General Average and Average throughout where the words refer to a maritime Average. When referring to a mathematical average, I have used lower case.

---

[4] This is following the usage of Giuseppe Felloni, who noted the potential of GA as a source of historical economic data in the 1970s. See Giuseppe Felloni, 'Una fonte inesplorata per la storia dell'economia marittima in età moderna', *Atti della Società Ligure di Storia Patria, nuova serie* 38 (1998), 843–60.

They that go down to the sea in ships,
that do business in great waters;
These see the works of the Lord,
and his wonders in the deep.

Psalm 107:23–4
(King James Version)

Introduction

It is no coincidence that the word 'risk' emerged from the world of maritime trade.[1] Few activities regularly undertaken by human beings are more unpredictable or dangerous than seafaring. We might assume that the sea has been tamed – that the great boats of today really plough the waves with the same calm indomitability with which an ox ploughs a field. In reality, commercial seafaring is still considered the second-most dangerous profession in the world and deep-sea fishing the first.[2] In past ages the peril was exponentially greater. Despite such concerns, life and limb have generally been ventured fairly freely in the pursuit of wealth from across the sea (not that those venturing have always had much say in their choice of occupation). But those risks that pertain to bodies also pertain to cargoes and to ships, to capital sunk into rigging, sails, and commodities. These latter are subject to further uncertainties: to the vagaries of price and persons hundreds of miles away. Few have the appetite for that sort of wager. It is thus not surprising that the maritime sector spawned many of the institutions and practices that manage risk – institutions which still undergird and shape the global economy today.

Risk management is a crucial element in the success of a maritime economy, and it has attracted a great deal of attention from economic historians looking to explain why the European maritime sector was quite so successful in the early modern period. Premium insurance is unsurprisingly seen as a key innovation in this respect. Invented in late medieval Italy, the institution whereby risk was transferred to third parties in exchange for the payment of a premium gradually spread to other parts of Europe.[3] Historians who have examined insurance, however, have been at pains to point out that early

---

[1] Andrea Addobbati, *Commercio, rischio, guerra: il mercato delle assicurazioni marittime di Livorno, 1694–1795* (Rome: Edizioni di storia e letteratura, 2007), pp. 7–8.

[2] Rose George, 'Worse things still happen at sea: the shipping disasters we never hear about', *The Guardian* (10 January 2015) <www.theguardian.com/world/2015/jan/10/shipping-disasters-we-never-hear-about> [accessed 2 Februrary 2024]. See also Rose George, *Deep Sea and Foreign Going* (London: Portobello Books, 2013), pp. 20–1.

[3] Luisa Piccinno, 'Genoa, 1340–1620: early development of marine insurance', in Adrian Leonard (ed.), *Marine Insurance: Origins and Institutions, 1300–1850* (Basingstoke: Palgrave Macmillan, 2016), 24–45.

modern underwriters certainly did not avail themselves of modern statistical methods as is sometimes assumed.[4] It is a key argument of this book, moreover, that other neglected risk-management institutions – considered 'archaic' in the economic literature if indeed they are considered at all – continued to be widely used even after the advent of premium insurance, and structured the European maritime economy in important ways. The 'modern' institutions are not so modern, nor the 'archaic' institutions so static as has been supposed. The linear narratives of change and modernisation that economic historians have tended to write are called into question by the continued use and developments of these techniques.

The 'archaic' institution that is the chief protagonist of this book is the institution now known as General Average – GA for short. While premium insurance is a risk-shifting device that transfers risk to a non-participant in the venture, GA is a risk-sharing one that distributes risk amongst those who already have a stake in the outcome in accordance with the size of their investment. Its underlying principle (at least as it exists today) can be expressed succinctly in the following axiom: 'That which has been sacrificed for the benefit of all shall be made good by the contribution of all'.[5] GA is 'declared' when some part of the ship or cargo has been reasonably sacrificed in order that the remainder of the ship or cargo might be saved from peril.[6] Every party with a financial interest in the voyage is then called upon to contribute to this extraordinary expense in proportion to their original investment. If the sacrifice represented 20 per cent of the total value of the maritime venture, for instance, then each stakeholder shall be deemed liable to bear a loss amounting to 20 per cent of the value of their investment, with those whose property has survived reimbursing those whose property has been lost. The underlying principle is thus one of beautiful – and deceptive – simplicity. The classic example of a GA event is a jettison. To avoid sinking, a shipmaster orders some of the cargo to be thrown overboard to lighten the ship, thus saving the ship and the remainder of the goods. In this circumstance, it would be unfair if the owner of those goods bore the cost of the jettison since everyone else benefitted from their sacrifice.

The heart of the procedure might thus be considered ethical. A sacrifice – individual loss, made consciously to save the property of another – demands reciprocation. On a ship the force of these moral obligations is starkly evident.

---

[4] See the collection of essays in Adrian Leonard (ed.), *Marine Insurance: Origins and Institutions, 1300–1850* (Basingstoke: Palgrave Macmillan, 2016).

[5] Richard Cornah, *A Guide to General Average* (London: Richards Hogg Ltd, 1994), p. 6. The definitive modern-day practioner text (or 'GA Bible') is Richard Cornah, John Reeder, Richard Lowndes, and George R. Rudolf, *Lowndes and Rudolf: The Law of General Average and the York-Antwerp Rules* (London: Sweet & Maxwell, 2013).

[6] 'York-Antwerp Rules' (2016), <https://comitemaritime.org/work/york-antwerp-rules-yar/> [accessed 18 August 2021], Rule A.

The ship is the ultimate common enterprise. It is no coincidence the 'ship of state' should be one of the oldest and most enduring metaphors for the polis, a community of reciprocal rights and obligations that stands or falls together.[7] Even more than the walls of a city, the hull of a ship creates a collective. The heart of the procedure is moral, then, but there are utilitarian benefits as well. Firstly, GA rules ensure right action in a crisis. If it is known beforehand that such sacrificial losses can be shared, potentially fatal delays resulting from self-interested reluctance are avoided. At the same time, GA provides players with a form of mutual insurance. If the GA principle is established, at least some of the losses associated with maritime transport are shared between stakeholders, blunting the financial impact of maritime disasters on any single interested party. The larger the number of situations to which GA can be applied, the wider the remit of this insurance. Finally, as will be shown, GA produced and to some extent continues to produce unexpected benefits for a certain interested party – ship-owners – especially in the domain of cost management. The archival evidence on GA also highlights the extent to which other 'archaic' instruments remained crucial, including the sea loan, an arrangement whereby a merchant would provide a shipmaster with cash up front to finance the voyage or pay an expense and would thus take some of the sea risk upon himself.[8] In examining GA and other 'archaic' instruments such as sea loan, sometimes used in tandem with premium insurance and sometimes in its stead, this book sheds light on the broader risk-management strategies of early modern merchants and ship-owners, for whom premium insurance was just one weapon in the arsenal.

GA's neglect at the hands of both economic and legal historians is in part due to contemporary factors. Premium insurance has spread to almost all domains of business activity and is thus highly visible, whilst GA remains quietly at work only in the maritime sector. Modern GA, moreover, can by its very nature only cover partial losses – since a total loss of ship and cargo would leave no surviving property to make good the loss – and, of those partial losses, it can only share those made deliberately for the common benefit. GA viewed from the vantage point of our own time thus appears the archytype of a niche instrument, playing its small part in the vast machine of global shipping, no doubt, but not in a way that should merit any attention from

---

[7] Norma Thompson, *The Ship of State: Statecraft and Politics from Ancient Greece to Democratic America* (New Haven & London: Yale University Press, 2001), pp. 167–74.

[8] Raymond De Roover, 'The organization of trade', in M.M. Postan, E.E. Rich, and Edward Miller (eds), *The Cambridge History of Europe, Volume III: Economic Organization and Policies in the Middles Ages* (Cambridge: Cambridge University Press, 1963), 52–9; Andrea Zanini, 'Financing and risk in Genoese maritime trade during the eighteenth century: strategies and practices', in Maria Fusaro, Andrea Addobbati, and Luisa Piccinno (eds), *General Average and Risk Management in Medieval and Early Modern Maritime Business* (Cham: Springer, 2023), 335–59.

non-specialists. Most of all, its neglect is due to two misconceptions: firstly, that GA is an ancient and 'archaic' instrument, and secondly, that it was fundamentally uniform across time and space.

In the scholarly world, these misconceptions have been fed by two powerful grand narratives in legal and economic history respectively. On the legal side, GA has been cited as evidence of the medieval lex mercatoria (or its subset, the lex maritima) – the supposedly universal customs of the sea that applied everywhere before the early modern national state began meddling in their operation. GA, ancient and apparently ubiquitous, seems to provide much-needed evidence of the existence of such a body of law, which tends to be dismissed by archival historians but continues to find favour among certain legal theorists.[9] The assumption that GA was essentially unchanging has had the effect of depressing any further interest in its operation and development. Even non-legal historians completely uninterested in the theories of the 'mercatorists' have similarly invoked GA and its uniformity as evidence of a common commercial culture that united the Mediterranean. In *The Donkey and the Boat*, for example, a highly comprehensive and erudite reassessment of the medieval 'commercial revolution', Chris Wickham leans heavily on GA's supposed fundamental uniformity as evidence of a 'common culture' that transcended traders' regional origins.[10]

In economic history, GA's 'archaic' status is reinforced by historians who stress the role of institutions in economic development. These accounts tend to give consideration to older risk-management practices only to the extent that they supposedly prefigured more 'sophisticated' modern technologies. In some popular histories, serious risk management only begins when Lloyd's Coffee House emerges as a marine insurance centre in eighteenth-century London.[11] Most scholarly accounts do give consideration to earlier techniques but tend to view these as 'proto' instruments. Of particular interest here is the work of New Institutional Economics (NIE) and particularly Douglass North's 'evolutionary story of risk', updated and rearticulated in several more recent works.[12] This can be crudely summarised as a modernity narrative, whereby older institutions – 'community'-based, relatively simple, widely diffused throughout most of the globe – were replaced by modern, impersonal institutions perfected in North-Western Europe, which drew on but then superceded

---

[9] See Orsolya Toth, *The Lex Mercatoria in Theory and Practice* (Oxford: Oxford University Press, 2017), pp. 6–30.

[10] Chris Wickham, *The Donkey and the Boat: Reinterpreting the Mediterranean Economy, 950–1180* (Oxford: Oxford University Press, 2023), p. 648.

[11] Peter L. Bernstein, *Against the Gods: The Remarkable Story of Risk* (New York: John Wiley & Sons, 1996), pp. 18–19, 58–60.

[12] Douglass North, *Institutions, Institutional Change, and Economic Performance* (Cambridge: Cambridge University Press, 1990), p. 127.

these older practices. GA in this conception is the amoeba – an instrument with a self-evident quality that legislates against its being given any further consideration: much better, and certainly more eye-catching, to study the innovations that supposedly made the difference. GA certainly has a long pedigree: if it can indeed be traced back to the ninth-century BC Rhodian laws of jettison, as Justinian's *Digest* suggests, then it is a practice with an almost 3,000-year continuous history.[13] It is certainly not the case, however, that ideas and practices about risk sharing remained fixed.[14] This stadial account of institutional development is curiously mirrored in a contemporary debate among maritime industry professionals, a small number of whom have launched strident criticisms of GA on the basis that it is a costly anachronism maintained only thanks to inertia and vested interests.[15] These contemporary considerations will be reflected upon further in the conclusion to this book.

The evidence presented here shows how GA was a more capacious instrument than even contemporary normative sources lead us to believe. The archetypal GA situation may be one of imminent peril in which ship and cargo are 'saved', but it can in fact be argued that any extraordinary expense made to bring ship and cargo safely to their destination performs a similar 'saving' function, even in a situation that is not obviously perilous. In other words, the 'common safety' interpretation of GA – with eligible expenses restricted to those made to directly remove the ship and cargo from peril – has usually been broadened to a 'common benefit' interpretation, admitting all expenses required to see the ship safely resume its journey.[16] This remains a point of potential controversy in modern-day GA cases.[17] Early modern Tuscan GA fully subscribed to the latter logic, at least in operational practice, as indeed has been the case for most of GA's history. Whereas the 'unit' of the GA as it existed in Roman law was the ship, in early modern GA it was the voyage which needed to be saved. The effect of this dynamic is that GA was – and arguably still is – a shipmasters' and ship-owners' instrument, notwithstanding the fact that the archetype of the GA is the jettison of cargo. GA was a tool for recouping extraordinary expenses, and, as we will see, some ordinary ones as well. GA was therefore a key tool for the early modern transport sector – a somewhat neglected element in most historical considerations of maritime institutions, in which the protagonist is invariably the merchant.

---

[13] D.14.2; Alan Watson, *The Digest of Justinian*, 4 vols (Philadelphia: University of Pennsylvania Press, 2011), vol. 2, pp. 419–22.

[14] Proshanto Mukherjee, 'The anachronism in maritime law that is general average', *WMU Journal of Maritime Affairs* 4 (2005), 195–209, at p. 195.

[15] Mukherjee, 'The anachronism in maritime law'.

[16] Cornah, *A Guide*, p. 8.

[17] Xie Ming, 'Legality, rationality of general average for MV Ever Given' (2022), <https://law.asia/legality-and-rationality-mv-ever-given/> [accessed 10 Aug. 2023].

Furthermore, this study demonstrates that GA practices varied not only across jurisdictions but also across time. Even the principles that lay behind it were not universally agreed upon. To write a history of 'GA' remains something of an anachronistic exercise until the sixteenth century, and arguably right up to the close of this study in the early eighteenth century, for there was still no agreement among theorists as to what GA actually was. The practices that we might with hindsight heuristically identify as 'GA' varied depending on time, place, economic conditions, the economic and political power balance between 'ship' and 'cargo' interests, the business arrangements that bound the different players involved, and the development and use of other risk-management tools. Rather than being a simple proto-institution that birthed modern premium insurance, GA continued to change and adapt alongside newer instruments, whilst remaining a useful tool in a domain that is still not just relatively dangerous but fundamentally unpredictable. This raises an epistemological challenge that both New Instutional economists and proponents of the lex mercatoria ignore: whether to group similar but diverse practices under the rubric of a single, stable 'institution'.

The Evolutionary Story of Risk

The 'evolutionary story of risk' is rooted in the 'New Institutional Economics' (NIE) approach that has enjoyed considerable success in the last 50 years. NIE has successfully convinced many – as evidenced by receipt of several Nobel prizes[18] – that cultural, social, and political institutions, collectively constituting the so-called 'rules of the game', are at least as important as factor endowments, the environment, and technology in pointing whole societies towards growth or stagnation. This reintegration of institutions into the writing of economic history was originally championed by Douglass North in the 1970s.[19] North was dissatisfied with the approach of the dominant neo-classical school, which he felt lacked historical awareness and was unable to explain change over time, that is, to explain economic divergence between one place and another. American economists, moreover, were becoming more aware of the importance of non-market organisation in the economy thanks to their discovery of the work of British economist Ronald Coase.[20] Coase pointed out that even free-market economies did not leave coordination decisions

---

[18] E.g. Ronald Coase in 1991, Douglass North in 1993, and Oliver Williams and Elinor Ostrom in 2009.

[19] Douglass North, 'Beyond the New Economic History', *Journal of Economic History* 34 (1974), 1–7.

[20] Claude Ménard and Mary Shirley, 'The contribution of Douglass North to new institutional economics' in Sebastian Galiani and Itai Sened (eds), *Institutions, Property Rights, and Economic Growth* (Cambridge: Cambridge University Press, 2014), 11–29, at p. 15.

entirely to the market but engaged in economic planning by means of a range of different structures – not least through the ubiquitous firm.[21]

Institutions here were conceived of broadly. They were no less than the 'rights associated with the use and transfer of resources', which were as present and relevant in socialist economies as capitalist ones.[22] Or, as North put it elsewhere, institutions were the 'humanly-devised constraints', both formal and informal, that structure exchange, determine production and transaction costs, and provide the incentive structure in an economy.[23] Social and political rules (or their absence) determined who could transact and in what way, what people hoped to achieve by transactions, and what they could expect from other parties. This could point whole societies towards productive or unproductive behaviours in the long term. On the basis of this observation, North suggested that economic historians should focus more on the non-market phenomena that were involved in economic decision making and resource allocation: the household, voluntary organisations, the state, the firm.[24] Following Coase, he also encouraged a focus on transction costs in order to explain economic change. These were the costs not directly associated with production, labour, and transportation, but with the process of 'ordering exchange'.[25]

North's ideas went further than simply proposing a new methodological framework, however. Indeed, the very importance he attached to this framework came from his notions about the origins of global growth and the divergence between the West and the rest. North's argument was that Europe and its North American colonies had experienced higher levels of growth thanks to the development of a number of institutions that had ensured their economic divergence from the rest of the world by enabling greater capital mobility, information exchange, and risk sharing.[26] In this respect, North singled out constitutional structures and impersonal legal systems which safeguarded property rights on the one hand, and the invention of joint-stock companies and premium insurance allowing for the management of risk on the other.[27] In fact, premium insurance arguably fulfilled all three of North's growth-enhancing functions, not only managing risk, but encouraging both information sharing, in the form of circulars such as Lloyd's list, and increasing the mobility of capital by reducing the amount that need be stockpiled to cover unfortunate

---

[21] Ronald Coase, 'The nature of the firm', *Economica* 4 (1937), 386–405.

[22] North, 'Beyond the New Economic History', p. 3.

[23] Douglass North, 'Institutions', *Journal of Economic Perspectives* 5 (1991), 97–112, at p. 98.

[24] North, 'Beyond the New Economic History', pp. 4–5.

[25] North, *Institutions*, pp. 97–8.

[26] North, *Institutions*, p. 105; Douglass North and Robert Thomas, *The Rise of the Western World: A New Economic History* (Cambridge: Cambridge University Press, 1973), p. 3.

[27] North, *Institutions*, pp. 100–6.

eventualities.[28] Convinced of the importance of such developments, North encouraged economic historians to concentrate less on the nineteenth and twentieth centuries and instead give greater attention to the centuries immediately preceding the industrial revolution, when these undergirding institutions had first emerged.

North's understanding of these institutions was presented through the prism of the 'evolutionary story of the institutionalisation of risk', which stretched 'from the *commenda* ... through its evolution at the hands of Italians, to the English joint-stock company'.[29] This was a stadial theory of institutional evolution which posits that the maritime economies of Europe were transformed by a successive series of innovations. Though applied most conspicuously to the evolution of the partnership/company, it is taken to pertain more generally to all risk-sharing institutions. Medieval Italian merchants in this conception provided the prototypes which were then perfected in the Netherlands and England. This story has recently received a sophisticated and wide-ranging rearticulation in Ron Harris's book, *Going the Distance*, which attempts a global study of institutional development.[30] Harris proposes a tripartite schema: 'endogenous' institutions are similar institutions that emerge locally and independently to tackle similar problems; 'migratory' institutions are those which emerge in one or perhaps two places and are then transplanted as new players are exposed to them and realise their efficacy; and 'embedded' institutions are complex endogenous institutions that are unable to easily migrate because they depend upon a particular institutional matrix in order to flourish. The book argues for the joint-stock company as the ultimate embedded institution, conceived of and nurtured in a social and political matrix specific to England and the Netherlands.

Yet though Harris's study is much more sophisticated and historically aware than much of the early NIE work, it still effectively posits the same basic narrative: simple institutions everywhere (such as GA), then moderately sophisticated instruments emerging in Italy becoming somewhat diffused, and these providing the foundation for highly sophisticated instruments in Northern Europe. It is of course undeniable that somewhere along the line, the institutional landscape changed and that we now have better systems for managing

---

[28] Adrian Leonard, 'Introduction: the nature and study of marine insurance' in Adrian Leonard (ed.), *Marine Insurance: Origins and Institutions, 1300–1850* (Basingstoke: Palgrave Macmillan, 2016), 2–22, at p. 10.

[29] Francesca Trivellato, 'Renaissance Florence and the origins of capitalism: a business history perspective', *Business History Review* 94 (2020), 229–51, at p. 243; North, *Institutions*, p. 127. Robert Fredona and Sophus Reinert, 'Italy and the origins of capitalism', *Business History Review* 94 (2020), 5–38.

[30] Ron Harris, *Going the Distance: Eurasian Trade and the Rise of the Business Corporation, 1400–1700* (Princeton: Princeton University Press, 2020).

risk than we did before. The problem, as Francesca Trivellato points out, is that NIE tends to assume its history from the theoretical predicates rather than the other way around.[31] The argument runs backward: already convinced *a priori* of the importance of institutions by the theory, and considering the success of the maritime economies of North-Western Europe in the early modern period, it is then concluded that that success was rooted institutional development, which is taken to justify the theoretical predicate. Moreover, despite using the language of 'evolution', which in biological terms suggests gradual and even imperceptible change, NIE tends to see the different institutional solutions for risk management as very discrete and well-defined entities and posits something more akin to a series of mini institutional-revolutions putting certain socities on the path to growth.

Harris has in fact directly applied this historical NIE schema to GA, explicitly taking a theory-led approach to historical change.[32] Here he draws on Frank Knight's distinction between risk (calculable and hence priceable) and uncertainty (unquantifiable and unknowable).[33] Harris argues that transition from one economic reality to another is in fact characterised by the transition from GA to premium insurance. GA as an 'ex-post' solution belonged not to a world of 'risk' but one of 'uncertainty' – unknown unknowns. The advent of premium insurance supposedly followed an increase in predictability in the global economy, which in turn allowed risk to be successfully priced and sold to a third party.[34] GA and premium insurance thus belong to different economic environments, one of primitive unknowing, the other of predictable risks.

Such a view seems to take it for granted that the survival of GA until our own times is an anachronism. Yet even modern-day merchants do not always make use of our supposed ability to calculate risk. In 2021, the 224,000-tonne ship *Ever Given* made headlines when it became stuck in the Suez Canal, blocking global shipping traffic. This event would occasion a GA claim reportedly worth around half-a-billion dollars, mostly for fees levied by the Suez Canal Authority. As industry magazine *The Marine Insurer* reported with consternation, it is likely that as much as a quarter of the cargo was not insured at all, while much of the remainder would have been under-insured.

---

[31] Francesca Trivellato, *The Familiarity of Strangers: The Sephardic Diaspora, Livorno, and Cross-Cultural Trade in the Early-Modern Period* (New Haven: Yale University Press, 2009), p. 15.

[32] Ron Harris, 'General Average and all the rest: the law and economics of early modern maritime risk mitigation', in Maria Fusaro, Andrea Addobbati, and Luisa Piccinno (eds), *General Average and Risk Management in Medieval and Early Modern Maritime Business* (Cham: Springer, 2023), 33–60.

[33] Frank Knight, *Risk, Uncertainty and Profit* (Boston and New York: Houghton Mifflin, 1921), p. 17.

[34] Harris, 'General Average and all the rest', p. 59.

Its (very many) owners were thus made directly liable for the payment of the GA contribution.[35] The magazine noted that a lack of insurance remains a 'persistent problem' in the industry, estimating that 80 to 90 per cent of containers lack adequate coverage.[36] An archaic instrument was thus called into action, whilst its sophisticated contemporary descendent was, for some unfortunate merchants, conspicuously absent.

Without denying that the development of premium insurance was a process of considerable historical importance, this study argues that there is little axiomatically 'modern' about risk shifting and nothing inherently 'archaic' in risk sharing. Indeed, the difference between them was not starkly evident in early modern trade, where merchants would often act as both underwriters and buyers of insurance, and premium insurance would not necessarily shift risk far outside of the merchant community.[37] Merchants did not transition to exclusive use of premium insurance after it had been 'invented'. Instead, they used it alongside existing instruments like GA and sea loan to create a very wide dispersal of risk. Each risk-management tool, moreover, responded to different exigencies. While cargo owners often used premium insurance by the end of our period, ships were rarely insured. Shipmasters and ship-owners instead found that sea loan and GA responded better to their particular demands. The continued importance of P&I clubs in the maritime world today (another understudied phenomenon from a historical perspective) is continued testament to the fact that risk sharing and collective mitigation have an important part to play in an environment in which Knightian 'uncertainty' has never really gone away.[38]

Lex Mercatoria and the Autonomy of Merchant Law

Legal scholars likewise have generally considered GA to be an uncomplicated procedure with an equally straightforward history.[39] Here, they may have been beguiled not only by the simplicity of the animating principle,

---

[35] Richard Sarll, 'The "Ever Given": not your average dispute', *The Marine Insurer* 7 (2021), 8–9.

[36] Johnny McCord, 'The Ever Given: one gut punch after another', *The Marine Insurer* 6 (2021), 48–9.

[37] Addobbati, *Commercio, rischio, guerra*, p. 10.

[38] Helen Doe and Robin Pearson, 'Organizational choice in UK marine insurance', in Robin Pearson and Takau Yoneyama(eds), *Corporate Forms and Organizational Choice in International Insurance* (Oxford: Oxford University Press, 2015), 47–67, at pp. 60–5.

[39] William Tetley, 'The general maritime law: the lex maritima (with brief reference to the *ius commune*) in arbitration law and the conflict of laws', *Syracuse Journal of International Law and Commerce* 20 (1994), 105–45, at pp. 105, 128–9.

but also by assumptions about the immutability of merchant custom under the influence of the aforementioned lex mercatoria. This is the highly influential concept propagated by some contemporary legal scholars that medieval Europe, or perhaps an even wider area, once shared a body of universal customary merchant law administered without the help or interference of the state.[40] This notion has been variously defined but is usually discussed in very vague and general terms: the legal scholar, Nikitas Hatzimihail, compares the lex mercatoria to the proverbial *Arlésienne*: everyone talks about her, but we never actually get to see her in person.[41] One influential articulation of the idea can be drawn from the work of Clive Schmitthoff, who, along with Berthold Goldman, helped to resurrect interest in the lex mercatoria in the early 1960s.[42] Schmitthoff claims that 'international commercial law ... arose in the Middle Ages in the form of the law merchant, a body of truly international customary rules governing the cosmopolitan community of international merchants who travelled through the civilized world from port to port and fair to fair'.[43] This medieval law merchant 'owed its international character mainly to four factors: the unifying effect of the law of the fairs, the universality of the customs of the sea, the special courts dealing with commercial disputes, and the activities of the notary public'.[44]

Whatever its vagaries, the lex mercatoria idea has powerful contemporary resonances, since it has been used to argue for a 'return' to private ordering in global trade, sometimes called the 'new' lex mercatoria.[45] The

---

[40] See Toth, *The Lex Mercatoria*, pp. 6–30 for the state of the art regarding the new lex mercatoria debate.

[41] Nikitas Hatzimihail, 'The many lives – and faces – of lex mercatoria: history as genealogy in international business law', *Law and Contemporary Problems* 71 (2008), 169–90, at p. 169. Hatzimihail explains that the French expression *L'Arlésienne* refers to someone about whom there is much talk but who never shows her face. The phrase originates from an 1872 play by Alphonse Doudet about the doomed love of a young man for a girl from Arles who never appears on the stage.

[42] Hatzimihail, 'The many lives – and faces', pp. 175–88; Stefania Gialdroni, 'Gerard Malynes e la questione della lex mercatoria', *Zeitschrift der Savigny-Stiftund für Rechtsgeschichte* 126 (2009), 38–69, at pp. 38–9.

[43] Clive Schmitthoff, 'The law of international trade, its growth, formulation and operation', in Clive Schmitthoff (ed.), *The Sources of the Law of International Trade* (London: Stevens & Sons, 1964), pp. 105–6.

[44] Schmitthoff, 'The law of international trade', p. 106.

[45] Bruce Benson, *The Enterprise of Law: Justice without the State*, 2nd edn (Oakland: Independent Institute, 2011), pp. 30–6; Leon Trakman, 'From the lex mercatoria to e-merchant law', *The University of Toronto Law Journal* 53 (2003), 265–304, at pp. 265, 269, 275–6; Ana Lopez Rodriguez, *Lex Mercatoria and Harmonisation of Contract Law in the EU* (Copenhagen: DJOF Publishing, 2003). This is a small fraction of the works which adhere to the notion of a historical *lex mercatoria*. See

increasing involvement of states in maritime law across the early modern period is generally seen by mercatorists as a negative development. While some theorists, such as Schmitthoff, saw the lex mercatoria's absorption into national state law as a fairly unproblematic process which did not change its fundamental character, others, led by Goldman, saw the takeover of state law as bowdlerisation.[46] Some jurists impressed by this latter vision have then used the lex mercatoria as part of a wider argument to the effect that non-state actors have, when allowed to thrive, provided more efficacious solutions to the problem of 'justice'. Here the medieval lex mercatoria represents, it is claimed, the 'best example of what a system of customary law can achieve'.[47] Similar claims are made regarding a lex maritima, a universal maritime law which is sometimes presented as a subset of the lex mercatoria.[48] These scholars present a private ordering as the natural solution for mercantile justice, a commercial Garden of Eden since disordered by the baleful interference of states.

GA has been cited by the supporters of the lex mercatoria idea – so-called 'mercatorists' – as evidence for these claims, especially with regard to Schmithoff's second pillar, the 'universality of the customs of the sea'. GA, with its ancient antecedents, and commonly practised across European jurisdictions, would seem at first glance the perfect example of the lex maritima.[49] The earliest expression of the law of GA is usually taken to be the *Lex Rhodia de Iactu* (the Rhodian Law of Jettison) collected in Justinian's *Digest*, and which thus forms part of the *Corpus Iuris Civilis* – the authorative texts at the centre of the *ius commune*, that is the system of civil and canon law which formed the substratum of all legal regimes in continental Europe in the medieval and early modern periods.[50] This was the 'learned' law that was

---

the bibliography in Emily Kadens, 'The myth of the customary law merchant', *Texas Law Review* 90 (2012), 1153–206, at pp. 1153–4.

[46] Hatzimihail, 'The many lives – and faces', p. 187. See also Benson, *The Enterprise of Law*.

[47] Benson, *Enterprise of Law*, p. 87.

[48] William Senior, 'The history of maritime law', *The Mariner's Mirror* 38 (1952), 260–75; Tetley, 'The general maritime law'. On the distinction between these two terms see Albrecht Cordes, 'Lex maritima? Local, regional and universal maritime law in the Middle Ages', in Wim Blockmans, Mikhail Krom, and Justyna Wubs-Mrozewicz (eds), *The Routledge Handbook of Maritime Trade around Europe 1300–1600* (London: Routledge, 2017), 69–85.

[49] For example, Tetley, 'The general maritime law', p. 128. On this, see Jolien Kruit, 'General average – general principle plus varying practical application equals uniformity?', *Journal of International Maritime Law* 21 (2015), 190–202, at p. 191.

[50] See Manlio Bellomo (trans. Lydia Cochrane), *The Common Legal Past of Europe, 1000–1800* (Washington, DC: Catholic University of America Press, 1995), pp. 78–90; Tamar Herzog, *A Short History of European Law: The Last Two and a Half Millennia* (Cambridge, MA: Harvard University Press, 2018), pp. 76–93.

taught to law students at universities from the twelfth century onwards, and was the law that jurists turned to when positive local law seemed to provide no solution to a legal problem. Since even the English admiralty courts used continental civil law, this meant that European jurists were, in theory, provided with a common reference point.[51] The fact that something called 'Average' apparently existed everywhere ostensibly gives substance to the idea of a unified merchant customary law. The argument has a tendency to become circular, because once this 'proof' of the lex mercatoria has been found in the form of GA, the 'fact' of the lex mercatoria, unchanging and universal, discourages further scrutiny of GA itself.

GA in its modern form is also an excellent example of 'stateless' law, since it derives its force not from international conventions, but rather by clauses inserted into freight and insurance contracts.[52] The rules which regulate it today are maintained and amended by a non-governmental organisation, the *Comité Maritime International*, with the input of international shipping and insurance associations.[53] It has therefore been taken up by mercatorist scholars as evidence for their claims and has, moreover, been presented as an instance of the lex maritima, immutable since ancient times. It is safe to say that one departing from the mercatorist position would have little reason to further examine GA, because its supposed staticity would render its 3,000-year history unilluminating – as well as very dull.

In response to the claims of mercatorists, historians of medieval and early modern trade have argued that a lex mercatoria neither existed nor needed to exist. Emily Kadens has shown that merchants had no use of a uniform substantive law, Edda Frankot has found that maritime customary collections in North Sea ports varied greatly, whilst Albrecht Cordes, Maura Fortunati, and Stefania Gialdroni trace most references to the 'law merchant' to a highly localised English discourse ultimately rooted in seventeenth-century antipathy between the common and civil law courts.[54] GA has even been called to the witness stand at times to show that norms were heterogeneous at a doctrinal

---

[51] Bellomo, *The Common Legal Past of Europe*, p. 81.

[52] Kruit, 'General average', p. 192.

[53] See 'CMI: About Us', <https://comitemaritime.org/about-us/> [accessed 23 February 2020]; 'General Average: York-Antwerp Rules', <https://comitemaritime.org/work/york-antwerp-rules-yar/> [accessed 23 February 2020].

[54] Kadens, 'The myth'; Albrecht Cordes, 'Lex maritima?'; Albrecht Cordes, 'The search for a medieval lex mercatoria', *Oxford University Comparative Law Forum* 5 (2003), <https://ouclf.law.ox.ac.uk/the-search-for-a-medieval-lex-mercatoria/> [accessed 2 February 2024]; Maura Fortunati, 'La lex mercatoria nella tradizione e nella recente ricostruzione storico giuridica', *Sociologia del diritto* 2–3 (2005), 29–41; Gialdroni, 'Gerard Malynes e la questione della lex mercatoria'; Edda Frankot, *Of Laws of Ships and Shipmen: Medieval Maritime Law and its Practice in Urban Northern Europe* (Edinburgh: Edinburgh University Press, 2012).

level. Albrecht Cordes has argued for at least two families of GA practice in Europe, one 'Southern' and one 'Northern'.[55] Jolien Kruit, meanwhile, has conducted a comparative study of GA in historic normative collections of European/Mediterranean maritime law starting with Justinian's *Digest* in the fifth century AD and ending with Louis XIV's *Ordonnance de la Marine* of 1681.[56] She finds that while the GA principle finds a place in all of them, there is no agreement between them as to the circumstances in which the apportionment of damages should take place. Yet precisely because the mercatorists claim that the lex mercatoria was composed of unwritten customs, it is almost unfalsifiable from the point of view of municipal and state collections. It is therefore necessary to turn to archival records that might shed light on the interplay between 'state' law and merchant practice.

A wider issue is the autonomy which maritime justice enjoyed from other legal regimes. This is a question that the lex mercatoria debate, with its focus on the autonomy of merchant law from the state, both hints at and distracts from. *Ancien régime* merchants did sometimes claim for themselves a special semi-autonomous place in the legal order of things, especially with regards to the *ius commune*. The idea of a 'lex mercatoria' was often invoked in English legal discourse as a means of expressing this.[57] What is more, much mercantile justice in the medieval and early modern periods was conducted using summary procedure, which required, amongst other things, that judges base their decisions on 'the nature of things'. As Simona Cerutti points out, the doctrine of the 'nature of things', drawing ultimately on the philosophy of Thomas Aquinas, posited a teleological vision of the world in which each 'fact' was a font of its own legitimacy.[58] Early modern mercantile cases were usually adjudged according to the principle of good faith and in a 'mercantile style'. This approach, as Tijl Vanneste so elegantly puts it, 'considered [what was] reasonable and equitable in law as the legal consequence of what was considered reasonable and fair behaviour in trade'.[59] So it turns out that 'what merchants did' could be of considerable normative importance.[60]

The seventeenth century is a key period of witness in this respect. Where the mercatorists have seen increasing balkanisation, some prominent legal

---

[55] Cordes, 'Lex maritima?', p. 76.

[56] Kruit, 'General average'.

[57] Mary Elizabeth Basile, Jane Fair Bestor, Daniel R. Coquillette, and Charles Donahue, *Lex Mercatoria and Legal Pluralism: A Late Thirteenth-Century Treatise and its Afterlife* (Cambridge, MA: Ames Foundation, 1998), pp. 139–46.

[58] Simona Cerutti, 'Fatti e fatti giudiziari: il consolato di commercio di Torino nel XVIII secolo', *Quaderni Storici* 34 (1999), 413–45, at p. 420.

[59] Tijl Vanneste, *Intra-European Litigation in Eighteenth-Century Izmir: The Role of the Merchants' Style* (Leiden: Brill, 2021), pp. 4–5.

[60] Kadens, 'The myth, p. 1164.

historians have seen a move towards greater European unity. It is undeniable that the centralised national state was on the move in this period in the domain of maritime law, and this resulted in the circulation of new printed doctrinal collections. Albrecht Cordes has argued that the influence of texts such as Louis XIV's *Ordonnance de la marine* (1681), produced under the auspices of Jean-Baptiste Colbert, as well as the publication of other influential collections, such as the 'Hanseatic ship and sea law' (1614) gave impetus to a gradual process of identification and consolidation.[61] Perhaps even more importantly, this was an era in which learned jurists began to seriously interest themselves in maritime law and in which printed texts on the subject emerged in increasing numbers, and this had the potential to promote a shared understanding of institutions like GA across Europe and to bridge the gap between different legal orders. Peter Peck the Elder, Quentin Weytsen, and Mattheus De Vicq in the Low Countries, Charles Molloy in England, and Francesco Rocco, Carlo Targa and Giuseppe Casaregi in Italy are just some of the authors who published on issues related to GA in the sixteenth and seventeenth centuries.[62]

From this it follows that a key theme in this book will be the dialogue between various written norms and the practice that emerges from the seventeenth-century archival documents. Was it the increasing 'professionalisation' of maritime law and centralising legislation from above, or shifting maritime practice and organisation of trade 'from below' that was driving legal change and determining how risk was to be shared? This was, moreover, also a faultline running through the tribunal that is the focus of this study: the Court of the *Consoli del Mare di Pisa* (Consuls of the Sea in Pisa), the foremost maritime-commercial court in Tuscany.[63] The court of the *Consoli* represents a kind of weather front where two legal regimes meet. It was a court with a commercial remit authorised to use summary procedure, and its judges were Florentine nobles without legal training, chosen, at least in theory, because they had some experience in commerce; and yet the court was staffed, at least in part, by learned lawyers schooled in the *ius commune* who looked to Roman law as the ultimate font of legitimacy.

---

[61] Cordes, 'Lex maritima?', p. 82.

[62] Quintin Weytsen and Mattheus De Vicq, *Tractatus de avariis* (Amsterdam: Henricus & Theodorus Boom, 1672), p. 23; Petrus Peckius, Arnold Vinnius, and Johannes Laurentius, *Ad rem nauticum pertinentes* (Amsterdam: Joannis Henrici Boom, 1708), pp. 188–297; Charles Molloy, *De iure maritimo et navali or A Treatise of Affairs Maritime and of Commerce* (London: Walthoe, 1744), p. 280. For the Italian authors, see pp. 65–76 in this book.

[63] Alessandro Lo Bartolo, 'The *Consoli del Mare* of Pisa, 1550–1750: an institutional and social profile', in Jake Dyble, Alessandro Lo Bartolo, and Elia Morelli (eds), *Un mare connesso. Europa e mondo islamico nel Mediterraneo (secoli XV–XIX)* (Pisa: Carocci, 2024), 177–200.

One particularly striking result to emerge from this study is fractures that existed between the 'GA' of the normative material, including tracts by learned jurists, and the GA that was used by early modern practitioners. The provisions of the *Digest* had a clear impact on Tuscan GA cases, but this remained quite superficial. GA was quite a different instrument to the institution posited in the *Lex Rhodia*, or even in the *Llibre del Consolat de Mar*, another important collection of norms in the Mediterranean context.[64] This tension posed few problems for practitioners but was a knotty issue for legal theorists and technicians versed in the *ius commune*, who were painfully aware of the dissonance between the traditions. Yet their systematisation efforts, as evidenced both by the activities of the court and the publications of learned jurists, had not produced much in the way of results even by the end of our period. There was still no commonly agreed upon typology of maritime Averages, nor an agreed upon definition of GA. Though Cordes is entirely correct to identify the period as tending towards harmonisation and consolidation, it should thus be noted that this remained an incomplete and contested process as late as 1700. Nor, on the basis of this evidence, is it wholly true to say, as Donahue does, that 'the effective legal system for the Italian merchants was the *ius commune*' as far as GA is concerned.[65]

Though the mercatorists are sometimes criticised for overstating the distance between commercial law and other legal orders, some autonomy for merchant practice thus emerges.[66] Ultimately, however, this cannot be considered to support the central mercatorist claims, since a certain deference to merchant practice does not imply the existence of a coherent corpus of unwritten doctrine understood by all merchants. On the contrary, this study demonstrates how commercial law, particularly the procedural element, was very susceptible to local conditions and contingency.[67] In the free port of Livorno, Tuscany's main international port in the period, the lack of a native mercantile elite was conducive to the emergence of a laissez faire approach on the part of the court, in contrast to places like Venice.[68] Procedural advantages were offered – informally, and off the record – to English and Dutch merchants

---

[64] Germà Colon and Arcadi García (eds), *Llibre del Consolat de Mar: edició del text de la Real de Mallorca, amb les variants de tots els manuscrits coneguts* (Barcelona: Fundació Noguera, 2001); Giuseppe Lorenzo Maria Casaregi, *Consolato del mare colla spiegazione di Giuseppe Maria Casaregi* (Venice: Silvestro Gnoato, 1802).

[65] Donahue, 'Lex mercatoria', p. 33.

[66] Donahue, 'Lex mercatoria', pp. 34–6.

[67] A similar conclusion is reached by Roberto Zaugg in *Stranieri di antico regime. Mercanti, giudici e consoli nella Napoli del Settecento* (Rome: Viella, 2011).

[68] Maria Fusaro, *Political Economies of Empire in the Early Modern Mediterranean: The Decline of Venice and the Rise of England 1450–1700* (Cambridge: Cambridge University Press, 2015), pp. 106–7.

and shipmasters operating in the port. This was not only done to keep these commercially important actors satisfied, but also to resist diplomatic pressures being exerted on the Grand Duchy by their home states.

The Study

The humble GA procedure is the perfect vehicle both to re-assess the 'evolutionary story of the institutionalisation of risk' posited by NIE, and to discuss the autonomy of mercantile law from other early modern legal orders. GA, if one does not look too closely, is both the example *par excellence* of the lex mercatoria and the ultimate 'archaic' institution. In actual fact, it fits neatly into neither grand narrative.

Though this book makes reference to GA laws and practices across Western Europe and the Mediterranean, the case study adopted here will be the port of Livorno in the Grand Duchy of Tuscany, which allows for a particularly pertinent and detailed engagement with these questions. One reason for this is practical: Tuscany is possessed of an especially rich documentary patrimony regarding GA which allows the operational side – the practice itself – to be illuminated in a way that is not possible for most other jurisdictions. The archive of the *Consoli del Mare di Pisa* preserves many GA cases in full, including the original calculations. The richness of the available data concerning the actual operation of GA is matched only by surviving Genoese documentation.[69] Four different years from across the period were examined in full – 1600, 1640, 1670, and 1700 – rendering 50 case studies in total. A number of other archival documents are brought to bear in order to fully contextualise these cases, whilst Chapter 4 presents a microhistorical reconstruction of a case which became the subject of a diplomatic dispute between England and Tuscany, an example of what Edoardo Gredi called an 'exceptional normal', whereby exceptionally rich evidence helps us uncover the normal dynamics which structured these institutions.[70]

There is also a compelling methodological case for exploring the Tuscan experience – or more accurately, for exploring the experience of the merchants and shipmasters of many different origins who found themselves at this Mediterranean crossroads. First of all, Italy occupies a special place in the institutional teleology posited by North.[71] Italy in the NIE schema

---

[69] Antonio Iodice, 'General average in Genoa: between statutes and customs', in Maria Fusaro, Andrea Addobbati, and Luisa Piccinno (eds), *General Average and Risk Management in Medieval and Early Modern Maritime Business* (Cham: Springer, 2023), 259–96.

[70] Edoardo Grendi, 'Micro-analisi e storia sociale', *Quaderni Storici* 12 (1997), 506–20, at pp. 509, 512.

[71] North, *Institutions*, p. 127.

is the institutional *homo erectus* to England's *homo sapiens*, furnishing the 'proto' institutions later perfected in North-Western Europe. Secondly, the operational reality we encounter in Tuscany was particularly complex since in the 'free port' of Livorno a significant proportion of resident merchants – and the overwhelming majority of shipmasters – were foreigners, who might conceivably import, along with their merchandise, their own notions of how GAs should be carried out.[72] As well as being home to significant numbers of Sephardic Jewish, Greek, and Armenian merchants, Livorno was particularly important for the English and Dutch, who formed large and influential communities in the seventeenth-century free port.[73] Hence the Tuscan context provides a privileged vantage point through which to examine a meeting of GA customs. If the Mediterranean has been described as a 'laboratory' of legal history, bringing a number of legal traditions into close contact, Livorno represents a particularly rich petri dish.[74] In short, it is especially germane for studying the meeting of Western Mediterranean and North-Western European traditions, since Livorno was an important player in what Fernand Braudel famously termed the 'Northern Invasion' of the Mediterranean trade circuits.[75]

The first chapter of the work will set the scene by elucidating this context in greater detail. The second will explore the GA that emerges from early modern normative sources, especially those pertinent to the Western Mediterranean, beginning with the *Lex Rhodia* in Justinian's *Digest*. Here we will see not only that GA has been far from stable over the centuries, but even that the animating principle of 'GA' before the early modern period was not universally shared. The very idea of a history of GA is in some ways a retrospective framework imposed upon a range of similar practices that were not yet grouped under

---

[72] Albrect Cordes and Stefania Gialdroni, 'Introduction', in Stefania Gialdroni, Albrecht Cordes, Serge Dauchy, Dave De ruysscher, and Heikki Pihlajamäki (eds), *Migrating Words, Migrating Language, Migrating Law: Trading Routes and the Development of Commercial Law* (Leiden: Brill, 2020), 1–9, at p. 2.

[73] Gigliola Pagano De Divitiis (trans. Stephen Parkin), *English Merchants in Seventeenth-Century Italy* (Cambridge: Cambridge University Press, 1998), pp. 144–52; Fusaro, *Political Economies of Empire*, pp. 64–88.

[74] See Guillaume Calafat, *Une mer jalousée: contribution à l'histoire de la souveraineté* (Paris: Éditions du Seuil, 2019), back matter; Maria Fusaro, 'The global relevance of the legal history of the early modern Mediterranean', *Cromohs*, Current Debates (2023), <https://oajournals.fupress.net/index.php/cromohs/article/view/14575> [12 August 2023].

[75] Colin Heywood, 'The English in the Mediterranean, 1600–1630: a post-Braudelian perspective on the northern invasion' in Maria Fusaro, Colin Heywood, and Mohamed-Salah Omri (eds), *Trade and Cultural Exchange in the Early Modern Mediterranean: Braudel's Maritime Legacy* (London: I.B. Tauris & Company, 2010), 23–44.

an agreed typology. The third chapter will compare these written norms with the seventeenth-century practice that emerges from the Pisan archive: GA-as-practised was much more capacious than the normative sources suggest, and merchants held quite different core assumptions to the lawyers about what the institution was for. The fourth chapter uses a microhistorical case study – a diplomatic dispute between the English and Tuscans over GA – in order to demonstrate the extent to which GA rules and procedures were inflected by political economy and contingent upon the balance of economic power, as well as discussing the implications of the procedure's inherently international nature. The final chapter will discuss the implications for the history of economic institutions, demonstrating how GA was used in concert with a range of other risk-management instruments and exploring the risk-management strategies of individual merchants and shipmasters working in the free port. The concluding remarks will consider the future of GA and the lessons that the GA of the past hold for practitioners in the present, as well as for historians of commercial law and early modern trade.

1

The Free Port of Livorno and its Pisan Court

The 'Free Port' and the Emergence of Livorno

Livorno's peculiar history makes the Grand Duchy of Tuscany a particularly rich case study for an examination of GA. Founded virtually from scratch through the initiative of the Medici Grand Dukes in the sixteenth century, Livorno quickly became the chief port of the Tuscan state and one of the leading ports of the seventeenth-century Mediterranean.[1] The importance of foreign merchant communities in Livorno and the diverse origins of the port traffic mean that the GA cases processed there form a remarkably diverse core sample of actors hailing from different national-religious communities. In this respect, the port represents in microcosm the potential of the Mediterranean as a whole for examining the historical interaction of different legal cultures and systems. Though the gaze of Anglophone early modern scholarship has traditionally been fixed upon the Atlantic and Indian Oceans, the comparative neglect of the Mediterranean is hardly justified by the evidence.[2] The Mediterranean remained an important economic zone in its own right even as people and goods began to circulate globally in the sixteenth and seventeenth centuries, and was, moreover, a crucial naval and commercial theatre for all maritime European nations, including those of Northern Europe.[3] To

---

[1] Some classic academic studies of the early modern port include Jean-Pierre Filippini, *Il porto di Livorno e la Toscana (1676–1814)*, 3 vols (Naples: Edizioni Scientifiche Italiane, 1998); Mario Baruchello, *Livorno e il suo porto. Origini, caratteristiche e vicende dei traffici livornesi* (Livorno: Editrice Riviste Tecniche, 1932); a recent single-volume history of the port is Lucia Frattarelli Fischer's *L'arcano del mare: un porto nella prima età globale: Livorno* (Pisa: Pacini editore, 2018). Further bibliography will be outlined below.

[2] Maria Fusaro, 'After Braudel: a reassessment of Mediterranean history between the Northern Invasion and the Caravane Maritime', in Maria Fusaro, Colin Heywood, and Mohamed-Salah Omri (eds), *Trade and Cultural Exchange in the Early Modern Mediterranean: Braudel's Maritime Legacy* (London: I.B. Tauris & Company, 2010), 1–22, at p. 3.

[3] David Ormrod, *The Rise of Commercial Empires: England and the Netherlands in the Age of Mercantilism, 1650–1770* (Cambridge: Cambridge University Press,

give some idea of its economic and political and importance to these states, we might consider that the English (and later the British) had more troops stationed in the Mediterranean than in both North America and India combined until the 1750s.[4]

It is the quality of the Mediterranean experience, however, quite apart from its economic weight, which makes it a particularly interesting setting for a GA case study.[5] In the Mediterranean it would prove impossible for any single state – or even for the states of Christian Europe considered collectively – to achieve anything amounting to political or economic hegemony. The Mediterranean was a contested zone in which no one power held sway.[6] Moreover, it was a zone of intense diversity: religious, linguistic, cultural – and legal. Economic rivalry between states intersected with religious rivalries, sometimes in surprising ways.[7] The Mediterranean was the active frontier of a long-standing conflict between Christianity and Islam, but this barrier was permeable and the conflict itself generated interaction and even trade across religious boundaries.[8] The entry of the English and the Dutch into Mediterranean shipping in large numbers in the late sixteenth century rendered the Mediterranean even more complex in terms of language, legal traditions, and diplomacy.[9] For this reason, it has been argued that the Mediterranean provides a kind of 'laboratory' for the study of legal, social, and political interaction across boundaries in the early modern period, a place in which a number of global cultures, and global-historical currents, found expression

---

2009), pp. 7–10; Richard Unger, 'Overview. Trades, ports, and ships: the roots of difference in sailors' lives', in Maria Fusaro, Bernard Allaire, Richard Blakemore, and Tijl Vannesste (eds), *Law, Labour and Empire: Comparative Perspectives on Seafarers, c. 1500–1800* (London: Palgrave Macmillan, 2015), 1–17, at p. 3.

[4] Trivellato, *The Familiarity of Strangers*, p. 6.

[5] Peregrine Horden and Nicholas Purcell, *The Boundless Sea: Writing Mediterranean History* (London: Routledge, 2019), pp. 3–4.

[6] Molly Greene, 'Beyond the northern invasion: the Mediterranean in the seventeenth century', *Past & Present* 174 (2002), 42–71, at p. 43.

[7] Molly Greene, *Catholic Pirates and Greek Merchants: A Maritime History of the Early Modern Mediterranean* (Princeton: Princeton University Press, 2010).

[8] Wolfgang Kaiser and Guillaume Calafat, 'The economy of ransoming in the early modern Mediterranean' in Francesco Trivellato, Leor Halevi, and Catia Antunes (eds), *Religion and Trade: Cross-Cultural Exchanges in World History* (Oxford: Oxford University Press, 2014), 108–30.

[9] Heywood, 'The English in the Mediterranean, 1600–1630'; Maria Fusaro, 'The invasion of northern litigants: English and Dutch seamen in Mediterranean courts of law', in Maria Fusaro, Bernard Allaire, Richard Blakemore, and Tijl Vannesste (eds), *Law, Labour and Empire: Comparative Perspectives on Seafarers, c. 1500–1800* (London: Palgrave Macmillan, 2015), 21–42, at p. 23.

in close physical proximity.[10] Few places embodied this diversity to a greater extent than the free port of Livorno.

The presence and importance of foreign operators in Livorno was even more marked than in other Mediterranean port cities. It is traditional when discussing this cosmopolitanism to pay homage to a rare coin, issued by the Grand Duke Ferdinando II.[11] This large gold *tollero* was minted in 1656 and bears an image of the harbour of Livorno filled with shipping. It was imprinted with the legend '*diversis gentibus una*' – from diverse peoples, one. For the contemporary reader it evokes a whole number of associations, not least the motto of the United States, *e pluribus unum*. This parallel with the 'land of the free' only intensifies an anachronistic impression that Livorno was a haven for Europe's persecuted, a cultural melting pot where toleration reigned.[12] In actual fact, the tolerance extended to different national and religious groups, while remarkable in some respects, was neither uniform nor, in many cases, extensive.[13] Toleration was not a good in itself, and integration was not a hallmark of Livornese society.[14] Boundaries between different groups were rigorously policed and possibly even sharpened by the experience of living in

---

[10] Wolfgang Kaiser and Guillaume Calafat, 'Violence, protection and commerce: corsairing and *ars piratica* in the early modern Mediterranean', in Stefan Eklöf Amirell and Leos Müller (eds), *Persistent Piracy: Maritime Violence and State-Formation in Global Historical Perspective* (London: Palgrave Macmillan, 2014), 69–92, at p. 69.

[11] Corey Tazzara, *The Free Port of Livorno and the Transformation of the Mediterranean World* (Oxford: Oxford University Press, 2017), pp. 1–2; Lucia Frattarelli Fischer, 'Lo sviluppo di una città portuale: Livorno, 1575–1720', in Marco Folin (ed.), *Sistole/Diastole: episodi di trasformazione urbana nell'Italia delle città* (Venice: Istituto veneto di scienze, lettere ed arti, 2006), 271–334, at p. 304.

[12] Andrea Addobbati and Marcella Aglietti, 'Premessa', in Andrea Addobbati and Marcella Aglietti (eds), *La città delle nazioni: Livorno e i limiti del cosmopolitismo (1566–1834)* (Pisa: Pisa University Press, 2016), 11–25, at p. 13.

[13] Francesca Trivellato, 'Credito e tolleranza: i limiti del cosmopolitismo nella Livorno di età moderna', in Andrea Addobbati and Marcella Aglietti (eds), *La città delle nazioni: Livorno e i limiti del cosmopolitismo (1566–1834)* (Pisa: Pisa University Press, 2016), 39–50; Stefano Villani, 'Religious pluralism and the danger of tolerance: the English nation in Livorno in the seventeenth century', in Federico Barbierato and Alessandra Veronese (eds), *Late Medieval and Early Modern Religious Dissents: Conflicts and Plurality in Renaissance Europe* (Pisa: Edizioni il Campano Arnus University Books, 2012), 97–124; Elena Fasano Guarini, 'Livorno nell'età moderna: mito e realtà', in Adriano Prosperi (ed.), *Livorno 1606–1806: luogo di incontro tra popoli e culture* (Turin: Alimandi, 2009), 19–30.

[14] Stefano Villani and Lucia Frattarelli Fischer, '"People of every mixture". Immigration, tollerance, and religious conflicts in early modern Livorno', in Ann Katherine Isaacs (ed.), *Immigration and Emigration in Historical Perspective* (Pisa: Edizioni Plus, 2007), 93–107; Stefano Villani, 'Religione e politica: le comunità protestanti a Livorno nel XVII e XVIII secolo', in Daniele Pesciatini (ed.), *Livorno dal medievo all'età contemporanea. Ricerche e riflessioni* (Pisa–Livorno: Banco di Sardegna, 2003), 36–64.

the free port.[15] Another coin, issued at the same time and with the same design, comes closer to the truth of the matter, making the less contentious claim of '*et patet et favet*' (it/he both stands open and supports). If, as seems likely, it refers not to the port itself but to the Grand Duke imprinted on the other side, then this inscription is even more apt. The minority groups that lived and operated in the port did so thanks to the personal protection of the Grand Duke.[16] It was he, not a general spirit of toleration, which reigned in Livorno.[17]

The coin was correct in one essential respect, however: Livorno was home to a great many different peoples. This was in part the result of conscious policy on the part of the Medici Grand Dukes who pioneered a series of radical institutional innovations that soon became associated with a new idea: the 'free port'.[18] It was these innovations, combined with an extraordinary initial outlay on infrastructure, which transformed Livorno from a fortress between a swamp and the sea in the sixteenth century into the Mediterranean boom town of the century in the seventeenth.[19] Livorno has a strong claim to be the world's first free port, though since there was, and is, no agreed definition of the term, it is impossible to make any definitive pronouncements in this respect. We might begin by saying that a free port, at least in its perfect platonic form, was a place where goods could be imported, exported, and exchanged without the payment of customs duties and/or where merchants of whatever religion and nationality could trade on an equal footing.[20] In order to reflect this dual conception of the free port, Thomas Kirk helpfully adopts the terms 'entrepôt' and 'emporium' to distinguish between free movement of goods (entrepôt) and free settlement of people (emporium).[21] Livorno's innovative and highly successful example was to have important implications for world trade. By the mid-eighteenth century, several Mediterranean ports had declared

---

[15] Trivellato, *The Familiarity of Strangers*, p. 275.

[16] Addobbati, *Commercio, rischio, guerra*, pp. 21–2.

[17] Ibid.

[18] Tazzara, *The Free Port of Livorno*, pp. 49–55; Michela D'Angelo, 'Livorno 1421–1606: da villaggio a città-porto mediterranea', in S. Adorno, G. Cristina, and A. Rotondo (eds), *VisibileInvisibile – Economie urbane* (Syracuse: Tyche, 2013).

[19] Lucia Frattarelli Fischer, 'I bandi di Ferdinando I. La costruzione e il popolamento di Livorno dal 1590 al 1603', in Aleksej Kalc and Elizabetta Navarra (eds), *Le populazioni del mare: porti franchi, città, isole e villaggi costieri tra età moderna e contemporanea* (Udine: Forum, 2003), 87–98; Lucia Frattarelli Fischer, 'Livorno città nuova: 1574–1609', *Società e storia* 11 (1989), 873–93; Paolo Castignoli, 'Livorno da terra murata a città', in *Atti del convegno Livorno e il Mediterraneo nell'età medicea* (Livorno: Bastogi, 1978), 32–9; Lucia Frattarelli Fischer, 'Livorno. Dal pentagono di Buontalenti alla città di Ferdinando I', *Nuovi Studi Livornesi* 19 (2012), 23–48.

[20] Tazzara, *The Free Port of Livorno*, p. 3.

[21] Thomas Allison Kirk, *Genoa and the Sea: Policy and Power in an Early Modern Maritime Republic 1559–1684* (Baltimore: John Hopkins University Press, 2013), pp. 189–98.

themselves free ports, including Marseille and Genoa.[22] The free port model was further developed in the Caribbean and in Asia, finding its modern-day descendant in the 'export processing zone', of which examples can be found all over the world.[23]

In the first half of the seventeenth century, the 'emporium' facet of the Livornese free port was more in evidence than the 'entrepôt' dimension. Fiscal exemptions were employed from the start, chief among them the so-called *benefizio libero* (free benefit) which allowed goods to be stored in Livorno for a year without the payment of any taxes.[24] Though this reduced the burden of customs duties, however, it did so in a somewhat arcane and complicated fashion, with many exceptions remaining. Duties payable on goods were actually increased by the Grand Duke in 1643 in order to meet expenses incurred during the Thirty Years War.[25] It was only with the reform of 1676 that Livorno became a free port in the modern understanding of the term, with the complete abolishment of customs duties.[26] Before this, the emphasis of the free port was more on personal protections and liberties. The emblematic instrument here – though its actual influence is debated – was the *livornina*, the famous declaration by Ferdinando I inviting 'all merchants of whatever nation – Easterners, Westerners, Spanish, Portuguese, Greeks, Germans, Italians, Jews, Turks, Moors, Armenians, Persians, and [those] of other states' to settle in the town, initially made in 1591 and reissued in 1593.[27] It encouraged

---

[22] Kirk, *Genoa and the Sea*, p. 11; Thomas Allison Kirk, 'Genoa and Livorno: sixteenth and seventeenth-century commercial rivalry as a stimulus to policy development', *History* 86 (2002), 2–17; Junko Takeda, *Between Crown and Commerce: Marseille and the Early Modern Mediterranean* (Baltimore: John Hopkins University Press, 2011), p. 48.

[23] Francis Armytage, *The Free Port System in the West Indies. A Study in Commercial Policy, 1766–1822* (London: Longmans, Green, & Co, 1953); John McIntyre, Ranjeesh Narula, and Len Trevino, 'The role of export processing zones for host countries and multinationals: a mutually beneficial relationship?', *International Trade Journal* 10 (1996), 435–66.

[24] There were various exceptions to this, however. For example, the goods had to be coming from more than 100 miles away, a distance which thus excluded goods coming from Genoa. See Tazzara, *The Free Port of Livorno*, p. 123.

[25] Tazzara, *The Free Port of Livorno*, p. 84; Carlo Cipolla, *Il burocrate e il marinaio: la 'sanità' Toscana e le tribolazioni degli Inglesi a Livorno nel 17. secolo* (Bologna: Il Mulino, 2012), pp. 25–6.

[26] Lucia Frattarelli Fischer, 'Livorno 1676. La città e il porto franco', in Franco Angiolini, Vieri Becagli, and Marcello Verga (eds), *La Toscana nell'età di Cosimo III* (Florence: EDIFIR, 1993), 45–66.

[27] Frattarelli Fischer, 'I bandi di Ferdinando I'; Stephanie Nadalo, 'Populating a "nest of pirates, murtherers etc.": Tuscan immigration policy and "Ragion di Stato" in the free port of Livorno', in Timothy Fehler, Greta Kroeker, Charles Parker, and

these would-be settlers with promises of safe-conduct from debts contracted elsewhere, freedom from criminal prosecution, and a series of tax breaks.[28] In the event, however, the initial settling of the town was achieved not so much through expansive rhetorical declarations, or even new taxation rules, but through a much more targeted immigration policy. The Medici government utilised letters of invitation, Grand Ducal hospitality, and an overseas network of agents to encourage the 'right sort' of economic migrant, targeting prominent Sephardic Jewish traders in particular.[29] There was also a significant process of internal migration from the Tuscan hinterland besides the better-known top-down efforts by the Grand Ducal administration.[30]

Whatever the precise influence of the *livornina* itself, the vision it represented did indeed come to pass, and the town's economic success was dependent on the presence of foreign operators.[31] Over the seventeenth century, English and Dutch merchants and shipmasters became increasingly important in trade with and within the Mediterranean.[32] They were particularly important to Livorno and helped it to carve out a role as a major port of deposit: thanks to the 'free benefit', it became a major centre of redistribution.[33] The port was notably engaged in 'horizontal' trade with the Levant and Northern Europe, but also enjoyed substantial 'vertical' connections with North Africa, as well as fulfilling an important role in trade along the Italian peninsula: the so-called

---

Jonathan Ray (eds), *Religious Diasporas in Early Modern Europe: Strategies of Exile* (London: Pickering and Chatto, 2014), 31–45; Lucia Frattarelli Fischer, 'La Livornina. Alle origini della società livornese', in Adriano Prosperi (ed.), *Livorno 1606–1806: luogo di incontro tra popoli e culture* (Turin: Alimandi, 2009), 43–62.

[28] Daniele Edigati, 'Aspetti giuridici delle franchigie di Livorno: l'immunità personale *in criminalibus* ed il problema dell'estradizione (secoli XVI–XVIII)', *Nuovi Studi Livornesi* 17 (2010), 17–41.

[29] Benjamin Ravid, 'A tale of three cities and their raison d'etat. Ancona, Venice, Livorno and their competition for Jewish merchants in the sixteenth century', *Mediterranean Historical Review* 6 (1989), 138–62.

[30] Marco Della Pina, 'La popolazione di Livorno nel Sei-Settecento: le componenti toscane' in Adriano Prosperi (ed.), *Livorno 1606–1806: luogo di incontro tra popoli e culture* (Turin: Alimandi, 2009), 149–57.

[31] Frattarelli Fischer, 'Livorno città nuova', pp. 875–6; Filippini, *Il porto di Livorno*, vol.1, pp. 75–102; Fernand Braudel and Ruggiero Romano, *Navires et marchandises à l'entrée du port de Livourne (1547–1611)* (Paris: Librairie Armand Colin, 1951), p. 25.

[32] This was Fernand Braudel's famous 'northern invasion'. For recent reflections on this see the first three contributions to Maria Fusaro, Colin Heywood, and Mohamed-Salah Omri (eds), *Trade and Cultural Exchange in the Early Modern Mediterranean: Braudel's Maritime Legacy* (London: I.B. Tauris & Company, 2010).

[33] Renato Ghezzi, 'Il porto di Livorno e il commercio mediterraneo nel Seicento', in Adriano Prosperi (ed.), *Livorno 1606–1806: luogo di incontro tra popoli e culture* (Turin: Alimandi, 2009), 324–40.

'*cabotaggio*'.[34] As was the case in lots of medieval and early modern trading centres, many of the foreigners resident in the port were organised into *nationes* (*nazioni* or 'nations'): Francesca Trivellato defines these *nationes* as 'foreign and ethno-religious communities on which sovereign authorities conferred a distinctive collective legal status that came with specific rights and obligations designed to integrate them into the fabric of local society and the economy while setting them apart from the majority of the population'.[35] By 1640, Livorno was home to communities of English, French, German, and Dutch traders, as well as Armenians and Greeks, all of which were organised into recognised *nationes* by the end of the century.[36] The most prominent of the

[34] Gigliola Pagano De Divitiis, 'Livorno: porto della Toscana?', in Adriano Prosperi (ed.), *Livorno 1606–1806: luogo di incontro tra popoli e culture* (Turin: Alimandi, 2009), 341–9.

[35] Trivellato, *The Familiarity of Strangers*, p. 43. See Frédéric Mauro, 'Merchant communities, 1350–1750', in James Tracy (ed.), *The Rise of Merchant Empires: Long Distance Trade in the Early Modern World, 1350–1750* (Cambridge: Cambridge University Press, 1990), 255–86, at pp. 262–6; Roberto Zaugg, 'On the use of legal resources and the definition of group boundaries. A prosopographic analysis of the French nation and the British factory in eighteenth-century Naples', in Georg Christ, Stefan Burkhardt, Wolfgang Kaiser, Franz-Julius Morche, and Roberto Zaugg (eds), *Union in Separation – Diasporic Groups and Identities in the Eastern Mediterranean (1100–1800)* (Rome: Viella, 2015), 699–714.

[36] Frattarelli Fischer, 'Lo sviluppo di una città portuale', p. 303. On the Armenians see Renato Ghezzi, 'Mercanti armeni a Livorno nel XVII secolo', in *Gli Armeni lungo le strade d'Italia: atti del convegno internazionale: Torino, Genova, Livorno, 8–11 marzo 1997: giornata di studi a Livorno* (Pisa: Istituti editoriali e poligrafici internazionali, 1998), 43–53. On the German-Dutch *natio* see Renato Ghezzi, *Livorno e l'Atlantico: i commerci Olandesi nel Mediterraneo del Seicento* (Bari: Cacucci, 2011); Marie-Christine Engels, *Merchants, Interlopers, Seamen and Corsairs: The 'Flemish' Community in Livorno and Genoa (1615–1635)* (Hilversum: Verloren, 1997); Magnus Ressel, 'La nazione Olandese-Alemanna di Livorno e il suo ruolo nel sistema mercantile europeo del XVIII secolo', in Andrea Addobbati and Marcella Aglietti (eds), *La città delle nazioni: Livorno e i limiti del cosmopolitismo (1566–1834)* (Pisa: Pisa University Press, 2016), 309–35. On the Greek communities of Livorno see Giangiacomo Panessa, *Le comunità greche a Livorno. Tra integrazione e chiusura nazionale* (Livorno: Belforte, 1991). On the English in Livorno see Michela D'Angelo, *Mercanti inglesi a Livorno, 1573–1737: alle origini di una British factory* (Messina: Istituto di studi storici G. Salvemini, 2004); Barbara Donati, *Tra inquisizione e granducato: storie di Inglesi nella Livorno del primo seicento* (Rome: Edizioni di storia e letteratura, 2010); Stefano Villani, 'Una finestra mediterranea sull'Europea: i "nordici" nella Livorno della prima età moderna', in Adriano Prosperi (ed.), *Livorno 1606–1806: luogo di incontro tra popoli e culture* (Turin: Alimandi, 2009), 158–77; Stefano Villani, '"Una piccola epitome di Inghilterra". La comunità inglese di Livorno negli anni di Ferdinandi II: questioni religiose e politiche', *Cromohs* 8 (2003), 1–23.

foreign communities was the Jewish *natio*, chiefly made up of Sephardic Jews who had been expelled from the Iberian peninsula.[37] Ferdinando I extended even greater autonomy to these Sephardic migrants, resulting in privileges unknown to Jews in any other Catholic state. Sephardic Jews would make up around 10 per cent of Livorno's population throughout the early modern period.[38] Muslims from the Ottoman and North African world also made up between 5 and 10 per cent of the population during the seventeenth century, but almost exclusively as slaves rather than the recipients of new freedoms.[39] These were almost all prisoners captured as part of the *corso* – the ceaseless conflict against the infidel that still simmered in the seventeenth-century Mediterranean, Tuscany's famous neutrality never extending to the Muslim world.[40]

The significance of the free port setting, however, cannot be captured from the exclusively top-down perspective of Grand Ducal policy making.[41] The Grand Dukes did not even explicitly set out to create a 'free port' as such. The term had many meanings for contemporaries and in the Livornese case was applied retrospectively to conditions that had already been arrived at in

---

[37] Renzo Toaff, *La nazione ebrea a Livorno e Pisa* (Florence: Olschki, 1990); Lucia Frattarelli Fischer, *Vivere fuori dal ghetto: Ebrei a Pisa e Livorno (secoli XVI–XVIII)* (Turin: Silvio Zamorani, 2008); Lucia Frattarelli Fischer, 'Ebrei a Pisa e Livorno nel sei e settecento tra inquisizione e garanzie granducali', in Aleksej Kalc and Elisabetta Navarra (eds), *Le popolazioni del mare: porti franchi, città, isole e villaggi costieri tra età moderna e contemporanea* (Udine: Forum, 2003), 87–98; Giuseppe Marcocci, 'I portoghesi a Livorno nei secoli dell'età moderna', in Adriano Prosperi (ed.), *Livorno 1606–1806: luogo di incontro tra popoli e culture* (Turin: Alimandi, 2009), 405–17; Francesca Trivellato, 'Stati, diaspore e commerci mediterranei: mercanti ebrei tra Livorno, Marsiglia e Aleppo (1673–1747)', in Adriano Prosperi (ed.), *Livorno 1606–1806: luogo di incontro tra popoli e culture* (Turin: Alimandi, 2009), 361–74.

[38] Trivellato, *The Familiarity of Strangers*, p. 5.

[39] Cesare Santus, *Il 'Turco' a Livorno: incontri con l'Islam nella Toscana del Seicento* (Milan: Officina Libraria, 2019); Tazzara, *The Free Port of Livorno*, p. 53; Trivellato, *The Familiarity of Strangers*, p. 70.

[40] See Santus, *Il 'Turco' a Livorno*; Cesare Santus, 'Crimini, violenza e corruzione nel bagno di Livorno: gli schiavi "turchi" in alcuni processo del XVII secolo', in Andrea Addobbati and Marcella Aglietti (eds), *La città delle nazioni: Livorno e i limiti del cosmopolitismo (1566–1834)* (Pisa: Pisa University Press, 2016), 93–108; Cesare Santus and Guillaume Calafat, 'Les avatars du "Turc". Esclaves et commerçants musulmans en Toscane (1600–1750)', in Jocelyne Dakhlia and Bernard Vincent (eds), *Les Musulmans dans l'histoire de l'Europe, tome 1. Une intégration invisible* (Paris: Albin Michel, 2011), 471–522; Andrea Addobbati, 'La neutralità del porto di Livorno in età medicea', in Adriano Prosperi (ed.), *Livorno 1606–1806: luogo di incontro tra popoli e culture* (Turin: Alimandi, 2009), 91–103.

[41] Addobbati, *Commercio, rischio, guerra*, p. 64.

a far more piecemeal and untidy fashion than the single term might suggest. Even in the late eighteenth century, when the two leading Livornese jurists, Francesco Pierallini and Ascanio Baldasseroni, were asked to define the '*porto franco*', they answered that such a thing would be impossible: the definition of a free port could not be fixed but was rather a matter of what particular laws had been laid down in each port.[42] The two lawyers restricted themselves to arguing that the making of the free port had begun with the *livornina* of 1591 and had been perfected with the customs reform of 1676. Corey Tazzara, meanwhile, has argued that a bottom-up process of negotiation between merchants and local authorities combined with a lack of central oversight was equally if not more important in the creation of the free port.[43] As has been noted, the 'freedom' of the port in the first half of the century consisted in a patchwork of piecemeal exemptions, privileges, licences, and special grants, rather than in more general liberties.[44] Rather than digging into archives to find precedents, officials preferred to deal directly with interested parties to manage disputes and assess requests.[45] This meant that matters were resolved not through reference to the 'rules' as such, but rather with reference to usage, half-remembered grants, 'common sense', commercial utility, and officials' desire for personal enrichment. Petition to the Grand Duke became a potential short cut to definitive resolution, and these petitions became an administrative tool as much as a tool of justice.[46]

In all these discussions the idea of a 'free port' was frequently invoked very loosely. Rather than being used in reference to specific institutions, the 'free port' was instead used in a more rhetorical fashion to invoke Livorno's unwritten constitution or compact. In essence, this constitution established that disputes be regulated in an informal manner by merchants and the local authorities without strict interpretation of the rules.[47] Port authorities were largely congenial to this way of thinking, grounding their decisions in this unwritten constitution even after the wide-ranging reforms of 1676.[48] Officials often extended privileges which only applied to certain groups to all users of the port. Freedom from existing debts, for example, was technically offered

[42] Addobbati, *Commercio, rischio, guerra*, pp. 65–6.

[43] Tazzara, *The Free Port of Livorno*; Corey Tazzara, 'Managing free trade in early modern Europe: institutions, information and the free port of Livorno', *Journal of Modern History* 86 (2014), 493–529.

[44] Tazzara, *The Free Port of Livorno*, pp. 83, 113.

[45] Tazzara, *The Free Port of Livorno*, pp. 186, 197.

[46] Tazzara, *The Free Port of Livorno*, pp. 85–98, 127; Guillaume Calafat, 'La somme des besoins: rescrits, informations et suppliques (Toscane, 1550–1750)', *L'Atelier du Centre de recherches historiques* 13 (2015), <https://journals.openedition.org/acrh/6558> [accessed 2 February 2024].

[47] Tazzara, *The Free Port of Livorno*, p. 127.

[48] Ibid.

only to those who intended to settle and become citizens. In practice, protection was often offered to ordinary merchants who had no intention of settling.[49]

These informal aspects of Livorno – the 'culture of collaboration' and the 'lax rules and careless scrutiny' – were equally as important to define what it meant to be a free port.[50] Even after the relative simplification of procedures in 1676, there were other pressures which encouraged a generous interpretation of the rules. Competition between the Mediterranean ports to attract traffic exerted a downwards pressure on port authorities, both precipitating more generous arrangements for merchants and discouraging the enforcement of existing constraints even further, lest merchants decide to move to greener pastures.[51] Marseille and Genoa were Livorno's particular rivals in this respect, and the threat to decamp, however empty, was leveraged with some success by foreign consuls at various points in the early modern period.[52]

The extent to which a 'culture of collaboration' was a specifically Livornese phenomenon is debatable: all early modern polities suffered to a certain extent from unenforceable rules, corrupt officials, and *ad hoc* solutions.[53] Administration-as-justice was likewise not an unusual phenomenon, as we shall see.[54] Nevertheless, whatever the singularity of the Livornese *modus operandi*, we see a similar attitude to the one described by Tazzara prevailing in GA cases presided over by the court of the *Consoli*. A similar permissiveness can be observed in the way GA cases were handled, despite the fact that the court was located outside of Livorno in nearby Pisa. If anything, the court's location outside of the port intensified this dynamic. The motivation was similar: a tendency to take the path of least resistance combined with a desire to protect the commercial vitality of the court and a willingness to accept outcomes negotiated by the participants themselves. The chief difference was that the benefit was chiefly felt not by foreign merchants resident in the port but rather the shipmasters.

Fiscal and administrative concerns were not the only part of Livorno's appeal. The attention given to the administrative architecture of the free port tends to overshadow the concrete naval infrastructure that was created specifically to cater to maritime traffic. Across the sixteenth and early seventeenth centuries, Livorno was availed of plenty of space for the unloading

---

[49] Tazzara, *The Free Port of Livorno*, pp. 78–80; Edigati, 'Aspetti giuridici delle franchigie di Livorno', pp. 17–18.

[50] Tazzara, *The Free Port of Livorno*, pp. 96, 127.

[51] Tazzara, *The Free Port of Livorno*, p. 8.

[52] Cipolla, *Il burocrate e il marinaio*, pp. 103–6; Kirk, 'Genoa and Livorno', p. 17: Fusaro, *Political Economies of Empire*, p. 95.

[53] Clemente and Zaugg, 'The grand narrative of new institutional economics', p. 125.

[54] See Luca Mannori and Bernardo Sordi, *Storia del diritto amministrativo*, new edn (Rome: Laterza, 2013), pp. 52–6.

and warehousing of merchandise, facilities for ship repair, and piers for the protection of vessels.[55] Several *lazeretti* were built in order to quarantine men and merchandise considered at risk of introducing plague, and these were accompanied by excellent health regulations.[56] Modern advocates of the free port as a tool of regional development might do well to consider Livorno not so much a successful example of a free port, but rather as the manifestation of the adage 'build it and they will come'. This effort to cater to the maritime transport sector on which the commercial economy depended is likewise something that seems to be reflected in the authorities' attitude towards GA.

Perhaps the most important consideration for our purposes, however, is simply the fact that Livorno was a new city, one that lacked a powerful native mercantile elite with well-entrenched political influence. The dynamic that this created between economic and political power in the port was the single most important influence on the way that maritime-legal cases like GA unfolded and explains the majority of differences we observe with nearby international ports such as Genoa. It is true that many members of the Florentine partriciate continued to participate in commerce right through the Medici period into the eighteenth century, both as passive investors and, sometimes, as active managers of their own commercial capital – we will have occasion to meet some of these figures in the following pages – but, overall, their capital was increasingly invested in Tuscany itself rather than in foreign trade.[57]

The situation in Livorno was therefore very different to the one that prevailed in other major Italian port centres like Genoa and Venice.[58] Livorno was not the capital of the state it was located in. Tuscan businessmen, moreover, were not central to its vitality, and those that were operating there did not have the whip hand in influencing commercial policy. In Genoa, meanwhile, trade remained concentrated in the hands of a mercantile oligarchy, who also constituted the judicial and political elite of the republic. This political economy pushed the form and substance of GA procedures in a different direction, as we will see in the following chapters. Whilst the Grand Dukes naturally wished to promote Tuscan commerce and industry, the private interests of native merchants were not always the regime's first consideration. Livorno was an important source of prestige and revenue for the Grand Duke, but the great

---

[55] L. Frattarelli-Fischer, 'Merci e mercanti nella Livorno secentesca', in Silvana Balbi de Caro (ed.), *Merci e monete a Livorno in età granducale* (Livorno: Cassa di Risparmio di Livorno, 1997), 65–104, at p. 66.

[56] See Cipolla, *Il burocrate e Il marinaio*.

[57] Robert Burr Litchfield, *The Emergence of a Bureaucracy: The Florentine Patricians, 1530–1790* (Princeton: Princeton University Press, 1986), p. 211.

[58] Fusaro, *Political Economies of Empire*, pp. 89–109.

free port experiment worked no corresponding economic miracle in the rest of the region. Indeed, one of the most striking elements in the history of the free port is that, while the rest of the world looked on in envious admiration at apparent Tuscan success, the Tuscans themselves were growing increasingly frustrated at the apparent inability of the free port to stimulate broader development in the Tuscan economy.[59]

The Court of the *Consoli del Mare* in Pisa

Another peculiarity of the Tuscan situation is that its most important maritime tribunal lay outside of the city where most of the maritime commerce was actually taking place, much to the frustration of Livorno-based merchants. This was the court of the *Consoli del Mare* (the Consuls of the Sea), which stood just over 20 km away from Livorno in the ancient maritime republic of Pisa. Despite its undoubted contemporary importance and rich archival patrimony, little scholarship exists that directly concerns this important court.[60] There is also currently no modern-day index of cases for the voluminous documentation that the *Consoli* produced, which makes working with the sources more difficult than it might otherwise be. While this situation leaves a lot to be desired, and further research in this area would be welcome, it is nevertheless possible to sketch out an administrative history of the institution, albeit largely from the top-down perspective of the Grand Ducal government.

The early modern court of the *Consoli* was a Medici resurrection of an ancient Pisan institution. During the Middle Ages, the court had been the most senior element of the *Ordo Maris*, a powerful corporate body with responsibility for all maritime matters and which remained the principal economic governing body even after the conquest of Pisa in the 1400s.[61] Having been briefly abolished under the rule of Alessandro de' Medici, the first Duke of Tuscany, the court was refounded in 1551 by Cosimo I, this time with two *Consoli* based in Pisa. Both were to be Florentine citizens and ideally would be possessed of some commercial experience. The court was twinned with

---

[59] Lisa Lillie, 'Commercio, cosmopolitismo e modelli della modernità: Livorno nell'immaginario inglese a stampa, 1590–1750' in Andrea Addobbati and Marcella Aglietti (eds), *La città delle nazioni: Livorno e i limiti del cosmopolitismo (1566–1834)* (Pisa: Pisa Univerity Press, 2016), 337–57; Tazzara, *The Free Port of Livorno*, pp. 202–31.

[60] Andrea Addobbati, 'La giurisdizione marittima e commerciale dei consoli del mare in età medicea', in Marco Tangheroni (ed.), *Pisa e il Mediterraneo: uomini, merci, idee dagli Etruschi ai Medici* (Milan: Skira, 2003), 311–15; Calafat, 'La somme des besoins'; Massimo Sanacore, 'I consoli del mare a Pisa, dall'età medicea alle riforme leopoldine' (unpublished MA thesis, University of Pisa, 1983); Lo Bartolo, 'The *consoli del mare*'.

[61] Addobbati, 'I consoli del mare', p. 311.

the Florentine *Mercanzia*, the Florentine court with jurisdiction over both commercial cases and those between Florentine citizens and foreigners. This meant that the two courts were meant to enjoy the same jurisdiction in their respective cities.[62] It was declared by Cosimo I that the *Consoli* should have the same competences as their republican forebears, but in 1557 and 1561 it was necessary to issue reforms to define what this actually meant in practice. This 1561 reform was a key piece of legislation.[63] Originally, it gave the *Consoli* a role in the management of the city and surrounding countryside, though this was reduced over the course of the seventeenth century.[64] Significantly for our purposes, the reform also gave the *Consoli* jurisdiction over all maritime cases between shipmaster and merchants or the master and his mariners, with the Captain (later Governor) of Livorno retaining only disputes between mariners themselves. Since GAs always involved a master and merchants, this meant that GA fell squarely in the Consular remit.[65]

The judgements issued by the *Consoli* were in theory unappealable, but an important change for the court occurred in 1600 with the creation of the *Consulta Regis* based in Florence, which provided a means of effectively overturning them.[66] The basis of this transformation was Grand Ducal ideology, which cast the prince as *paterfamilias* of his people, a site of justice and clemency that transcended the rigid strictures of the law.[67] Any judgement issued by a Tuscan court, even one that was considered immediately executive and unappealable, could be overruled by the prince if he felt it was unjust or if he felt that clemency should prevail. In reality, petitions were soon too numerous for a single Grand Duke to manage. Manned by three jurists of considerable experience, the *Consulta* would therefore decide on behalf of the Grand Duke to which court petitions should be 'delegated' for further consideration.[68] The original court, meanwhile, might be required to provide 'information' (*informazioni*), justifying its original decision. Cases coming

---

[62] Sanacore, 'I consoli del mare a Pisa', pp. 57–8.

[63] ASF, *Auditore poi Segretario delle Riformagioni*, 116.

[64] Sanacore, 'I consoli del mare a Pisa', pp. 51–79.

[65] The Captain of Livorno was given the right to redact *consolati* in 1577. See Guillaume Calafat, 'Livorno e la camera di commercio di Marsiglia nel XVII secolo: consoli francesi, agenti e riscossione del cottimo', in Andrea Addobbati and Marcella Aglietti (eds), *La città delle nazioni: Livorno e i limiti del cosmopolitismo (1566–1834)* (Pisa: Pisa University Press, 2016), 237–76, at pp. 242–3.

[66] Sanacore, 'I consoli del mare a Pisa', pp. 178–9; Addobbati, 'I consoli del mare', pp. 311–12; Luca Mannori, *Lo stato del granduca, 1530–1859: le istituzioni della Toscana moderna in un percorso di testi commentate* (Pisa: Pacini Editore, 2015), pp. 70–1; Calafat, 'La somme des besoins', pp. 4–6; Burr Litchfield, *The Emergence of a Bureaucracy*, p. 89.

[67] Calafat, 'La somme des besoins', p. 3.

[68] Calafat, 'La somme des besoins', p. 4; Mannori, *Lo stato del granduca*, p. 70.

from the Consular court in Pisa would almost always be delegated to the Florentine *ruota*, the highest civil court in Tuscany.[69] On the advice of this tribunal, the Grand Duke would give his response in the form of a rescript (*rescritto*), written on the original petition itself. This might ask the *Consoli* to 'reconsider' or 'revise' their original judgement, thus recognising their formal right to issue final and unappealable pronouncements but in effect ordering that it be overturned.

Despite the fact that the location of the court in Pisa made life difficult for Livorno-based merchants, the *Consoli* managed to retain and even increase their ample maritime jurisdiction throughout the seventeenth century. Though there were periodic disputes over jurisdiction between the *Consoli* and the Governor's Court in Livorno, the Florentine authorities almost always sided with the *Consoli*.[70] In 1623, it was decided that the court of the *Consoli* was the sole court of appeal for cases coming from the Governor's court; previously, his decisions could also have been appealed directly to the *ruota*.[71] It was also possible to appeal to the *Consoli* from the Governor of Livorno's tribunal for all civil lawsuits with a value greater than 100 *lire* (later increased to 200 *lire*).[72] In 1632, exclusive Consular jurisdiction over insurance cases was confirmed.[73] There was a particular crisis point in the 1650s as Consular executive powers and maritime jurisdiction were challenged by the Governor's court, but the *Pratica Segreta* – the body responsible for resolving jurisdictional questions in the Grand Duchy – eventually ruled that the Governor's court should not impede the activities of the *Consoli* in any way.[74] The only decision that went against this general direction of travel during this century was that of 1684, which established that cases involving corsairs could be resolved in Livorno, not being strictly 'commercial' in nature.[75] The jurisdictional

---

[69] On the Florentine *ruota* see Giuseppe Pansini, 'La ruota Fiorentina nelle strutture giudiziarie del Granducato di Toscana sotto I Medici', in Leo Olschki (ed.), *La formazione storica del diritto moderno in Europa* (Florence. Società italiana di storia del diritto, 1977), 533–79.

[70] See Massimo Sanacore, 'Le fonti giurisdizionali Pisano-Livornesi e i conflitti di competenze nei secoli XVI–XVII', *Studi Livornesi* 4 (1989), 77–93.

[71] Addobbati, 'I consoli del mare', pp. 314–15; Sanacore, 'I consoli del mare a Pisa', p. 56; Calafat, 'La sommes des besoins', p. 9.

[72] Sanacore, 'I consoli del mare a Pisa', p. 56.

[73] Sanacore, 'I consoli del mare a Pisa', p. 215.

[74] Sanacore, 'I consoli del mare a Pisa', pp. 216–17; the *Pratica Segreta* was an advisory council created by Cosimo I to advise on fiscal, administrative, and jurisdictional questions. Its members were chosen by the Grand Duke and usually included the *auditore fiscale*, the *auditore delle riformagioni*, and the *auditore della giurisdizione*. See Furio Diaz, *Il Granducato di Toscana. I Medici* (Florence: UTET, 1976), pp. 97–8.

[75] Sanacore, 'I consoli del mare a Pisa', p. 219; Addobbati, 'I consoli del mare', pp. 314–15.

boundaries regarding GAs were therefore fairly clean cut. Since requesting a GA involved a shipmaster and receiving merchants, this fell squarely into the Consular remit. If a merchant wished to challenge a GA, he had to submit a petition to the Grand Duke and in these instances the case would go to the Florentine *ruota*.

As will be explained further in Chapter Two, the foundational 1561 reform offered no clarification as to how GA cases ought to be dealt with by the court, despite its comprehensive nature, with the original reform document containing more than 400 different directives. In this respect, Tuscany stands in contrast to some other states who were reforming their GA procedures in the same period. Amsterdam had instituted a new Chamber of Insurance and Average in 1598, after merchants complained that they were causing too many problems to be handled by the 'wise men' who had previously resolved such disputes.[76] The three Commissioners of this court were generally experienced merchants who retained their position for six years in order that the court should avail itself of considerable experience in judging cases. Similarly in Genoa there was an attempt to add new certainty to Average procedures in 1588 with the institution of a new office, the *Calcolatori* (Office of the Calculators), who were to be specifically instituted to adjudicate and award Averages and to assess damages.[77] In both these cases, the creation of new bodies was accompanied by the creation of new statutes which were to clarify the norms and procedures surrounding Averages.[78] The Genoese innovations were admittedly not destined to remain unaltered for long, with the *Conservatori del Mare* (a body manned by members of the nobility) first taking the independent calculators under their aegis, then gradually robbing them of many of their competences over the course of the seventeenth century.[79] It is, nevertheless, curious that we see no similar moves in the Tuscan case, with GA remaining, as we will see, something of an uncharted blank space on the juridical and statuatory map.

---

[76] See Sabine Go, 'The Amsterdam Chamber of Insurance and Average: a new phase in formal contract enforcement (late sixteenth and seventeenth centuries)', *Enterprise & Society* 14 (2013), 511–43; Sabine Go, 'GA adjustments in Amsterdam: reinforcing authority through transparency and accountability (late sixteenth–early seventeenth century)', in Maria Fusaro, Andrea Addobbati, and Luisa Piccinno (eds), *General Average and Risk Management in Medieval and Early Modern Maritime Business* (Cham: Springer, 2023), 389–414.

[77] Iodice, 'General average in Genoa', p. 280; Go, 'GA adjustments in Amsterdam', p. 394.

[78] Iodice, 'General average in Genoa', p. 279; Go, 'GA adjustments in Amsterdam', p. 395.

[79] See Iodice, 'General Average in Genoa'.

The Court Personnel

An unflattering perspective on the court *Consoli del Mare* has come down to us from the seventeenth century in the unexpected form of a musical comedy. On 2 March 1661, the city of Florence was celebrating *carnivale*, a night of levity on the eve of the lean Lenten season. Members of the *Accademia degli Immobili*, among them Cardinal Giancarlo de' Medici, brother of the Grand Duke, were hurrying up to the newly opened *teatro della pergola* to mark the festivities. That evening's offering was a comedy by Giovanni Andrea Moniglia, replete with music and dancing and promising 'fun' and 'innocent recreation' to its patrons.[80] Its hero was already well known to the members of the academy from Moniglia's previous 'civil dramas': Anselmo Giannozzi, Florentine citizen, reluctant civil servant, dirty old man, and all-round buffoon.[81] This time, Anselmo found himself ensnared by the charms of the young and beautiful Drusilla. Unfortunately, tiresome administrative responsibilities insisted on getting in the way, for Anselmo had been landed with the unenviable role of *Console del Mare di Pisa*.

> *Anselmo*: Quick, draw a slip of paper from my hat.
> *Drusilla*: And why should I?
> *Anselmo*: We have us two merchants who are locked in dispute, today is the day I must choose 'tween the two. Who cares about gold, and who cares about honour, the name that you pull from my hat is the winner!
> *Drusilla*: Oh, poor Justice!
> *Anselmo*: Come on.
> *Drusilla*: You pick.
> *Anselmo*: Meliachim the Armenian. I declare him a dear and noble fellow. As long as I adopt such procedures, the loser can only blame his bad luck, and never the Consulate!
>
> [*Ans*. Cava presto
> Fuor del Cappello un Polizzino. *Drus*. E questo
> Perché? *Ans*. Son due mercanti
> Ch'hanno una lite; il giudice son io.

---

[80] 'La Serva nobile' (1661) in Giovanni Andrea Moniglia, *Delle poesie drammatiche* (Florence: Alla Condotta, 1689), vol. 3, pp. 173–259. In his preface to this and other plays in the same collection, Moniglia recommends that 'divertimento degli animi sia onorato, nobile il sollievo, la ricreazione innocente'; see vol. 1, p. ix. On Moniglia and his civil dramas, as well as the context of the performances, see Marco Catucci, 'MONIGLIA, Giovanni Andrea', in *Dizionario Biografico degli Italiani* (Rome: Istituto dell'Enciclopedia Italiana, 2011), vol. 75 <www.treccani.it/enciclopedia/giovanni-andrea-moniglia_(Dizionario-Biografico)/> [accessed 2 February 2024].

[81] For example, *Il pazzo per forza* (1658) and *Il vecchio balordo* (1659), see Catucci, 'MONIGLIA, Giovanni Andrea'.

> Oggi va la sentenza.
> Ch'importa onore et oro,
> Ho scritto i nomi loro
> In due facciole, e messe nel cappello.
> Tirane un fuora, e quel
> Che esce abbia ragione.
> *Drus.* Oh, povera giustizia! *Ans.* Presto. *Drus.* Pigli.
> *Ans.* Meliachim Armeno.
> L'ho caro, è galant'uomo. In questa forma
> Mentre farò, la colpa
> Dar deve il sentenziato
> Alla Fortuna, e non al Consolato.][82]

Moniglia's *Commedia del Console*, as it became known, does not suggest a particularly high regard for the *Consoli del Mare* or their procedures; it certainly transmits a rather dim view of the justices themselves. Having spent several years in Pisa as a student, Moniglia's decision to make the court the butt of his joke may not have been entirely random.[83] Yet though the upstanding nature of individual *Consoli* is impossible to establish, more sober evidence than Moniglia's 'innocent recreation' suggests that the central Tuscan authorities were in fact fairly conscientious in their efforts to choose candidates with appropriate experience for the role.

Anselmo had been landed with his unwelcome new role as judge thanks to the fact that he was a member of the Florentine nobility: all *Consoli* were required to be Florentine citizens and had to possess sufficient property to qualify them for payment of the *decima* tax.[84] They would preferably be members of the *Consiglio dei Quarantotto* or senate – a council created by the Medici comprising 48 members drawn from the most important families of Florence.[85] They would also, ideally, have some experience in commercial matters.[86] Candidates were obliged to move out of the capital to the palace of the *dogana* (customs house) in Pisa so that cases would not be delayed (no doubt some of Anselmo's real-life counterparts shared his chagrin on

---

[82] *La Serva Nobile*, Act III, Scene 25, pp. 248–9.

[83] Catucci, 'MONIGLIA, Giovanni Andrea'.

[84] Sanacore, 'I consoli del mare a Pisa', p. 48. On the 'nobility' see Marcella Aglietti, 'Patrizi, cavalieri e mercanti. Politiche di nobiltà tra Toscana e Spagna in età moderna', in Marcella Aglietti (ed.), *Istituzioni, potere e società. Le relazioni tra Spagna e Toscana per una storia mediterranea dell'Ordine dei Cavalieri di Santo Stefano* (Pisa: Edizioni ETS, 2007), 339–77.

[85] Addobbati, 'I consoli del mare', pp. 314–15; Jonathan Davies, *Culture and Power: Tuscany and its Universities, 1537–1609* (Leiden: Brill, 2009), p. 40.

[86] Addobbati, 'I consoli del mare', pp. 314–15; Sanacore, 'I consoli del mare a Pisa', p. 48.

this score) and their appointments were to last a year with the possibility of a six-month extension at the discretion of the Grand Duke.[87]

A list of *Consoli* and their officials found in the Pisan archive confirms that this pattern of appointments was indeed adopted in practice across most of the century, at least until the accession of Cosimo III in 1670.[88] Across the first three quarters of the century, we find two *Consoli* being appointed for one-year terms in May and November, respectively: 1617 is the only exception, in which three *Consoli* were appointed in a single year, two of whom were appointed only for six months each. A few candidates served multiple terms: Vettorio Nelli, for example, served as *Console* in 1640, 1643, and 1647, and a few others served twice. Nevertheless, the contrast with the Amsterdam Chamber is clear. While the Commissioners in Amsterdam served for a full six consecutive years, in order that they might accumulate valuable judicial nous, the judges in the Tuscan case acquired, at most, a few years of comparable experience. In the majority of cases, they had only a year in which to orientate themselves in their new role. Their familiarity with the court's activities was thus entirely dependent on their own personal experience as merchants.

Satirical attacks at the hands of dramatists notwithstanding, however, it seems that the Tuscan authorities really did try to ensure that these figures were possessed of some commercial experience in making the appointments. A preliminary prosopographical study of the court by Alessandro Lo Bartolo, comparing the list of *Consoli* with the records of *accomandite* (bilateral, limited business partnerships) in Florence, shows that at least half the *Consoli* in the period 1550–1750 were directly involved in trade themselves or had a confirmed close relative who was, whilst a further 40 per cent had family names which appear in the *accomandita* register (of which some may in fact have been close relatives).[89] The real extent of Consular involvement in commerce is most likely higher, since investing in *accomandite* was by no means the only way of getting involved in business. Eventually, the Tuscans also seem to have tried to give the judges more experience by extending their terms, a phenomenon that began gradually during the reign of Cosimo III.[90] From May 1674 to June 1676, Luigi Ulbaldini appears to have been the sole *Console*. Camillo Gherardini held his post for two years, from 1685 to 1687. From November 1687 until May 1695, both posts were held by Lodovico Alamanni and Carlo Poltri, respectively, with Poltri remaining in office until 1698 alongside Ruberto del Beccuto. By the end of the century, the custom of nominating two new *Consoli* a year had completely broken down. There is no clear way to interpret this development. Our source, an official list of

---

[87] Sanacore, 'I consoli del mare a Pisa', p. 49.
[88] ASP, MM, 112.
[89] Lo Bartolo, 'The *consoli del mare*', pp. 191–2.
[90] ASP, MM, 112.

Consoli housed in the archives, records not that the holder was granted a tenure of a specific number of years but notes on a rolling basis every time that the term was extended, six additional months at a time. The administration could, of course, have been continually putting off making new appointments by simply proroguing the current appointee's term, suggesting a lack of interest in the role. It seems more likely, however, that the opposite was true, and that the administration recognised the need to give judges more experience at a time when the volume and complexity of maritime-commercial cases was increasing.[91] The unusual way of recording appointments is probably simply an attempt to preserve form, given that the 1561 statutes envisaged only six-month extensions on the annual term.[92]

In theory, the commercial experience of the *Consoli* was not the only thing that gave the justice of the court a 'mercantile' character. If a case which was worth more than 300 *scudi* reached its fortieth day, a procedure known as '*ricorso*' could be initiated.[93] A college of judges was drawn up, comprising the *Consoli*, the commissioner (*commissario*) of the city of Pisa, and either four, six, or eight merchants, whose names were to be drawn from the *borse di ricorso* – the *ricorso* lists, or, literally, the 'bags of the *ricorso*'. One bag contained the names of eight Florentine merchants, the other contained eight Pisan merchants, and these names were changed every three years. While the former were Florentine citizens, the 'Pisans' were simply inhabitants of the city and could be foreigners. However, this system does not seem to have been widely used. Even the 1561 statutes gave litigants the option to avoid it and to force the *Consoli* to arrive at a judgement within the original 45-day limit.[94] A later government report on the court of the *Consoli* produced in 1744 for the incoming Lorraine dynasty reports that judgements arrived at through *ricorso* usually depended not on mercantile custom, but rather on the eloquence of the laywers employed or each side, or else rivalries among the merchants.[95] It was therefore little used, and interested merchants had begun to resort to 'written practices', that is producing written statements of mercantile customs countersigned by a number of their fellows. We know that the *borse* continued to exist until at least the 1650s, because, as we will see, the calculators in GA cases were drawn from them.[96] After this time, they seem to disappear from the record.

---

[91] Andrea Addobbati, 'Until the very last nail: English seafaring and wage litigation in seventeenth-century Livorno', in Maria Fusaro, Bernard Allaire, Richard Blakemore, and Tijl Vanneste (eds), *Law, Labour and Empire: Comparative Perspectives on Seafarers, c. 1500–1800* (London: Palgrave Macmillan, 2015), 43–60, at pp. 49–50.

[92] Sanacore, 'I consoli del mare a Pisa', p. 47.

[93] See Sanacore, 'I consoli del mare a Pisa', pp. 101–3.

[94] Addobbati, 'I consoli del mare', pp. 313–14.

[95] Lo Bartolo, 'The *consoli del mare*', pp. 185–6.

[96] pp. 82–3.

This is not to say that the *Consoli* determined the outcomes of cases unaided. The court was also possessed of a permanent staff of officials – legal 'technicians' who aided the *Consoli* in their deliberations. Of particular importance was the chancellor (*cancelliere*) of the court, known as the secretary (*segretario*) from the 1660s onwards. In protracted disputes an assessor (*assessore* or *avvocato*) could also be called upon by the litigants, who was always a Doctor of Law who lectured at Pisa University.[97] And as the 1744 report mentions, the parties were sometimes represented by attorneys (*procuratori*).[98]

The weight of these figures within the court set up was considerable, probably greater than that of the *Consoli* themselves. In particular, the chancellor's authority over procedures not only allowed him control over the information on which a judgement was based, as we will see further in Chapter 3, but also allowed him to direct the activities of the court more broadly.[99] This balance of power is suggested in the difference between the 1561 statutes and the wording of the 1604 reform. Whereas the 1561 statutes had held both *Consoli* and employees of the court responsible for procedural mistakes (threatening them with a fine), the equivalent stipulation in the 1604 reform holds only the Chancellor responsible, recognising an effective diminution of the Consular remit.[100] This was made even clearer in a Grand Ducal *rescritto* of 1662 which named the chancellor as 'secretary for the tribunal' (*segretario al tribunale*), explicitly limiting the role of the *Consoli* to the hearing and judgement.[101] In contrast to the *Consoli*, the list of appointees to the court shows that the chancellors were men of considerable experience. Agapito Titio held the role from 1562 to his death in 1598. His son Lorenzo then held it until 1617.[102] Later chancellors did not linger quite so long, but still performed long terms of service, often as a stepping stone in an illustrious career in public administration. Emilio Luci was chancellor from 1659 until 1669, when he was appointed *auditore fiscale*, the highest authority in the Tuscan legal system and defender of the state's fiscal interests in all criminal cases.[103] Tommaso Cepparelli likewise held the position from Luci's departure until at least 1676, eventually becoming *luogotenente fiscale*, the other main officeholder in the *congregazione del fisco*.[104] Benedetto Mochi was appointed

[97] ASF, *Auditore poi Segretario delle Riformagioni*, 116, § 24; Calafat, 'La somme des besoins', p. 9.

[98] Lo Bartolo, 'The *consoli del mare*', p. 186.

[99] Sanacore, 'I consoli del mare a Pisa', pp. 66–7, 92, 97.

[100] Sanacore, 'I consoli del mare a Pisa', pp. 167–74.

[101] Sanacore, 'I consoli del mare a Pisa', p. 191; Addobbati, 'I consoli del mare', pp. 313–14.

[102] ASP, MM, 112.

[103] Emilio Luci to Cardinal Leopoldo de Medici (6 April 1671), ASF, MM, 358-17.

[104] For a summary of both of these roles see Burr Litchfield, *Emergence of a Bureaucracy*, p. 85.

for at least two years before becoming *auditore* (chief legal official) of the Governor's court in Livorno in 1691.[105] It was not strictly necessary that the chancellor be a Doctor of Law, though it is clear that, in practice, this was always the case.[106] The chancellor at the time of the reform, Agapito Titio, is explicitly listed as doctor *in utroque*.[107] A memorandum from 1662, moreover, notes that the chancellor was already carrying out the role of legal consultant (*consultore legale*), which would have necessitated the election of a jurist to the position.[108] The *Consoli*, on the other hand, would probably not have received a legal education. Since many of the top positions in the Tuscan bureaucracy and judiciary that required legal training were actually not open to Florentine citizens, going to university was not a priority for high-ranking Florentines who wished to embark on a career in public administration.[109]

The attorneys meanwhile were quite a limited number and consequently must have become very well-acquainted with one another. In fact, we find only two regularly conducting GA cases at any one time during our period.[110] These men would naturally have received a legal education, and it has also been claimed that the attorneys who worked in the court of the *Consoli* in the seventeenth century were notaries.[111] This seems to have indeed been the case in the first half of the century. We find all three proctors named in the sources from 1600 and 1640 in the index of notarial protocols housed in the state archive in Florence: Amadio Ghibellini (acting as a notary in Pisa between at least 1595 and 1613), Lorenzo Zucchetti (1634–58), and Vincenzo Frosini (1617–49).[112] In the second half of the century, on the other hand, the attorneys appear not to have been notaries themselves. Michelangelo Frosini, a proctor from 1670, could have been the father of the notary, Giovanni Vincenzo Frosini, active in Livorno from 1663 to 1670 and bearing the patronymic 'Michelangelo'. He might also have been a relative of Alessandro Frosini, a notary active in Pisa in the same period: he himself, however, is not to be found in the index. Many of the Frosini family appear to have held positions at Pisa University.[113] A government report on GA from the late eighteenth

---

[105] ASP, MM, 112.

[106] ASP, MM, 112; Lo Bartolo, 'The *consoli del mare*', p. 184.

[107] ASF, Auditore poi Segretario delle Riformagioni, 116, f. 1r.

[108] Sanacore, 'I consoli del Mare a Pisa', p. 191.

[109] Burr Litchfield, *The Emergence of a Bureaucracy*, pp. 158–62.

[110] ASP, CM, AC, 198-17 (13 August 1640), Citation; ASP, CM, AC, 320-7 (28 May 1670), Citation; ASP, CM, AC, 417-27 (23 March 1699/1700), Citation; ASP, CM, AC, 417-16 (9 February 1699/1700), Judgement.

[111] Guillaume Calafat, 'Jurisdictional pluralism in a litigious sea (1590–1630): hard cases, multi-sited trials and legal enforcement between North Africa and Italy', *Past & Present* 242 (2019), 142–78, at p. 169.

[112] ASF, Inventario N/484, 'Notarile Moderno: Inventario sommario dei notai che hanno rogato in Toscana dal 1569 al 1860'.

[113] See Marta Battistoni, 'Molina di Quosa e la casa di Michele'. A copy of this unpublished study was given to me by Professor Andrea Addobbati.

century suggests that all cases were handled with the help of these attorneys, but in the seventeenth century it is not possible to definitely establish their presence in every case. For they year 1600 they were present for at least one of the parties in 9 of the 13 cases, for 8 of the 10 cases in 1640, for 5 of the 19 cases in 1670, and for 5 of the 12 cases dealt with in 1700. Sometimes they are recorded as having represented one part of the other only aurally ('*in voce*').[114] Sometimes they are explicitly mentioned in the court summons along with the part they represent; sometimes their presence can be inferred from the fact that a fee is levied in their name at the end of the procedure.[115] In those cases where neither indiciation is present, the parties probably did not avail themselves of the services of an attorney.

The mixed composition of the court – merchant litigants, patrician-merchant *Consoli*, and university-educated officials – allows us a perspective on a central problem in the history of commercial law, namely the relative importance of the *ius commune* in the actual operation of commercial justice during the early modern period, a question which in turn directly pertains to the issue of commercial law's autonomy. Though educated jurists had in fact often written on commercial subjects in the medieval period, it is undoubtedly the case that the early modern period saw increasing 'professionalisation' in the field of private commercial law, a development which increased the potential relevance of *ius commune* principles and even the substantive rules contained within its authoritative texts. Learned jurists became increasingly interested and involved in mercantile cases, and the publication of *De mercatura seu mercatore tractatus* (Treatise on commerce or the merchant) by Benvenuto Stracca in Venice in 1553 heralded a new era in which university-educated jurists published increasing numbers of treatises dedicated exclusively to commercial and maritime law.[116] The other major development in this period was the increasing importance of centralised courts whose decisions were published in printed collections, with the activities of the Genoese *Rota* being considered particularly important for maritime and commercial law.[117] Whilst the *Rota* sought to uphold existing Genoese mercantile custom, explicitly maintaining the principle of *mercatorum observantia facit ius* (the observance of merchants makes law), the judges of the *Rota* naturally carried forward their own experience and education as jurists to the cases they encountered.[118]

---

[114] ASP, CM, AC, 198-17 (14 August 1640).

[115] ASP, CM, AC, 199-16 (15 November 1640); ASP, CM, AC, 198-17 (14 August 1640).

[116] Benvenuto Stracca, *De mercatvra, sev mercatore tractatvs*, ed. Marco Cian (Turin: Giappichelli, 2024).

[117] Mario Ascheri, *Introduzione storica al diritto moderno e contemporaneo* (Turin: Giappichelli, 2008), pp. 134–46.

[118] Vito Piergiovanni, 'The rise of the Genoese civil rota in the XVIth century: the "decisiones de mercatura" concerning insurance', in Vito Piergiovanni (ed.), *The Courts and the Development of Commercial Law* (Berlin: Duncker & Humbolt, 1987), 24–39.

One might assume that the university-educated officials at the court of the *Consoli* would have brought the attitudes, concepts, and even doctrine that they had learned as law students and professional lawyers to bear on the cases unfolding in the tribunal. Some scholars have given this increasing involvement of jurists a positive valence: the result was largely one of continuity, accompanied by 'a technical refinement of language and concepts'.[119] On the other hand, a commonplace in merchant manuals of the period is that the sophistry of the civil lawyers and their *ius commune* was entirely unsuited to mercantile justice and was to be avoided as far as possible, as it tended to unnecessarily complicate affairs and introduce new and pedantic requirements that mattered little to the pratical people of commerce: 'full of quillets and distinctions, overcurious and precise ... they doe more regard certain subtleties than the trueth of the fact or matter', as the Anglo-Flemish merchant Gerard Malynes colourfully put it in 1622.[120] This attitude likewise resonates into the present, finding a modern-day counterpart, among others, in articulations of the lex mercatoria idea. A study of the court of the *Consoli del Mare* sheds further light on how these different legal attitudes and traditions actually interacted in practice, as part of a debate that is not without emotional charge and that even today tends to get mixed up with questions of professional pride and identity.

The Use of Summary Procedure

The tribunal of the *Consoli*, like its medieval forebearers, had been granted the privilege of using summary procedure.[121] This was a truncated form of judiciary procedure designed to expedite the lengthy and expensive process of going to court. Summary procedure remains somewhat understudied, and recent work is only just beginning to reveal the variety of forms that it could take.[122] It originated in the medieval period and owed its existence to the precepts of canon law, which placed foreigners, including merchants, in the category of the 'weak', and thus worthy of special dispensation.[123] Particularly

---

[119] Vito Piergiovanni, 'Genoese civil rota and mercantile customary law', in Vito Piergiovanni (ed.), *From Lex Mercatoria to Commercial Law* (Berlin: Duncker & Humblot, 2005), 191–206, at p. 192.

[120] Gerard Malynes, *Consuetudo vel lex mercatoria*, 3rd edn (London, 1685, originally published 1622), pp. 3–4.

[121] Lo Bartolo, 'The *consoli del mare*', pp. 184–5.

[122] Simona Cerutti, *Giustizia sommaria: pratiche e ideali di giustizia in una società di ancien régime* (Milan: Feltrinelli, 2003); Cerutti, 'Fatti e fatti giudiziari'; Roberto Zaugg, 'Judging foreigners. Conflict strategies, consular interventions and institutional changes in eighteenth-century Naples', *Journal of Modern Italian Studies* 13 (2008), 171–95.

[123] Mario Ascheri, 'Il processo civile tra diritto comune e diritto locale da questioni preliminari al caso della giustizia estense', *Quaderni Storici* 34 (1999), 355–87, at p. 363; Vito Piergiovanni, 'Il mercante e il diritto canonico medievale: "mercatores in

important in the establishment of summary procedure were the fourteenth-century papal decretals *saepe contingit* (promulgated somewhere between 1312 and 1314) and *dispendiosam* (1312).[124] These both described summary procedure as 'plain, without the clamour and form of a trial' (*de plano, sine strepitu e forma iudicii*).[125] Neither document was very clear about what exactly should be omitted, however, and summary procedure was therefore primarily defined by what it was not, rather than what it was.[126] Summary procedure soon spread throughout Italy and thence to the rest of Europe, and came to be seen as an efficacious solution to the problem of commercial justice where cases needed to be resolved quickly.[127] This was especially urgent as litigation increased in line with greater literacy and social mobility. In some places, it is clear that it was deployed selectively and strategically as a political-economic tool in order to favour certain groups: in Venice, for example, English litigants were unable to access summary procedure as the Venetians (correctly) identified them as the chief threat to their own commercial interests in the Levant.[128] In some courts, the procedures were very truncated indeed, with the two sides presented orally, and without either the production of witnesses or the intervention of laywers to represent the sides.[129] In other cases, the 'form of a trial' was more evident, with the presentation of a libel by the plaintiff, the production of evidentiary documents, the examination of witnesses, and the cross-examination of these by means of interrogatories (i.e., lists of questions to be put to the witnesses), thus making affairs far less 'summary'.[130] Attorneys might also be employed to argue the case. The summary procedure on offer at the court of the *Consoli* was of this latter kind.

---

itinere dicuntur miserabiles personae"', *Atti della Società Ligure di Storia Patria*, nuova serie 52 (2012), 617–34.

[124] Javier Belda Iniesta, 'The Clementines Dispendiosam and Saepe Contingit and the evolution of the medieval summary procedure', *Journal on European History of Law* 10 (2019), 46–67, at p. 58.

[125] Belda Iniesta, 'The Clementines Dispendiosam and Saepe Contingit', p. 54.

[126] Charles Donahue, 'Procedure in the courts of the *Ius Commune*', in Wilfried Hartmann and Kenneth Pennington (eds), *The History of Courts and Procedure in Medieval Canon Law* (Washington, DC: Catholic University of America Press, 2017), 127–58, at p. 116; Francesca Trivellato, '"Usages and Customs of the Sea": Étienne Cleirac and the making of maritime law in seventeenth century France', *The Legal History Review* (2016), 193–224, at p. 198.

[127] Ascheri, 'Il processo civile', p. 361.

[128] Maria Fusaro, 'Politics of justice/politics of trade: foreign merchants and the administration of justice from the records of Venice's Giudici del Forestier', *Mélanges de l'Ecole Francaise de Rome* 126 (2014), 139–60, at pp. 145–7; Ascheri, 'Il processo civile', p. 361.

[129] Cerutti, 'Fatti e fatti giudiziari', p. 415.

[130] Calafat, 'La somme des besoins', p. 9.

Technically, judges were not bound by strict rules in forming their judgements but were free to interpret evidence with the sole purpose of establishing the truth, answering to their conscience alone.[131] Summary justice based itself on 'the truth of the matter' and 'the nature of things'.[132] The utility of the judicial process lay not in the full reconstruction of an indisputable truth, but rather in the cessation of hostilities between parties.[133] Simona Cerutti has argued that these imperatives represented a distinct judicial attitude drawing upon a framework originally provided by Thomas Aquinas and theories of natural law.[134] In alluding to the 'nature of things', it embodied a view of the world which saw each thing moving towards a full expression of itself which was inherently just. The 'equity' that this justice guaranteed was not an equality of subjects, which would have been a contradiction in terms, but rather responded to each subject's concrete essence. Such jurisprudence was clearly capable of regarding practices as fonts of their own legitimacy.[135] In concrete terms, it is easy to see why this procedure would have appealed to commercial practitioners, who might thus achieve a swift outcome responding to commercial practice and avoid becoming embroiled in abstract points of law. Judgements based on the 'nature of things' brought to the fore the central mercantile concept of good faith (*bona fides*), a viewpoint that considered what was 'reasonable and equitable in law as the legal consequence of what was considered reasonable and fair behaviour in trade'.[136]

---

[131] Andrea Addobbati, 'When proof is lacking: a ship captain's oath and commercial justice in the second half of the seventeenth century', *Quaderni Storici* 153 (2016), 727–41, at p. 730.
[132] Cerutti, 'Fatti e fatti giudiziari', p. 415.
[133] Cerutti, 'Fatti e fatti giudiziari', p. 417; Addobbati, 'When proof is lacking', p. 727.
[134] Cerutti, 'Fatti e fatti giudiziari', p. 417.
[135] Cerutti, 'Fatti e fatti giudiziari', p. 420.
[136] Vanneste, *Intra-European Litigation*, pp. 4–5.

2

Defining Average in Early Modern Italy and Europe

Overview

From the sixteenth century onwards, both professional jurists and increasingly centralised states across Europe started to show a greater interest in commercial and maritime law.[1] Their involvment was not entirely new. Doctors of the *ius commune* had touched upon commercial and maritime questions in the past, while municipal statutes or municipally sponsored collections of maritime customs are well known.[2] However, the increased level of engagement by these actors, sparked not least by a growing awareness of the importance of commerce to political economy, signals a new phase in the history of maritime law. This chapter will consider the development of GA in formal sources of law with a focus on those sources that might conceivably have regulated GA in early modern Tuscany.

During this period, learned jurists increasingly began to publish printed works dedicated exclusively to maritime and commercial law, drawing on the *Corpus Iuris Civilis* (the texts of Roman law), authoritative collections of maritime customs, and the work of other jurists across the continent, as well as their own experience as lawyers who specialised professionally in maritime litigation. This historical development furnishes us with a range of printed evidence, ostensibly describing how GA functioned. In actual fact, as we will see, these texts more often were prescriptive rather than descriptive in nature, outlining how GA ought to have functioned according to the author in question. This chapter examines this evidence and charts the changing taxonomy of

---

[1] Italo Birocchi, *Alla ricerca dell'ordine: fonti e cultura giuridica nell'età moderna* (Turin: Giappichelli, 2002), pp. 246–53; Francesco Galgano, *Lex mercatoria*, 5th edn (Bologna: Il Mulino, 2010), p. 78.

[2] Rodolfo Savelli, 'Modelli giuridici e cultura mercantile tra XVI e XVII secolo', in Franco Angiolini and Daniel Roche (eds), *Cultures et formations négociantes dans l'Europe moderne* (Paris: Editions de l'école des hautes études en sciences sociales, 1995), 403–20; Giuseppe Speciale, 'Diritto e mercato. Il "diritto che viene dalle cose". Dallo ius mercatorum al mercato in blockchain', in Aldo Andrea Cassi (ed.), *Le danze di Clio e Astrea. Fondamenti storici del diritto europeo* (Turin: Giappichelli, 2023), 459–512.

risk sharing that emerges, especially from the work of learned jurists, paying particular attention to the material relevant to the Tuscan situation. Tuscany itself, somewhat unusually, did not itself produce anything in the way of normative material on GA in the early modern period: neither statutes, state-sponsored collections, nor native jurists who dealt with GA, at least until the work of Ascanio Baldasseroni in the late eighteenth century.[3]

From this survey, and a comparison with operational practice to take place in the next chapter, three things become clear. Firstly, the word Average (*avaria*) was not in wide use in formal sources of law until the sixteenth century, at which point it seems to have gained currency very quickly. As for late medieval practices in the Western Mediterranean, some form of collective contribution for jettison remained a constant, but this existed alongside a range of different arrangements for risk- and cost-sharing, and the word 'Average' was rarely used to describe them. It is therefore in a strict sense quite difficult to talk of a history 'Average' before the early modern period. Secondly, a principle of 'General Average' which grouped all damages incurred for the general benefit together and mandated the same modality of contribution to make them good, did not emerge until the early modern period. Though this had largely emerged in the Low Countries in the sixteenth century, it was not articulated elsewhere until the late seventeenth century and not convincingly theorised by Italian jurists until the eighteenth. To this should be added the caveat that the modality of contribution towards extraordinary or semi-regular expenses made for the general benefit – sometimes grouped under 'Small' or 'Common' Average – remained a point of uncertainty.

Finally, as we will see in the following chapter, all of these developments were anticipated in practice, with the jurists trying to theorise in its wake. Even by the beginning of the eighteenth century, contemporary Italian jurists schooled in the *ius commune* had not fully managed to reconcile the sometimes anachronistic inheritance of earlier and discordant authoritative collections – the *Lex Rhodia* and especially the *Llibre del Consolat de Mar* – with the risk-sharing institution that they observed on the ground in a way that they found satisfactory. Earlier collections did not articulate a clear legal principle of GA but presented a range of situations in which collective or group contribution was required. As early modern Italian jurists attempted to crystalise a theory of 'Average', they were clearly unsettled by the lack of support which merchant practice found in existing authoritative texts. At the turn of the eighteenth century, there was no unified response to these dissonances, and Italian jurists attempted to rationalise them in different ways. Only the work of Giuseppe Casaregi, influenced in particular by juridical discussion emerging out of the Netherlands, pointed the way to a taxonomy that more closely resembles our modern theory of Average.

[3] Ascanio Baldasseroni, *Delle assicurazioni marittime*, 5 vols (Florence: Bonducciana, 1786–1803).

Sources of GA Doctrine in Tuscany

During the period under consideration, the Tuscan authorities, unlike their counterparts in Amsterdam and Genoa, did not issue any formal laws concerning GA.[4] The statutes and reforms concerning the court of the *Consoli* make no mention of Average or jettison.[5] Nor are there references to Average or jettison in the *Statuti di sicurtà*, enacted between 1523 and 1529 to govern Tuscan insurance practices, other than to note that jettison was one of the eventualities which was to be covered by the new standard-issue printed insurance contract.[6] There is one stipulation contained here which would seem to very distantly resemble GA, namely the practice whereby the five officials in charge of insurance could incur expenses for the recovery of items lost in a shipwreck or other disaster for the 'universal benefit', and subsequently divide the expenses between parties as they saw fit. There is, however, nothing amounting to a doctrine of maritime Averages. The medieval maritime republic of Pisa had in fact been a precocious maritime legislator, compiling the collection known as the *constitutum usus*, promulgated in 1160: yet though this does contain some brief references to jettison, these are never referenced in an early modern context.[7]

This is not to say that there existed no relevant written normative material which had at least the potential to influence the outcome of GA cases. First and foremost, there existed provisions regarding collective contribution in the *Digest* of the sixth-century Byzantine emperor, Justinian, one of the foundational texts of the learned *ius commune* tradition. This was the *Lex Rhodia de Iactu* (the 'Rhodian Law of Jettison'), the title given to section 14.2 of the collection. The other major normative authority for maritime cases in seventeenth-century Tuscany was the *Llibre del Consolat de Mar*, a collection of maritime customs originally compiled in medieval Catalonia which held considerable authority in the Western Mediterranean, and the only collection

---

[4] Go, 'GA adjustments in Amsterdam', p. 395; *Degli statuti civili della Serenissima Repubblica di Genova* (Genoa: Giuseppe Pavoni, 1613), pp. 139–41.

[5] See ASF, *Auditore poi Segretario delle Riformagioni*, 116; Lorenzo Cantini, *Legislazione Toscana: raccolta e illustrata dal dottore Lorenzo Cantini*, 32 vols (Florence: Pietro Fantosini e Figlio, 1802), vol. 4, pp. 157–66, 'Riformazione della Dogana di Pisa pubblicata il di 28 Aprile 1561, ab Incarnat.'

[6] Addobbati, *Commercio, rischio, guerra*, pp. 118–19. The *statuti* can be found reprinted in Jean-Marie Pardessus, *Collection de lois maritimes antérieures au 18. siècle*, 6 vols (Paris: L'Imprimerie Royale, 1837), vol. 4, pp. 598–605.

[7] Antonio Lefebvre D'Ovidio, 'La contribuzione alle avarie dal diritto romano all'ordinanza del 1681', *Rivista del Diritto della Navigazione* 1 (1935), 36–140, at pp. 88–90; Paola Vignoli, *I costituti della legge e dell'uso di Pisa (secolo XII). Edizione critica integrale del testo tràdito dal 'Codice Yale' (ms. Beinecke Library 415)* (Rome: Istituto storico italiano per il Medioevo, 2003).

of norms explicitly referenced directly in Tuscan GA cases in the archive.[8] In some jurisdictions, such as the Republic of Genoa, some even considered this compilation to have been received as *lex* and therefore to have the status of enacted law.[9] This chapter will analyse both of these sources in turn as part of a chronological survey of normative works.

These provisions were in turn an important reference point for the commentaries on GA produced by early modern learned jurists, most of whom were practising maritime lawyers themselves. Tuscany, again, did not itself produce any native jurist who would publish a work dedicated to maritime law until the late eighteenth century. In this respect, it seems that Richard Lassels, an English travel writer, was correct when he asserted in the 1660s that the primary goal of Livornese residents was 'good bargains, not good books'.[10] Ascanio Baldasseroni's treatise on insurance (*Trattato delle assicurazioni maritime*) published in 1786 was the first time that a Tuscan would write publically on the subject of Averages. Even in this treatise, however, Baldasseroni takes it for granted that his reader knows what Averages are and does not provide an explicit definition. Moreover, Baldasseroni's implicit definition is not normative: it does not make any judgements on the circumstances that *should* give rise to a GA. The term 'Average' (*avaria*) usually appears in Baldasseroni's treatise without any qualification, used to mean any kind of damage which falls short of a total loss (*sinistro*). Recognising that each jurisdiction has its own rules as far as risk sharing is concerned, Baldasseroni then uses the term General Average (*avaria generale* or, very occasionally, *avaria grossa*) for any loss that, in the jurisdiction in question, is shared by all participants in the venture, and the term Particular Average (*avaria particolare*) for any damage borne by the affected individual(s). Yet there were other Italian jurists who did consider the question of Average in more depth during the seventeenth century, whose texts would enjoy circulation throughout the peninsula as the eighteenth century progressed. It is clear, moreover, that at the outset of the eighteenth century, such attempts were still beset by uncertainty about how to resolve contradictions between existing authoritative texts (the *Digest* and the *Llibre*) and current practice. Before beginning a chronological survey of this normative inheritance, however, let us first briefly establish our bearings by reviewing the modern-day theory of Average and the risk-sharing taxonomy it envisages.

---

[8] Colon and García (eds), *Llibre del Consolat de Mar*.

[9] Giuseppe Lorenzo Maria Casaregi, *Discursus legales de commercio*, 2nd edn, 2 vols (Florence: Io. Cajetanum Tartinium, & Sanctem Franchium, 1719), vol. 1, p. 280.

[10] Quoted in Stefano Villani, 'Livorno – diversis gentibus una', in Giovanni Tarantino and Paola Von Wyss-Giacosa (eds), *Twelve Cities – One Sea: Early Modern Mediterranean Port Cities and their Inhabitants* (Rome: Edizioni Scientifiche Italiane, 2023), 37–53, at p. 50.

Modern-Day Averages

Today, there exist two main types of Average.[11] As in Baldesseroni's treatise, this division is between General Average (GA) and Particular Average (PA). GAs are shared between all participants in a venture whilst PAs are borne by the directly affected party. PAs are effectively defined by exclusion (all damages that are not GA are automatically considered PA). The participants in the case of a GA are today defined as the ship-owners and cargo owners. These parties may then be covered by their insurers, with underwriters usually being held liable for GA contributions.

GA is regulated by the York-Antwerp Rules (YAR), which derive their force from their being inserted into freight contacts. These emerged only in the second half of the nineteenth century after the 1864 'York Conference' and the 1877 follow-up in Antwerp, both held under the auspices of the 'Congress of the Association for the Reform and Codification of the Law of Nations'.[12] Instead of being enshrined in legislation, as originally envisaged, the rules would be inserted into freight contracts as an intermediary solution. Like lots of intermediary solutions in the history of international cooperation, it has proved remarkably durable. Somewhat remarkably, the original rules did not even define what GA was. The YAR quickly gained traction nevertheless and were 'all but universally adopted' by 1890.[13] They continue to be regularly updated, though there are still periodic contentions to resolve. The tensions that the reformers encountered had a long history – nor did they ever really go away even after their supposedly definitive resolution via YAR.[14]

Rule A of the 2016 YAR defines a GA act as follows: 'there is a general average act when, and only when, any extraordinary sacrifice or expenditure is intentionally and reasonably made or incurred for the common safety for the purpose of preserving from peril the property involved in a common maritime adventure'.[15] On this basis, Richard Cornah, a contemporary Average adjuster, identifies four conditions which an expense or damage must meet for an act to be declared a GA: firstly, it must be extraordinary and not part of the ordinary fulfilling of the freight contract; secondly, it must be intentionally made and not

---

[11] 'York-Antwerp Rules'.

[12] Richard Morrison, 'General Average', *The Assurance Magazine, and Journal of the Institute of Actuaries* 12 (1866), p. 350; Richard Cornah, 'The road to Vancouver: the development of the York-Antwerp Rules', *Journal of International Maritime Law* 10 (2004), 155–66, at p. 161.

[13] Cornah, 'The road to Vancouver', p. 162.

[14] For discussion on the limitations of the York-Antwerp Rules see Jolien Kruit, *General Average, Legal Basis and Applicable Law: The Overrated Significance of the York-Antwerp Rules* (Zutphen: Paris Legal Publishers, 2017).

[15] 'York-Antwerp Rules'.

an inevitable loss that would have followed without any human intervention; thirdly, it must be for all participants and not just for the salvation of a part of the property; and finally, it must be made in a situation of peril. Cornah admits that this last criterion involves making some subtle distinctions.[16] He states that while the peril in question might not be 'immediate' it must be 'real and substantial': precautionary acts are therefore not admitted. To this we should also add the criterion contained within the rule paramount of the YAR: that a sacrifice or expenditure must be 'reasonably made or incurred'. The YAR thus avoids the more probablematic criterion that a GA act be recognised as 'necessary' for the salvation of the ship, a somewhat awkward element, as we will see.

These five criteria or variations upon them – extraordinary, intentional, for all participants, in a situation of peril, and reasonable – have been important normative considerations to various extents across the history of risk sharing. There was, however, for most of the history of trade, a much wider typology of Averages than the binary one that we adopt today, resulting in a heterogenous patchwork of different risk- and cost-sharing practices.

Contribution in Ancient Rome and Byzantium: The Rhodian Law of Jettison

The name *Lex Rhodia de Iactu* (the Rhodian Law of Jettison) given to section 14.2 of Justinian's *Digest* hints at its perceived antiquity even in Roman times.[17] The *Digest* is a collection of juridical opinions collected from about 40 different Roman jurists.[18] Though Justinian transformed such opinions into *lex* – enacted law – by promulgating the *Digest* in the sixth century, it is important to remember that its provisions did not enjoy this status at the time of their writing. If section 14.2 of the *Digest* itself is to be believed, the Roman Emperors deferred in matters maritime to the ancient Rhodian 'law of the sea', at least as long as this did not contradict Roman laws, thus placing its origins some 3,000 years ago.[19] As the name further suggests, the law itself is primarily concerned with jettison, but does state that common contribution is due in some situations other than the throwing of cargo overboard. These include ransoms paid to pirates or enemies, masts cut during a storm, and a situation in which cargo is unloaded into lighters so that the ship can enter a river or port and then one or more of the lighters is subsequently lost. Wear and tear to the ship incurred during the course of a voyage is explicitly ruled

---

[16] Cornah, *A Guide*, pp. 6–7.

[17] D.14.2; Watson, *Digest*, vol. 2, pp. 419–22.

[18] Ennio Cortese, *Le grandi linee della storia giuridica medievale* (Rome: Il Cigno, 2000), p. 68.

[19] D.14.2.9; Watson, *Digest*, vol. 2, p. 421.

out, with the Roman jurist Paul offering a memorable analogy: 'the damage arising when a smith breaks his anvil or hammer would not be charged to the customer who gave him the work. But a loss at sea falls to be made good if it arises from a decision of the cargo owners or a reaction to some danger'.[20] The damage must therefore clearly be an extraordinary sacrifice.

There is no mention of 'Average' in Roman law which talks only of contribution (*contributio* or *collatio*). Furthermore, the *Lex Rhodia* does not explicitly express an overarching legal principle that lies behind these different situations. The opening provision comes close when it states that 'the Rhodian law provides that if cargo has been jettisoned in order to lighten a ship, the sacrifice for the common good must be made good by common contribution'. However, the *Lex* itself is, as with the rest of the *Digest*, a compilation of the opinions of different Roman jurists discussing jettison and contribution – there are ten fragments in all compiled here – and there is no explicit attempt to make these opinions cohere. It is therefore unclear whether we should consider the examples it provides to be an exhaustive list of specific cases where contribution is due, or whether they are intended as illustrations of a more general rule.[21] J.J. Aubert suggests that the original Roman position probably changed over time, moving from a 'specific, narrow, and rather strict application towards a wider, more flexible, and gradually encompassing use'.[22]

Despite the fact that there is no statement of a legal principle, the resulting collection diplays a coherent shared understanding of the division between intentional and inevitable damage, one that is not so far removed from our own contemporary understanding of Average. The idea that common contribution occurs only in a situation of peril also seems to be a point of agreement between the Roman jurists. Paul says that what is given for all must be made good by all (*omnium contributione sarciatur quod pro omnibus datum est*), which, in isolation, would seem to suggest that any act which is made for the benefit of all should be made good, regardless of whether the situation was perilous.[23] Later on, however, Paul says that a loss suffered at sea is to be made good if it arises from 'a decision of the cargo owners or in response to some danger'. Other stipulations strongly suggest that common good on its own is not a sufficient object, and that the ship must be saved from peril, with 'common danger' mentioned both by excerpts from the laywers Papinian and

---

[20] D.14.2.2.1; Watson, *Digest*, vol. 2, p. 419.

[21] Kruit, 'General average', p. 193.

[22] J.J. Aubert, 'Dealing with the abyss: the nature and purpose of the Rhodian sea-law on jettison (Lex Rhodia de Iactu, D 14.2) and the making of Justinian's Digest', in J.W. Cairns and P.J. du Plessis (eds), *Beyond Dogmatics: Law and Society in the Roman World* (Edinburgh: Edinburgh University Press, 2007), 157–72, at p. 170.

[23] D.14.2.2.1 in Watson, *Digest*, vol. 2, p. 419; *The Digest of Justinian* (Latin original), <www.thelatinlibrary.com/justinian.html> [accessed 18 August 2021].

Hermogenian.[24] This is also suggested by Callistratus's remark to the effect that to qualify for contribution, goods must have been sacrificed to 'save a sinking ship'.[25] Even the contribution due when goods are unloaded into lighters and subsequently lost, which might be classified as an act for the 'general benefit' rather than a situation of peril, is linked to the salvation of the ship. Callistratus, when relating this scenario, says that the cargo is loaded into lighters 'lest the ship come to harm outside of the river'.[26] However unconvincing we might find this, Callistratus clearly connects the act of lightening the ship by means of lighters to a situation of immediate danger.

There are, however, some problematic elements that arise when examined closely. Though the *Lex* – specifically the jurist Paul – asserts that contribution after jettison is 'extremely fair' (*aequissimum*), Roman law has problems outlining how an obligation might be generated between two merchants who are not linked to one another through contract. The solution in the *Lex* is therefore somewhat convoluted: the owner of the goods should sue the master on their contract, and the master then brings an action on his contract against those whose goods have been saved.[27] The two parties are thus joined together in a triangular fashion by means of their separate contractual relationships with the master. Furthermore, the *Lex* does not regulate several aspects of GA that would be of concern to later jurists. Unlike the YAR, the *Lex Rhodia* makes no suggestion that the sacrifice should be reasonable or necessary for the salvation of the ship. There is also little in the way of procedural norms. Most procedural information concerned with how cargo should be valued for the purposes of determining contribution (contributing property at its market value, sacrificed property at its cost price since 'what is to be made good is loss suffered not gain forgone').[28] However, there is nothing concerning the procedure to be adopted during the jettison itself, an element which would become prominent in GA jurisprudence in the medieval and early modern periods, as we will see.

Though it had no direct bearing on cases in the early modern Mediterranean, it is worth at this point making mention of another normative text: firstly because it can be easily confused with the Roman *Lex Rhodia de Iactu*, and secondly because its provisions prefigure several elements that we will find in later collections and practices, illustrating an important new direction of travel. This collection is the *Nomos Rhodion Nautikos* (the Sea Law of the Rhodians or Rhodian Sea-Law), a compilation made sometime in the 600s or 700s AD in the Byzantine Empire. [29] These provisions would later be

[24] D.14.2.5.1; Watson, *Digest*, vol. 2, p. 421.
[25] D.14.2.4.1; Watson, *Digest*, vol. 2, p. 420.
[26] Ibid.
[27] D.14.2.2; Watson, *Digest*, vol. 2, p. 419.
[28] D.14.2.2.4; Watson, *Digest*, vol. 2, p. 420
[29] On the *Nomos Rhodion* and 'Average' see Daphne Penna, 'General average in

incorporated into the collection known as the *Basilica* around the year 900 AD, the last major collection of Byzantine law to be issued. Here it would sit alongside Greek translations and glosses of Justinian's Latin *Digest*, thus furnishing two different normative texts covering the subject of contribution.

For those looking to recover a doctrine of 'Average' from the *Nomos Rhodion*, their anachronistic task is even more fraught here, for provisions on contribution are scattered in a number of different places across Part III of the work and are, moreover, closely entwined with other maritime issues such as shipwreck, partnership, and piracy.[30] A number of new elements are introduced. Chapter 9 of Part III introduces a procedural rule, whereby any master who is considering a jettison must first consult with his passengers and organise a vote among them before starting. This consultation, for all the practical, operational difficulties it undoubtedly presented in reality, would become an important element of risk-sharing jurisprudence. The chapter also introduces a curious element closely connected with partnership law, whereby if there has been an 'agreement to share profit in common' (*kerdokoinonia*) then each man will bear the loss of a jettison according to his share of the profit. Most strikingly, Chapters 35 and 38 seem to uncouple contribution from the idea of voluntary sacrifice and transform it into a form of mutual insurance. Chapter 35 states that a jettisoned mast, 'whether it breaks or has been cut down', will be made good by all parties; Chapter 38 states that if a cargo of grain is damaged by a storm and there is no negligence on the part of the crew, then all parties shall bear the loss, with the master and crew given some salvage rights in compensation.[31] We will find several of these elements echoed in later collections.

'Average': A Polysemic Term

During the Middle Ages, a new term gradually gained currency which would eventually become central to practices of maritime risk sharing. The origin of the word 'Average' has been much discussed and never convincingly established. The modern English term 'average' meaning a mathematical mean is derived from the maritime term rather than the other way around.[32] A whole host of possible origins have been proposed, the most accredited being that

---

Byzantium', in Maria Fusaro, Andrea Addobbati, and Luisa Piccinno (eds), *General Average and Risk Management in Medieval and Early Modern Maritime Business* (Cham: Springer, 2023), 95–119.

[30] Penna, 'General average in Byzantium', p. 104.

[31] Penna, 'General average in Byzantium', pp. 110–11.

[32] 'Average', in T.F. Hoad (ed.), *The Concise Oxford Dictionary of English Etymology* (Oxford: Oxford University Press, 1996) <www.oxfordreference.com/display/10.1093/acref/9780192830982.001.0001/acref-9780192830982-e-1034> [23 February 2021].

'Average' is of Arabic or Byzantine origin.[33] The Arabic thesis points to the word *awār*, meaning damage, from which can be formed awārīya, or 'the thing damaged'.[34] The suggested conduits here are either Italian, the Mediterranean *Lingua Franca* (a pidgin language based largely on northern Italian dialects), or Catalan, mediating between the Romance languages and the Arabic of the Iberian peninsula.[35] The Byzantine hypothesis on the other hand suggests that the origin could lie with the Greek *bàros*, pronounced with a 'v' sound rather than an English 'b', meaning 'weight', and hence *abàros*, meaning to 'de-weight', presumably referring to the process of jettison. Another possible origin is the related adjective *bareîa* meaning 'onerous', being a shortened form of *sumbolè bareîa*, 'onerous contribution'.[36]

As has been noted, the sixth-century *Lex Rhodia de Iactu* and the seventh-century Byzantine *Nomos Rhodion* do not use any version of the term Average.[37] The first use of the term occurs in a Genoese contract from 1200 with the meaning of 'added expense for maritime taxes'.[38] The first reference in a normative text that we can date with certainty, meanwhile, is found in chapter 89 of the Venetian *Statuta et Ordinamenta Super Navibus* (1255) and reads 'si alicui navi vel ligno evenerit quod Deus avertat, de arboribus antenis & timonibus dapnum, illud (non) sit in varea' ('if to any ship or vessel should happen that which God should prevent – damage to the masts, yards, or rudders – that should (not) go into Average').[39] Ultimately, it should also be noted that in European languages, all of which seem to have adopted some derivative form of the word *avaria* by the end of the sixteenth century, the word was used to mean both the 'damage' which had been sustained and the process of 'contribution' which made good that damage, a thing which renders arbitrating between the two theories virtually impossible.[40] A fifteenth-

---

[33] Steven Dworkin, *A History of the Spanish Lexicon: A Linguistic Perspective* (Oxford: Oxford University Press, 2013), pp. 93–4.

[34] Khalilieh, *Islamic Maritime Law: An Introduction* (Leiden: Brill, 1998), p. 101.

[35] On *Lingua Franca* see Guido Cifoletti, 'Lingua franca and migrations', in Stefania Gialdroni, Albrecht Cordes, Serge Dauchy, Dave De ruysscher, and Heikki Pihlajamäki (eds), *Migrating Words, Migrating Language, Migrating Law: Trading Routes and the Development of Commercial Law* (Leiden: Brill, 2020), 84–92.

[36] Dworkin, *Spanish Lexicon*, pp. 93–4.

[37] Lefebvre D'Ovidio, 'La contribuzione alle avarie', pp. 130–40.

[38] Andrea Addobbati, 'Principles and developments of general average: statutory and contractual loss allowances from the *Lex Rhodia* to the early modern Mediterranean', in Maria Fusaro, Andrea Addobbati, and Luisa Piccinno (eds), *General Average and Risk Management in Medieval and Early Modern Maritime Business* (Cham: Springer, 2023), p. 147, note 8. There are several similar Genoese examples from around the same time.

[39] Pino Musolino, 'A relic of the past or still an important instrument? A brief review of General Average in the 21st Century', *Il Diritto Marittimo – Quaderni I – New Challenges in Maritime Law: de lege lata e de lege ferenda* (2015), 257–88, at p. 262, and especially note 8. The presence of 'non' in the original is a matter of scholarly debate.

[40] Casaregi, *Discursus legales de commercio*, vol. 1, p. 278.

century maxim from the Low Countries which we find cited in court records (*'werping is averij'* – jettison is [General] Average) attests to the word's transfer beyond the Mediterranean basin.[41] The first mention of the term in a written normative source outside the Mediterranean occurs in the 1538 Burgos *Ordonnance* (issued in Castille); the 1551 *Ordonnance* of Charles V for the Low Countries also makes mention of the term.[42]

The etymological puzzle of Average is made even more difficult by the wide array of 'Averages' which exist and have existed. Like many of the 'technical' terms associated with medieval trade, 'Average' is polysemic, i.e. a term with many meanings. What is more, these different uses of the term are usually implicit in contemporary operational sources and helpful labels for the different variants come from a later juridical tradition which is not usually reflected in the operational documents. As well as the GA/PA distinction already discussed, a number of other variants existed in the late medieval and early modern periods. There was the 'Small' or 'Petty' Average: eventually it was determined that the Small Average refered to ordinary fees associated with the voyage that could be foreseen at the outset (pilotage, stallage fees, and so on), and the bearer of these costs was usually determined by the freight contract.[43] In earlier periods there was some doubt about whether Small Average – also sometimes known as 'Common Average' – referred to ordinary or extraordinary fees or both. Then there were other forms specific to more local settings. In English freight contracts the master might expect to be paid his 'primage and average', a kind of bonus given to him in reward for good service.[44] In the very unusual Spanish case, the *avería de Indias* was a duty levied on all the ships of the American fleets in order to fund protection for the convoy: that is, a contribution levied *a priori* to prevent misfortune, rather than a contribution levied after the fact.[45] Many other *averías* existed in the Spanish case.[46] The Biscayar and Castilian merchant *nationes* operating in the

---

[41] Dave De ruysscher, 'Maxims, principles and legal change: maritime law in merchant and legal culture (Low Countries, 16th Century)', *Zeitschrift der Savigny-Stiftung für Rechtsgeschichte. Germanistische Abteilung* 137 (2021), 260–75, at p. 262.

[42] Gijs Dreijer, *The Power and Pains of Polysemy: Maritime Trade, Averages, and Institutional Development in the Low Countries (15th–16th Centuries)* (Leiden: Brill, 2023), p. 67.

[43] James Allan Park, *A System of the Law of Marine Insurances* (London: His Majesty's Law Printers for T. Whieldon, 1787), pp. 112–13.

[44] Park, *Marine Insurances*, pp. 113–14.

[45] Miguel Luque Talaván, 'La avería en el tráfico maritimo-mercantil indiano: notas para su estudio (siglos XVI–XVIII)', *Revista Complutense de Historia de América* (1998), 113–45.

[46] See Gijs Dreijer, 'General average, compulsory contributions and Castilian normative practice in the Southern Low Countries (sixteenth century)', in Maria Fusaro, Andrea Addobbati, and Luisa Piccinno (eds), *General Average and Risk Management in Medieval and Early Modern Maritime Business* (Cham: Springer, 2023), 193–214.

Low Countries in the sixteenth century, for example, demanded the payment of an 'Average' by its members to meet the expenses incurred by the organisation (a practice more commonly referred to as a *massaria* by Italian merchant *nationes*).[47] This is yet further evidence that the history of maritime Averages is more tangled – and interesting – than the lex mercatoria theory suggests.

The *Llibre del Consolat de Mar*

In addition to the *Digest*, the other major normative reference point for GA cases in the Western Mediterranean was medieval: the *Llibre del Consolat de Mar*. This collection of maritime customs had been compiled in Catalonia in the early fifteenth century, bringing together various rules and practices employed in the Western Mediterranean.[48] It derived its name from the tribunal of the *Consolat de Mar*, a mercantile court under the authority of the Aragonese crown.[49] It was first printed in Barcelona in 1502, and the first Italian translation was published in 1519 in Rome under the influence of the Florentine *natio* and dedicated to the Medici Pope Leo X.[50] Giuseppe Casaregi, a Genoese jurist whose work we will shortly examine, published a new Italian edition in 1719, noting in his introduction that having been maintained for eight centuries, the *Llibre* was now 'generally maintained' in all the countries of Europe.[51] He also states that the *Llibre*, though originally a collection of customs, had been received as *lex* by the *ius commune*.[52] Almost all editions of the *Llibre*, including that of 1519 and Casaregi's of 1719, are prefaced with the so-called *cronica de les promulgacions* – a fantastical list of dates in which the provisions of the *Llibre* had supposedly been 'received' in various Mediterranean cities: Rome is listed as having recognised them in 1075, Pisa in 1118, and Genoa in 1187.[53]

---

[47] Dreijer, *The Power and Pains*, p. 77.

[48] Lefebvre D'Ovidio, 'La contribuzione alle avarie', pp. 103–6.

[49] Elena Maccioni, *Il Consolato del Mare di Barcellona. Tribunale e corporazione di mercanti (1394–1462)* (Rome: Viella, 2019).

[50] Lorenzo Tanzini, 'Le prime edizioni a stampa in italiano del Libro del Consolato del Mare', in Rossana Martorelli (ed.), *Itinerando. Senza confini dalla preistoria ad oggi. Studi in ricordo di Roberto Coroneo* (Perugia: Morlacchi Editore, 2015), 965–78, at pp. 968–71; Salvatore Corrieri, *Il consolato del mare: la tradizione giuridico-marittima del Mediterraneo attraverso un'edizione italiana del 1584 del testo originale catalano del 1484* (Rome: Associazione nazionale del Consolato del mare, 2005).

[51] Casaregi, *Consolato del mare*, p. iv. On Casaregi, see Vito Piergiovanni, 'Casaregi, Giuseppe Lorenzo Maria', *Dizionario Biografico degli Italiani* (Rome: Instituto dell'Enciclopedia Italiana, 1978) vol. 21, <www.treccani.it/enciclopedia/giuseppe-lorenzo-maria-casaregi_(Dizionario-Biografico)> [2 February 2024]; p. 72.

[52] Casaregi, *Discursus legales de commercio*, vol. 1, pp. 97, 280.

[53] Casaregi, *Consolato del mare*, pp. vii–viii.

The *Llibre* is the only juridical text that we find cited with regularity in the GA documentation found in the Consular archive. We find explicit reference to the *Llibre* (usually referred to as the *capitoli di Barcellona* or the *ordini di Barcellona*) in 2 of our 13 GA cases from 1600, 2 of the 8 cases from 1640, and 2 of the 19 ordinary cases from 1670.[54] The *Llibre* was not straightforward to interpret, however. Casaregi's edition offers a series of 'explanations' for the *Llibre*'s 294 chapters in recognition of the text's difficulty: 'the strange and contorted rewinding of words, disconnected and wandering ... so that to get to the true meaning has been the subject of profound, and ... almost ethical speculation'.[55]

The *Llibre*, however, does not outline anything amounting to systematic treatment of maritime Averages or a concept of 'General Average'. Jettison is treated at several different points in the collection, and arguably in contradictory ways. Where other non-jettison examples of contribution are introduced, moreover, they are not explicitly linked to jettison or to a single overarching concept. Like the Byzantine *Nomos Rhodion*, the provisions that we might anachronistically categorise under the heading 'GA' are scattered throughout the compilation. The chapters that touch upon practices which we would recognise as dealing with issues of GA are 93–8 (jettison), 109 (jettison in the absence of merchants), 110 (extraordinary expenses), 184 (jettison when cargo is placed on board fraudulently), 192 (ships that beach themselves), 227 (ransom payments to pirates), 279 (delays caused by intervention of authorities), and 281 (jettison, once more).[56] Unlike the *Lex Rhodia*, there is no overarching principle that could conceivably unite these instances in which contribution is due. The word 'Averages', moreover ('*averies*' in the original Catalan), is only used to refer to certain extraordinary expenses which are borne only by the cargo owners.[57]

Like the *Nomos Rhodion*, the *Llibre* seems to place considerable store by the consultation with merchants and/or crew to be carried out before a sacrifice. There has been some scholarly disagreement, however, about why the *Llibre* insists on consultation and whether, indeed, all consultations fulfil the same role. This debate, in turn, has implications for our understanding of risk-sharing practices more broadly in this period. The consultation is mentioned several times in the *Llibre*, most strikingly in Chapter 97 (jettison), in Chapter 281 (jettison again), and in Chapter 192 (when the ship is beached). Chapter 97 states that before making a jettison the master must gather the merchants, the boatswain, and all those who are in the ship together and make the following declaration:

---

[54] ASP, CM, AC, 319-20 (18 March 1669); ASP, CM, AC, 321-14 (23 July 1670); ASP, CM, AC, 196-37 (2 January 1639); ASP, CM, AC, 197-29 (26 April 1640); ASP, CM, AC, 25-22 (5 May 1600); ASP, CM, AC, 25-28 (8 April 1600).

[55] Casaregi, *Consolato del mare*, p. iv.

[56] Chapter numbers are those given in Casaregi's translation of the *Llibre*: Casaregi, *Consolato del mare*.

[57] Colon and García, *Llibre del Consolat de Mar*, vol. 1, pp. 65, 87, 116, 128–9, 136, 163. Vol. 2, pp. 87, 89, 206.

> 'Merchants, if we do not jettison, we are faced with losing both persons and property, and everything on board, and, if you merchants desire the jettison, with the will of God we would be able to save persons and a great part of our property; and if we do not jettison, we are faced with losing ourselves and all our property'. And if the merchants will agree to jettison everything, or the greater part, then they can jettison it.[58]

As in the case of the *Nomos Rhodion*, it is difficult to imagine that anyone would actually have had the opportunity to indulge in prolix speeches and direct democracy with the ship in the grips of a potentially deadly storm. This fact is recognised in the *Llibre* but not in Chapters 93–7. Instead, it caters for these circumstances in Chapter 109 and again much later on in Chapter 281, which provides details entirely absent in Chapter 109.[59] Chapter 281, which makes no explicit reference to the earlier provisions, states that if the merchants have jettisoned without the permission of the master, then they have no right to call the ship into contribution.[60] If the master makes a jettison of all or almost all of the cargo without the permission of the merchants, however, this is licit but cannot be regarded as a regular jettison (*getto piano*). The chapter declares that this jettison is instead actually someway between jettison and shipwreck. In the latter case there is common contribution but with the rates of contribution adjusted. Whereas in the case of a *getto piano* the ship should be counted for half its value; in a case of 'nearly shipwreck', the ship contributes for two-thirds, thus increasing the burden on the ship-owners (which, especially in this period, might include the master). The motivation behind this is presumably to incentivise the transport sector with a reduced contribution but to disincentivise jettisons in all but the direst circumstances if the merchants are not present to monitor the situation. Chapter 281 states that the master's freight comes into contribution but only if he insists on payment in full, including for the cargo that has been jettisoned.[61]

Chapter 192 ('Of a ship that, for act of God or other such case, has to make for the land') would at first sight seem to be an instance of exactly the same phenomenon. Here, too, the master makes a speech to the assembled company of the ship in anticipation of an imminent threat:

> *Signori*, we cannot hide the fact that we cannot do no other than beach the ship, and I propose the following: that the ship should go upon the cargo, and the cargo upon the ship. If all the merchants, or the greater part, should concede it and the ship is beached and breaks, or if it should sustain some damage, in this case, with some misadventure having occurred, [the ship] should be estimated at that which it was worth before being beached ...[62]

---

[58] Casaregi, *Consolato del mare*, p. 29.
[59] Casaregi, *Consolato del mare*, pp. 113–14.
[60] Ibid.
[61] Casaregi, *Consolato del mare*, p. 115.
[62] Casaregi, *Consolato del mare*, p. 56.

The speech then continues, increasingly less plausible as it goes on, with several other procedural stipulations for how contributing elements should be valued and by whom.

The reknowned German jurist and legal historian Levin Goldschmidt argued that the consultations in both 93–8 and 192 were the same and had a contractual function, uniting participants in a 'company against danger'.[63] Antonio Lefebvre D'Ovidio and Andrea Addobbati, on the other hand, have convincingly argued that the two consulations are actually quite different, seeing the beaching example as contractual, but the jettison consultation as no more than formal proof of both the opportunity and necessity of performing the jettison act.[64] The wording of the two stipulations certainly seems to support the idea that the two acts are distinct. Chapter 97 is about choosing whether or not to take a certain action: 'if you merchants desire the jettison, with the will of God we would be able to save persons and a great part of our property; and if we do not jettison, we are faced with losing ourselves and all our property'.[65] In the consultation of 192, the master presents no such choice: 'we cannot hide the fact that we can do no other than beach the ship'.[66] In this second example, there is no discussion over the action itself and no mention of the merchants 'consenting' to the beaching. Instead, the merchants' choice is whether or not to accept the master's proposal for what happens *after* the beaching. In Chapter 192, unlike Chapter 97, we find a whole series of conditions and minutiae regarding the way the two interests should contribute after the inevitable disaster: if the parties cannot agree on correct valuations then two 'good men' should be elected to perform the valuations and their decision should be respected; if the ship should be wrecked then the value of any equipment salvaged should be deducted from the value of the ship, but that value should be the price of the ship before the accident; however, if the ship survives, then it should contribute its full value, but the value should be of the ship in its current condition; and so on.[67] Such stipulations not only give the act a more contractual flavour but clearly distinguish this act from the jettison, where the ship is valued at half its value for 'regular jettison' and two-thirds for 'nearly shipwreck'.

---

[63] Levin Goldschmidt, 'Lex Rhodia und Agermanament der Shiffsrat: Studie zur Geschichte und Dogmatik des Europäischen Seerechts', *Zeitschrift für das gesammte Handelsrecht* 35 (1888), 37–90, 321–95.

[64] Lefebvre D'Ovidio, 'La contribuzione alle avarie', p. 114; Andrea Addobbati, 'Principles and developments', pp. 145–66.

[65] Casaregi, *Consolato del mare*, p. 29.

[66] Casaregi, *Consolato del mare*, p. 56.

[67] Ibid.

Addobbati's reading of Chapter 192 also points to an important semantic link between this and Chapter 229, which discusses the payment of freight on cargo which has been stolen by enemies. Chapter 229 states that the merchants can agree that the ship will go over the cargo ('*nau vaia sobre los havers*' in the original Catalan) but the shipmaster cannot 'brother' the ship with the cargo ('*lo senyor de la nau non agermanara la nau ab laver*'). The use of this verb *agermanar*, probably from Catalan *germà* (*hermano* in Castilian), is the key to the link between Chapters 192 and 229.[68] Chapter 229 makes reference to the possibility of an agreement between the master and merchants before the voyage begins whereby the parties have agreed to share the costs of unforeseen accidents equally: a '*germinamento*'.[69] In short, Chapter 229 envisages the possibility of a mutual insurance agreement between the parties before the start of the voyage. It suggests, moreover, that this agreement might be made mid-voyage if an enemy is sighted in the distance. The master's proposal in Chapter 192 is therefore also a mutual insurance pact: an *ad hoc* arrangement to share damages in the face of certain but as yet undetermined harm which could conceivably pertain to both ship and cargo interests. This is not an 'Average' event akin to jettison.

Finally, Chapter 109, dealing with jettison in which the merchants are not present, makes it clear that the jettison consultation is not strictly necessary, undermining the idea that it has a contractual function. Chapter 109 states that if a master makes a jettison in order to defend himself or because of an Act of God (*fortuna del mare*), it will be valid 'as if all the merchants were present' (thus somewhat undermining the discussion in Chapter 281 about 'regular jettison' and 'nearly shipwreck').[70] In the absence of the merchants, the master is to consult with those who are present on board and the merchants must subsequently accept whatever 'pacts' they have made and contribute to the damages. The *scrivano* (ship's scribe) is to write down these pacts; if he is not present, the absent merchants will have to be content with the testimony of the crew. The same even applies if the master decides to beach the ship. Though the *Llibre* seems uneasy with the idea that the merchants are not on the ship – the passage imagines that the merchants are not on the ship because some misfortune has forced the master to depart without them – it is clear that their assent is not necessary for the jettison to go ahead.

Addobbati is thus surely correct to conclude that a strict interpretation of the *Llibre* reveals the existence of an institution of mutual insurance which he distinguishes from the rules of 'General Average'.[71] As we will see, this distinction caused some confusion for jurists for whom the prevalence of

[68] Casaregi, *Consolato del mare*, pp. 73–4.
[69] Casaregi, *Consolato del mare*, p. 73.
[70] Casaregi, *Consolato del mare*, p. 32.
[71] Addobbati, 'Principles and developments', p. 163.

such mutual insurance agreements was no longer operational reality. It should be noted, however, that adjudicating between these positions is not straightfoward, since arguments built on the idea that the *Llibre* is an internally coherent collection of rules inevitably rest on a shaky premise, as the differences between the different chapters on jettison suggest. In particular, there is more than a hint of contradiction between Chapter 109, which declares that a jettison made in the absence of the merchants is valid 'as if they had been present', and Chapter 281, which declares that such a jettison is in fact 'nearly shipwreck' and follows different procedures.

It is, moreover, doubtful that we can yet speak of a doctrine of 'General Average' in the *Llibre*. Chapter 192 is not the only chapter in which the 'common benefit, common contribution' maxim is not adopted. Chapter 110 ('the payment of extraordinary expenses'), the only contribution-like situation in which the word 'Average' is used, outlines a situation in which we might expect to find contribution from all parties, but in fact the ship interests do not contribute at all. The chapter mentions two concrete situations which are very similar: when a ship has entered a port of refuge to 'escape from an act of God' or when a ship has remained blocked in port by the weather or enemies. The chapter states the ensuing expenses (*'averies'*) should be paid proportionally with only the contribution of the saved merchandise.[72] Since the ship clearly benefitted, this would seem to directly contradict that central principle of GA that 'the sacrifice for the common good must be made good by the common contribution'. In this conception, jettison (*'git'*) and *'aueries'* would appear to be two separate things, with the latter resembling what later Dutch jurists would refer to as 'small Average'.[73] The word *aueries* is also used to refer to all those extraordinary expenses which the merchants have consented to pay by prior agreement, thus echoing the meaning of 'additional payment for maritime taxes' found in thirteenth-century Genoese contracts.

In fact, the only scenario in the *Llibre* where there is a situation comparable to that of jettison (and, again, jettison is not explicitly referenced) is the payment of ransom to an armed ship in Chapter 227. In this situation, the *Consolato* establishes that the ransom cost is to be borne by all interested parties, with the ship counting for half. The ransom has to be agreed by everyone on board, but if there are no merchants on the ship then a consultation with the crew is sufficient and the merchants will be obliged to pay anyway.[74] The word 'Average' is not used in connection with this situation.

The *Llibre* thus provides us with a snapshot of medieval risk-sharing practices in the Western Mediterranean during a period of change. The resulting image is somewhat blurred: perhaps because practices were changing as the work was

[72] Casaregi, *Consolato del Mare*, p. 33.
[73] p. 63.
[74] Casaregi, *Consolato del Mare*, p. 72.

being compiled, perhaps because quite different practices were in use contemporaneously. We can, however, discern a more heterogenous situation than that which would prevail from the early modern period onwards. A wide range of risk-sharing practices are outlined. There are some circumstances in which ship and cargo contribute (i.e. ship-owners and merchants), and others in which only the cargo contributes (i.e. just merchants). There are different rates of contribution for the ship depending on whether the merchants give their assent to the jettison or not (though their assent or otherwise is elsewhere declared to be irrelevant in a contradictory passage). Rules about compulsory contribution (we might anachronistically say 'GA') coexist alongside the possibility of contractual agreements between merchants and masters to share damages, even in situations with no sacrifice of property. There are no expressions of legal principle but rather a series of concrete examples that may or may not illustrate a rule with more general applicability.

The most important change in this heterogenous situation appears to be operational: its compilers were coming to terms with a maritime economy in which merchants and their representatives (supercargoes) were ever less likely to be accompanying their goods. This created some unease on a practical level because merchants had to repose more trust in the master, but also on a juridical level, because it was now necessary to explain how an obligation might be created upon someone unable to assent to an act supposedly made in their interests. Such questions could be avoided in a context in which merchants were physically present but now became increasingly difficult to ignore. An absence of merchants also left little opportunity for *ad hoc* mutual insurance agreements such as the *germinamenti*, and these soon fell out of use, leaving an interpretative puzzle for jurists no longer familiar which such practices. In short, a new, practical maritime context was already altering risk-sharing practices before the beginning of the early modern period, independent of the advent of new risk institutions like premium insurance and the increased interest of learned jurists in maritime questions.

Developments in the Low Countries

Several important developments affecting the future GA then took place in Northern Europe in the sixteenth century, in the cities of Bruges, Antwerp, Amsterdam, and other smaller centres. As Gijs Dreijer has shown, the period saw a shift from the 'rules of thumb' contained in medieval collections to general legal principles.[75] These abstracted general rules from the specific instances outlined in earlier norms, with both educated jurists and the state in the Low Countries taking a precocious interest in these questions.[76] For the first time, a typology of maritime Averages emerged in legal theory, one which we might find broadly recognisable today.

---

[75] Dreijer, *The Power and Pains*, pp. 89–133.
[76] Dreijer, *The Power and Pains*, p. 89.

The tendency observed across medieval collections from the Low Countries is a gradual increase in the number of situations in which collective cost sharing was explicitly authorised. Laws stipulating contribution after jettison and mast cutting had already been incorporated into the municipal law of Bruges in the fourteenth century, with the fifteenth-century *Ordonnantie* of Amsterdam adding further admissible expenses such as using lighters when the ship could not make it to port and extraordinary pilotage, as well as payment for a pilgrimage promised to thank God for aid during a storm.[77] The *Ordonnantie* also allowed the shipmaster to jettison when merchants were not present (unlike in the Mediterranean, shipmasters could choose whether to contribute to the GA with their freight or with the value of the ship). Dave De ruysscher thinks it likely that instances of collective contribution were in practice restricted to these specific instances, and that practitioners did not accept other instances by analogy with these maxims.[78]

A particularly important step was then taken with the issue of a series of princely legislation on this and other topics by the Habsburg rulers of the Low Countries in the 1550s, occasioned by disputes over the costs of protecting trade from Spain to the Low Countries and particularly by the State's desire to curb the controversial use of premium insurance. For the first time these collections actually sought to define GA rather than simply providing examples. According to the *Ordonnance* of 1551, all damage suffered for the common benefit of the ship had to be shared over the ship and cargo as per 'the old customs of the sea'.[79] This was to also include costs associated with seamen who had died or been wounded when fighting off attackers. The *Ordonnance* also defined Small Average (*gemeyne avarye*): these were operational costs such as ordinary pilotage, port duties, and customs costs. Though the shipmaster advanced these costs, Small Average was usually paid by merchants in proportion to the value of their cargo: the development of Small Average probably points to a change in the role most commonly carried out by the master, as he moved from participant in the venture to agent of the merchants.[80] Dreijer argues that by keeping such costs separate from freight, the cost of the voyage could remain largely fixed whilst the master was allowed some flexibility if he had to make a stop, though it should be pointed out in this respect that making unforeseen stops would incur costs more obviously understood as extraordinary.[81] This provision seems somewhat similar to Chapter 110 of the *Llibre del Consolat de Mar*, which states that only the merchants are liable for the costs of emergency stops rather than the collective: the *Llibre*'s version of Small Average *ante literram*. The 1553

---

[77] Dreijer, *The Power and Pains*, p. 99.

[78] De ruysscher, 'Maxims, principles and legal change', p. 265.

[79] Dreijer, *The Power and Pains*, p. 107.

[80] Dreijer, *The Power and Pains*, pp. 80, 107; De ruysscher, 'Maxims, principles and legal change', p. 274.

[81] Dreijer, *The Power and Pains*, p. 80.

issue of the *Ordonnance* then toughened penalties for masters who had acted fraudulently, probably so as to attempt to offset the new discretionary powers that were awarded to him to make GA sacrifices as he saw fit: as in the Western Mediterranean *Llibre*, Northern European legislation was having to come to terms with the absence of merchants and their supercargoes. The costs of running the ship aground were also explicitly included in GA, a novelty in Northern Europe, perhaps inspired by Southern European practice.[82] Another major legislative development occurred in 1570 when Phillip II issued the Castilian *Hordenanzas* as princely legislation, thus affirming the existing practice of making insurers liable for both PA and GA payments.[83] The 1608 *Costuymen* of Antwerp was the first municipal collection to contain a typology of Average, distinguishing GA (*Averij-grosse*), PA (*simple Averij*), and Small Average (here, rather confusingly, referred to as *Averij-commune*).[84] Italian jurisprudence (though not practice, as we will see) would arrive at such a neat typology somewhat later.

The attempt in the state legislation to explicitly distinguish between different types of GA was supported by the work of a learned jurist, Quintin Weytsen, who wrote a treatise on GA entitled *Een Tractaet van Avarien*. First printed in 1619, it was probably originally written in 1564 or 1565 as a kind of scientific companion to the 1563 princely legislation.[85] Weytsen's approach was the new, legal-humanistic method of *emandatio*. Rather than relying on the explanatory commentaries of earlier jurists, he drew upon both the authorative works of the *Corpus Iuris Civilis* but also merchant practice to find the 'true meaning' or 'pure' content of existing rules: this was in contrast to those scholars who simply aimed to produce hermetic, textual commentaries.[86] The effect of this approach was to bend and shape those rules towards consistency and was thus an important spur to legal development.[87] Weytsen was the first to distinguish between GA and Small Average, providing examples.[88] He was also the first to offer a clear definition of GA:

> Average is the common contribution of the things found in the ship in order to make good the damage voluntarily inflicted upon items, whether belonging to merchants or the ship, to the end that lives, ship, and the remaining goods should escape unscathed.[89]

---

[82] Dreijer, *The Power and Pains*, p. 112.

[83] Dreijer, *The Power and Pains*, p. 117.

[84] Dreijer, *The Power and Pains*, p. 118. De ruysscher, 'Maxims, principles and legal change', p. 263.

[85] Dreijer, *The Power and Pains*, p. 127.

[86] De ruysscher, 'Maxims, principles and legal change', p. 267.

[87] De ruysscher, 'Maxims, principles and legal change', pp. 261–2.

[88] Dreijer, *The Power and Pains*, p. 127.

[89] Weytsen and De Vicq, *Tractatus de avariis*, p. 1.

Italian Jurists on Averages

The legal-humanistic approach employed by Weytsen would eventually become consolidated north of the Alps but would find less long-term success in the Italian peninsula: hence the label *mos gallicus* ('French style') to describe the humanist method, and the label *mos italicus* ('Italian style') to describe a scholastic method that focused more on the elaboration of authoritative texts. It is perhaps thanks to this greater respect for the relevant texts, the *Digest* and the *Llibre*, that Italian jurists had more difficulty reconciling the different provisions they contained with the practices that they encountered daily as active maritime lawyers. The process of 'technical refinement of language and concepts' that characterised this period was still something of a work in progress.[90]

For a while, Italian jurists did little more than briefly repeat provisions contained in the *Digest*. Though he is occasionally cited in the GA cases in the Tuscan archive, the Neapolitan jurist Francesco Rocco, for example, contented himself with a few scattered references to the *Lex Rhodia de Iactu* in a section on 'ships and freights' in his *Responsorum legalium cum decisionibus* (1655).[91] Most of the little he did write on the subject, moreover, was gleaned from a reading of the Spanish jurist Juan de Hevia Bolaño.[92] Only at one point does he report an incidence of contribution not explicitly mentioned in the *Lex Rhodia*, when, citing Bolaño and the *Llibre del Consolat*, he notes that contribution is due from the master of the ship and the merchandise when a ship is beached to avoid a storm, thus providing us with the first explicit conflation of the contractual *germinamento* (no longer a part of contemporary practice) with a GA-style contribution as described in the *Lex Rhodia*.[93] Nowhere does Rocco make reference to the terminology of Average which was already current in Italian practice.

By the end of the century, however, jurists like Carlo Targa and Giuseppe Casaregi were making an effort to flesh out a doctrine of 'Average'. Both men were influential in Italy and beyond, and though Targa passed his entire career in Genoa, Casaregi would have a direct influence on Tuscan judicial practice when he was appointed to the Florentine *ruota* in 1717 – the supreme court of civil appeal.[94] Yet the typologies of Average which emerge from the work of Carlo Targa and Giuseppe Casaregi are substantially and surprisingly different, despite the fact that both of them were Genoese maritime lawyers whose careers substantially overlapped. Neither of their treatments of GA reflects practices attested by the Tuscan archives, as we will see.

---

[90] Piergiovanni, 'Genoese civil rota', p. 192.

[91] Francesco Rocco, *Responsorum legalium cum decisionibus*, 2 vols (Naples: Luca Antonio Fusci, 1655), vol. 2, pp. 363–85.

[92] See Juan de Hevia Bolaño, *Labyrinthus commercii terrestris et navalis* (Florence: Petrus Antonius Brigonci, 1702) (originally published in Spanish, 1617).

[93] Rocco, *Responsorum*, vol. 2, p. 376.

[94] Piergiovanni, 'Casaregi, Giuseppe Lorenzo Maria'.

Carlo Targa (1615–1700) was born in Genoa, the son of a Genoese merchant and a noblewoman.[95] After studying in Pavia and Bologna he became a doctor *in utroque iure* (i.e., in both civil and canon law). His posthumous fame rested principally upon the publication, towards the end of his life, of *Ponderationi sopra la contrattazione marittima* ('Reflections upon maritime contracting'), published in 1692 and written in Italian.[96] His perspective cannot be described as a view from an ivory tower. Targa's extraordinarily long legal career in Genoa was passed in various tribunals and state bodies of the republic but above all as a lawyer dealing with maritime cases in the magistracy of the *Conservatori del Mare*. He was thus intimately acquainted with maritime practice and his work has been lauded as a 'faithful mirror … of the maritime custom of these times' which 'described summarily but comprehensively … the maritime institutions of the age'.[97] Yet in actual fact Targa's vocation as a practising maritime lawyer alone is no guarantee of his account's descriptive value. As his treatments of Averages show, Targa's intentions must have been in part prescriptive, an attempt to gently redirect practice into line, above all with the provisions of the *Lex Rhodia* and *Llibre del Consolat*. The systemising intent was ultimately not so different to Weytsen's synthesis of textual sources and maritime customs, though with rather less success as far as Averages are concerned.

One area in which Targa does lift the veil of legal theory to reveal a different operational reality concerns the consultation prior to a jettison, which he conflates with the *germinamento* of the *Llibre del Consolat*. As mentioned, the word *germinamento*, an Italianisation of the original Catalan *agermanar*, most likely derives from the Catalan *germà* meaning 'sibling', and thus it might be best understood as an act of 'twinning'. Targa provides a more fantastical derivation from the French *germiner*, itself purportedly springing from the idea of *unum germen*, a 'single shoot', and thus indicating that the venture has become 'a union, and a single body as far as those interested are concerned'.[98] He goes on to write:

> The most frequent case in which the *germinamento* arises is when there is a jettison to lighten the ship, and to save it from shipwreck … however, in many other cases there is a *germinamento* prompted by other types of disaster, but it is always done to avoid a greater danger by confronting a lesser one, as when it is decided to beach a ship for fear of being sunk, when a vessel finds itself too close to the shore, as in the *Consolato* Chapter 192.[99]

---

[95] For a biography, see Maura Fortunati, 'Targa, Carlo', *Dizionario Biografico degli Italiani* (Rome: Instituto dell'Enciclopedia Italiana, 2019), vol. 95 <www.treccani.it/enciclopedia/carlo-targa_%28Dizionario-Biografico%29/> [accessed 18 December 2023].

[96] Carlo Targa, *Ponderationi sopra la contrattazione marittima* (Genoa: Lampadi, 1750).

[97] Enrico Bensa, *Il diritto marittimo e le sue fonti* (Genoa: Cenni, 1889), p. 35; Fortunati, 'Targa'.

[98] Targa, *Ponderationi*, p. 175.

[99] Ibid.

By this point, the contractual risk-sharing agreement that had originally been described by the word *germinamento* was no longer an operational reality and had passed beyond living memory. It is understandable that Targa confuses the two institutions and sees both as a kind of *ad hoc* formation of a risk-sharing community. He goes on to write that the consultation itself was in fact no longer a part of maritime practice (though we might doubt that it ever had been). Targa remarks that in over 70 years of work as a professional maritime lawyer, he recalled only four or five cases of 'regular jettison' (i.e. a jettison that was prefaced by a consultation with the crew), and that in each of these cases the very fact that these regularities had been observed had prompted criticism that the jettison was premeditated.[100] As we will see, the operational GA documentation from Tuscany did continue to pay lip service to the consultation before a jettison, but even here, consent tended to be assumed even in the absence of these formalities.[101]

Less straightforward to interpret is the typology of Averages set out in the *Ponderationi*. Targa's treatment of the subject is in fact highly idiomatic and seems to find no equivalent in any other work. First of all, we should note that Targa treats jettison, *germinamento*, 'Averages', and contribution under separate headings rather than as different facets of the same phenomenon.[102] In the section on Averages, he then distinguishes between ordinary Average (*avaria ordinaria*), extraordinary Average (*avaria straordinaria*), and 'mixed' Average (*avaria mista*), which is a blend of the two.[103] He goes on to explain that ordinary Average is the bonus which is paid customarily to the master for his custody of goods which come 'from beyond the straits [of Gibraltar] for here': since this, 'like all customary payments' is an 'ordinary' damage, they are known as 'ordinary Average'.[104] This type would appear to be similar to the 'primage and Average', a customary payment made to the master for good service which was customarily awarded in England. In its 'ordinariness' it also somewhat resembles what Weytsen called Small Average.[105] What Targa calls 'extraordinary' Average, on the other hand, is that which we would understand as PA: when wind and weather damage some part of the ship or cargo and the cost lies where it falls.[106]

One might therefore expect Targa's 'mixed Average' to be directly equivalent to GA, but this is not the case. This is not 'mixed' in the Aristotelian sense

---

[100] Targa, *Ponderationi*, p. 72.
[101] See pp. 92–3.
[102] Targa, *Ponderationi*, Chapter 60 '*Dell'Avarie, e loro diversità*', pp. 142–4; Chapter 76 '*Del germinamento*', pp. 175–7; Chapter 77 '*Della contribuzione*', pp. 177–81; Chapters 58–9, '*Del gettito in mare*', pp. 138–41.
[103] Targa, *Ponderationi*, p. 142.
[104] Targa, *Ponderationi*, p. 143.
[105] Park, *Marine Insurances*, pp. 112–13.
[106] Targa, *Ponderationi*, p. 142.

of a sacrifice which is both forced and voluntary; it is rather an 'extraordinary, voluntary' Average (*avaria straordinaria voluntaria*).[107] This mixed Average takes place, according to Targa, when the ship has 'stumbled into' an unfortunate situation out of the participants' control (he uses the unusual phrase '*quando s'inciampa in un fortunio*'), and some extraordinary collective expense that depends on a voluntary negotiation (*spesa che dipende da negotiato voluntario*) must be made in order to extract the ship from this situation. Such expenses include when a ship encounters an armed vessel (presumably a ransom payment in order to escape unscathed), when a ship shelters under the cannons of a fort for safety (presumably some payment for this service would be due), or when a ship has been abandoned for fear of corsairs and must later be recovered.

Into this 'mixed' category fall several further sub-categories. Targa first outlines an 'Average of the Indies' (*avaria dell'indie*), which he says is used in both the ports of Brazil and the Levant. He describes a situation in which two or three ships are loading in a far away port in competition with one another. 'In order not to damage one another', the masters collectively agree to set the freight rate between themselves, splitting the cargo between them and effectively creating a temporary cartel.[108] The freight is then split between the masters and their crews, with expenses first deducted. Targa next describes an Average 'of the English and Dutch usage', which consists of the gift of a *reale* to the master for every valuable parcel he brings, three *reali* per tonne for large parcels, and one and a half for every tonne of bulk cargo.[109] This seems to be another iteration of the 'primage and Average', or something very similar to it, notwithstanding the fact that Targa has already outlined a very similar situation under the rubric of 'ordinary Average'.

Finally, Targa outlines something which we might term GA, though it is not GA as we know it. The phrase used here is *avaria grossa* (gross Average), though it is telling that Targa on this occasion somewhat distances himself from the term, as if he does not quite want to take ownership of it: 'another Average can be found which they call *avaria grossa*'.[110] Later on in the paragraph, he refers to it indiscriminately as *avaria commune* (common Average).[111] This Average involves common contribution from ship, freight, and merchandise. This is used for a scenario in which a 'vessel [...] remains deliberately in a port or under a fortress for some time to avoid a meeting with corsairs or

---

[107] Targa, *Ponderationi*, p. 143; for Aristotle on the subject of jettison as a 'mixed' act that is both voluntary and involuntary, see Addobbati, 'Principles and developments', p. 153.
[108] Targa, *Ponderationi*, p. 143; see pp. 93–4.
[109] Targa, *Ponderationi*, pp. 143–4.
[110] Targa, *Ponderationi*, p. 144.
[111] Ibid.

enemies to save itself and the cargo'.[112] As this would seem to be exactly the type of scenario that Targa has just placed under the heading of mixed Average, it seems that Targa considers GA to be an improperly named subset of mixed Average. There is no mention of jettison. Targa does, however, exclude unintentional damages from this GA when 'the delay was not voluntary but was forced'.[113] (In practice, as will be shown, such damages were often made good through the mechanism of GA through a careful wording of claims.)

In his section on 'contribution', meanwhile, Targa does not outline a general principle, nor does he connect contribution at any point to the word 'Average'. He instead provides a list of seven situations in which collective contribution is due: when there has been a *germinamento*, when there has been a jettison even without *germinamento*, when there has been a ransom to enemies and corsairs, when cargo has been unloaded to lighten the ship and is lost, when expenses have been incurred in combat with enemies so long as there has been *germinamento* (with damages sustained in combat to be excluded), when the small boat, anchor, rope, or some other appurtenance has been abandoned to escape danger, and, finally, when some of the merchandise has been lost and the rest has become mixed up and it is not clear to whom the remaining merchandise belongs.[114] In short, only instances of contribution which are explicitly supported either by the *Lex* or the *Llibre* are admitted. The only two exceptions to this are the final example of the lost merchandise and the combat expenses. Yet these latter expenses at least are justified because there has been explicit agreement between parties in the form of *germinamento*. We might note that there is some contradiction between the chapter of 'contribution' and the chapter on 'Averages', since Targa's chapter on Averages states that *avaria grossa* requires contribution, but it gets no mention here.

This was not a faithful mirror of practice. The Tuscan operational documents, as we will see in the following chapter, show that practice had long before moved to a binary intentional/unintentional, GA/PA distinction between damages that were to be made good collectively, and those that lay where they fell. In the documentation there is no hint of ordinary, extraordinary, and mixed Averages, Averages of the Indies, and Averages of English and Dutch usage (nor have these terms been found in Genoese operational documents, for that matter).[115] The most frequent 'Average' in operational terms, moreover, is jettison, the supposedly archetypal instance that Targa in fact excludes.

---

[112] Ibid.
[113] Ibid.
[114] Targa, *Ponderationi*, pp. 177–8.
[115] Antonio Iodice, 'Maritime average and seaborne trade in early modern Genoa, 1590–1700' (unpublished PhD thesis, University of Exeter/University of Genoa, 2021), p. 185.

Table 1. Typology of maritime averages outlined in Carlo Targa's *Ponderationi sopra la contrattazione maritima* (1692). Source: Targa, *Ponderationi*, pp. 138–44, 175–81.

Average Type	Sub-Type	Literal English Translation	Possible Equivalents	Circumstances	Paid by
Avaria ordinaria		Ordinary Average		Customary payment for masters coming from beyond Gibraltar	Merchants
Avaria straordinaria		Extraordinary Average	Particular Average	Damage directly sustained through wind or weather	Affected party
Avaria mista/ Avaria straordinaria voluntaria		Mixed Average (Extraordinary Voluntary Average)		Negotiated payments (e.g. ransoms, money paid to forts)	(Collective?)
	Avarie delle Indie	Average of the Indies		Ad-hoc cartelization between several ships in one port	Shipmasters
	Avarie all'uso inglese ed olandese	Average of the English and Dutch Usage	Primage and Average	Customary payment of one *reale* to the shipmaster	Merchants
Avaria grossa/ commune*		Gross/Common Average		Expenses when taking refuge from enemies voluntarily in a port	Ship & Freight & Cargo
Contribuzione		Contribution		*Germinamento*	Half Ship & Freight minus expenses & Cargo

Jettison (even without *germinamento*)	Half Ship & Freight minus expenses & Cargo
Cutting of apurtanances (mast, rope, anchor)	Half Ship & Freight minus expenses & Cargo
Ransom paid to enemies	Half Ship & Freight minus expenses & Cargo
Part of cargo unloaded into small boats which are then lost	Half Ship & Freight minus expenses & Cargo
Combat expenses (only with *germinamento*)	Half Ship & Freight minus expenses & Cargo
Part of cargo lost, the rest with uncertain ownership	Half Ship & Freight minus expenses & Cargo

Targa's juridical treatment was well aware of practice but somewhat awkwardly trying to make this fit with the two most important normative authorities, the *Lex Rhodia* and the *Llibre del Consolat*. These spoke of contribution, mostly in reference to jettison, but did not use the language of Average. Practice, meanwhile, spoke of Averages, but sometimes did so 'improperly' by trespassing on territory already regulated by the texts. Averages, with improper elements excluded, was then elaborated in an idiosyncratic way. The result was an elaboration and systematisation which, because it did not historicise the authoritative texts, could not synthesise text and practice successfully in the way that Weytsen had done.

The efforts of Giuseppe Casaregi (1670–1737) to reconcile practice, custom, and textual norms produced yet different results. His attempt is perhaps more coherent than Targa's and seems to have been influenced in particular by Weytsen, whose work on Averages had been available in Latin (and thus rendered accessible to jurists outside the Low Countries) since 1672. Like Targa, Casaregi had passed his career in Genoa, as an attorney, consultant, arbitrator, and judge, when he published the first 50 of his *Discursus legales de commercio* in 1707, including provisions on Average.[116] Later, in 1717, Casaregi would be invited by the Tuscan Grand Duke to become a judge of the *ruota* of Siena, soon moving up to the more prestigious Florentine *ruota*, the highest civil court in Tuscany.

Casaregi begins by declaring that he will omit any pointless discussion of whether the term 'Average' comes from the 'Greeks, Arabs, or even the Scythians' and simply note that the term is used everywhere. Casaregi then, for the first time in Italian jurisprudence, offers a definition of Average, much reminiscent of, though not identical to, Weytsen's:

> Average is the collective *pro rata* contribution of all merchandise or things in the ship in the time of danger, to be repartitioned for the restoration of the damage to other goods, of the merchants or shipmaster, which is made to the end that life, ship, and the rest of the goods might be saved.[117]

In the definition, Casaregi only mentions the contribution of merchandise, but he then goes on to remark that in fact both the freight and the ship also contribute. The freight contributes because it is earned thanks to the fact that the property was saved, and this is a 'general rule'. The ship, meanwhile, contributes thanks to the provisions of the *Llibre del Consolat*, commonly observed everywhere and received as a '*lex*'. Casaregi then goes on to divide 'proper' from 'improper' Averages. Damages 'improperly' called Average include the customary 'Primage and Average' bonus sometimes paid to

---

[116] Casaregi added to his *Discursus* over time in successive editions. The *discursus* on Average and jettison examined here were, however, published as part of the first edition in 1707. See Piergiovanni, 'Casaregi, Giuseppe Lorenzo Maria'.

[117] Casaregi, *Discursus legales de commercio*, vol. 1, p. 279.

shipmasters and – 'even more improper' – the custom of calling any accidental damage an 'Average' (i.e. Particular Average). It is hard not to agree with Casaregi that avoiding use of the word 'Average' in these circumstances would have made the situation much clearer.

'Proper' Averages, meanwhile, are found in two varieties according to Casaregi: 'Gross' and 'Common'. Whereas Targa uses the term Common Average (*avaria commune*) and Gross Average (*avaria grossa*) interchangeably, Casaregi places a divide between them. Here he was in part influenced by Weytsen's definition of Small Average (which, it should be remembered, was sometimes called Common Average in a Dutch context) and perhaps, though he does not cite it, by Chapter 110 of the *Llibre* which assigns extraordinary expenses for entry into a port to the merchants alone. Common Average, for Casaregi, covers payments 'devoted to preserving the ship and merchandise from danger'.[118] The instances he gives are when some money is given to local 'practical people' in return for assistance, when the master pays a sum passing through a river or a port, or when the shipmaster pays convoy money to a ship of war.[119] Here, the ambiguity that bedeviled 'Small' or 'Common' Average is illustrated well, for the first instance is likely to be an extraordinary expense, the second is likely to be an ordinary one, and all three could conceivably be either. In situations of Common Average, Casaregi states that only the merchandise needs to contribute, and that the ship is excluded.[120] He notes, however, that by custom the ship also usually contributes to Common Average. Common Average is, moreover, 'practiced differently according to regional variations or national styles'.[121] Gross Average, meanwhile, takes place 'when certain things are thrown into the sea on account of a labouring ship having to be lightened'; in these cases, contribution from merchandise, ship, and freight is due.[122]

When we examine the Tuscan operational documents, we will see all of these expenses being indiscriminately partitioned through GA without distinction, with half of the ship contributing, and a third of the freight. As Casaregi himself goes on to note:

> It is true that this division is trivial and not much used today. That said, I am not able to approve it, because Average, or rather maritime contribution, does not have a proper place unless there should be a cut or a jettison in order to lighten a labouring ship ... if there ought to be contribution in cases similar to that of jettisoned merchandise, it would be better if Average were divided into 'proper' and 'improper', with Gross Average understood as the former and Common Average as the latter.[123]

---

[118] Casaregi, *Discursus legales de commercio*, vol. 1, p. 281.
[119] Ibid.
[120] Ibid.
[121] Ibid.
[122] Casaregi, *Discursus legales de commercio*, vol. 1, pp. 281–2.
[123] Casaregi, *Discursus legales de commercio*, vol. 1, p. 281.

Casaregi thus rejected the extention of the provisions of the *Lex Rhodia* by analogy. For his own part, he felt it unfair that expenses under Common Average had to be made good by merchants 'since they are done more for fitting out and repairing the ship than serving the merchandise'.[124] This was the first instance of a complaint that we will encounter multiple times and is borne out by the operational evidence: that Average in its seventeenth-century form was a useful tool for defraying the costs of running a ship, including those that might better be understood as ordinary costs of business. But it also speaks to some tricky uncertainties at the heart of the procedure. The first is the 'subtle distinction' that modern GA makes between non-immediate peril and precautionary acts (a distinction easily eroded by a cleverly constructed master's accident report). The second related distinction is even more fundamental: the difference between what Richard Cornah labels the 'common safety' and the 'common benefit' approach to GA.[125] The former, associated in the nineteenth century with English maritime law but also favoured here by Giuseppe Casaregi, adopts a narrow view of GA and admits claims for contribution only where there have been expenses to avoid an imminent and immediate danger; the latter, associated with later American and French maritime law, recognises that cargo that is 'safe' hundreds of miles away is as good as lost, and thus admits extraordinary expenses in order to bring the voyage to a successful conclusion.[126]

Casaregi, for his part, was clearly perturbed by the lack of authoritative support in existing authoratitive texts for the practices he witnessed as a maritime lawyer. The payment of extraordinary expenses could be partly rationalised as 'Common Average', but this was at the same time intuitively unsatisfactory because it required the merchants to pay for what more obviously pertained to the ship. Ultimately, Casaregi felt that Average ought to be reduced to the *ius commune*, i.e. the Roman law of jettison; what he called 'Gross Average' – the jettisoning of cargo or the cutting of ropes or masts – was the only Average worthy of the name. Far from dividing jettison and Average as Targa does, Casaregi puts jettison at the conceptual centre of 'Gross Average' (*avaria grossa*) in his *Discursus*. Indeed, for Casaregi, jettison and mast cutting are the only true, legitimate form of 'GA'. These considerable differences between the accounts of two Genoese contemporaries demonstrate how far away jurisprudence was from successfully reconciling existing norms and what was going on in maritime practice. It also explains why in Casaregi's translation of the *Llibre* we find no reference to 'Average'. Since the word '*aueries*' in the *Llibre* is never found in relation to jettison but refers to specific, extraordinary expenses borne by merchants, translating

---

[124] Ibid.
[125] Cornah, *A Guide to General Average*, p. 8.
[126] Ibid.

these as 'Averages' would have disturbed the careful schematisation Casaregi was trying to outline with the help of Weytsen and the *Digest*, placing jettison firmly at the conceptual heart of General Average. He thus translates *aueries* as 'extraordinary expenses' (*spese straordinarie*). Doing otherwise risked introducing futher 'impropriety' into an already confused landscape.[127]

---

[127] E.g. Casaregi, *Consolato del Mare*, p. 33.

Table 2. Typology of maritime averages outlined in Giuseppe Casaregi's *Discursus legales de commercio* (1707). Source: Casaregi, *Discursus*, pp. 279–82.

Average Type	Sub-Type	Literal English Translation	Possible Equivalents	Circumstances	Paid by
Avaria impropria	praemii speciem magistro navis	Sort of bonus for the shipmaster	Primage and Average	An optional payment to the shipmaster for looking after the goods	Merchants
	omne damnum quod casu fortuito…	Any damage arising accidentally	Particular Average	Damage arising accidentally	Affected Party
Avaria propria	avaria commune	Common Average	Small Average	Expenses to preserve ship and cargo from danger	Ship & Freight & Cargo
	avaria grossa/ contribuzione marittima	Gross Average/ maritime contribution		Jettison or mast cutting	Ship & Freight & Cargo

3

Average in Practice: The Evidence from the Pisan Archive

Overview

It is now time to turn our attention to the operational evidence: the documents, preserved in the state archive in Pisa, produced as part of real risk-sharing procedures carried out in Tuscany from 1600 to 1700. Thanks to Livorno's status as a particularly cosmopolitan port inserted into international trade networks, these documents bring us into contact with shipmasters and merchants hailing from a wide range of national and religious backgrounds who presented their case to the court of the *Consoli del Mare*.[1]

The most striking thing to emerge from this documentation is the sheer range of different types of damages that were shared between merchants, ship-owners, and the master through the use of a single instrument: what we can already call GA. These damages were not just classic cases of jettison and mast cutting that were well embedded in the normative material. These included the deliberate beaching of the vessel, expenses and damages sustained in fighting off corsairs, legal costs for freeing the ship when illegally captured, bribes to local officials, expenses for hiring local assistance of various kinds and in various situations, as well as financial exactions imposed by local and consular authorities. There is no hint in our sources of the separate 'Common' or 'Small' Average which sometimes appears in the normative sources.[2] This very wide use of GA was in part made possible by a largely unavoidable structural imbalance in the procedure: the strong interest that the shipmaster had in the outcome, and his near-total control over information. Technical personnel of the court aided masters in posing their requests in a legally valent way designed to trigger a GA declaration, but GA-as-practised in some ways contravened juridical stipulations, and there was not even necessarily agreement on the central juridical principle of 'common benefit, common contribution'.[3]

---

[1] Adriano Prosperi (ed.), *Livorno 1606–1806: un luogo dell'incontro tra popoli e culture* (Turin: Allemandi, 2009).
[2] See p. 101.
[3] See p. 105.

The result of the master's control of information was that GA was, above all, a tool that benefitted the transport sector, in a way that was generally acceptable and perhaps even desirable at the beginning of our period but became more contentious towards the end of the *ancien regime*. Some later eighteenth-century Tuscan reformers – not wholly inaccurately – portrayed GA as an inbalanced procedure in which the attorneys and shipmasters colluded to push through spurious claims. The second half of the chapter will thus explore the theme of merchant representation, particularly the progressive 'streamlining' of procedures that happened over the century, with less and less material dedicated to the defence of merchant interests. Rather than representing a diminution in the quality of representation, however, it will be shown that this was simply a stripping away of extraneous material, most likely in response to the well-attested growth in commercial-maritime litigation across Europe in the last third of the seventeenth century. The quality of defence, and the procedure more generally, remained largely stable across the century. The changes merely revealed GA cases for what they usually were: not legal investigations or 'trials' but rather processes of certification – administration-as-justice – in which the important decisions usually happened outside of the courtroom.

The Limitations of Private Resolution

Before examining the court documentation, it is first worth briefly noting that the cases we find in the archive do not represent all GA cases carried out in Tuscany during this period. It was, in fact, possible for GAs to be resolved privately without any involvement by the court, albeit in a limited set of circumstances. Though such cases by their very nature tend not to make an impression on our source base, we do have one case in which private resolution is explicitly referenced. A master from Pisa requested a GA before the *Consoli* in December 1599 for his ship, *San Torpè*, including in his *testimoniale e domanda* the detail that between him and the merchant 'there had always been the intention to reach an accord on this business without disputes ... and with a month having past it became clear that nothing was being decided ... instead it was necessary to resort to their lordships [the *Consoli*], as he has done'.[4] Having initially turned to the *Consoli*, it then seems that the case was committed to arbitrators the following February. But this too failed, and the *Consoli* ended up adjudicating the case themselves almost a full year after it started.

This example demonstrates several things. It firstly reminds us that requesting a GA before the *Consoli* was not compulsory and that private resolution was possible, whether through informal agreement between the parties themselves or through arbitration. It should be remembered in this latter

---

[4] ASP, CM, AC, 27-30 (31 November 1600), *Testimoniale*.

regard that turning to arbitration was not an 'informal' means of resolving a dispute: an arbitration process was both binding on the parties involved and recognised in courts of law.[5] Secondly, it shows that the court could be flexible, and responded to instructions from the parties about how to proceed: in this example, the case was initiated, then paused while arbitration took place, then restarted when arbitration failed. Though we know about this example precisely because these alternative routes to resolution failed, it is likely that most of the time they worked without issue.

The most salient point about this case, however, is that we are dealing with an unusually restricted circle of participants: the master (a native of Pisa, which was in itself unusual) and a single merchant based in Livorno. In circumstances like these it would have been easy to coordinate the parties and reach an amicable settlement. Other voyages, however, might involve hundreds of interested parties. Moreover, if there were receivers based in other ports, it would have been necessary to present evidence of an official judgement by a competent authority to those receivers in order to ensure payment, since even formal arbitration could only bind participants who had actually been party to the agreement.[6] This immediately ruled out the arbitration or private arrangements for any GA that involved a receiver based in another jurisdiction, a common occurrence in a port-of-transit like Livorno.[7] It should also be noted that the attractiveness of arbitration or informal agreement would most likely decline as a number of participants in a GA increased, even when all did hail from a single jurisdiction. Merchant preference for an informal or arbitrated settlement is often asserted by historians, but the coordination problems involved in reaching an agreement between all players would likely outweigh the benefits of avoiding court fees in a larger case because shared administrative costs became progressively smaller for each individual player as the number of participants in a GA increased.[8]

---

[5] Christian Burset, 'Merchant courts, arbitration, and the politics of commercial litigation in the eighteenth-century British empire', *Law and History Review* 34 (2016), 615–47, at pp. 621–2; Ana Belem Fernandez Castro, 'Handling conflicts in long-distance trade: a view of the Mediterranean through the experience of merchants operating in the Kingdom of Valencia in the late sixteenth century', in Louis Sicking (ed.), *Conflict Management in the Mediterranean and the Atlantic, 1000–1800* (Leiden: Brill, 2020), 237–59, at pp. 248–52.

[6] Fernandez Castro, 'Handling conflicts', p. 250.

[7] Andrea Addobbati and Jake Dyble, 'One hundred barrels of gunpowder. General average, maritime law, and international diplomacy between Tuscany and England in the second half of the 17th century', *Quaderni Storici* 168 (2021), 823–54, at pp. 843–4.

[8] Nevenka Bogojevic-Gluscevic claims that in the medieval eastern Adriatic, arbitration was the preferred mode of resolution. See Nevenka Bogojevic-Gluscevic, 'The law and practice of average in medieval towns of the eastern Adriatic', *Journal of Maritime Law and Commerce* 36 (2005), 21–60, at p. 59. For the preference of

We can therefore be fairly certain that we have all or almost all of those cases involving receiving merchants in more than one jurisdiction: this is underlined by the fact that all those cases in which we have evidence of private agreement were cases involving just Livorno-based merchants.[9] It is, however, impossible to know how many cases of GA were declared in a certain year and what proportion of the total cases went before the *Consoli del Mare*. Moreover, it is also one of the arguments of this study that even in cases that were resolved 'formally', a great deal of negotiation happened outside the courtroom that only leaves a very faint impression in our evidence base, and that the court in turn was very responsive to this. These dynamics will be fully reconstructed in a single case study examined in Chapter 4.

The Court Procedures: The Evidentiary Phase

An early modern GA case that came before the *Consoli* rested on two principal documentary pillars. The first were the accident reports, known in English as 'sea protests'. A sea protest was a master's account of the voyage with a focus on the vicissitudes that had led him to a request for GA. In Tuscany, most cases actually contain two versions of this report, which were not always identical. The first is generally called a *consolato*. This had to be made by the master as soon as possible on arrival in the closest available port after the accident, a thing that all the narrative documents are at pains to emphasise.[10] This fact usually meant that the court or official drawing up the *consolato* had no jurisdiction with regard to any litigation arising from the mishap. The name *consolato* derives from the custom of producing the document in the chancellery of a national consul or other local official in a port: if made in Livorno they were made before the Governor of the city and his auditor. When a ship found itself making land far away from a port with the facility to create *consolati*, masters sometimes provided an affidavit signed by a local castellan, before making the *consolato* at a later point.[11] The *consolati* are

---

merchants for arbitration or informal resolution over recourse to the courts see Adrian Leonard, 'London 1426–1601: marine insurance and the law merchant', in Adrian Leonard (ed.), *Marine Insurance: Origins and Institutions, 1300–1850* (Basingstoke: Palgrave Macmillan, 2016), 150–75, at pp. 161–3; Trivellato, *The Familiarity of Strangers*, pp. 153–4.

[9] ASP, CM, AC, 27-30 (31 November 1600); ASP, CM, AC, 418-11 (14 May 1700).

[10] See for example ASP, CM, AC, 25-8 (30 May 1600), *Testimoniale*; ASP, CM, AC, 197-29 (26 April 1640), *Consolato*; ASP, CM, AC, 320-7 (28 May 1670), *Testimoniale*. This requirement is discussed in Guido Rossi, 'The liability of the shipmaster in early modern law: comparative (and practice-orientated) remarks', *Historia et Ius* 12 (2017), 1–47, at p. 33.

[11] E.g. ASP, CM, AC, 25-3 (28 June 1600).

almost all supported by the testimony of witnesses, usually three in number, almost always members of the crew.[12] Most of these *consolati* would be made as a precautionary measure and would not result in any further action. If a master even suspected damage, water damage from a storm for example, it was prudent to make a declaration so that he would have the means to indemnify himself if damage was discovered later.[13]

The second version of the report which we find in the archival cases is usually referred to as the *testimoniale e domanda*. This also purported to be the verbatim testimony of the master, who had come personally before the Pisan court to explain what had happened in the voyage (the *testimoniale* part), and to make a formal request for absolution and for GA (the *domanda* part).[14] As we will see, however, the master's presence was not actually guaranteed at this stage.

While the court procedure was initiated with the presentation of the *testimoniale e domanda* along with the original *consolato*, a number of other documents might then be produced and make their way into the file deposited in the archive. These include summons (*citazioni*), notifying interested parties of the case and of the submission of new documentation; exceptions (*eccezioni*) and interrogatories (*interrogazioni*), which were used as part of the judicial investigation to test the veracity of the master's account; and the final judgement (*sentenza*) of the *Consoli* declaring the GA. As the judgements do not state the underlying reasons for a particular outcome, however, they are of limited value in understanding how GA cases worked. Only one thing from the judgements needs to be borne in mind here: that the judgement of the *Consoli* in cases of GA was in fact two-fold. Firstly, they declared that the master was not liable for the damages and expenses incurred (*assolviamo detto capitano, sua nave, e gente di essa*), and only then did they declare that it was a case of GA (*condennando ... à dover concorrere in avaria*).[15] The interest of the master in the case was not only that GA be declared, but that he and his crew be absolved of any potential personal liability for what had gone wrong.

---

[12] There appears to be no discernible pattern regarding the selection of witnesses. Sometimes a mixture of crew and officers are selected, sometimes all officers, sometimes all crew.

[13] See the many *consolati* which have remained in Livorno, preserved in ASL, *Governatore e Auditore*, Atti Civili; Rossi, 'The liability of the shipmaster', p. 33.

[14] This nomenclature is not rigidly observed by the sources. The *consolato* is sometimes referred to as a *testimoniale* and vice versa. Sometimes the *consolato* is also referred to as a *relazione* or *dichiarazione*. They are, however, the most common labels applied to these documents, and they are used here for the sake of clarity.

[15] ASP, CM, AC, 321-30 (30 August 1670), Judgement.

The Court Procedures: The Evidentiary Phase

The other main pillar of a GA case, and the final formal act in the procedure, was the calculation (*calcolo*). This would only be drawn up in the event that the *Consoli del Mare* concluded that there was in fact grounds for common contribution. Two calculators would create a document listing all the property involved in the voyage and the interested parties to whom it belonged and assign this property a value, including the value of the ship and the value of the freight to be paid to the master. In Tuscany the ship would count for only half of its value, and the freight for a third. The result of this was to lessen the burden on the ship-owners and master and increase the eventual burden on the receiving merchants. This is just one of the ways in which the procedure was tilted in favour of the ship interests.

After establishing the value of all the property involved in the voyage, the calculators would then list and value the expenses or damages incurred. By dividing the total damages by the total value of the voyage, they would arrive at a contribution rate. This would be expressed as 'X pieces for every 100 Tuscan golden *scudi*/pieces of eight' (depending on the currency being used), meaning that for every 100 *scudi*/pieces of property invested in the voyage, the interested party contributed X amount towards the loss, damage, or expense. The calculation finishes with the signatures of the calculators and is counter-signed by the *Consoli*, who reserved the right to change the values arrived at by the calculation.[16]

This was the end of the procedure as represented in the documentation. It seems likely that, more often than not, the final stage of reimbursement – in which it was decided who specifically owed what to whom and money actually changed hands – was coordinated by the master, who took the required contribution from each party, and, if the loss had been suffered by cargo interests, would then distribute the money to the affected parties in lieu of delivery of the goods. Often, in the case of damage to the ship or the payment of expenses, it would be the master himself who was out of pocket; he might even have been forced to take out a sea loan during the voyage in order to pay for expenses of repairs.[17]

The identity of the calculators changed over our period. A government report of 1785 states that the calculations were drawn up by two employees of the Pisan customs house, for a fixed fee of two pieces of eight.[18] This was not, however, the system in place at the beginning of the seventeenth century, nor, it would seem, at the end. In the 1600 and 1640 samples we find that the calculators were drawn from the *borse di ricorso*, the pool of merchants who,

---

[16] ASP, CM, AC, 25-24 (13 April 1600), *Testimoniale*.
[17] See p. 174.
[18] ASL, *Governo civile e militare*, 977, f. 28r.

according to the 1561 reforms, could be drawn on to form a judgement if a case before the tribunal was reaching the 45-day limit. One calculator would be drawn from the Florentine *borsa*, the other from the Pisan one. On one occasion only one calculator was elected.[19] In the early part of the period, then, it was recognised merchants who were responsible for valuing the cargo.

Sometime between 1640 and 1670, the *borse* appear to have been dissolved: we can probably narrow this window down even further when we consider that, in 1662, a report for the *Consulta* relates that the 'special judgement of *ricorso*, done with the participation of merchants, had by now fallen into disuse'.[20] Since there is a case involving *ricorso* as late as 1652, the change most likely occurred in the 1650s.[21] This probably reflects a decline in native merchant corps, especially in Pisa, given that most merchants, native and foreign, had moved to Livorno by 1640: it may simply have been impossible to maintain a fresh supply of recognised merchants every three years.

After the dissolution of the *borse*, it is unclear how *Consoli* elected the calculators, but it does not seem that they were using members of the customs house. In 1670, we find 15 different individuals appearing as calculators, a large number considering the fact that the *Consoli* elected only two calculators for each calculation, and that only 16 GA calculations were drawn up that year.[22] None of the names are to be found in the indices of notarial protocols, ruling out the possibility that they were notaries. Though the customs house would be the obvious place to find candidates with the requisite skills, 15 seems an improbably large number of estimators working in the customs house at Pisa. It is possible that the *Consoli* nominated Livornese merchants on an *ad hoc* basis to work as calculators.[23]

The method of valuation adopted is one of the main practical ways in which GA rules, ostensibly similar in theory, could vary greatly in practice.[24] The normative material deals with the problem of valuation in part, but different authorities provide contradictory assertions on what practice should be adopted. The *Lex Rhodia* states that contributing goods should be valued at the price which they can fetch, i.e. the market price at the destination, while sacrificed goods should be valued at their purchase price 'since what

---

[19] ASP, CM, AC, 27-26 (1 September 1600).

[20] Sanacore, 'I consoli del mare', p. 192.

[21] ASP, CM, AC, 239-5.

[22] The other cases either had no calculations or were the enforcement of calculations drawn up elsewhere: ASP, CM, AC, 321-25 (25 August 1670); ASP, CM, AC, 322-16 (9 November 1670).

[23] ASP, CM, AC, 321-30 (30 August 1670). See Chapter 4 for further discussion.

[24] On valuation in Tuscan GA cases see also Jake Dyble, Antonio Iodice, and Ian Wellaway, 'The technical challenges of measuring maritime trade in the early modern Mediterranean: Livorno and Genoa', *Histoire & mesure* 38 (2023), 135–62, at pp. 143–4.

is made good is loss suffered not gain foregone'.[25] The *Llibre del Consolat de Mar*, on the other hand, states that jettisoned cargo should be valued at the price of the port of origin (i.e. the purchase price) if lost in the first half of the voyage and at the destination (selling) price if lost in the second half.[26] This 'rule of halves' accords greater respect to the idea of an inherent value, with 'value added' to the cargo by virtue of its being transported to another part of the world, while the Roman jurists see the matter in terms of personal loss and gain, with loss being concrete and definite, and gain always hypothetical and thus not worthy of recompense. As with other aspects of GA, however, regional practices abounded. One record from 1670 preserved in Pisa includes an original calculation made in Marseille where the calculator adopts a much more complicated procedure than in Tuscany.[27] The GA itself is for various extraordinary fees paid to the French consulate on leaving the Levant. The contributing cargo is explicitly valued according to the current price on the Marseille piazza, but then expenses such as the freight paid on each item, 'percentage of the city', quarantine payments, and similar charges are deducted.[28] The rationale would appear to be that the cargo had an inherent value at the time of the incident, one which included some value added in the form of profit but which did not yet include various port charges which would be factored into the eventual selling price: the freight, meanwhile, had already paid GA and should likewise be excluded.

Whatever the exact rationale in the Marseille example, it at least illustrates there were many different theories about how values should be fairly arrived at, and that normative rules were not always followed. Nor did these rules cover every eventuality. The *Llibre*, for example, seems to envisage a simple journey from point A to point B, with no provision for a ship making multiple stops. It only refers to the valuation of jettisoned cargo and is not clear about how the passive mass should be valued: whether the cargo should be valued at the selling price at the destination, as in the *Lex Rhodia*, or whether the 'rule of halves' applies to the passive mass, too. Applying the rule of halves would presumably be the more consistent approach, but the *Consolat* is certainly not explicit about this.

The Tuscan calculations themselves provide scant detail about how values were obtained or the process which lay behind their creation. The preambles to many of the 1600 calculations say that the calculators have been elected to 'estimate, calculate, and repartition' the damages (*stimare, calcolare e ripartire*), but nothing is said about the passive mass (and it is at any rate

---

[25] D.14.2.2.4; Watson, *Digest*, vol. 2, p. 420.
[26] Casaregi, *Consolato del mare*, p. 28.
[27] ASP, CM, AC, 322-16 (9 November 1670).
[28] ASP, CM, AC, 322-16 (9 November 1670), Calculation.

clear that the calculators are often *not* the ones estimating the damage).[29] What we can glean from the sources shows that no single approach was adopted across all cases. Among all the GA cases surveyed, we only find the 'rule of halves' explicitly adopted twice for the sacrificied cargo.[30] These two cases occurred in 1600 and 1700, which suggests that the rule remained current throughout the period even if it was not adopted in the majority of cases. There are several cases where we would expect to see the rule of halves applied, but there is no indication that this was so. It is interesting to note, however, that in 1600 the rule of halves is explicitly applied to both the active and the passive mass; since the accident happened in the first half of the journey, all cargo is valued at the price in the port of origin. In the 1700 example, on the other hand, it is clearly being applied only to the jettisoned cargo.[31] Whereas in 1600 the logic of the *Consolat* is adopted (value is added to the cargo thanks to its being transported), in 1700 it would appear to be that of the *Lex Rhodia* (concretely realised gains contribute while ephemeral unrealised gains are not eligible for compensation).

Judging by the layout of the calculations, it seems likely that the calculators worked on the basis of a bill of lading provided by the shipmaster, and that, in the majority of cases, cargo was valued at the current going rate in Livorno, as was clearly practised in Marseille. This was surely the only approach which was practical in cases in which Livorno was an intermediary stop and there were many cargoes destined for many different ports. Calculators seem to have occasionally taken account of the report of the two merchant 'deputies' (*deputati*) who were sent to inspect the cargo and reported damages. Deputies, also sometimes called 'assistants' (*assistenti*), were often elected to supervise the unloading of the ship, and were sometimes requested by the shipmaster.[32] They were not elected in every case, however, and there does not appear to have been a consistent logic behind their participation. They often provided details on what was present, giving information on weights and merchant marks, and sometimes reporting if certain cargo had been damaged.[33] It was only occasionally, however, that they gave a monetary value to damage which the cargo had sustained, and still more infrequently did they provide a value for the cargo in good condition to be incorporated into the calculation, though this did sometimes take place.[34] In one example from 1670, Carlo Benassai

---

[29] E.g. ASP, CM, AC, 25-21 (16 May 1600), Calculation.

[30] The cases where we find the rule: ASP, CM, AC, 27-26 (9 September 1600); ASP, CM, AC, 418-21 (1 July 1700); cases where we would expect to find the rule and do not: ASP, CM, AC, 318-26 (22 January 1669); ASP, CM, AC, 197-43 (6 July 1640).

[31] ASP, CM, AC, 418-21 (1 July 1700), Calculation.

[32] ASP, CM, AC, 322-27 (9 December 1670), Request for deputies.

[33] ASP, CM, AC, 322-27 (9 December 1670), Report.

[34] ASP, CM, AC, 319-3 (30 January 1669), Report; ASP, CM, AC, 418-12 (25 May 1700), Report.

and Guglielmo Van Weltrusen claimed that their cargo of hides had received water damage: deputies were sent to assess the damage and this was duly incorporated into the calculation.[35] In the case in question, however, there were many receivers who had received hides, which were most likely similarly damaged, but this was never brought to light and no adjustment was made to the value of their cargo with respect to any hypothetical damage. This suggests that, in this case at least, valuation was being made without reference to the receiving merchants or the deputies unless the merchants specifically requested it. Since for most of the century most of the goods would have been valued for the purpose of levying customs charges, this could also have plausibly provided a ready source of values. Using a valuation different from that of the customs house, moreover, would have occasioned disputes. However, after 1676 the port no longer levied customs charges, instead demanding a flat fee for every parcel of goods.[36]

Ultimately, the important thing in evaluating the passive mass was not complete accuracy in valuation but rather a just proportionality between interests.[37] An overvaluation of all items in the passive mass by 10 per cent, for example, would have no effect on GA contributions, since the amount to be paid in damages remained the same: one's contribution to that amount depended on the *proportion* of the overall venture in which one was interested. This did not render the method used for valuing the passive mass completely irrelevant – some cargoes would have gained more value thanks to their being transported than others – but it certainly must have removed some of the urgency from the question. That contemporaries thought the same way is demonstrated by an unusual case from 1692 in which it was discovered that the bill of lading was missing crucial details.[38] It was impossible to discover who had had which cargoes and, consequently, who owed what. The calculators solved the problem by using the freight that each party had paid to work out the GA, since these would reflect, albeit imperfectly, the proportional interest of each player.

As for damages to the ship, there were two principal ways in which damages were valued: the court could send two experts (*periti*) to inspect the damages, or the master might submit the values himself. If expert assessment was adopted, the *Consoli* would send to the governor's court commanding their election: for each year we find that the same two experts were elected in every case. In 1640 and 1670, these were master shipwrights (the *capo maestro de calafati* and *capo maestro de capi d'ascia*) attached to the Grand Duke's fleet of galleys.[39] In 1700, it is impossible to tell exactly what professional group the experts

---

[35] ASP, CM, AC, 318-26 (22 January 1669).
[36] See Frattarelli Fischer, 'Livorno 1676'.
[37] Addobbati and Dyble, 'One hundred barrels of gunpowder', p. 838.
[38] ASP, CM, AC, 393-81 (12 November 1692), Judgement.
[39] ASP, CM, AC, 319-25 (25 August 1670); ASP, CM, AC, 196-37 (2 January 1639).

belonged to as they did not state their roles, though one of them is sometimes given the title 'captain' (*capitano*), suggesting that they might have been a commander of one of the Grand Duke's galleys.[40] These experts would make an inspection of the ship and deliver a written report, including a suggested value for the damages. The 'self-assessment' method, on the other hand, could take a few different forms. Sometimes a 'suggested' value would be incorporated into the *testimoniale* itself: for example, in 1600, a master 'was forced to cut away six oars that were attached to the outside of the said ship, which could be worth around £3.10 Sterling or around 14 *scudi* in Florentine money'.[41] Alternatively, masters could submit more detailed breakdown of damages submitted in a separate document, apparently on their own authority. These more procedurally dubious methods will be discussed further in Chapter 4.

These two avenues – master's submission or expert valuation – were the two principal means of evaluating damages which we find in the procedures, but they were not the only ones. In one example from 1700, the case of the *Sante Anime del Purgatorio*, the evaluation of the damages is done consensually by both parties. A document submitted to the court lists the damages, and the master and the merchants both provide the values they think should be attached to each one.[42] A compromise figure was then chosen between these two values, and we learn in the judgement that this mediation was facilitated by Rafaello Medina, described as a 'mutual friend' of the two parties.[43] In another case from the same year, which started as an arbitrated case, four members of the Jewish *natio* were chosen to provide all values required for the GA, including the estimation of the ship.[44] Eventually they handed the case on to the *Consoli*, unable to reach a satisfactory decision as to whether articles stored on deck should be included in the passive mass (see below).[45] Yet the values that they had already established for ship and cargo remained in use. This is also, interestingly, the first and only time in which we find the word 'adjust' used to describe the resolution of an average case (*aggiustare*), i.e. the modern verb used in English to describe the process of resolving a GA.[46] It may not be a coincidence that we find the word being used in a context closely analogous to modern GA resolution, i.e. recourse to a trusted third party made up of private specialists.

---

[40] ASP, *CM*, AC, 417-5 (19 January 1699), Judgement.
[41] ASP, CM, AC, 25-28 (8 April 1600), *Testimoniale*.
[42] ASP, CM, AC, 418-7 (6 April 1700), Estimation of damages.
[43] ASP, CM, AC, 418-7 (6 April 1700), Judgement.
[44] ASP, CM, AC, 418-11 (14 May 1700).
[45] ASP, CM, AC, 418-11 (14 May 1700), Statement, List of Reasons.
[46] See Cornah, *A Guide*, pp. 10–11.

The Creation of Sea Protests

Though some historiography has been struck by the drama and immediacy of sea protests, when analysed in bulk it quickly becomes clear that these were drawn up with the help of legal professionals in a formulaic fashion.[47] What is more, it is clear that the *testimoniale e domanda* was drawn up by a Pisan court official on the basis of the original *consolato*, who sometimes 'touched up' the *consolato* narrative – itself hardly a spontaneous account of the voyage – to regularise the GA using the most salient legal vocabulary. This mediating function therefore played by the university-educated technicians has important implications for how we read and understand this evidence.

The reality behind the legal formalities is naturally difficult to reconstruct, but the evidence we have suggests the master was often not in fact present. Each *testimoniale* begins with the same formulaic proem (with slight and inconsequential variation) suggesting that he actually presented himself in court to deposit his testimony: 'before the most illustrious *Consoli del Mare* of the city of Pisa, their honourable office and audience, ship's master X presented himself, master of the vessel named Y, and he says how in the weeks passed he found himself in the port of Z …'.

On at least one occasion, however, in a case from 1670, we can be certain that the master was not physically in Pisa on the day that the *testimoniale* was presented. Coming from England, a place recently infected by the plague, shipmaster Stephen Dring could technically only have disembarked once he received permission from the *Magistrato di Sanità* in Florence, recognising the validity of the quarantine certificate he had received in Alicante. That permission of the *Magistrato* is dated 21 August: but Dring had already supposedly appeared before the *Consoli* on 20 August, the day after he arrived on 19 August.[48] The enforcement of these regulations may have been somewhat lax, but allowing Dring to disembark, travel to another city, and physically present himself before a court of law would have made a complete mockery of the procedures. It is unlikely that Dring's was an isolated case in this respect.

Furthermore, clues from the documents themselves show that the *testimoniale* was not his verbatim account but was made on the basis of the written *consolato*. The fact that the two documents are near identical is in itself an

---

[47] Marcello Berti, 'I rischi nella circolazione marittima tra Europa nordica ed Europa Mediterranea nel primo trentennio del Seicento ed il caso della seconda guerra anglo-olandese (1665–67)', in Simonetta Cavaciocchi (ed.), *Ricchezza del mare, richezza dal mare, secc. XIII–XVIII* (Florence: Le Monnier, 2006), 809–25.

[48] ASP, CM, AC, 321-30 (30 August 1670), *Testimoniale*; ASL, *Magistrato poi Dipartimento di Sanità*, 68-338, Panciatichi to Serristori (21 August 1670); Jake Dyble, 'Divide and rule: risk sharing and political economy in the free port of Livorno', in Maria Fusaro, Andrea Addobbati, and Luisa Piccinno (eds), *General Average and Risk Management in Medieval and Early Modern Maritime Business* (Cham: Springer, 2023), 363–87, at p. 381.

indiciation of this, and we also find mistakes in the *testimoniale* that can only have resulted from copying the *consolato*. In a case from 1600, for example, the *consolato* makes reference to events which happened in 'this current month', which was February; the *testimoniale* keeps these references to the 'current month', even though the *testimoniale* was drawn up in March.[49] On another occasion the author of the *testimoniale* decided it was necessary to record the date of the arrival in Livorno, which the *consolato*, made in Malta, naturally did not provide. The author leaves a blank of the date of arrival, suggesting that there was no one from the voyage present who might have provided the information.[50] Who was responsible for preparing the *testimoniale* document? The most likely candidates are the chancellor of the court (*cancelliere*), the vice-chancellor (*sottocancelliere*), and the notary whom the chancellor was obliged to retain.[51] One of the *testimoniali* finishes its narrative with the phrase 'he made his *consolato* which is produced in the chancellery of their [the *Consoli*'s] magistrate and court, and again is reproduced to justify the above [events]'.[52] Whoever was precisely responsible, the figure who drew up the *testimoniali* had benefitted from a legal education and can thus be expected to have some familiarity with the *ius commune* and with the provisions of the *Lex Rhodia*.[53]

Jettison and Mast Cutting

Analysing the precise wording (and significant silences) of these sea protests ultimately reveals tensions between the relevant normative material on contribution and the way that GA was used by early modern merchants. As we saw in Chapter 2, the two salient normative touchstones – the *Lex Rhodia* and the *Llibre del Consolat de Mar* – were built above all around the example of jettison, with some discussion of mast and rope cutting, and limited discussion of other kinds of property sacrifice. The *Lex Rhodia* was not explicit about how far the GA principle could be extended, though it does mention ransoms and cargo lost in lighters, whilst the *Llibre* apparently treats jettison, ransom, beaching, and extraordinary expenses as different instances, each with their own specific rules for collective defrayment rather than as part of a single institution like GA.

When it came to jettison and mast cutting, therefore – the majority though not the vast majority of our cases – shipmasters and, more pertinently, the legal technicians of the court could draw upon a fairly rich normative inheritance. Here, the *consolati* and especially the *testimoniali* are very explicit

---

[49] ASP, CM, AC, 25-3 (28 June 1600).
[50] ASP, CM, AC, 25-8 (30 May 1600).
[51] ASF, *Auditore poi Segretario delle Riformagioni*, 116, 'Dogana e Consoli di Mare di Pisa con la riforma del 1561', f. 11r.
[52] ASP, CM, AC, 25-26 (10 April 1600), *Testimoniale*.
[53] p. 40.

about these expenses and go into great detail into order to properly justify them as per the *Lex Rhodia* and the *Llibre del Consolat de Mar*, as well as *ius commune* presumptions about carrier's liability that had been crystallised in preceding centuries. In these circumstances there is clear emphasis on the coercive nature of the circumstances in the accident reports: 'it was necessary', 'it was forced', 'it was not possible to resist' are all phrases which recur time and time again in the narratives.[54] At other times it is the imminent danger that suggests the effective impossibility of other action in the circumstances: 'with evident danger of sinking' or 'the shipwreck was clearly imminent'.[55]

This emphasis on constraint by circumstances reflects *ius commune* assumptions about the shipmaster's liability. A prime concern of the shipmaster, and a necessary preliminary to a GA declaration, was to divest himself of any liability. Guido Rossi, moreover, has shown how the civil law considered the master of a vessel to be a *conductor* under *culpa levissima*, which, the name notwithstanding, actually held shipmasters to an incredibly high standard of care for the merchandise they were carrying.[56] In effect, this placed the burden of proof on the master if there was an accident to show that he was not liable. By the seventeenth century, however, and in many ways to avoid thorny problems about the nature of causation, civil lawyers and courts had brought about the crystallisation of a series of presumptions about liability, essentially outlining a list of situations in which the master was and was not presumed liable. Significantly for GA, in any case of *casus fortuitus* the master was presumed not to be responsible.[57] This explains why we see so much emphasis on the constraints posed by storms, wind, and in generally being 'forced' to do things by the elements, though this may on a philosophical level exclude the possibility of voluntary action. Once *casus fortuitus* was established, the master was absolved of an otherwise formidable burden of proof. A telling example of this can be found in the case of the *Madonna delle Grazie* brought before the *Consoli* in 1670.[58] The ship had jettisoned in order to get off the shoal on which it had become stuck while sailing in shallow waters. Sailing in a dangerous area could call the conduct of the master into question and could be argued to be an act of negligence.[59] It is unsurprising, therefore, that in this case the narrative makes sure to foreground the fact that there was not only a wind rising, but that the master had only entered those shallow waters in order to escape from two square-rigged ships which he thought had been corsairs.[60]

[54] E.g. ASP, CM, AC, 199-23 (20 November 1640), *Consolato*; ASP, CM, AC, 319-13 (28 February 1669) *Testimoniale*; ASP, CM, AC, 319-3 (30 January 1669), *Testimoniale*.
[55] ASP, CM, AC, 319-20 (18 March 1669), *Testimoniale* and *Consolato*; ASP, CM, AC, 319-28 (28 April 1670), *Consolato*.
[56] Rossi, 'The liability of the shipmaster', p. 19.
[57] Rossi, 'The liability of the shipmaster', p. 23.
[58] ASP, CM, AC, 319-25 (18 April 1670).
[59] Rossi, 'The liability of the shipmaster', p. 22.
[60] ASP, CM, AC, 319-25 (18 April 1670), *Testimoniale*.

It is somewhat surprising that, by contrast, explicit reference to the voluntary nature of the sacrifice only emerges once in the entire data set, even if the voluntariness clearly constituted the conceptual divide between the GA and PA (as mentioned, the sources use the term *avaria* for both).[61] The importance of the voluntary criterion clearly emerges from the only GA case among our samples which was refused by the *Consoli*. A *consolato* submitted in 1670 by the master of the *Madonna del Carmine* recorded that 'thanks to the storm we lost the main mast'.[62] When it came to the judgement, the *Consoli* refused to award the GA on the grounds that it was 'not the place for a demand for Average for the broken mast'.[63] Yet the sole explicit reference to the voluntariness occurs in a set of merchant objections which claims that the mast was broken by the wind and was therefore not liable for GA.[64] The voluntary nature of the sacrifice is never explicitly alluded to in any of the *consolati* or *testimoniali*, in contrast to the repeated emphasis on the circumstances which 'forced' the sacrifice or made it 'necessary'. The interested merchants in this case were two Englishmen, 'Giovanni Barcher' and 'Tommaso Mun' (the same Thomas Mun who would one day write *England's Treasure by Forraign Trade*, based in part on his experience as a factor in Livorno).[65] The case involved a broken mast which, according to the master, had been cut away during a storm. The merchants, however, maintained that 'for its poor quality and defects [the mast] broke in that instant, meaning that the defendants should not be held to account for it, as indeed they are not, it being *casus fortuitus*; in this way it seems that it was fortune and not a voluntary cut'.[66] The two merchants were, however, unsuccessful in convincing the *Consoli*.

The Consultation in the Tuscan Documentation

If the voluntariness of an action was the dividing line between individual responsibility for damages and collective contribution, why do we only find it explicitly mentioned once in documentation explicitly designed to justify a declaration of GA? Only part of the answer lies in the fact that Tuscan sea protests cleaved formalistically to the need for a pre-jettison consultation between master and crew, a fact that presupposed voluntary action and obviates the need to mention it explicitly. In this they seem to have been anxious to follow the letter of the normative material. Indeed, the insertion or foregrounding of a consultation between master and crew is the prominent

---

[61] For example, there is a clear division of damages between GA and PA within the same sea-loan case in ASP, CM, AC, 322-27 (9 December 1670), Calculation.

[62] ASP, CM, AC, 321-25 (25 August 1600), *Consolato*.

[63] ASP, CM, AC, 321-25 (25 August 1600), Judgement.

[64] ASP, CM, AC, 25-28 (8 April 1600), Exceptions.

[65] ASP, CM, AC, 25-28 (8 April 1600); Thomas Mun, *England's Treasure by Forraign Trade* (London: J.G. for Thomas Clark, 1664).

[66] ASP, CM, AC, 25-28 (8 April 1600), Exceptions.

instance of 'improvement' carried out by the court technicians when drawing up the *testimoniale*. Despite Carlo Targa's assertion that he had only ever come across four or five cases with a consultation in Genoa, in Tuscany we find that most jettison cases continue to mention it, even if its presence becomes a little less marked as the century progresses.

In all the 1600 and 1640 samples, we find that the *testimoniale* makes reference to the consultation in every single case of jettison, usually using the wording 'with the required consultation' (*con la debita consulta*).[67] In this respect they strengthen this element in the *consolati* which is often hinted at more vaguely: the *consolati* use a greater variety of wordings to express this idea, vaguely referencing either a conference (*consiglio*) or stating that the jettison was made 'by common agreement' (*di commune accordo*).[68] In other cases the *testimoniali* actually depart from the *consolati* narratives in order to insert the consultative element. One particularly resonant example is the case of the *Santa Maria della Nunziata* (1600), which made its *consolato* in Gaeta before the Genoese consul after a jettison of grain. This *consolato* simply records that 'in order to avoid drowning and losing the vessel and the merchandise we were of the opinion that a jettison should be carried out, for which reason it was done and we began to jettison', hinting only very distantly to a consultation or the common consent of the ship's company.[69] The *testimoniale*, however, recounts the jettison in the following way: 'they were faced with the shipwreck and loss of the ship, merchandise, and persons, for which reason, and with the required consultation, it was resolved upon to begin to jettison for the universal salvation and benefit'.[70]

In the second half of the century, this attention to the consultation is rather less present, though is still clearly a relevant consideration, and the pre-jettison consultation remains present in the majority of cases. In the 1670 samples, we do find that most jettisons were still (ostensibly) undertaken after a consultation: four of the seven jettisons reported in that year had explicit reference to a consultation in both *consolato* and *testimoniale*.[71] There is even one case where the rather weak 'they resolved themselves to [jettison]' (*si risolvorno*) of the *consolato* was transformed by the *testimoniale* into the much less ambiguous statement that the master ordered the jettison 'with the counsel of his crew' (*con il consiglio dei suoi marinai*).[72] Though this leaves three

---

[67] E.g. ASP, CM, AC, 197-29 (26 April 1640); ASP, CM, AC, 198-17 (14 August 1640).

[68] E.g. ASP, CM, AC, 197-4 (14 February 1639), *Consolato*.

[69] ASP, CM, AC, 27-26 (9 September 1600), *Consolato*.

[70] ASP, CM, AC, 27-26 (9 September 1600), *Testimoniale*; See ASP, CM, AC, 25-3 (28 June 1600) for a very similar modification.

[71] Jettisons in that year which include a consultation: ASP, CM, AC, 319-3 (30 January 1669/70); 319-18 (10 March 1669/70); 319-25 (18 April 1670); 322-39 (23 December 1670).

[72] ASP, CM, AC, 319-18 (10 March 1669/70).

cases in which there was no reference to a consultation in either document, there were admittedly still more regular jettisons in a single year than Targa claimed to have seen in a lifetime of practice.[73] Likewise in 1700, five of the cases involving a jettison mentioned the consultation in the *testimoniale*, with one even referring to a 'consultation and parliament'.[74]

That the consultation was just beginning to come into question is illustrated by the case of the *Madonna di Monte Nero*, a GA awarded in 1671 which was then challenged by means of a petition sent to the Grand Duke; the case was subsequently delegated to the Florentine *ruota*.[75] We can infer from documents submitted in defence of the master that one of the merchants' objections was that the jettison had been done without consultation: the *consolato* (which was made at Zante) apparently made no mention of it.[76] In response, the master's defence argued that, on the contrary, there was no need of a consultation before a jettison: since the jettison was carried out 'in response to an effective need' (*seguito al certo bisogno*), consent could in fact be presupposed, and indeed, the jettison would not have been carried out if there had not been consensus.[77] Nevertheless, taking the belt-and-braces approach typical of the legal argumentation we find in the archive, the memorandum goes on to emphasise that, despite its omission from the original narrative, the four witnesses to the *consolato* did in fact mention that a consultation preceded the jettison.[78] The issue was thus clearly something of a grey area, and while the memorandum's author was clearly willing to argue against the need for consultation, he still felt it prudent to erect a second line of defence by insisting on its having been made. This is further evidence that, though the situation was moving in the direction Targa described, the consultation had not yet been abandoned completely in Tuscany.

The Advantage of the Master

This idea that necessity actually presupposes common consensus is perhaps the more important reason why voluntariness or intentionality is not foregrounded and is a curious philosophical take on a problem originally posed by Aristotle: how can an act be forced and voluntary at the same time, both freely undertaken

---

[73] Jettisons of 1670 which did not include a consultation: ASP, CM, AC, 318-26 (22 January 1669/70); 320-2 (9 May 1670); ASP, CM, AC, 322-30 (15 December 1670).

[74] ASP, CM, AC, 418-7 (6 April 1700); ASP, CM, AC, 418-20 (1 July 1700); ASP, CM, AC, 418-21 (1 July 1700); ASP, CM, AC, 419-27 (11 September 1700); ASP, CM, AC, 420-14 (9 November 1700).

[75] ASP, CM, S, 985-333 (8 February 1671). On petitions to the Grand Duke see Guillaume Calafat, 'La somme des besoins'.

[76] ASP, CM, S, 985-333 (8 February 1671), Master's objection.

[77] ASP, CM, S, 985-333 (8 February 1671).

[78] Ibid.

and yet dictated by circumstances?[79] Aristotle approached the problem from a somewhat unexpected angle that sheds light on the emphases we find in the sea protests. He proposes a division between voluntary and involuntary based on our appraisal of the action itself: voluntary actions are those which we praise or blame, while involuntary ones are those that we pardon or pity.[80] Aristotle then further defines the involuntary as an action to which the agent contributes nothing, which would seem to make a jettison voluntary, but this is inconsistent precisely because we would *not* be inclined to blame the master in these circumstances. Aristotle thus introduces the concept of the 'mixed action': a case in which someone chooses something harmful through fear of a greater evil or for some noble purpose. In such cases it is open to question whether such things are voluntary or involuntary.[81] As we have already seen, what seems to have concerned early modern contemporaries above all was the question of the master's liability: in other words, whether the master could be blamed for the loss or damages through negligence or ill intent, especially when this involved jettisoning the property of others in his custody. It is perhaps no surprise then that our sources foreground the necessity and even inevitability of what the master did, almost to the extent of portraying GA as an involuntary act.

In fact, once the necessity of an act had been established, its intentionality was both unproblematically assumed and very widely defined, a thing which, at a single stroke, massively increased the potential of the procedure as far as the master was concerned. Anything which could be described as resulting from a forced act undertaken by the master seems to have been placed into GA, and since it was the master and his crew members who were coordinating the describing, this did not turn out to be particularly difficult. Almost all mast damage described in all our *consolati* and *testimoniali*, for example, was made through some deliberate action. Only once, in all the accident reports, is a mast simply blown over by the wind.[82] There is of course some selection bias at work here: one does not request GA in the first place if one does not believe that one's sacrifice could plausibly be a GA. Nevertheless, the complete absence of accidentally damaged masts is suspect. We never find a mast broken by natural forces even in cases in which the principal expense in the GA was something other than the mast: an extraordinary expense incurred in port, for example. One would expect that, at least on a few occasions, there would be a mix of PA and GA damage to a vessel: maybe some expenses,

---

[79] Aristotle (trans. Terence Irwin), *Nicomachean Ethics* (Cambridge, MA: Hackett Publishing Company, 2019), Book III, Chapter 1, §§1–7 (1009b–1010a), pp. 35–6.

[80] Aristotle, *Nicomachean Ethics*, p. 35; see also Frederick Adrian Siegler, 'Voluntary and involuntary', *The Monist* 52 (1968), 268–87, at p. 269.

[81] Aristotle, *Nicomachean Ethics*, p. 35.

[82] ASP, CM, AC, 321-25 (25 August 1670).

and then accidental storm damage later in the voyage. The fact that we do not find this is thanks to the fact that, from the right point of view, any event could be made to seem the result of voluntary sacrifice. The case of the French ship *Cavallo Marino* is a case in point, demonstrating how damage resulting from a storm might be recast as the result of human action, with a few narrative convolutions:

> And because [bailing out] was not enough, there being always more water in the bilge in such a way that the ship was in evident danger of sinking and being lost with all its cargo, with, however, the advice of his officers and mariners and for the universal benefit, to save the ship, he resolved to run before the wind towards Baffa [Paphos], and in order to round the point that he found there, and thus enter into the harbour, he made to make all sail, during which [manoeuvre] the mizzenmast broke.[83]

We cannot be sure whether all sail was necessary or not; the *Consoli* could not be sure either and that was partly the point. What is clear is that an event which might more obviously be described as the direct result of natural forces ('storm breaks mast') could equally be presented as the result of human endeavour ('master breaks mast through evasive actions during a storm'). Being fundamentally unfalsifiable, it was enough in the vast majority of cases that the voluntary aspect be simply asserted. Since choosing to do something is an action which is internal and unobservable, it would have been impossible to prove or disprove, even had the witnesses to the event been impartial.[84] It was therefore possible to cloak certain damages to the ship which might more obviously be PA – and thus borne by the ship-owners – as GA, which were then borne by the collective.

This is not to say that there was no point in objecting to a master's GA demand, or that masters' control of information automatically and inevitably resulted in their being granted everything they asked for. If this were so, we would not find any conflict surrounding GA declarations, when in fact GA cases were the subject of contestation, conflict, and, occasionally, full-blown litigation: this will be given due consideration below. It should nevertheless be noted that conclusively disproving the master's testimony was almost impossible in the majority of cases, and that the master thus entered any litigation at a distinct advantage. Merchants might claim that the master's version of events was implausible, but they could not prove it wrong, and such objections never resulted in the case being dismissed outright in the cases examined. It is thus not surprising that the outcome of contested cases was generally a readjustment of the amount awarded, rather than the case's outright

---

[83] ASP, CM, AC, 319-20 (18 March 1669), *Testimoniale*.
[84] Addobbati, 'Principles and development', p. 154.

dismissal.[85] Though the first phase of the procedure – the production of the *testimoniale* and other evidentiary documents – was intended to determine whether or not a GA was appropriate, in actual fact this was very often taken for granted: the realistic object of merchant objection seems to have been to ameliorate their lot through a reduced contribution rate, rather than to overturn the judgement. Since the facts of the case could only be proved or disproved with great difficulty, this turned GA procedures from a forensic exercise into something which more resembled a negotiation. It is revealing that, in the two major pieces of GA litigation examined later in this book, the merchants' primary objection was not that the GA demanded was unjust in and of itself, but that it was 'exorbitant', i.e. out of the ordinary line of cases.[86]

The relatively unreflective attitude towards the voluntary criterion comes into sharper relief in those cases in which the *casus fortuitus* which blocked the ship's progress was an irresistible force of a human power. In the case of the *Sante Anime del Purgatorio*, the ship, commanded by a French shipmaster and presumably flying a French flag judging by subsequent events, had left Livorno in July 1699 bound for Tétouan in North Africa.[87] It then met two French warships which compelled the master to shelter in the port of Gibraltar. The King of Meknes had taken all the French merchants and the French consul to Meknes for as-yet unclear reasons: until it was safe to proceed the warships 'forced' the *Sante Anime* to remain in the harbour. This incurred considerable expenses of food, salaries, anchorage, and the expense of sending a man to the French consul at Cadiz to certificate this event, all of which were later placed into GA and defrayed by common contribution. Despite the fact that the master had had no effective say in the matter, the GA was presumably justified here on the grounds that the action had thus ensured the 'security' of the ship and cargo.

We will recall that a recurring doubt regarding GA is the object or end of a GA sacrifice: whether this is for the 'general safety' (a situation of peril) or the 'general benefit' (enabling the ship to complete the voyage). Though sea protests are in no way clinically precise about the employment of these terms, what is clear is that the early modern Tuscans clearly adhered to the latter, wider definition, and that any loss of property incurred for the general benefit was considered a legitimate GA. 'Universal benefit' (*benefizio universale*) is in fact the phrase used by *testimoniale e domanda* when formally demanding the GA to describe the loss or damage, and this phrase also occurs more often than not in the judgement. The example from the *testimoniale* of the *San Spirito e San Pietro Buona Ventura* in 1640 is typical:

[85] See for example ASP, CM, AC, 320-7 (28 May 1670).
[86] ASP, CM, S, 985-333 (8 February 1671); ASF, MM, 358-17, John Finch to Cosimo III (4 February 1671).
[87] ASP, CM, AC, 418-11 (14 May 1700).

... condemning furthermore the said receiving merchants to come together in Average, *lira* and *soldo*, with the value and estimate of the said *tartana* [the vessel] and the master with the value and estimate of half of the said *tartana* and a third of the freight, for the restitution and restoration of the [jettisoned items], all jettisoned into the sea, left and lost for the universal benefit ....[88]

As well as the classic examples of jettison and mast cutting, sacrifices admitted to GA in Tuscany include other deliberate acts for the ship's safety (the deliberate beaching of the vessel, hiring local assistants to help the ship off a shoal, the expense and damages sustained in fighting off corsairs) but also expenses not arising from situations of peril, some of which can only tenuously be described as intentionally incurred: seamen's wages and legal costs while sequestered in port, bribes to local officials, some specific local taxes, as well as even more unexpected costs such as divers' fees and expenses incurred sending messengers with warnings.[89] One of the more striking examples of the 'common benefit' approach comes from a case from 1640. Lorenzo Buonaccorsi, the owner of the *Santo Domenico*, was awaiting his ship's return from Lisbon with cargo for several Livornese merchants, including members of the Sephardic-Jewish Ergas family (the cargo and its value is unfortunately unknown because the calculation is missing from the file).[90] When he found out that the hostile French Armada was abroad in the waters around Livorno, Buonaccorsi sent a felucca (a small wooden sailing vessel) captained by Giovanni Pietro Mattei as far as Barcelona to find the ship and warn it of the French Armada's position. This mission was successful, and the master, Paolo Maria Cardi, took the *Santo Domenico* into Genoa instead. The French had not yet moved their fleet however, so Buonaccorsi sent a messenger on foot to Genoa to tell Cardi not to sail for Livorno until he received further instructions. When the Armada moved to the bay of Ponsa, another felucca was then sent to Genoa to tell Cardi to come down to Livorno with the good weather. The felucca was sent off to the bay of Gorgona to keep a look out for the return of the French. With the ship securely in port, Buonaccorsi, the ship-owner, brought a GA case to share the expenses between all interested parties. In this case, the *testimoniale* argues that the expenses were made 'for the benefit of the ship and cargo' and 'as an expedient' (*per spediente*).[91] Such

---

[88] ASP, CM, AC, 196-38 (2 January 1639), *Testimoniale*.
[89] ASP, CM, AC, 25-26 (10 April 1600); ASP, CM, AC, 318-26 (22 January 1699); ASP, CM, AC, 321-30 (30 August 1670); ASP, CM, AC, 314-9 (16 March 1668); ASP, CM, AC, 319-20 (18 March 1669); ASP, CM, AC, 321-14 (23 July 1670); ASP, CM, AC, 199-16 (15 November 1640).
[90] Trivellato, *Familiarity of Strangers*, pp. 23–34.
[91] ASP, CM, AC, 199-16 (15 November 1640).

an expense was considered legitimate – and apparently raised no objections among the merchants – even though they were clearly precautionary rather than sacrifices to save the ship certain peril.

Though the term 'general benefit' is the one most commonly found in the documentation, it should be noted sea protests did not use the terms 'safety' and 'benefit' with too much consistency. In the cases from 1640, every single judgement and *testimoniale* contain this phrase (8 out of 8). In the cases from 1670 just over half (10 out of 19) of the *testimoniali* contain it, as do around a third of the judgements (6 out of 19). In the 1700 cases 11 out of the 12 judgements contain a reference to the universal benefit, and it is mentioned in either the *testimoniale* or the *consolato* in 9 of those cases. The exception to the rule is, interestingly, the cases from 1600, where it finds its way into only 3 *testimoniali* or *consolati* out of a possible 12 cases and is mentioned in only 1 judgement. Sometimes they instead talk about the 'saving' or 'safety' of the ship (*per salvare, salvezza, salute*, or similar).[92] Less commonly, we are left to infer salvation from the conditions described immediately preceding the action: 'in great danger of drowning', for example (*gros pericolo di annegarsi* [sic]).[93] Many cases use both 'benefit' and 'safety'.[94] There is not, however, a clear link between physical damage and 'salvation' on the one hand and extraordinary expenses and 'benefit' on the other. In the case of the *Mercante Fiorentino* which came loose from its moorings during a storm while anchored in Livorno, we are told in both the *consolato* and the *testimoniale* that the crew cut an anchor rope for the 'universal benefit', and then beached the ship, also for the 'universal benefit'.[95]

Mercantile and Juridical Conceptions of GA

This clear preference for a 'common benefit' definition of GA renders it strange that we find another class of acceptable expenses which are accepted into GA but never get mentioned at all in the sea protests. These might be collectively termed 'irregular financial impositions': extraordinary expenses imposed by political or administrative bodies which needed to be paid in order that the voyage be brought to a successful conclusion.

First in this category are payments of the French *cottimo*. The *cottimo* was a levy introduced by the French state to be made on all ships flying the

[92] E.g. ASP, CM, AC, 196-38 (2 January 1639); ASP, CM, AC, 319-13 (28 February 1669); ASP, CM, AC, 25-28 (8 April 1670).

[93] ASP, CM, AC, 199-23 (20 November 1640).

[94] ASP, CM, AC, 196-37 (2 January 1639); ASP, CM, AC, 196-28 (2 January 1639); ASP, CM, AC, 197-4 (14 February 1639); ASP, CM, AC, 197-29 (26 April 1640); ASP, CM, AC, 197-43 (6 July 1640); ASP, CM, AC, 198-17 (14 August 1640); ASP, CM, AC, 199-23 (20 November 1640).

[95] ASP, CM, AC, 319-28 (28 April 1670).

French flag which entered a Levant port.[96] This tax was ostensibly to pay the expenses of the French *nationes* and for the maintanence and improvement of the French consular apparatus there. It was originally envisaged as an *una tantum*: a one-off. In reality, it became a long-standing duty and even took on a protectionist aspect, as it would be waived if a ship returned directly from the Levant to Marseille (with Livorno as the unspoken target). Guillaume Calafat finds that this Navigation Act *à la français* was not very successful, and in fact we find several instances in the 1670 sample of French ships stopping at Livorno and splitting the cost of the *cottimo* through GA.[97] What is strange, however, is that we do not find such costs justified in the *consolati* or *testimoniali*. We do find attestations in the GA file (*attestazioni* or *relazioni*) signed by the French consul in the port that certify that such payments were indeed levied and paid, but though it was clearly important to provide proof that payment of such expenses actually took place, there is no attempt to justify these under the rubric of GA.

The same thing occurs with another 'political' imposition. These were the costs associated with the so-called 'avanias'. Avanias, still little understood by historians, were large demands levied by the Ottoman authorities on individual European traders or European trading *nationes* resident in the Empire.[98] The European sources, which are the only ones to use the term 'avania', present these as unwarranted and unjust demands, effectively depicting them through an Orientalist lens as examples of Ottoman despotism and tyranny. There is reason to believe, however, that these were more like fines that were levied when disputes between Europeans and the authorities spiralled out of control.[99] In the French case, at least, the costs of avanias borne by the *natio* were then passed on to its shipping. In a manner not dissimilar to the approach used for the *cottimo*, ships flying the French flag were assessed by the *natio* (on exactly what criteria it is not clear) and awarded a portion of the avania that the master was then obliged to pay.[100] The French *nationes* thus operated a

---

[96] Calafat, 'Livorno e la camera di commercio di Marsiglia', pp. 238–9.

[97] Dyble, 'Divide and rule', pp. 374–8.

[98] Merlijn Olnon, 'Towards classifying avanias: a study of two cases involving the English and Dutch nations of seventeenth century Izmir', in Alastair Hamilton, Alexander H. de Groot, and Maurits H. van den Boogert (eds), *Friends and Rivals in the East: Studies in Anglo-Dutch Relations in the Levant from the Seventeenth to the Early-Nineteenth Century* (Leiden: Brill, 2000), 159–86; Maurits van den Boogert, *The Capitulations and the Ottoman Legal System: Qadis, Consuls, and Beratlıs in the 18th Century* (Leiden and Boston: Brill, 2005), pp. 117–41.

[99] Olnon, 'Towards classifying avanias', pp. 169–75.

[100] ASP, CM, AC, 319-20 (18 March 1669); ASP, CM, AC, 322-33 (16 December 1670); ASP, CM, AC, 322-39 (23 December 1670).

kind of meta-GA, a system of collective contribution across all French ships trading in the Ottoman Empire (and via GA, the interested merchants back in Europe). In the first instance, the sum demanded was paid by the master, usually with the help of local merchants who lent him the money at interest via a sea loan (later the interest would also be put into the GA). On one occasion, the French *natio* even demanded contribution for payments for gifts to the Turkish officials on the basis that otherwise the Turks might levy an avania.[101] This raises the intriguing possibility that the French *nationes* used the avania as an excuse to defray the ordinary expenses of maintaining good relations with their hosts.[102]

As mentioned, we do not find either the payment of the *cottimo* or contribution to avanias justified in the sea protests, or even mentioned. All of these cases had a *consolato* and *testimoniale*, but these focused on other tribulations suffered on the voyage such as broken masts and jettisons. In the aforementioned case of the *Cavallo Marino* coming from Alexandretta in 1670, for example, the *testimoniale* relates various tribulations involving a series of storms, yet the narrative accounts completely fail to mention the two large payments levied by the French *natio* in Aleppo for the *cottimo* and Avania, even though these constituted the bulk of the GA. (Nor does it mention the payment of bribes to local officials which we find surreptitiously entered only in the master's list of expenses.)[103]

The reason for this is probably connected to the fact that expenses like avanias and *cottimi* sit awkwardly somewhere between ordinary and extraordinary expenses, and between sacrifices for the benefit of the ship and obligatory levies. This made it difficult to square these costs with existing GA norms. Expenses that were clearly extraordinary and directly pertained to 'liberating' the ship were not problematic: bribes, for example (usually described as 'gifts'), were often required to get a ship moving again after an accident or sequestration in port, and these are sometimes mentioned in the sea protest, albeit not consistently.[104] But apart from their clearly extraordinary nature, bribes were often directly associated with a *casus fortuitus* (putting into a port after a storm or corsair attack, for example). The *cottimo* on the other hand had originally been an *una tantum*: seven years later, could it still be considered as such? The avania was an irregular one in every sense of the word, at least from the European point of view, but it was also a sort

---

[101] ASP, CM, AC, 319-20 (18 March 1669).

[102] See Jake Dyble, 'The threat of the "avania": financial risk in European–Ottoman trade and the growth of an Orientalist discourse, 1660–1710', in Jake Dyble, Alessandro Lo Bartolo, and Elia Morelli (eds), *Un mare connesso: Europa e mondo islamico nel Mediterraneo (secoli xv–xix)* (Pisa: Carocci editore, 2024), 109–31.

[103] ASP, CM, AC, 319-20 (18 March 1669), Calculation.

[104] ASP, CM, AC, 322-16 (9 November 1670), Calculation.

of tax, especially given that it was levied by the French *natio* and was not actually directed at the ship in question. In a way, payments to *avoid* an avania fitted better into the logic of Average, though here too the risk to the parties interested in the voyage was distant and indirect.[105] These were thus verging towards being ordinary costs, but from a pratical point of view it was difficult to deal with these expenses in advance. In the case of avanias, it was presumably not always certain that they would be levied; even if the *cottimo* itself could be predicted, it was not known what payment the ship would incur, since the *natio* apparently carried out an *ad hoc* assessment based on what other similar ships had been charged. It was thus impractical in many cases to deal with such costs at the outset via clauses in the freight contract.

If Giuseppe Casaregi's 'not-much-observed' distinction between Gross Average and Common (or Small) Average had been in force, avanias and *cottimi* taxes would probably would have been regarded as Common Average (even if, as has been noted, there does not seem to have been clear agreement on whether this was for ordinary or extraordinary expenses.) We might also remember that the *Llibre del Consolat* had actually assigned extraordinary expenses incurred during stops to the merchants, not to all parties interested in the voyage. Yet in the seventeenth century, all instances of common contribution had been subsumed under the rubric of General Average with the same modality of contribution in all cases. Given this, they had to fall under GA, as it was unthinkable from a practical point of view to let such costs lie where they fell. Masters and ship-owners did not want to be left footing huge bills. No one wanted to see ships stuck in sequestration because masters and ship-owners refused to pay those bills. If semi-regular eventualities like these could not always be dealt with in the freight contract before the voyage, GA allowed them to be dealt with in a predictable manner. This is almost certainly why the narrow definition of GA called for by Casaregi was never adopted in our period, and we never find an instance of merchants objecting to the principle of these expenses. By helping masters and merchants to share the burden of the *cottimo*, moreover, the court of the *Consoli* helped to defend Livorno against the protectionist measures favouring Marseille.[106]

The use of GA in these cases thus created little concern, certainly for masters and merchants. But the sea protests were drawn up with the help of legally trained professionals. Thanks to their knowledge of the normative material, they were aware that such expenses were dubious, or even, in the case with the French *cottimo*, verging on the indefensible from a strictly theoretical point of view. Since the use of common contribution was apparently accepted by all parties, the court officials would certainly not have objected, especially

---

[105] On the possible connection between GA and the presentation of avanias see Dyble, 'The threat of the "avania"', p. 123.

[106] Dyble, 'Divide and rule', p. 365.

because GA cases brought in fees for the court and its employees. Rather than explicitly justifying these expenses according to the principles of GA, however – tricky, perhaps, but not impossible given that Tuscan GA allowed expenses aimed at the 'universal benefit' – they decided not to mention them at all. The sea protest is in itself then an expression of the way that the GA of normative theory diverged from practice.

The archival documents reveal other ways in which GA practice diverged from theory and indeed give some limited credence to the mercantile refrain that the *ius commune* lawyers should be kept far away from commercial cases on the grounds of being 'overcurious and precise ... [more regarding] certain subtleties than the trueth of the fact or matter', as Gerard Malynes alleged.[107] One conspicuous example of this is the question of whether a GA can be carried out after a ship has been declared unseaworthy. This was an important issue given that shipmasters that wished to declare GA had probably suffered a great deal of damage. Carlo Targa, the contemporary Genoese maritime lawyer, insists that a ship which is no longer seaworthy cannot be the beneficiary of an Average: 'From that moment it is no longer within the bounds of Average but comes to be total loss. The reason proceeds from the rule that the doctors adduce, that everything takes its being and name from that of which it chiefly participates'.[108] In other words, if a ship (a '*nave*') were declared unseaworthy ('*innavigabile*') it could no longer be considered a ship and should therefore be considered lost.

In actual fact, it was not necessary to write off an expensive investment simply because it was temporarily unable to participate in that activity from which it took its name and being. This is neatly illustrated by a remarkable case from the archive. In 1670, the Livornese shipmaster, Giuseppe Reali, had just left port with *La Madonna del Rosario* when the ship (for reasons unstated in the sea protests) began to take on water.[109] The ship hurried back to the pier where it was possible to unload a small proportion of the valuable textiles on board before the vessel sank. Even if we do not accept the sophistry of the doctors, this might at first sight appear a good example of a total loss. In actual fact, given that the vessel went down in port, the ship and some of the remaining merchandise could be recovered (at considerable expense) by divers. The master claimed to have decided to save the valuable merchandise rather than his less valuable ship: this seems to have been his justification for putting the costs of the refloating into GA.[110] We will have reason to revisit this case further on, as it perhaps unsurprisingly was objected to by the merchants, and the amount requested by the master was in the end substantially reduced.

[107] See above, p. 42.
[108] Targa, *Ponderationi*, pp. 142–3.
[109] ASP, CM, AC, 321-14 (23 July 1670).
[110] ASP, CM, AC, 321-14 (23 July 1670), *Testimoniali*.

The master was, however, allowed to recoup some of his costs, thus implicitly recognising the right to request GA in such circumstances. Unseaworthiness, even to the point that the ship rested on the seabed, was no barrier to a GA.

In some cases we even find a GA declared after an official, legally documented declaration of unseaworthiness; indeed, declaring unseaworthiness was the prerequisite for the GA because the ship was originally not meant to terminate its journey at Livorno. Declaring a GA in an unscheduled destination where there were no receivers was highly suspect, but claiming that the ship was unable to go on apparently legitimised such an irregularity. The four 1670 cases which involved a declaration of unseaworthiness all show suspicious similarities: all four were grain ships whose destination was Genoa, and in each of these cases the ship was given permission to terminate its journey, liquidate the cargo, and perform a GA.[111] Since there was a market for grain everywhere, and since political authorities were presumably keen to gain greater access to this essential and politically sensitive commodity, it may not have been difficult to obtain the necessary declaration.[112] In any case, the 'unseaworthiness' was clearly no barrier to performing a GA: perhaps we can designate this one of the effects (and advantages) of summary procedure, which allowed judges to procede according to 'the nature of things'.[113]

It was not only over 'subtleties' that practice and norms disagreed. There is even indication that merchants themselves understood the principle of the GA procedure in a wholly different light. This is an important consideration for those commentators who see GA as a fundamentally universal procedure because the principle was common everywhere even if the mechanisms adopted in the procedures were not. It is particularly relevant for those who argue that GA attests the existence of a lex mercatoria or a common mercantile 'culture' in the Mediterranean.[114] An alternative conception of the principle emerges from a case we have already had cause to examine several times, a GA declared by the master of the *Sante Anime del Purgatorio* on his ship's return from Tétouan in 1700.[115] As has been noted, this case was originally proceeding through arbitration rather than in front of the court. There was a particular sticking point in the process, however, which necessitated bringing the case before the *Consoli*: whether cargo owned by the master, supposedly

---

[111] ASP, CM, AC, 319-25 (18 April 1670); ASP, CM, AC, 320-2 (9 May 1670); ASP, CM, AC, 321-25 (25 August 1670).

[112] Fusaro, *Political Economies of Empire*, pp. 93–108.

[113] p. 44.

[114] Tetley, 'The general maritime law', p. 128; Wickham, *The Donkey and the Boat*, p. 648.

[115] ASP, CM, AC, 418-11 (14 May 1700). This case is also analysed in Jake Dyble, 'General average, human jettison, and the status of slaves in early modern Europe', *The Historical Journal* 65 (2022), 1197–220, at pp. 1209–11.

stored above deck, should contribute to GA. The master claimed that his own goods should not contribute, because 'these were loaded under the bridge and not in the hold, for which fact according to Chapter 183 of the *Llibre del Consolat de Mar* they are excluded'.[116] When we examine the *Llibre*, however, it does not in fact state that cargo stored above deck does not contribute to GA. What it says is that cargo loaded above deck without the permission of the merchants cannot be indemnified and that the master will have to bear the whole cost of any losses.[117] In other words, it suggests that the loss or damage of this cargo could not be defrayed by common contribution; it does *not* suggest that the same cargo should be excluded from contribution when someone else's property has been lost or damaged. This is rather something that the master felt was implicit in the stipulation.

Even more surprisingly, this logic appears to have been accepted by the merchants, at least initially. The dispute revolved not around the principle of excluding the cargo on the bridge but around the truthfulness of the master's account. The merchants claimed that the master was simply lying about where he had stored his goods, as the amount of cargo he had on board would not have fitted there.[118] The master, in turn, produced an affidavit signed by the customs officials that backed up his statement about the loading of the goods.[119] It was only after both sides had already submitted two sets of documents on the matter that questions over the principle of exclusion were raised. In their third and final list of objections submitted to the court, the merchants argued that things stored above deck should contribute after all, because 'by means of the jettison they had been saved'.[120] They thus switched to the logic of GA with which we are familiar, outlined in the *Lex Rhodia*: even if things loaded on deck could not have been indemnified through GA, they nevertheless should contribute because they benefitted from a jettison. In their final judgement, the *Consoli* sided with the merchants and declared that the cargo stored above deck should contribute, but it is clear that the merchants themselves were not familiar with the logic of the *Lex Rhodia* until very late on in the process.[121] It is possible that they may have sought new legal counsel in creating this last submission.

What is clear is that all concerned on both sides were initially convinced that Chapter 183 of the *Llibre del Consolat* implied that cargo stored out of the hold was excluded from GA entirely. Both the master and the merchants thus held that, if their property did not to receive the protection of GA in certain circumstances, then that same cargo should not have to contribute

---

[116] ASP, CM, AC, 418-11 (14 May 1700), Master's Second Set of Reasons.
[117] Casaregi, *Consolato del mare*, p. 51.
[118] ASP, CM, AC, 418-11 (14 May 1700), Master's Second Set of Reasons.
[119] ASP, CM, AC, 418-11 (14 May 1700), Affidavit of Customs Officials.
[120] ASP, CM, AC, 418-11 (14 May 1700), Affidavit of Iuda Crespino.
[121] ASP, CM, AC, 418-11 (14 May 1700), Judgement.

to the protection of other cargo. They were therefore viewing GA not as a one-time obligation rooted in a benefit received at someone else's expense but were rather viewing it as a form of mutual insurance that followed a logic of reciprocity: I will help defray your losses today in the knowledge that you would be compelled to do the same for me if the positions were reversed. It is likely this same logic accounts for the fact that only one cargo of slaves was found in the Tuscan GA cases, despite the fact that Livorno hosted the most important slave market in the Christian Mediterranean after Malta.[122] Both the *Lex Rhodia* and the writings of contemporary European jurists legislated against the jettison of slaves, and ships in the Mediterranean did not in any case have to deal with the practical challenges that occasioned human jettisons in the Atlantic slave trade: provisioning, rebellion, and rampant disease, the results of oceanic distances, the industrial scale of the slavery, and the more desperate and irreversible position of the enslaved. The one time we do find slaves included (as contributing property rather than sacrificed property) this was the result of special circumstances and was the object of a successful legal challenge.[123]

The GA principle was thus not as widely shared by practitioners as has sometimes been suggested. Whilst we should refrain from claiming on this basis that there was a monolithic 'merchant' conception of GA in opposition to the juridical one, there were nonetheless clearly different ideas in play about what made GA 'fair'. This evidence should also alert us to the dangers of associating a communitarian mindset or attitude with the use of GA or contrasting this with a more individualistic economic modernity. The quite transactional GA principle implicitly adopted by the merchants and master in the case of the *Sante Anime del Purgatorio* does not, after all, suggest a particularly collectivist attitude towards the maritime venture.

Eighteenth-Century Critics of Tuscan GA

The structural advantages enjoyed by the master went unremarked upon during the seventeenth century. Already at the beginning of the eighteenth century, Giuseppe Casaregi seems to make a critical allusion to this phenomenon when he remarks that 'I do not believe that these expenses [those usually placed into Common Average] ought to be made good by the merchants or the owners of the goods, which are done more for the fitting out and repairing of the ship than for the sake of saving the merchandise'. It was not until the 1780s, however, that there were robust criticisms of the way that GA was routinely carried out. Virgilio Andrea Sgazzi, a failed merchant turned accountant, laid out his views on GA (as well as a great many other topics) in a series of 'reflections'

---

[122] Kaiser and Calafat, 'The economy of ransoming', p. 113.
[123] The subject of slaves and GA is discussed in depth in Dyble, 'General average, human jettison'.

which he sent to the governor of Livorno in 1785.[124] Sgazzi considered that the *Consoli* were not up to the job of administering GA, and abetted the abuses of shipmasters by agreeing to believe whatever story was put before them. Masters could thus hide routine expenses by pretending that they had been made for the benefit of all. Sgazzi instead suggested that a group of judges should be drawn up on a case-by-case basis, with the judges in question to be specialists in the particular commodities involved.

Sgazzi's ideas had little immediate impact, but the governor of Livorno did pass on his reflections to the city's energetic auditor, Francesco Giuseppe Pierallini.[125] Pierallini's precise role was in fact that of *auditore consultore*, providing advice on political and economic matters.[126] During his tenure he not only effectively appropriated the mediating and consulting role traditionally carried out by the governor himself, but even appropriated a substantial portion of the governor's archives, moving it into rooms adjoining his own personal apartments.[127] His review of insurance practices was undertaken at the behest of the Tuscan secretary of state in 1785, and Pierallini decided to go to Pisa personally to conduct his investigation into GA procedures at the Consular court.[128]

More insightful and better informed than Sgazzi, Pierallini realised that existing GA procedures suffered from two systematic problems: a problem of transparency and a problem of proof.[129] The problem of proof was the one that we have already observed based on the seventeenth-century sea protests. It was often impossible to prove or disprove the master's version of events, and while the *consolato* had to be corroborated by the testimony of witnesses, these were usually members of the crew, who, unsurprisingly, duplicated their master's testimony.[130] Current Tuscan procedures made matters worse. Although the accident had to be publicised within 24 hours of arrival, the deadline for presenting the *consolato* proper was a far more generous three months. By the time the three months had expired, any witnesses who were not members of the crew would no longer be available for cross-examination. The result was that many ordinary expenses might be masked as extraordinary ones. Ascanio Baldasseroni, writing in the same year, was likewise

---

[124] Addobbati, *Commercio, rischio, guerra*, p. 226.

[125] Marcella Aglietti, *I governatori di Livorno dai Medici all'unità d'Italia* (Pisa: Edizioni ETS, 2009), pp. 105, 129, 149–5, 157, 160–70.

[126] Marcella Aglietti, 'Il governo di Livorno: profili politici e istituzionali nella seconda metà del Settecento', in Adriano Prosperi (ed.), *Livorno 1606–1806: un luogo dell'incontro tra popoli e culture* (Turin: Allemandi, 2009), 95–106, at p. 96.

[127] Aglietti, *I governatori di Livorno*, p. 166.

[128] ASL, *Governo civile e militare*, 977, f. 27r.

[129] Addobbati, *Commercio, rischio, guerra*, p. 226; ASL, *Governo civile e militare*, 977, ff. 18r–32r.

[130] Addobbati, *Commercio, rischio, guerra*, p. 229.

perturbed by this issue. It seemed, he remarked acerbically, that the masters had discovered the secret of the Galley of Salamis, the ship of Theseus which was 'preserved' in Athens for more than a thousand years without decaying because all its component parts were continually and surreptitiously replaced: 'In our times', meanwhile, 'such miracles happen only to the detriment of insurers'.[131] Indeed, Baldasseroni seems to have taken the issue of fraudulent GA particularly to heart, mentioning its injurious effect on insurers on at least four separate occasions and in particularly strong terms.[132]

Pierallini thought he had identified a further problem: Sgazzi was indeed correct in supposing that collusion existed and that it favoured the masters, but he was wrong to put the blame squarely at the feet of the *Consoli*. Rather it was the attorneys who represented the conflicting interests who were primarily at fault. Since there were only four attorneys dealing with Averages – namely 'Papanti, Castinelli, Braccini' and, 'beginning to involve himself in these sorts of cases, Vannucchi' – they came into frequent contact with one another, sometimes on one side, sometimes on another.[133] Furthermore, fees for court officials and attorneys alike were linked to the size of the GA case in question. The master's attorney would receive a fee of one piece of eight for every 1,000 pieces of passive mass (i.e., the value of all the cargo, half of the ship, and a third of the freight). The chancellor would receive payment at two thirds of this rate. The merchant's proctor would be paid the same, but only if there had been a deduction in the damages requested by the master; otherwise, he would receive nothing. The fee of the *curatore* would amount to a quarter of the amount paid to the chancellor and merchant's attorney. Two officials attached to the Pisan customs house would carry out the eventual calculation *ex officio*. For this, they would be paid a flat fee of two pieces. In short, everyone's fee, apart from the calculators', was determined by the value of the cargo, ship, and freight of the case in question.

Since the attorneys of the receiving merchants would only receive a fee if they succeeded in getting the GA payment reduced, the other attorneys would help out their colleagues in the knowledge that the shoe would soon be on the other foot.[134] Thus, according to Pierallini, the attorneys for the shipmaster would agree to deduct a nominal portion of the fees and their colleagues opposite them would agree to waive through the greater part of the damages.[135] A single list of exceptions listing all possible objections pertaining to the awarding of the GA was produced by the attorney of the receiving

---

[131] Baldasseroni, *Delle assicurazioni marittime*, vol. 3, p. 15.
[132] Baldasseroni, *Delle assicurazioni marittime*, vol. 1, pp. 212, 266, 269, vol. 2, p. 239.
[133] ASL, *Governo civile e militare*, 977, f. 29v.
[134] ASL, *Governo civile e militare*, 977, f. 29v.
[135] Addobbati, *Commercio, rischio, guerra*, p. 227.

merchants in order to maintain form.[136] The result would be presented to the *Consoli* as a happy consensus. This suited the master, who had a lot to lose if he was found liable, and who was therefore deeply invested in the outcome. The receiving merchants on the other hand, whose portion was small and usually covered by insurance, did not have the same incentive to raise objections.[137] According to Pierallini, Livornese merchants, already generally reluctant to attend to disputes and willing to entrust everything to their attorneys, were even less willing to burden themselves as individuals with a 'communal affair' like GA.[138] In any case, in the event of any complaint from the merchant side, the attorneys could always shrug and cite the judgement of the *Consoli*: hence a lack of transparency abnegated individual responsibility. Here too, however, procedures could be somewhat improved to partly remedy the situation. Pierallini thus advised that the *Consoli* refrain from giving a judgement based on 'consensus' unless it was signed by all the interested parties – a change which was in fact enacted.[139]

The problem of transparency and the more general problem of coordination between the merchants is therefore a question which we should pose to the evidence of the court records. The final section of this chapter will therefore consider the problem of merchant representation and coordination, especially in light of a superficial reduction in the care paid to safeguarding merchant interests.

Merchant Representation and Objection

The most obvious way that merchant objection manifested itself, but by no means the most meaningful, was the production of official legal interventions contesting the master's claims. Pierallini noted in his report that 'only a single list of exceptions' was produced on behalf of the merchants.[140] In the first half of the seventeenth century, meanwhile, the procedure appears, at least on the surface, far more detailed and rigorous. Many of the documents contain not only a list of exceptions, but also a full list of interrogatories and *capitoli* ('headings'); both types of document were designed to protect merchant interests and root out false declarations.[141] Exceptions were technically meant to be what we would now call affirmative defences. Exceptions were used when the defendant conceded the validity of a claim but would argue

---

[136] ASL, *Governo civile e militare*, 977, ff. 27r–28v.
[137] Addobbati, *Commercio, rischio, guerra*, p. 227.
[138] ASL, *Governo civile e militare*, 977, f. 29r.
[139] Addobbati, *Commercio, rischio, guerra*, p. 228.
[140] ASL, *Governo civile e militare*, 977, ff. 27r–28v.
[141] One case is missing interrogatories (ASP, CM, AC, 25-28), one is missing exceptions (ASP, CM, AC, 25-26). A further case is clearly incomplete, and it is therefore impossible to say (ASP, CM, AC, 28-12).

that the plaintiff should nevertheless not recover.[142] The exceptions found in GA cases represent objections of every sort, but especially question the truth of the account. Interrogatories, meanwhile, were questionnaires to be submitted to the witnesses of the sea protest in order to test both the truth of the narrative and uncover information which might render the request invalid.[143] After swearing an oath, the witness would be subjected by the judge to questions. Andrea Addobbati states that the normal procedure was that the witness should first answer questions posed by the plaintiff and then by the defendants.[144] However, in our cases we do not find any questions from the master, at least under the heading of 'interrogatories'. These instead appear to have taken the form of the documents called 'headings'. This document divided the master's account into a series of individual points copied word for word from the *testimoniale* which the witness was required to confirm or deny. Since the witness had already been examined upon the master's original *consolato*, however, and had already confirmed it, this was necessarily something of a *pro forma* exercise. In 1600, ten out of the 12 cases contain exceptions, interrogatories, and *capitoli* together. By 1640, only half of cases had exceptions, though all of them still involved both interrogatories and *capitoli*.

When we arrive at 1670, however, there is a marked drop off in the number of documents being produced on behalf of the merchants. A full 14 of the 18 GA cases in that year do not have any exceptions, interrogatories, or *capitoli* at all. Of the four which include exceptions, only one includes interrogatories, and one other *capitoli*.[145] The situation is similar in 1700. Of the 12 cases adjudicated in that year, nine do not include any documents produced in defence of the merchants. One case includes just interrogatories, one includes just exceptions, and only a single case includes both.[146] The *capitoli*, appearing just once in the 1670 data set, have disappeared entirely. The impression from the numbers alone is that, from being well defended at the beginning of the century, procedures moved further and further in favour of the masters as the century progressed, with a case from the first half of the century showing markedly more representation of 'merchant interests' than the second half. The merchants of 1785 who apparently received a single sheet of exceptions would, in fact, appear to be doing considerably better than their counterparts of 1700 who frequently received no defence at all.

Examining the cases themselves, however, it seems that this change is more accurately interpreted as streamlining rather than a progressive diminution of

---

[142] Donahue, 'Procedure in the courts of the *ius commune*', p. 84.

[143] Addobbati, 'When proof is lacking', p. 142.

[144] Addobbati, 'When proof is lacking', p. 142.

[145] ASP, CM, AC, 319-25 (18 April 1670); ASP, CM, AC, 320-7 (28 May 1670); ASP, CM, AC, 321-14 (23 July 1670); ASP, CM, AC, 322-30 (15 December 1670).

[146] ASP, CM, AC, 417-16 (9 February 1700); ASP, CM, AC, 418-20 (1 July 1700); ASP, CM, AC, 419-27 (11 September 1700).

representation: it is not just the fact of being represented that counts but the quality of the representation on offer. We must ask how penetrating the exceptions and interrogations were, an investigation which necessarily involved a degree of subjective judgement, as well as examine the extent to which merchants were actually involved and interested in the cases themselves. Closer scrutiny of these documents shows that, in the first half of the century, the merchants' attorney produced documents for his party, regardless of whether there was an obvious case against the master; in the second half of the century these were only produced when the merchants had concrete cause for grievance. Whilst the procedures were thus less rigorous in one sense, the 'decline' was somewhat ephemeral. Given the difficulty of disproving a GA case without inside information, very little had been lost in practice from the merchants' point of view.

The first point to note here is that mounting a defence against a GA request by means of interrogatories was a very tricky exercise. The witnesses were seamen who worked with the master, and the master was able to send those seamen for examination who were most amenable to his cause. With the *testimoniale* arranged in a manner structurally favourable to the master, the best that the merchants' attorney could hope for was to try to trip up the witnesses and induce them to produce some inconsistency in the account. Given these limitations, the interrogatories from the first half of the century were probably about as penetrating as they could have been, mostly asking about the ship's condition, or for specific details about the voyage and accident in the hope that the witnesses might expose the case as a fiction. Shipmasters were legally held to a very high standard of care under *culpa levissima*; if it could be intimated that anything less than the highest standard of care had been taken, and that this in turn could have been behind the ship's difficulties, this would have been a good line of attack.[147] A typical example of a GA interrogatory asked when the ship was last careened and how much was spent on it, whether the portholes had been properly secured, and whether they had made the required consultation.[148] Though this made a certain degree of sense, one wonders whether the Pisan attorneys or *Consoli* had the expertise to make anything of these responses. The *Consoli* ideally had some commercial knowledge, but the idea that they had substantial seafaring knowledge is highly doubtful: who would have known that a master had underspent on the careening of his boat? Other questions were simply designed to expose inconsistencies in the testimony, asking the exact time of the jettison, how the jettison was made (by whom, from which part of the ship), and the direction of the wind at the time of the accident.[149] This was never achieved in our cases, though witnesses did occasionally claim to be unable to remember the details.[150]

---

[147] Rossi, 'The liability of the shipmaster', pp. 11–15.
[148] ASP, CM, AC, 25-8 (30 May 1600), Interrogatories.
[149] Ibid.
[150] Ibid.

Exceptions tended to be extremely generic and even irrelevant in the majority of cases. Most of the exceptions made in the first half of the century raise three or four points: that the libel was vague, obscure, and groundless; that the master was not legally competent to make the demand for GA; and that the things related by the master were not true.[151] Most of the exceptions from the first half of the century are comprised of only these three objections, and these were sometimes produced on the day of the citation to the judgement itself.[152] All this suggests that the majority of the exceptions were likewise for show and had no real bearing on the case. Only occasionally does a further, specific exception appear, and even in these cases, defence generally rested on casting aspersions on the quality of the equipment. An example is provided by the case of the *Francesca*, an English ship from London and 'Barbary' with cargo for Thomas Mun.[153] The ship had supposedly been forced to cut the mast while sheltering at the beach of 'Portolando'.[154] The final exception, which 'contradict[ed] more than anything' the master's account, was that

> it [was] not realistic that while he was anchored with good ropes in the port of Portolando that he should have had such misfortune that he was forced to cut the mainmast to save the ship, it being far more likely that is it was the winds, if indeed there were any, which was that which broke the mast, which broke for its poor quality and defects.[155]

Of the four cases from 1670 in which we find merchant exceptions, three present an obvious motive for intervention.[156] One case was a very large one (awarded damages of 4,832 pieces, the second largest award in that year) which impacted a large number of merchants (97, more than three times as many as any other case that year).[157] One was the case mentioned above in which a ship had become lodged on a shoal on account of sailing too close to the shore, a thing the master claimed had been done to avoid a corsair.[158] The third of these cases was perhaps the most egregious: the case of the

---

[151] ASP, CM, AC, 196-37 (2 January 1640).

[152] See ASP, CM, AC, 27-26 (9 September 1600).

[153] ASP, CM, AC, 25-28 (8 April 1600).

[154] It has not been possible to identify this port. The details of the *testimoniale* are particularly vague. The ship was on its way from London to 'Barbary' and thence to Livorno. The ship left London sometime in September and sheltered at the beach of 'Portolando' on 3 and 4 October. So, it was almost certainly outside of the Mediterranean, a thing also suggested by the fact that it was caught in another storm after loading in Barbary around the Cabo de Gatt of the southern coast of Spain.

[155] ASP, CM, AC, 25-28 (8 April 1600), Exceptions.

[156] The odd one out in this case is ASP, CM, AC, 322-30 (15 December 1670) which appears to be a fairly uncontentious jettison.

[157] ASP, CM, AC, 320-7 (15 December 1670).

[158] ASP, CM, AC, 319-25 (18 April 1670).

Livornese master, Giuseppe Reali, and his ship the *Madonna del Rosario*, which began to take on water near port and eventually sank in the harbour and was rescued by divers.[159] It is no surprise at all that the merchants had something to say about this particular case.[160] In fact, the master's responses to the interrogations give us a fairly good indication as to how a hole had mysteriously appeared in his boat. The numbered statements are those posed by the merchants (and/or their legal counsel) and the interpolations are the master's response which was inserted in the margin of the page:

> 3rd. When he departed from the pier, he had diverse friends aboard his ship that were due to return to Livorno that evening.
>
> *Objection, it was only that a little boat came to the pier with people from Livorno when the ship had sailed to the pier to pick up consignments.*
>
> 4th. With the aforesaid friends on board, he ate and drank and stood with them in conversation.
>
> *[Agreed,] once the boat was there, they came aboard the ship to give the master a good send off, and the same [master] gave them something to drink out of common decency ...*[161]

On this occasion the objection seems to have met with some rare success, with an original request for 1,014 pieces of eight being reduced in the final judgement to 351 pieces.[162] This is apparently typical of GA cases. Rather than being thrown out outright, claims favouring the master were reduced, either by exclusion of the more dubious claims or by a wholesale reduction of the requested figure.

Rather than the quality of representation declining then, GA cases – at least the more straightforward ones – appear to have become leaner over the course of the century, with merchant objections being raised when there was felt to be particular need. Pierallini's report suggests the way that court officials and attorneys were renumerated might explain this change. Expenses for a GA case were not paid for by one or other of the parties. They were instead added to the damages awarded and then partitioned over all players according to their interest, thus becoming part of the GA payment itself. Pierallini described a system in which the payment received by the key figures was linked to the value of the voyage once this had exceeded a certain base level. The 1561

---

[159] ASP, CM, AC, 321-14 (23 July 1670); see p. 102.
[160] ASP, CM, AC, 321-14 (23 July 1670), Positions.
[161] ASP, CM, AC, 321-14 (23 July 1670), Positions.
[162] ASP, CM, AC, 321-14 (23 July 1670), Expenses, Calculation.

reform of the court, on the other hand, include a price list which detailed what was due for each type of document that was submitted: 3 *soldi* 4 *denari* for 'every exhibition of a libel [e.g. a sea protest], exceptions, *capitoli* ... and list of supporting evidence'; 2 *soldi* for every summons; 3 *soldi* to be levied on every *capitolo* or interrogatory; and so on.[163] In short, a system where the expenses of the case were linked to the number of documents which were produced. This raises the possibility that in the earlier period attorneys were incentivised to submit more documents in order to receive higher fees, and that once this incentive was removed, extraneous documents vanished.

In actual fact, when we analyse the expenses levied over the period it appears that the system Pierallini describes did not exist in the seventeenth century and, what is more, that there is no causal link between changes to renumeration and the form taken by the procedures. Across the entire period, the expenses for the case remained fairly stable, and bear no relationship to the size of the case as Pierallini suggests. In most cases we have no indication of how the administrative fees of the case were levied but only have a single total figure for administrative expenses in the calculation. However, we can be certain that the system described by Pierallini was not in existence in 1600, because two of the cases include a full breakdown of the fees paid to various court officials.[164]

Table 3. Breakdown of expenses for two GAs in 1600 in Tuscan golden *scudi*. Archival References: ASP, CM, AC, 25-28 (8 April 1600), Calculation; ASP, CM, AC, 27-30 (31 November 1600), Calculation.[165]

	Francesca	**San Torpè**
Total value of the voyage	4,700.00	527.09
Total awarded in GA	41	126.17
Chancellery Fees	4.13	1.87
Master's Attorney	4	2
Merchants' Attorney	2.67	2

---

[163] ASF, Auditore poi Segretario delle Riformagioni, 116, §45.

[164] ASP, CM, AC, 25-28 (8 April 1600), Calculation; ASP, CM, AC, 27-30 (31 November 1600), Calculation. Why the full breakdown should have been provided in these cases is unclear. In one instance the breakdown corresponds to the lump sum for 'expenses of the case' in the calculation; in the other, the parties seem to have divided the expenses between themselves and, unconventionally, not entered them into the active mass.

[165] In the original documentation, the four expenses are given in *lire* while the

While it is unclear on this basis how the various fees were determined, we can see that the various items of expenditure show no obvious relationship either to one another, to the damages awarded, or to the contributing elements. It certainly does not appear that the fees were dependent on the financial import of the case.

This is confirmed when we analyse data from the entire period, where we find no discernible relationship between the total value of the voyage and administrative expenses. The graphs in Figures I–III plot the expenses of the case as recorded in the calculation against the passive mass. Tuscan golden *scudi* were used in the first half of the century and pieces of eight in the second, though since the same currency applies to both expenses and passive mass they can be placed on the same graph. If there were a system in place like the one which Pierallini describes, we would expect to see a flat line in Figure 1 for expenses up to a certain point (since cases where the voyage was worth less than 5,000 pieces levied a flat fee), and then to see an ascending line demonstrating a positive correlation between expenses and passive mass. In fact, we see only an extremely weak correlation between the size of the case and expenses, even no correlation for some years, demonstrating that fees remained similar even for cases which were very large in financial terms. If a system like that described by Pierallini were in place, expenses for the largest case (a voyage worth over 138,000 pieces) ought to have been in the hundreds, but the figure was instead less than 50 pieces. The data is presented twice, firstly using an arithmetic scale and then using a logarithmic scale (Figure 2), which allows for better visibility of the far more common smaller cases. Though the automatically generated trend lines using the logarithmic scale do initially appear to demonstrate the curve that we would expect if Pierallini's system were used, the lines bend upwards much later than they ought to, and the curve in fact disappears entirely when outliers are removed (Figure 3). While the rationale behind the levying of fees remains elusive – a great deal of data would have to be collected to overcome the limitations of the source material in this respect – we can at least say that the incentive structure Pierallini describes was not yet in place, and thus that the bureaucratic 'streamlining' was not the result of changes in the way that court functionaries were renumerated.

The most likely explanation for the gradual reduction in the documentation dedicated to merchant representation, therefore, is that this was a streamlining process brought about by the pressure being placed on the court by increased commercial litigation. As the century progressed, the *Consoli*, like all mercantile courts across Europe, faced an increasing number of litigants

---

active and passive mass are given in *scudi*. The *lire* have been converted using the rate of 7.5 *lire* to a *scudo* which is stated in the calculation. ASP, CM, AC, 25-28 (8 April 1600), Calculation; ASP, CM, AC, 27-30 (31 November 1600).

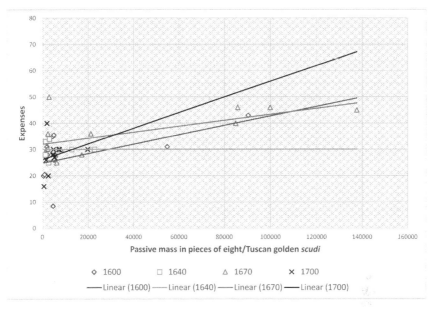

Figure 1. The relationship between the size of the case and expenses, 1600–1700 (arithmetic scale).

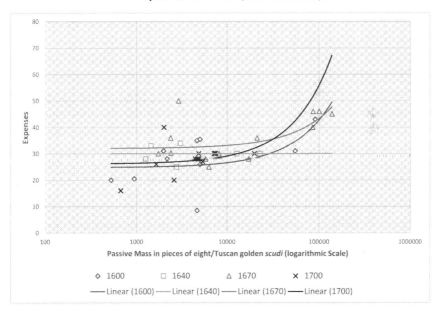

Figure 2. The relationship between the size of the case and expenses, 1600–1700 (logarithmic scale).

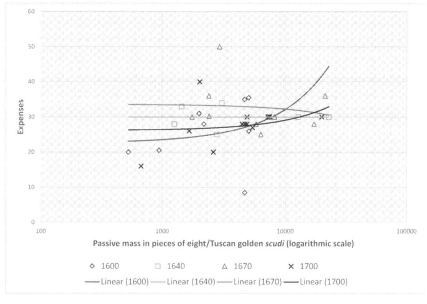

Figure 3. The relationship between the size of the case and expenses excluding the largest cases, 1600–1700.

wanting to go before the court, and there was greater pressure to resolve disputes quickly.[166] The change to merchant representation is therefore a superficial one. Merchants now needed to be active in their own defence, but this had always been the case, precisely because of the master's control over the information presented to the court. The case of the *Madonna del Rosario*, in which Giuseppe Reali hosted a party on board his vessel, provides us with a good illustration of this fact. Though the original narrative was admittedly suspect, ultimately, the most pertinent evidence against the master's case was local information, deliberately concealed in the original submission, of which a Pisan attorney could not be aware. A case which unfolded in 1640 demonstrates the point even more clearly.[167] The vessel *Annuntiata Buona Ventura* came from Algiers to Livorno carrying silver, feathers, and other merchandise, as well as a number of redeemed Christian captives. The ship endured two storms on its way back to Livorno and in both cases made a jettison of cargo. The ship arrived into Livorno on 29 March 1640, and the master made his *consolato* before the governor the next day and submitted

---

[166] Andrea Addobbati, 'Until the very last nail', pp. 49–50; Fusaro, 'Politics of justice/politics of trade', p. 152.

[167] ASP, CM, AC, 198-17 (14 August 1640).

his *testimoniale e domanda* to the *Consoli* on 3 April. A set of *capitoli* and interrogatories to be put to the witnesses were sent to the governor on 7 April: this examination took place on 12 April. At this point the case appeared clear cut. A month later, the master officially submitted a list of points in his favour (*ragioni*) in which he listed the *testimoniale*, the examination on the *capitoli* and interrogatories, and the generic and oft-invoked reference to 'every law, statute, reform, *capitolo*, and every other relevant thing'.[168] The judgement condemning the receivers to the payment of GA was issued on 2 June. At this point, we would expect to find the calculation as the final act in the case. Instead, on 19 July, without any explanation, a new *testimoniale* was submitted (though essentially identical to the first). A citation was issued for the merchants on 20 July, notifying them of this new *testimoniale* as well as a 'renunciation of acts' (*renuntia d'atti*).[169] New *capitoli* and interrogatories were submitted, as well as a new piece of evidence: two Dutch passengers, seamen of long experience, who claimed that the ship had been overladen when it left Algiers.[170] It is unclear who officially issued the 'renunciation of acts', but the only logical inference is that talk about the state of the ship had spread to the merchants and that they had forced the case to be reopened. Again, it was information circulating in the port which enabled the judgement to be challenged: the new interrogatories largely reflect the new evidence that had come to light, with questions about the tonnage of the ship, whether it had been overladen, and whether they thought that a jettison would have been necessary had the ship carried less cargo.[171] A successful challenge therefore generally depended on local fact finding, and, since the court was located in another city, this essentially depended on the merchants bestirring themselves, regardless of the quality of the legal defence provided in Pisa.

This example also alerts us to an important aspect of the way in which merchants interacted with GA cases. The timing of events is suggestive in this respect, particularly the long, unexplained periods in which nothing appears to be happening. The *testimoniale* was submitted on 3 April and the first interrogatories were sent back to Livorno just four days later: this does not seem much time to allow any evidence to emerge outside of the master's account. This, in turn, suggests that the attorney drew them up on the basis of the *testimoniale*, without any communication with the merchants. Between the examination of witnesses on the *capitoli* and interrogatories (12 April), and the production of the master's list of evidence (10 May), a whole month elapsed; more than a month elapsed between this and judgement (2 June); and a month and a half between this and the 'renunciation of acts' (19/20 July).

---

[168] ASP, CM, AC, 198-17 (14 August 1640), Reasons.
[169] ASP, CM, AC, 198-17 (14 August 1640), Summons 20 July 1640.
[170] ASP, CM, AC, 198-17 (14 August 1640), Passenger Statement.
[171] ASP, CM, AC, 198-17 (14 August 1640), Second Interrogatories, §§8, 18, 19.

The whole case took over three months, far longer, it should be noted, than the statutory 45 days. It seems unlikely that the rumours about the ship being overladen should have taken three months to reach the merchants. We do not have any positive evidence for why these long delays took place, but the most likely explanation is the merchants first confronted the master about the issue privately, and perhaps tried to pressure him into making a less onerous demand. It may be at this point that the master submitted his list of supporting points to the *Consoli* in an effort to force the delivery of a judgement. It was only when the informal talks failed that the merchants then decided to force an official re-examination of the case. While this is hardly conclusive evidence, it is our first hint of an important theme which we will see on other occasions: the use of semi-private forms of resolution, with out-of-court discussion and agreement having an important role but rarely making an impression on our evidence base. It is also notable that an ostensibly 'final' judgement by the *Consoli* was overturned in order to accommodate new evidence (though despite this seemingly important intervention by the merchants, the *Consoli* awarded the GA anyway).

Conclusions

By comparing the normative material analysed in Chapter 2 with the GA procedures from the archive, it becomes clear that the latter enjoyed a significant autonomy from the former. While the normative material did have an influence, most notably the way that jettisons were presented in GA documentation, this influence was only partial and, for the most part, formal. This was nowhere more true than with regards to the scope of GA, i.e., the different costs that it could repartition. The overall picture that emerges is of an operational GA which was very capacious, repartitioning a large number of extraordinary costs between ship and merchant interests, as well as many ordinary ones, thanks in part to the considerable structural and procedural advantages enjoyed by the shipmaster. GA was used in a wide range of scenarios, not only when the alternative to action was the physical loss of the vessel, but also when any outside circumstances had impeded the ship's progress. The 'unit' of the GA was not the physical ship and cargo, as it was in the *Lex Rhodia*, but was instead the voyage or venture. This finding offers something of a corrective to those who have argued that mercantile justice was unfolding firmly inside the tent of the *ius commune*.[172] In this sense, GA can probably be likened to another risk-management instrument: insurance. In neither case did learned

---

[172] Guido Rossi, *Insurance in Elizabethan England: The London Code* (Cambridge: Cambridge University Press, 2017), pp. 6–8; Piergiovanni, 'Genoese Civil Rota', p. 28.

jurists succeed in successfully theorising the merchant practice and reconciling it to the categories of the *ius commune*.[173]

The *Consoli* generally took the path of least resistance in their administration of GA. Their attitude was characterised by a certain passivity in reaching judgements and a willingness to countenance irregularities, especially over the way that damages were assessed. This was not because the *Consoli* were the work-shy and inexpert buffoons of Andrea Moniglia's musical comedies. The outward form of the procedure may have been adversarial (the cases are introduced as 'shipmaster X *versus* receiving merchants'), and the adjustment of a GA might even have involved contestation and conflict, with the merchants formally challenging the master's narrative with the production of interrogatories and exceptions, but the prime role of the *Consoli* was one of certification, simply recognising the fact of the GA in order that the obligation to contribute might be recognised in jurisdictions where absent interested parties resided. This was often administration in the form of justice, a concept foreign to our own world view, accustomed as we are to a clear separation of powers, and administrative machinery largely divorced from that of the judiciary.[174] The *Consoli* facilitated this process, favouring the master by default unless merchant resistance was particularly concerted, and it appears that court officials helped shape the master's testimony into a legally acceptable form. They therefore smoothed the way to GA declarations. The strange thing, in a way, is that we find any GA's that were rejected, and we are led to wonder what the master of the *Madonna del Carmine*, whose mast broken by the wind did not qualify for GA, had done to forfeit the court's assistance.

Finally, we have seen how merchants did not necessarily share jurists' views on GA, even at the level of broad principle. In a certain sense, it can also be said that practice was ahead of the jurists: a dichotomous GA/PA division had been established while jurists were trying to theorise older variants and procedures into the mix (the pre-jettison consultation, *germinamento*, Common Average). With that said, the various ways that cargo and damages were valued provides evidence that merchants were not availing themselves of a customary lex mercatoria, even on a procedural level. It should also be noted that the laissez faire approach of the court was not indiscriminate: some foreign groups were accorded more latitude than others, demonstrating that GA formed part of Livorno's wider political economy. This will be explored further in the next chapter.

---

[173] Guido Rossi, 'Civilians and insurance: approximations of reality to the law', *The Legal History Review* 83 (2015), 323–64.

[174] Mannori and Sordi, *Storia del diritto amministrativo*, pp. 52–6.

4

Commercial Justice and Political Economy: Stephen Dring's Tale

Overview

This chapter completes the picture of GA-as-practice begun in Chapter 3 by arguing for the importance of political economy in GA's functioning, and for the influence of political economy on commercial justice more broadly.[1] *Pace* proponents of a lex mercatoria, GA regulations varied from jurisdiction to jurisdiction but were generally accepted by players in other jurisdictions as *fait accompli*. What is more, regulations were applied differently even within the same jurisdiction in accordance with the dictates of political economy, both that of the home state and that of foreign powers. In making this argument, we will move away from a tight focus on documentation produced by the court to consider dynamics that only evidence from elsewhere can shed light upon.

This chapter is centred on the evidence provided by a single microhistorical case study, a GA which became the object of a complex and high-profile diplomatic dispute between England and Tuscany. The case analysed represents what Edoardo Grendi called an 'exceptional normal': 'exceptional inasmuch as it mirrors a normality, so normal that often it remains silent'.[2] Here we have an example for which exceptionally rich evidence from across several archival collections can be triangulated in order to establish the normal dynamics which underpinned GA resolution.[3] As a GA in and of itself, there was nothing overly distinctive about the case. The English ship *Alice and Francis* declared a GA in Livorno in the summer of 1670 after enduring a storm and combat with corsairs.[4] The original procedure in Pisa was resolved in a mere ten days. Months later, however, the *Alice and Francis* would find itself at the centre of another storm, this one diplomatic in nature, and another combat, as English representatives attempted to wrest GA jurisdiction from

---

[1] On GA and political economy see also Dyble, 'Divide and rule'.
[2] Grendi, 'Micro-analisi e storia sociale', p. 512.
[3] The case is reconstructed in Addobbati and Dyble, 'One hundred barrels of gunpowder' to a different analytical end.
[4] ASP, CM, AC, 321-30 (30 August 1670).

the Grand Duke. Diving deep into this single case, at once ordinary and extraordinary, uncovers the dynamics at play beneath the veneer of official form, and provides important insight into the way that GAs were actually resolved behind the scenes. Though the dispute was ostensibly about GA practices, we find that the real issue at stake was jurisdiction. The scrutiny was problematic for the Tuscan authorities, however, because the way that the case had actually been resolved was highly irregular in procedural terms. The important decisions in the *Alice and Francis* were not being made in the court, but rather outside of it. While the rhetoric of the dispute was confrontational, and concerned itself with rules and regulations, the resolution of the cases on the ground involved consensus, compromise, and, in this case, collusion. This is an important corrective to the 'official' account of GA cases which is presented in the court archive.

None of these dynamics were evident to the English diplomats, who accused the Tuscans of using GA as a political-economic ploy to attract traffic to the port. This accusation was levelled as part of a wider struggle to obtain consular jurisdiction in Livorno. In fact, the Tuscan 'hands-off' approach towards the 'Northern' merchants and shipping merely reflected the commercial importance of the Northerners to the port and the unwillingness of the Tuscan authorities to alienate this important interest group. While the court's approach was in many respects irregular, the English diplomats' failure to obtain their objectives reflected the fact that the state's desire to control English shipmasters and merchants ultimately did not align with the interests of those same actors.

From a comparison between English and Tuscan GA practices that this analysis requires, the countours of two distinct official attitudes towards maritime capitalism emerge. These two attitudes did not revolve around the question of the security of property rights – a question of particular interest to New Institutionalists.[5] Instead, while the Tuscan authorities maintained older regulations that favoured the interests and wellbeing of seamen, the English authorities instead adopted regulations that favoured merchant capital and increased the burden of risk – both financial and personal – upon the maritime labour force.

The English Complaint

The original English complaint about the *Alice and Francis* illustrates the various tensions embedded into GA's multilateral nature. The controversy started in February 1671 with a memorandum addressed to the Grand Duke by

---

[5] Daron Acemoglu and James Robinson, *Why Nations Fail: The Origins of Power, Prosperity, and Poverty* (London: Profile Books, 2013), pp. 77–83, 102–3; Douglass North and Barry Weingast, 'The evolution of institutions governing public choice in seventeenth-century England', *Journal of Economic History* 49 (1989), 803–32.

the English resident in Florence, Sir John Finch.[6] Some London merchants had made a representation to King Charles II, complaining of the 'exorbitant' GAs being awarded in Tuscany, and now the king wanted authorities over cases such as these transferred to the English consul in the port.[7] The complaints came at a sensitive juncture in relations between the two states – a disastrous visit by Charles's extraordinary ambassador the year before had only exacerbated long-standing tensions between the English in Livorno and the Tuscan authorities.[8] According to these unnamed London merchants, the *Consoli del Mare di Pisa* frequently granted outrageous damages to masters.[9] There were complaints about the frequency of Averages, and the length of time they took to resolve.[10] Cases were said to follow an irregular form arbitrarily determined by the *Consoli*, and the 'principal merchants' were unable to make objections. While these abuses were various, however, the motivation behind them was clear: 'the same *Consoli*, with every ease, agree unto the pretensions of the masters of the vessels to invite them to the port of Livorno, though with damage to those that employ them'.[11] The final straw for the London merchants had been a particularly egregious recent case, that of the ship named the *Alice and Francis*, whose master had been awarded damages totalling 1,800 pieces of eight for powder expended during a battle with Algerian corsairs, 'despite being in convoy with other English vessels'.[12]

What had happened to the *Alice and Francis*? As we will see, accounts varied. A broad outline of events is provided by the *London Gazette* of mid-August 1670, based on letters received from Cartagena dated 21 July 1670.[13] The ship had left England as part of a small convoy, two men of war, *HMS Advice* and *HMS Guernsey*, and two other merchant ships, the *Alicant Merchant* and the *Summer Island Merchant*. On entering the Mediterranean, the group had been attacked off the Cabo del Gatt in south-eastern Spain by seven Algerian men of war, three of them carrying between 56 and 60 guns, and the others 'no less than 40'. The Algerian Vice-Admiral's vessel, struck

---

[6] ASF, MM, 358-17, John Finch to Cosimo III (4 February 1671). On John Finch see Stefano Villani, 'Between anatomy and politics: John Finch and Italy, 1649–71', in Gaby Mahlberg and Dirk Wiemann (eds), *The Practice of Reform in Health, Medicine, and Science, 1500–2000* (Aldershot: Ashgate, 2005), 151–66; Dyble 'Lex mercatoria', pp. 691–3.

[7] ASF, MM, 358-17, John Finch to Cosimo III (4 February 1671).

[8] See Maria Fusaro and Andrea Addobbati, 'The grand tour of mercantilism: Lord Fauconberg and his Italian mission (1669–1671)', *English Historical Review* 137 (2022), 692–727.

[9] ASF, MM, 358-17, John Finch to Cosimo III (4 February 1671).

[10] Ibid.

[11] Ibid.

[12] Ibid.

[13] *The London Gazette*, n. 495 (11 August–15 August 1670).

in the hull, had retired from the combat, but the rest of the fleet returned the following morning to exchange cannon fire from afar. Only the oncoming darkness had finally allowed the convoy to escape. The convoy was saved, but the English had suffered losses. The commanders of the naval vessels had been killed, along with seven seamen of the *Advice*. Around 20 more had been wounded. Among these latter figures was the master of the *Alice and Francis*, 'struck on the arm with a splinter'.

This master, unnamed by the Gazette, was one 'Stephen Dring', a seasoned mariner with many years' sailing behind him. Beginning life as a simple seaman, Dring had risen to the rank of master six years earlier: a hard, violent individual it would seem, who had spent half or more of his 40 years at sea.[14] The *consolato* shows that the *Alice and Francis* had scheduled calls at Alicante, Livorno, and Messina, with a final destination at Izmir, where it would deliver cloth for private merchants flouting the monopoly privileges of the English Levant Company in the Ottoman Empire.[15] After the combat, the ship went to Alicante, where it proceeded to make a *consolato*. It then continued its voyage to Livorno, apparently alone. There Stephen Dring declared GA and was eventually granted damages: for the damage to the ship and rigging, for the powder and shot expended during combat, and compensation for his broken arm and the exertions of his crew under enemy fire.

Finch was doing more than simply demanding that the *Consoli* be brought into line: he demanded that jurisdiction over GAs involving Englishmen be transferred to the English consul in Livorno. Finch claimed that English laws on Averages were quite different to those of the Grand Duchy, never conceding damages worth more than 1.5 per cent of the entire value of the enterprise.[16] Stephen Dring was awarded damages at the slightly higher rate of 2.28 per

---

[14] Dring obtained his master's certificate from Trinity House on 28 September 1664: TNA, SP 46/137, f. 476. In 1659, he had appeared as a witness in a case before the Admiralty in London 'aged 23 years or thereabout', classified as a simple mariner: TNA, *High Court of the Admiralty*, 13/73, ff. 720v–721v. If he is the same Stephen Dring who commanded the *Elias of London* in 1668, he was involved in a court case in Massachusetts in 1668 against his Mate, Charles Thirston: three seamen declared to the court that 'Mr. Dring told their Mate Thirston that he could take his clothes and things he had in the ship and go ashore when he would for he looked upon him now as a passenger. Thurston said that he would go aboard Mr. Dobbin's ketch and get passage, to which Mr Dringe replied "Gooe & be Damd; what is due to you I will paye with manie other verrie incomely speeches"'; see *Records and Files of the Quarterly Courts of Essex County, Massachussets (1667–1671)* (Salem: Essex Institute, 1914), vol. 4, p. 28.

[15] ASP, CM, AC, 321-30, *Consolato*; *Calendar of State Papers, Domestic Series, of the Reign of Charles II*, vol. 10, p. 412, Levant Company to Consul Ricaut (1 September 1670).

[16] ASF, MM, 358-17, John Finch to Cosimo III (4 February 1671).

cent.[17] It was only right, argued Finch, that the English in Livorno should be able to resolve their own GA cases according to their own rules. If the situation continued, warned the letter, the King would not hesitate to overrule future rulings emerging out of Tuscany, such was his commitment to ensuring justice for his subjects.[18] A routine procedure for redistributing the extraordinary costs of a maritime voyage had captured the attention of princes and become the subject of diplomatic controversy. The claim that GA was being rigged in order to attract traffic to the port shows a clear awareness of Tuscany's broader economic strategy: encouraging commerce through institutional incentives, among which might be included a certain disregard altogether for rigorous and time-consuming rules and procedures.[19] At the very least, we can say that Livorno's reputation was preceding it.[20]

Evidence for English GA Procedures

In reality, however, the evidence that we have available suggests that the supposed gulf between English and Tuscan GA laws was not as large as had been made out. Finch's claims about the English procedures do not add up, and the idea that English law capped GAs at 1.5 per cent is implausible. If this really were the case, it would mean that those who had made a sacrifice to save the ship that was of greater value than 1.5 per cent would have to bear any loss in excess of this alone; this would have been a radical practice, unparalleled anywhere else in Europe, and yet it leaves absolutely no trace in contemporary GA jurisprudence. Charles Molloy, the Anglo-Irish lawyer who would publish a major and influential work on maritime law just a few years later in 1676, makes no mention of any such restriction, and the principles he outlines are broadly in line with those adopted elsewhere: that 'common calamity' should be made good by 'common contribution', with no reference to any arbitrary limit imposed by statute or ordinance.[21]

In fact, the 'laws of England' concerning GA, far from contradicting those in Tuscany, hardly seem to have existed at all.[22] English GA procedures were the least definite in Europe, relying almost exclusively on private agreement.

---

[17] ASP, CM, AC, 321-30, Calculation.
[18] ASF, MM, 358-17, John Finch to Cosimo III (4 February 1671).
[19] Tazzara, *The Free Port of Livorno*, p. 127.
[20] Lillie, 'Commercio, cosmopolitismo e modelli della modernità'.
[21] Molloy, *De iure maritimo*, p. 280.
[22] This would not be first time that Englishmen in the Mediterranean had tried to gain commercial advantage through reference to 'English laws' that turned out not to exist – at least not as 'laws' in the strict sense of the term. See Maria Fusaro, 'The invasion of northern litigants', p. 32.

As Nicolas Magens, a German London-based merchant and author of *An Essay on Insurances* (1755), remarked:

> As there are in London no Commissioners particularly appointed for the settling of Affairs relating to Insurances and Averages as at Amsterdam, nor a Person to adjust the same upon Oath as at Hamburgh [sic], neither are there any certain Laws relating to Assurances and Averages, therefore it is frequently submitted to private Opinions, especially when there is but a small Difference, whether it be calculated either in one Way or the other, and Things will now and then be misunderstood.[23]

Digging down into Finch's claims further, we find that the case of the *Alice and Francis*, far from being an 'exorbitancy, contrary to the laws of England', would almost certainly have been substantially accepted had the claim been made in London. The reference to a cap of 1.5 per cent on GAs, rather than an absolute limit on contribution rate, was probably referring in a confused or misleading way to a much more specific provision in a recent Act of Parliament: the 'Act to prevent the Delivery up of Merchant Shipps, and for the Increase of good and serviceable Shipping', first promulgated in 1664, and then renewed with several amendments in 1671.[24] It had come to the attention of Parliament that English seamen, rather than heroically defending their vessels against all comers, understandably considered discretion to be the better part of valour.[25] Rather than risk life and limb for someone else's cargo, the mariners were choosing to make over a portion of the goods freely in order to continue their journey in peace, a situation which certainly suited their would-be assailants who thus received plunder without firing a shot. Such conduct was even encouraged by some norms on GA. The *Lex Rhodia* rules, as we have seen, allowed ransoms paid to pirates and enemies to be shared out by means of GA.[26] The Act now made it a legal duty of seamen to offer resistance to such enemies. Any master who was found to have made a deal with the aggressor would be responsible for all damage and imprisoned for six months. Crew would forfeit all of their wages and any goods they had in the ship. By way of compensation for these exertions, the Act established that on the safe return of the ship, the merchants might present a gift to the crew of an amount that they 'shall judge reasonable', and in no case 'exceeding

---

[23] Nicolas Magens, *An Essay on Insurances* (London: J. Haberkorn, 1755), p. 171.

[24] 'Charles II, 1664: An Act to prevent the delivering up of Merchant Ships', in John Raithby (ed.), *Statutes of the Realm: Volume 5, 1628–80* (1819), pp. 521–2; 'Charles II, 1670 & 1671: An Act to prevent the Delivery up of Merchants Shipps, and for the Increase of good and serviceable Shipping', pp. 720–2. Addobbati and Dyble, 'One hundred barrels of gunpowder', p. 834.

[25] Addobbati and Dyble, 'One hundred barrels of gunpowder', p. 833.

[26] D.14.2.2.3; Watson, *Digest*, vol. 2, pp. 419–20.

the value of two per cent of the Shipp and Goods soe defended according to the first Cost of the Goods to be made appeare by the Envoice'.[27] This would then be distributed 'amongst the Captain, Master, Officers, and Seamen of the said Ship, or Widows and Children of the Slain'. Since the master of the *Alice and Francis* had been awarded a similar 'gift' in recognition of their engagement with the enemy, it seems likely that this was the statute Finch was referring to. The reference to 1.5 per cent rather than 2 per cent may be down to a miscommunication, a simple desire to place extra pressure on the Grand Duchy, or perhaps Finch's own weak grasp of the particulars of GA (he was a medic rather than a merchant by training).[28]

The Act had created a slim procedural difference between the two jurisdictions. In Tuscany, compensation for the crew after a combat was awarded, along with the rest of the GA, by an official body: the *Consoli*. The English act removed the 'gift' from the remit of GA and transformed it into an optional bonus to be given entirely at the discretion of the merchants, albeit working on the same principle of contribution. Rather than requiring the merchants to award these funds, the act had placed a statutory limit on their generosity: an unnecessary worry, it transpired, since in 1698–9 Parliament was forced to retract these discretionary powers from merchants, and mandate the appointment of 'four or more good and substantiall Merchants and such as are no Adventurers or Owners of the Shipp or Goods soe defended and have no Manner of Interest therein' to decide on fair compensation for the mariners.[29] Yet despite this procedural difference, the size of the gift decided upon by the *Consoli* in this case fell within the terms of the Act and did not even come close to exceeding the statutory limit of two per cent; it was certainly no 'exorbitancy'. The money paid to Stephen Dring for his broken arm and the compensation paid on account of the combat together came to 385 pieces of eight, a mere 0.44 per cent of the total value of the cargo and ship.[30] Nor was compensation for the crew unusual in a European context. Phillip II's 1563 maritime ordinances for the Low Countries, for example, made provision for a payment of damages to the wounded and any funeral costs of seamen killed in a combat to be included in GA.[31] The French *Ordonnance de la Marine* (1681) would establish that the cost of treatment of those wounded during a combat should likewise enter into

---

[27] 'An Act to prevent the delivery up of Merchants Shipps', Clause IX, p. 722.

[28] Peter Lely, 'Finch, Sir John (1626–1682)', *Oxford Dictionary of National Biography* (2004), <www.oxforddnb.com/view/10.1093/ref:odnb/9780198614128.001.0001/odnb> [18 August 2021].

[29] 'William III, 1698–9: An Act for the more effectual suppression of piracy', in John Raithby (ed.), *Statutes of the Realm: Volume 7, 1695–1701* (1819), p. 593.

[30] ASP, CM, AC, 321-30, Calculation.

[31] Ordonnance of Phillip II of 1563, Title IV, Article 2, quoted in Pardessus, *Collection de lois maritimes*, vol. 4, p. 79.

GA.[32] The master's decision to fight, and the subsequent award by the *Consoli*, were entirely in line with the spirit of the law, as expressed by the 1664 English Act of Parliament and by practice elsewhere in Europe.

Hypothetically, the Act had subtle and far-reaching implications because it arguably transformed the decision to enter into combat from a voluntary act (thus eligible for GA) into a compulsory duty: in other words, from an extraordinary into an ordinary expense. In reality, however, these implications had not been apprehended in contemporary English practice, a thing made clear by a nineteenth-century case which turned on precisely this issue. The case of Taylor vs Curtis came before the Common Bench in 1816 after a first hearing at the Guildhall, and concerned combat expenses put into GA.[33] Magens's view that there were no specific laws concerning Averages in England was clearly borne out by the progress of the trial, with both English legal opinion and eighteenth-century continental authorities providing contrary opinions, and little in the way of precedent found to resolve the matter.[34] Eventually, the judge ruled against the master and ship-owners – a decision made partly on the basis of the 'Act to prevent the Delivery up of Merchant Shipps', which was taken to place combat in the master's 'proper line of duty'.[35] The judgement was not based on merchant practice, which seems instead to have accepted combat expenses. It had been argued by the attorneys for the ship-owners that 'it being habitual with merchants to treat losses of this description as General Averages, it may be fairly inferred that the law is such'.[36] Even the lawyers for the merchants admitted that 'a wise policy might frequently have induced individuals to contribute to similar losses'.[37] Given the largely private nature of GA resolution in England, it is perhaps unsurprising there was little certainty on the point in terms of legal precedents. What is clear is that even in English practice it was common to treat combat expenses as a GA sacrifice. This further suggests that, had the GA of the *Alice and Francis* been adjusted in England, the outcome would have been the same, or, at the very least, it would not have attracted comment.

---

[32] René-Josué Valin, *Nouveau commentaire sur l'ordonnance de la marine*, 2 vols (La Rochelle: Legier & Mesnier, 1760), vol. 2, p. 165.

[33] W. Pyle Taunton (ed.), *Reports of Cases Argued and Determined in the Court of Common Pleas and Other Courts* (Boston: Wells & Lilly, 1823), vol. 6, pp. 608–25.

[34] While most of the commentators had argued that expenses incurred in combat with the enemy were eligible, the extremely influential Balthazar-Marie Émérigon had recently argued that they were not, a fact of which the counsel for the defence made much. See Taunton, *Reports of Cases*, pp. 615–16; Park, *Marine Insurances*, p. 140; Valin, *Nouveau commentaire* (1760), vol. 2, p. 153; Balthazard-Marie Émérigon, *Traité des assurances et des contrats à la grosse*, 2 vols (Marseille: Jean Mossy, 1783), vol. 1, p. 627.

[35] Taunton, *Reports of Cases*, p. 616.

[36] Ibid.

[37] Taunton, *Reports of Cases*, p. 611.

If English and Tuscan practices regarding combat expenses were substantially the same, what was the point of the complaint? The key to making sense of Finch's accusations is to contextualise it within a wider diplomatic game. Bad feelings between the English *natio* in Livorno and their Tuscan hosts had intensified for several years. English merchants had become increasingly frustrated by the restrictions and fees imposed on them by port authorities, especially the strict quarantine of their goods a full four years after the Great Plague.[38] The Tuscans for their part had suffered a number of humiliating slights at English hands. Recent judgements given by Tuscan tribunals had been challenged in London, casting aspersions on the Grand Duke's justice. Royal Navy ships had begun refusing to salute the port on entry from 1665, and ordinary English shipmasters soon followed suit – an unprecedented snub.[39] A visit by Lord Fauconberg, the extraordinary ambassador of Charles II, in the early summer of 1670 could have been an opportunity to pour oil on troubled waters, but the visit succeeded in achieving the exact opposite.[40] The ambassador arrived at an inauspicious moment, just days after Grand Duke Ferdinando II had died. When Fauconberg finally was able to meet the young Cosimo III, the ambassador concentrated his energies not on commercial questions, but rather pressed for English freedom of worship, a topic guaranteed to offend and impossible for the Grand Duke to grant even had he wanted to. The English party managed to add several *faux pas* to an already long list, holding a public Protestant wedding in Livorno, and celebrating the Stuart restoration with fireworks while the rest of the Florence was still in mourning. The task of taking forward negotiations in these difficult circumstances was left in the hands of John Finch.

This would render a difficult brief even more so: Finch had been charged with bringing disputes 'between English Merchants & Mariners' under the jurisdiction of the English consuls.[41] This was an issue of particular interest to English merchants, since the rules regarding wages applied in England and those in the Mediterranean varied considerably, with those in the Mediterranean in clear favour of the mariners. The *Llibre del Consolat de Mar* gave the seaman a degree of wage protection and a say in the modality of payment, and Englishmen serving in the Mediterranean were quick to seize upon these advantages.[42] Wage disputes were becoming increasingly common fixtures of Mediterranean maritime courts in the second half of the

---

[38] Addobbati and Fusaro, 'The grand tour of mercantilism', p. 706.
[39] Carlo Cipolla, *Il burocrate e il marinaio*, p. 109.
[40] Addobbati and Fusaro, 'The grand tour of mercantilism', p. 700.
[41] John Finch to Lord Arlington (10/20 January 1670/1), TNA, State Papers Foreign, Tuscany, 1582–1780, SP 98, vol. 12, part 1, f. 169v.
[42] See Addobbati, 'Until the very last nail', p. 826.

seventeenth century.[43] Only a few months before Finch was officially charged with the task, the English consul at Livorno, Thomas Clutterbuck, had raised the matter of English mariners with the governor, Antonio Serristori, claiming that English seamen should not be allowed to seek employment with foreign masters. Serristori, under strict orders from Florence that the demand 'should in no way be upheld', had responded that all seamen who were not in Naval service were 'free in the context of the port to make their fortunes however they see fit'. 'I hope that this topic', remarked Serristori acerbically, 'will not be brought up again'.[44]

This hope was in vain. Finch had his first meeting with the Grand Duke on this and other commercial questions on 2 November 1670.[45] The memorandum concerning GA was then presented as an addendum to these ongoing discussions.[46] It is this context that allows us to understand the true intent behind Finch's complaint. The letter drew attention to a procedure, Average, which was (supposedly) governed by two different sets of laws in the two countries. This was taken to benefit those employed in the transportation sector ('the pretensions of the masters'), to the detriment of merchants ('those who employ them'). The proposed solution was that the English enjoy the 'benefits of His Majesty's laws' on the subject, instead of being subjected to those 'extremely long' procedures in the Tuscan tribunals. The parallels with the dispute over wages are obvious. Having thus far enjoyed no success with the direct approach, it seems that Finch was trying a new angle of attack on the problem of wages. GA was the thin edge of the wedge. If the Tuscans could be embarrassed into conceding jurisdiction over GA, this could provide a useful precedent. Arguing by analogy, the English might then begin to once more angle for more general consular jurisdiction. At the very least, concessions over Average would give John Finch something to show for his efforts.

GA could thus be seen as a Trojan horse.[47] Any remaining doubt over Finch's true object is dispelled by his reference to 'articles of commerce' signed between the King of England and the King of Spain. Finch explained to the Grand Duke that the concession of 'the benefit of His [English] Majesty's laws' to English subjects was so far from prejudicing Cosimo's sovereignty that even the King of Spain and 'other kings and potentates' had agreed to such requests.[48] What exactly Finch had in mind by 'the benefit of His Majesty's laws' is suggested by his specific passing reference to 'article 19' of a treaty

---

[43] Addobbati, 'Until the very last nail', p. 50; Fusaro, 'The invasion of northern litigants', p. 37.
[44] ASF, *Serristori*, 438, Serristori to Bardi (1 August 1670).
[45] ASF, MM, 358-17, John Finch to Cosimo III (4 February 1671).
[46] ASF, MM, 358-17, John Finch to Cosimo III (4 February 1671).
[47] Addobbati and Dyble, 'One hundred barrels of gunpowder', p. 825.
[48] ASF, MM, 358-17, John Finch to Cosimo III (4 February 1671).

between England and Spain. The reference is, in fact, to the Anglo-Spanish treaty of 1667, an unexpected and highly advantageous commercial treaty which the Spanish hastily signed as part of wider diplomatic efforts to achieve peace with Portugal after the opening of hostilities with France.[49] When we examine the document, we find that article 19 was not in the least concerned with maritime Averages, but rather established, on a reciprocal basis, consular jurisdiction over disputes between 'captains, officers or mariners ... for their wages or salaries, or under any other pretence'.[50]

The Tuscan Response

At this point, the GA dispute appears nothing more than a cynical gambit to win consular jurisdiction over wages. But the Tuscan response suggests there was more to the matter. Rebutting Finch's arguments was easy enough: his interlocutors chose to play dumb, as though the dispute really was only about GA. This task fell to the *auditore fiscale*, the highest authority in the Tuscan legal system. This position was held by Emilio Luci, and there was no one better placed to refute the English arguments: Luci had been chancellor of the court of the *Consoli* from 1659 until the previous year.[51] Unlike Finch, he was intimately acquainted with maritime Averages, and his response to Finch's complaint was a model of reasonableness.[52] If jurisdiction over Averages involving English merchants and masters were given over to English consuls, he argued, then merchants would begin to game the system. Non-English merchants would ask Englishmen to trade their goods under their name, in order to benefit from less onerous rules on contribution. They may even pretend to be English, creating endless confusion and disputes about jurisdiction. It was, at any rate, very rare that a shipment should exclusively involve only traders of one nation. If merchants of other nations were involved, in which tribunal should the affair proceed? If the case had to proceed in two different tribunals there would be a doubling of costs, to the detriment of all involved, and there could be some absurd outcomes in which the same events were judged differently by two different courts. There would be no

---

[49] Jean McLachlan, 'Documents illustrating Anglo-Spanish trade between the commercial treaty of 1667 and the commercial treaty and the asiento contract of 1713', *The Cambridge Historical Journal* 4 (1934), 299–311; see also Zaugg, *Stranieri di antico regime*, pp. 59–71.

[50] 'Treaty of Peace and Friendship between Great Britain and Spain. Signed at Madrid 13/23 May, 1667', in Edward Hertslet (ed.), *Treatises and Tariffs regulating the Trade between Great Britain and Foreign Nations: Part V* (London: Butterworths, 1878), 25–43.

[51] ASP, MM, 112.

[52] ASF, MM, 358-17, Emilio Luci to Cardinal Leopoldo de' Medici (6 April 1671); Addobbati and Dyble, 'One hundred barrels of gunpowder', p. 839.

COMMERCIAL JUSTICE AND POLITICAL ECONOMY 131

superior court which could arbitrate between the two judgements. It would also play havoc with insurance, if the insurers were of a variety of nationalities, since they might not consider themselves bound by 'English' rules. In short, Luci's memorandum noted the thoroughly international nature of GA and the subsequent impossibility of applying national rules in all cases involving English subjects. Luci finished his memorandum by noting that the English Royal 'ordinances' would encourage the 'absurd' situation where the same thing was judged twice, with 'unfortunate consequences'.[53]

This effectively ended Finch's line of attack. Yet for all its cogency, Luci's memorandum contains a striking and revealing omission: not once does it mention the case of the *Alice and Francis*, the original spur for English complaint. This approach would not have been so strange had Finch not blatantly misreported the case in his original memorandum, a thing which could have been easily rebutted with reference to the original files. It is rendered still stranger by the fact that Luci did in fact use archival documents in his rebuttal. Finch had claimed that the *Alice and Francis* had been awarded a GA of 1,800 pieces, 'for the consumption of powder' used in the fight with the Algerians.[54] It is not clear from the letter whether the point at issue was the admission of powder itself, or rather the quantity that had been claimed, or both. Luci was not to know that powder would have been admitted in England too, but he tackled the question of admissibility by attaching a list of precedents from the Consular archive which showed that the repartitioning of combat expenses via GA was standard practice.[55] He did not, however, use the Consular archive to disprove Finch's contention that 1,800 pieces of eight had been spent on powder in the case of the *Alice and Francis*. This would indeed have been an absurd expense for powder alone, enough for any would-be Guy Fawkes to blow up the Houses of Parliament three times over.[56] When we examine the original files, however, we learn that powder was only part of the expense claim. The award, 1,875 pieces, 12 *scudi*, and

---

[53] ASF, MM, 358-17, Emilio Luci to Cardinal Leopoldo de Medici (6 April 1671).
[54] ASF, MM, 358-17, John Finch to Cosimo III (4 February 1671).
[55] ASF, MM, 358-17, 26-9.
[56] The gunpowder plotters reckoned that 36 barrels or maybe less would be sufficient. See 'The Gunpowder Plot', *Encyclopedia Brittanica*, <www.britannica.com/event/Gunpowder-Plot> [accessed 18 August 2021]. At the price on the expenses claim submitted by the officers of the *Alice and Francis* themselves (ASP, *CM*, 321-30, List of Expenses, £4 a barrel), 1,800 pieces of eight would have fetched 101 barrels of gunpowder. This figure has been obtained using a conversion rate of 1 piece to 4 shillings and 6 pence obtained from N.G. Merchant, *The Compleat Tradesman, or The Exact Dealers Daily Companion* (London: John Dunton, 1684), p. 173; Addobbati and Dyble, 'One hundred barrels', p. 825.

10 *denari* to be precise, not including 60 pieces in administrative costs, was not just for powder and shot expended, but also for damage to the ship, and compensation paid to the master and crew in recognition of their exertions and injuries sustained. In the master's estimation of damages submitted to the *Consoli* in August 1670, the consumption of powder and shot was estimated at £106 and 14 shillings, or approximately 536 pieces of eight: no more than a quarter of the total awarded.[57] Whether this was Finch's exaggeration or misrepresentation by the London merchants, the idea that the *Alice and Francis* had claimed 1,800 pieces for the consumption of powder was simply not true. And yet Luci chose not to bring the relevant evidence to light.

The reason for Tuscan diffidence soon becomes clear when we turn to the documents themselves. The case is a veritable Pandora's box of irregularities, which Luci, as a former chancellor of the court, knew better than to open.[58] We have already seen in Chapter 3 how the 'appearance' of the master before the *Consoli* was often no more than a legal fiction. Stephen Dring could not possibly have come before the *Consoli* on 20 August, as the *testimoniale* maintained, because the permission from the *Magistrato di Sanità* in Florence recognising the validity of his clean bill of health from the authorities in Alicante and therefore granting him permission to disembark was signed the next day.[59] While there may conceivably have been some laxity in the enforcement of the rules preventing masters from disembarking before receipt of the license, travel to another city in order to present oneself before a court of law would have been out of the question.

But this was only the first in a series of questionable procedural elisions. Of more concern to the English would have been the differences in content of the *consolato* which had been created in Alicante, and the contents of the *testimoniale* presented by some person other than Master Dring to the *Consoli* in Pisa. The Italian translation of the original *consolato*, made before Don Alexandro Pasqual, Assessor of the *Baile* of Alicante, states how the ship had left Gravesend on 27 July 1670.[60] Off the coast of Portugal, at a latitude of 43.5 degrees, the ship had been caught in 'a great storm of strong wind', with the sea striking the ship's sides and entering the hold.[61] The storm lasted 24 hours and the ship took on 'much water, which we were constantly having to bail out with the pump, and I carried on my journey continuing to bail out'.[62] When the ship

[57] ASP, CM, AC, 321-30, List of Expenses.
[58] Addobbati and Dyble, 'One hundred barrels of gunpowder', p. 828.
[59] ASP, CM, AC, 321-30 (30 August 1670), *Testimoniale*; ASL, *Sanità*, 68-338, Panciatichi to Serristori (21 August 1670); Addobbati and Dyble, 'One hundred barrels of gunpowder', p. 830.
[60] Addobbati and Dyble, 'One hundred barrels of gunpowder', p. 829.
[61] ASP, CM, AC, 321-30 (30 August 1670), *Consolato*.
[62] ASP, CM, AC, 321-30 (30 August 1670), *Consolato*. The change of person midway through the narrative is typical of the *consolati*.

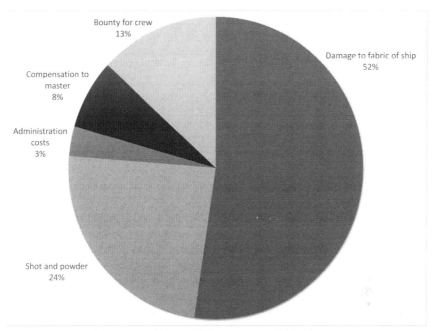

Figure 4. Breakdown of damages awarded in the case
of the *Alice and Francis* (pieces of eight).

met with the fleet of Algerian corsairs, therefore, it was already in a bad way. After a stop at Cadiz, the ship entered the Mediterranean and near the Cabo di Gatt they were set upon by 'seven Moorish vessels of war, which we fought, my own ship and those others of my convoy, until six hours later, that is 10 o' clock in the evening'.[63] Dring recalled that 'with the motion of the artillery, my aforementioned ship was taking on much more water than before, which we continued to extract with the pumps, and finding myself free from them, I continued my journey for this city [Alicante]'.[64] Dring's reference to the 'motion of the artillery' (*moto dell'artiglierie*) suggests that the damage received was primarily from the explosive force of his own cannons recoiling, rather than blows received directly from the enemy. This version of events was repeated word for word by the three witnesses, all of whom described themselves as helmsmen (*nocchieri*): George Bumpt, Buiardi Lestoch, and Carlos Dickinfield.

The *testimoniale*, however, had quite a different story to tell. Here, there is no mention of the storm off Portugal. The account skips straight to the combat, which is now described in much more dramatic terms. Rather than meeting 'seven Moorish vessels of war' the English convoy was set upon by 'seven ships, formidable Algerian corsairs':

[63] ASP, CM, AC, 321-30 (30 August 1670), *Consolato*.
[64] Ibid.

These straightaway came to face the English vessels, which, not being able to flee, were forced to go upon the defensive and to fight most furiously for the space of two days, for which they received much damage to the hull of the ship, and to its rigging, sails, and other equipment of the ship, and the plaintiff received injuries to his arm, shoulder, and chest which disabled his right arm, and finally, with the help of God and through the valour of the mariners and the daring and courage of the two warships of the convoy, notwithstanding the fact that the two captains were killed in the combat, the enemy vessels abandoned their attempt.[65]

Apart from the new sense of high drama (the size and aggression of the enemy, the courage of the mariners, the death of the captains) there are several new details, omissions, and straightforward changes to the account of the battle. Rather than lasting six hours, this 'most furious' combat was now said to have lasted two days. This difference in the length of time can be explained by the account in the *London Gazette*, which reports that the Algerian fleet, minus their commander, returned to fire at the convoy from afar on the second day: while the *consolato* reports only the six hours of close combat, the *testimoniale* counts this second day of long-range firing as part of the battle. The *testimoniale* makes it clear that the *Alice and Francis* had had no other option than to fight, a detail absent from the *consolato*. Rather than just damage to the hull as suggested by the *consolato*, the *testimoniale* suggests that every part of the ship received damage: hull, rigging, sails, and 'other' parts. The exact origin of the damage, moreover, is not stated: in lieu of other information one is left to assume that this was received at the hands of the enemy, and there is no mention of the 'motion of the artillery'. The master's injury had not been mentioned in the initial account but was described in detail in the *testimoniale*.

The difference between the two documents is an excellent illustration of the master's ability to manipulate the information on which a GA judgement was based, and of the court's willingness to couch the request in the appropriate terms. The differences between the two accounts can be easily explained with reference to the norms separating Particular Average (PA) and GA. In creating the original *consolato*, Dring's prime concern appears to have been to absolve himself of any responsibility for potential damage to the cargo. As the document itself remarks: 'It is suspected that for reason of the said storm and battle that the cargo of my ship may have suffered damage, notwithstanding that to repair it my mariners and I have carried out every possible diligence'.[66] The principal object was to excuse himself for any deterioration of the merchandise, the extent of which would only become clear when the cargo was unloaded. It is possible that the idea of declaring a GA had not

---

[65] ASP, CM, AC, 321-30 (30 August 1670), *Testimoniale*.
[66] ASP, CM, AC, 321-30 (30 August 1670), *Consolato*.

even occurred to Dring at this point. The *testimoniale*, on the other hand, was clearly aimed at triggering a GA declaration. Since non-voluntary damages received as the result of a storm could not be admitted in GA and might cast confusion on which damages were eligible for reimbursement, any reference to it was removed. A suggestion that the ship was already in a bad state prior to the battle might suggest liability: hence the reference to the motion of the cannons straining the timbers was also removed. This was especially important in the case of the *Alice and Francis*, a ship with its best years behind it: at least 13 years old at the time of the accident, it would be repurposed as a Royal Navy fire ship two years later – a disposable flaming hulk to be pushed into the oncoming enemy fleet.[67] The reference to their inability to flee, moreover, reinforces the sense of stark choice presented to the master: either fight, with all the risks and damages that entailed, or be captured with the complete loss of ship, cargo, and crew. The reference to the valour of the mariners and the injury to the master paved the way to the receipt of compensations for their exertions and sacrifices. The broadening of hull damage to encompass damage to all parts of the ship anticipated a reimbursement which might not only cover damage actually received in the combat, but any defect whatsoever in the ship's structure. Once again, Ascanio Baldassaroni's remark is brought to mind: through GA, masters were repeating the trick of the Galley of Salamis, which had ostensibly remained a thousand years in perfect condition while all the component parts were quietly replaced.[68]

The most generous interpretation we can give of the *testimoniale* is that it was replete with exaggeration and disingenuous omission. The differences between the two documents should have given the judges pause for thought. In the event, however, the entire case took only ten days to be concluded: the *testimoniale* was submitted on 20 August and the *Consoli* had approved the final calculation by 31 August (itself a rebuttal of Finch's claim that Tuscan

---

[67] The earliest mention of the *Alice and Francis* is found in an interrogation of George Ravenscroft, an English merchant in Venice, which was carried out by the Inquisition in order to obtain information on the arrival of a certain Quaker preacher. Ravenscroft admitted that the preacher had touched at Venice while travelling to the Ottoman Empire, where she had hoped to have an audience with the Sultan: the resident had sent her back to England. The ship on which she had arrived was the *Alice and Francis*, on its way to Constantinople. Kenneth Carroll, 'Quakers in Venice, 1657–8', *Quaker History* 92 (2003), 22–31, at p. 27; Henry Cadbury, 'Friends and the Inquisition at Venice, 1658', *The Journal of the Friends Historical Society* 52 (1968), 39–45, at p. 43; Stefano Villani, *Tremolanti e papisti: missioni quacchere nell'Italia del Seicento* (Rome: Edizioni di Storia e Letteratura, 1996), p. 95. On the ship's later career as a fire ship, see *Calendar of State Papers, Domestic Series, of the reign of Charles II*, vol. 12, pp. 169, 405; vol. 15, pp. 98, 100, 114, 125, 349.

[68] Baldasseroni, *Delle assicurazioni marittime*, vol. 3, p. 15.

cases took far too long to process).[69] This swift expedition was facilitated in part by the practice of 'self-assessment' which we have already encountered at the end of Chapter 3. In his response to Finch's letter, Luci pointed out that, if the English had their way, the 'experts' of one court might make a different estimation of the damages to the experts of another court, creating confusion and contention.[70] In this case, however, the account of the damages was not made by experts at all, but submitted directly by the master. As a legal document with probative value, it ought to have been presented to a notary before submission to the court. In the event, it was simply signed by ship's officers: Isack Shiltons, carpenter, Thomas Whincop, boatswain, Charles Durkenfelds, gunner, and several others.[71] They declared damage to the ship of £353, 14 shillings, which included the £106, 14 shillings for powder and shot expended, as well as damage to the hull, cabins, sails, rigging, and the value of things thrown overboard in preparation for combat. Nor was this the only example of the master and crew calling the shots rather than the Tuscan authorities. In Dring's *testimoniale*, he had already specified the amount he felt was fair as compensation for his arm: 140 pieces.[72]

Though the *Consoli* made a show of tempering the request, in reality the effect of this was negligible. In their judgement, the *Consoli* declared that they would award a 'reduced' amount of 1,875 pieces, 10 *soldi*, and 12 *denari*.[73] Once the discretionary gift and compensation to the master are removed, which were not included in the self-assessment, we are left with 1,490 pieces, 12 *soldi*, 10 denari. The officers of the *Alice and Francis* had estimated the remaining expenses at £353, 14 *soldi*. Using the near-contemporary conversion rate of 54 pence to each piece, this worked out as 1,572 pieces: the *Consoli* had reduced the request by a mere 81 pieces, a reduction of just over 5 per cent.[74] The rhetoric of the judgement thus suggested a careful process of probity and judgement in the interests of equity. In the event, however, the result was more or less what the officers of the *Alice and Francis* had originally demanded.

A similar dynamic can be observed in the representation offered to the absent merchants. Livorno was not the only scheduled stop on the journey of the *Alice and Francis*. According to the calculation, only 31.3 per cent of the cargo, as measured by value, was destined for Livorno. The rest was destined for Naples (21%), Messina (42.2%) and Izmir (5.4%).[75] As such, the

[69] ASP, CM, AC, 321-30 (30 August 1670), *Consolato*; *Testimoniale*.
[70] ASF, MM, 358-17, Emilio Luci to Cardinal Leopoldo de Medici (6 April 1671).
[71] ASP, CM, AC, 321-30 (30 August 1670), List of Expenses.
[72] ASP, CM, AC, 321-30 (30 August 1670), *Testimoniale*.
[73] ASP, CM, AC, 321-30 (30 August 1670), Calculation.
[74] Using conversion rate of 4 shillings and 6 pence per piece obtained from Merchant, *The Compleat Tradesman*, p. 173.
[75] ASP, CM, AC, 321-30 (30 August 1670), Calculation.

majority of merchants were not based in Livorno, but elsewhere. To reflect this, a *curatore* was appointed who could represent the interests of the absent interested parties. The choice of the court in the case of the *Alice and Francis* fell upon one Michele Moneta. This character was certainly no stranger to the *Consoli*, since we later find him attesting a citation in the position of vice-chancellor of the court.[76] No interrogatories were produced, and, as such, the *curatore*'s objections represent the only scrutiny offered of Dring's narrative. In his exceptions, Moneta railed rhetorically against the 'null and invalid request', which he solemnly promised to oppose in 'beginning, middle, and end', refusing to validate 'even one of the intentions of the present adversary'. He then made the following objections: that the things related in the *testimoniale* were not true; that the master had not made his request in the proper form; and that he had not proved that the *consolato* was true, but had rather done everything fraudulently.[77] That is to say, he made the most bombastic and least specific objections he possibly could have done. These three objections padded out numerous exceptions: they were entirely standard and, thus, fairly meaningless.[78] The irony, of course, is that the first two objections were true: the master had *not* made his request in the proper form, not being present before the *Consoli* as his *testimoniale* had claimed. The *testimoniale*, meanwhile, contained several untruths, or was at least so economical with the facts that it amounted to a deception. But in neither case did Moneta refer to the *testimoniale* itself to back up his assertions. It is clear that it was not his intention to expose these inconvenient truths. He did not offer any comment on the damages requested by the English master or their quantities, not once citing specific details of the case. His were objections that might be made in any GA case, indeed, to almost any case coming before the *Consoli*. Once again, we see lip service paid to judicial rigour and due process, but little in the way of concrete opposition to Dring's request.

In the light of this lack of scrutiny, Finch's accusations begin to seem somewhat plausible. The Pisan *Consoli* do indeed appear to have readily agreed to Stephen Dring's 'pretensions'. What is more, Dring seems to have specifically chosen Livorno as the place in which to demand GA. The most damaging thing to emerge from examination of the documentation is the fact that the ship had a scheduled stop at Alicante, where the original *consolato* was done, and yet still chose to carry out the GA at Livorno. This fact is glossed over in the *testimoniale*: Alicante does not appear in the list of scheduled ports. The *Alice and Francis* departs London with a cargo of 'diverse merchandise',

[76] ASP, CM, AC, 322-16 (9 November 1670); ASP, CM, AC, 322-27 (9 December 1670).

[77] ASP, CM, AC, 321-30 (30 August 1670), Exceptions.

[78] E.g. ASP, CM, AC, 320-7, Exceptions; ASP, CM, AC, 197-29 (26 April 1640); ASP, CM, AC, 196-37 (2 January 1639).

'part for Livorno, part for Naples, Messina, and Izmir', with Alicante nowhere to be found.[79] The only thing done in Alicante, according to the *testimoniale*, was the making of the *consolato*. The *consolato*, however, very clearly states that Dring loaded cargo for 'this city [i.e. Alicante], Livorno, Messina, and other places'.[80] The witnesses likewise confirm this fact. This omission was more than poor form: the result was unjust, placing a greater burden on the shoulders of those merchants with cargo for Izmir and the ports of the Italian peninsula, while the Alicante merchants were – literally – let off scot-free.[81] The cargo of the Alicante receivers had been saved by the 'sacrifice' of the combat, and yet they had not been required to pay towards the damages. The exact impact of this omission is impossible to quantify since, unsurprisingly, the cargo for Alicante was not included on the calculation contained in the file.

The Role of the Receiving Merchants

It should by now be very clear why Emilio Luci had no desire to lift the lid on the case of the *Alice and Francis*. The abuses and failings of the system were clear and numerous. Finch – whether he knew it or not – had been right about the *Consoli* agreeing to the pretensions of the masters. Yet why had complaints not been raised at the time? Why had the receiving merchants in Livorno allowed such abuses to take place without even offering a hint of objection?

The answer lies in a small note, scribbled in one corner of the *consolato*. The document that was presented to the *Consoli* was a translation into Italian, the original being written in Spanish. The translation should have been accompanied by a sworn declaration by the translator as to its accuracy as well as the attestation of a certified notary.[82] This translation, on the other hand, was simply signed by the translator, one 'Aron di Samuel Israel', who adds only that he had knowledge of both languages.[83] A note in the margin records that 'the original was returned to Niccolaio Pettinini, 13 September', a fortnight after the conclusion of the case.[84] This was the same Niccolaio Pettinini who was chosen by the *Consoli*, along with Ludovico Tiezzi, to draw up the calculation for the *Alice and Francis* just ten days after the submission of

---

[79] ASP, CM, AC, 321-30 (30 August 1670), *Testimoniale*.
[80] ASP, CM, AC, 321-30 (30 August 1670), *Consolato*.
[81] Gerard Malynes writes that Average was known by some in England as 'scot and lot'. These were community dues for church building, wall maintenance, poor relief, and the like. Malynes, *Consuetudo vel lex mercatoria*, p. 157. See Danby P. Fry, 'On the phrase "Scot and Lot"', *Transactions of the Philological Society* 12 (1867), 167–97.
[82] Addobbati and Dyble, 'One hundred barrels of gunpowder', p. 836.
[83] ASP, CM, AC, 321-30 (30 August 1670), *Consolato*.
[84] Ibid.

the *testimoniale*, and on the very same day as the judgement.[85] The original *testimoniale* had thus been 'returned' to a calculator who was not officially involved in the case until 30 August. This same calculator, according to official dating, had then managed to draw up the entire calculation in the space of a single afternoon. It is, in fact, strange that the calculator should have been in possession of the *testimoniale* at all. The function of the narrative document was to aid the *Consoli* in deciding whether absolution and Average should be awarded. Once this was done, the *testimoniale* no longer had a part to play: it was not used in the writing of the calculation which could be drawn up using the judgement with the final awarded figure and the bill of lading specifying the cargo onboard. The only logical conclusion to draw is that Pettinini must have been involved in the case from an earlier point, drawing up the calculation on the basis of the ship's bill of lading while the *Consoli* were still officially deliberating. He had been given access to the ship's paperwork earlier than the judgement, probably as soon as Dring arrived. Since he clearly had access to both the bill of lading and the *consolato*, it thus seems likely that it was he who had been responsible for depositing the *testimoniale* on 20 August, while Stephen Dring was waiting for permission to leave his ship.

It would have been impossible for Stephen Dring to have orchestrated these efforts alone on his arrival. He would not have had the local knowledge or contacts to engage the services of someone like Pettinini, nor in all likelihood the necessary language skills; he was, at any rate, officially confined to his ship until after the *testimoniale* had been deposited. It is thus extremely unlikely that he should have single-handedly set the case in motion by means of Pettinini just a day after his arrival. The most reasonable explanation for Pettinini's early involvement – indeed, the most reasonable explanation for the speed of the case in general and its lack of proper form and rigour – is that, far from being adversaries to the master's request, the receivers in Livorno were themselves coordinating it. They would have had more than a week's notice of the incident – we know from a letter of the English consul, Thomas Clutterbuck, that news of the battle had arrived in Livorno by 11 August.[86] Robert Foot, the receiving merchant entrusted with the reception of the ship in Livorno by the owners, would thus have had plenty of time to contact other interested parties in the port, and would have been expecting some kind of GA payment or declaration.[87] When Dring sailed into port on 19 August, Foot appears to have been ready to offer him a deal.

The exact nature of that deal can be reconstructed thanks to another case involving the same ship, preserved in the files of the Florentine lawyer, Andrea

---

[85] Addobbati and Dyble, 'One hundred barrels of gunpowder', p. 837.
[86] TNA, State Papers Foreign, Tuscany, 1582–1780, SP 98, vol. 11, pp. 508–10, Thomas Clutterbuck to Arlington (11 August 1670).
[87] Addobbati and Dyble, 'One hundred barrels of gunpowder', p. 842.

Capponi.[88] The day after the submission of the *testimoniale*, as the last of the cargo was being unloaded into little boats and conveyed to the warehouses of the receivers, the customs authorities decided to perform a spot check on the boat of one Tommaso del Frate. Hidden in the bottom of del Frate's vessel they found 14 packs of hides and 3 packs of wax, all undeclared. The boatman was arrested and imprisoned for fraud and the merchandise was sequestered. On 1 September – the day after the declaration of GA had been officially made by the *Consoli* – the English merchant Humphrey Sidney came forward and admitted to being the intended recipient, thus saving the boatman from serious reprisals.[89] A day later, Gisberto Seale and Carlo Benassai did likewise. This attempt to defraud the customs house could not have been attempted without the agreement of the master, Stephen Dring, who would have been supervising the unloading. Nor was it likely the only item that was being imported fraudulently. Wax and hides are heavy items. They were probably stored lower down in the ship's hold and were among the last things to be unloaded. By the time the authorities had apprehended the unfortunate boatman – perhaps alerted by the suspiciously ponderous movement of his covertly loaded vessel – a quantity of lighter undeclared merchandise had no doubt made it into the port undetected. The nature of the exchange is clear: the Livornese receivers had facilitated and supported Dring's GA claim in return for his cooperation in evading customs charges.[90]

The irony of the case of the *Alice and Francis* – an 'exorbitancy' contrary to the laws of England – is that it was actually resolved exactly as it would have been in London, that is by private agreement between master and merchants.[91] Somewhat ironic, too, was the Tuscan defence of their own procedures which, by their very laxity, had inadvertently facilitated an English attempt to defraud the native customs authorities. The agreement benefitted the English master and the English receivers in the port more than anybody. The master secured personal compensation for his injuries and exertions, while his vessel was repaired almost entirely at merchant expense. What the Livorno-based merchants lost in larger GA contributions they then made back in evaded customs charges. The losers in this deal were those merchants in other centres who paid an inflated GA contribution (except those of Alicante, who, as we

---

[88] ASF, *Auditore dei Benefici Ecclesiastici poi Segretaria del Regio Diritto*, 5682, document 40.

[89] Addobbati and Dyble, 'One hundred barrels of gunpowder', p. 842.

[90] It should be remembered that the free port did not fully abolish import and export duties until 1676. Though one could store goods for up to a year without paying customs if they were destined for re-export, this may not have been the English merchants' intention. See Frattarelli Fischer, 'Livorno 1676'; Tazzara, *The Free Port of Livorno*, pp. 107–45.

[91] Addobbati and Dyble, 'One hundred barrels', p. 843.

have seen, paid nothing) and the Tuscan state, which lost out on customs revenue. For all the ostensible differences between the private ordering in England and the very official and public procedures in Tuscany, these were less substantial in practice than one might think.

Tuscany's 'Northern' Policy

We are now in a position to say something about how GA and Livorno's political economy intersected. The idea that GA was used to entice masters to Livorno, as Finch had maintained, made little sense. However much masters might have wished to declare in Livorno, their wishes were irrelevant unless Livorno was already a scheduled stop. Long-term traffic flows were determined by the merchants who chartered the ships, which in turn were informed by commercial incentives. Masters decided where to declare GA only within very limited bounds. Since the actual adjustment of the GA should take place in a port in which there were some receivers, the choice was still effectively limited to the 'menu' of options provided by the master's freight contract. Furthermore, the number of GA declarations resolved formally – an average of 12.5 per year across our samples, roughly one a month – does not suggest that generous GA provisions would have had a huge impact on overall port activity. Here the work of Jean-Pierre Filippini, reconstructing data on port traffic for the late seventeenth and eighteenth centuries, can lend some sense of proportion. In the period 1683–1700, the port was visited by between 100 and 300 *navi* annually (large, square-rigged vessels built for medium- and long-distance trade); the number of small vessels would have been far greater.[92] As noted in Chapter 3, the court of the *Consoli* was more likely to be involved in GAs for these larger ships employed in longer voyages which had multiple stops involved, whilst smaller ventures were more likely to have been resolved privately, and thus be hidden from view. Even so, the GA numbers, while not insignificant, cannot be deemed decisive from the point of view of Tuscan commercial and maritime ambitions.

The only possible circumstances in which Tuscan authorities might have used GA procedures to actively attract traffic to the port (with no bearing on the case of the *Alice and Francis*) was in the case of grain ships. As already noted, there are several instances in the documentary evidence where grain ships destined for Genoa were allowed to declare unseaworthiness and carry out a GA in Livorno: the end result was that the grain was sold on the Livorno market.[93] The idea that this was a conscious policy has a certain plausibility within the broader contours of both Tuscan and Genoese political economy.

---

[92] Filippini, *Il porto di Livorno*, vol. 1, pp. 39, 44.
[93] ASP, CM, AC, 319-25 (18 April 1670); ASP, CM, AC, 320-2 (9 May 1670); ASP, CM, AC, 321-25 (25 August 1670).

Grain was a politically sensitive commodity, and both Livorno and Genoa competed as important regional distribution centres.[94] Indeed, the 'free port' institutions in Genoa were largely oriented around the need to encourage imports of grain.[95] In Livorno, meanwhile, grain imports formed an important part of the Grand Duke's income.[96] The authorities were thus surely happy to allow masters of vessels carrying grain to Genoa to carry out this deception, though it must be said that there is not positive evidence that the strategy was deliberate, and it may have simply been a function of the court's willingness to give shipmasters the benefit of the doubt.

In the *Alice and Francis*, however, the passivity of the Pisan court was not a way of attracting shipping per se but a way of privileging certain groups of merchants and masters who were already using the free port and played a critical role in maintaining its vitality. It is clear that the *Consoli* were more than happy to allow the English merchants and Stephen Dring to arrange the GA between themselves. They facilitated the process by tolerating procedural irregularities and even providing the guise of due process, appointing a *curatore* who made no substantial effort to oppose the master's request. Nor, crucially, was the *Alice and Francis* singular in this respect. By the second half of the seventeenth century, the *Consoli* seem to be treating 'Northern' masters – English, Dutch, and German – differently from the rest. Of the 18 GA cases administered in Pisa in the year 1670, five involved an English, Dutch, or German master; on each occasion – and on no others – the *Consoli* mandated a 'reduction' in their judgement.[97] These varied in size: deductions

---

[94] Fusaro, *Political Economies of Empire*, pp. 93–108.

[95] Kirk, *Genoa and the Sea*, pp. 151–85.

[96] See Anna Mangiarotti, 'La politica economica di Ferdinando I de Medici', in Silvana Balbi de Caro (ed.), *Merci e monete a Livorno in età granducale* (Livorno: Cassa di Risparmio di Livorno, 1997), 17–36.

[97] ASP, CM, AC, 318-26 (22 January 1669). *Speranza Incoronata*. Master and all three witnesses from Hamburg. List of damages submitted in Dutch and translated by the '*consule Amburghese*' in Livorno. The Dutch and Germans shared a consul in Livorno. See Ressel, 'La nazione Olandese-Alemanna'.

ASP, CM, AC, 319-13 (28 February 1669). *San Giovanne*. Master and all three witnesses from the Netherlands.

ASP, CM, AC, 319-28 (28 April 1670). *Mercante Fiorentino*. Master and all three witnesses from England. Final destination was London.

ASP, CM, AC, 320-7 (28 May 1670). *Principe Enrico Casimiro*. Ship bears a Dutch name. List of damages submitted in Dutch. Master from the Netherlands, two witnesses from the Netherlands, two from Hamburg. Final destination was Amsterdam.

ASP, CM, AC, 321-30 (30 August 1670). *Alice and Francis*. Master and all witnesses from England. Voyage began in London. Finch's letter attests the involvement of English merchants.

of 5%, 20%, 31%, 38%, and 57% on the original amounts requested in the masters' declarations. Whereas Italian masters continued to receive a visit from experts to assess damage, these masters were also all allowed to submit their own damage assessments. In two of the cases, the claim was not even notarised.[98] The decision to reduce the requested sum was clearly not a function of accident type, since these were various in nature: corsair encounters, masts being cut in a storm, ropes being cut, and the ship being beached during strong winds. This was a conscious policy of allowing Northerners to use different procedural forms.[99] At first glance, the 'reduction' suggests that the *Consoli* were rigorously safeguarding merchant interests. In fact, this reflects an agreement made between the parties themselves.

There thus clearly emerges a strategy designed to appease those Northern merchants and masters who were so important to the port's vitality.[100] Rather than being a stratagem to actively attract ships to the port, the Tuscan approach to GA was rather a way of privileging powerful foreign merchants whilst maintaining their own judges' role as ultimate arbiters. The Tuscans were allowing the Northerners the greatest possible latitude in resolving their own cases in actual practice while being careful never to concede the principle of their own jurisdiction. In this sense, the Tuscan approach to GA was in line with the political economy of the free port more broadly. Livorno's success was founded on the activities of powerful, foreign merchant communities who were enticed to the port with the promise of an extraordinary level of freedom and latitude as far their commercial activities were concerned.[101] With the Northerners in the ascendency in the Mediterranean in general, and in Livorno in particular, it was politic to keep English merchants and masters onside.[102] This may seem somewhat self-negating, like the King in Antoine de Saint-Exupéry's novella *The Little Prince*, who believes all things to be subject to him but only commands them to do what they were about to do

---

[98] Notarised self-assessment: ASP, CM, AC, 319-13 (28 February 1669); ASP, CM, AC, 320-7 (28 May 1670). Unnotarised self-assessment: ASP, CM, AC, 319-28 (28 April 1670); ASP, CM, AC, 321-30 (30 August 1670).

[99] Dyble, 'Divide and rule', pp. 378–84.

[100] Ghezzi, 'Il porto di Livorno', p. 96.

[101] Tazzara, *The Free Port of Livorno*, pp. 48–77; Frattarelli Fischer, 'Lo sviluppo di una città portuale'.

[102] Maria Fusaro, *Political Economies of Empire*, pp. 64–88; Ghezzi, 'Il porto di Livorno', pp. 324–8. On the Tuscan efforts to maintain the principle of their jurisdiction see Addobbati, 'Until the very last nail', pp. 49–51. See also Danilo Pedemonte, 'Deserters, mutineers and criminals: British sailors and problems of port jurisdiction in Genoa and Livorno during the eighteenth century', in Maria Fusaro, Bernard Allaire, Richard Blakemore, and Tijl Vanneste (eds), *Law, Labour and Empire: Comparative Perspectives on Seafarers, c. 1500–1800* (London: Palgrave Macmillan, 2015), 256–71.

anyway in order to avoid exposing the emptiness of his own pretensions.[103] In reality, it was a sound strategy in the circumstances: the Tuscan authorities kept the merchants onside while formally retaining their jurisdiction and the power to intervene if it was really necessary.

A close analysis of this case thus casts Finch's remark in a different light. The Tuscans were not neglecting the interests of merchants *inside their own jurisdiction*; the losers in this situation were those merchants in other centres who had no say in the negotiation of the GA figure, particularly those in Messina, and the principal merchants in London. The important difference between a GA adjusted in Livorno and one carried out in London was that the receivers who had negotiated the GA in Livorno typically represented just a fraction of the overall venture.[104] Livorno's importance for long-distance trade, it should be remembered, lay largely in its role as a Mediterranean redistribution centre.[105] Many of the resident foreign merchants were middlemen who made their money by receiving, storing, and re-exporting goods which belonged to merchants based in London, Amsterdam, and other major 'final destinations'.[106] When a GA was adjusted in London or another major terminus, most or all of the interested merchants could be present in order to be party to the agreement. In a waypoint like Livorno, this was not the case. This aspect should not be exaggerated, of course: Livorno was the starting point for numerous intra-Mediterranean voyages.[107] Yet it is undeniable that many of the ships that stopped at Livorno were often midway through a longer voyage, sometimes a voyage with many additional stops. Though agents bore full legal responsibility for the cargo of their principals, they may have been able to pass on these costs to their associates, directly or indirectly.[108] Even if they had to bear the cost personally, there was nothing to stop them striking a good deal for themselves, and damaging the interests of their associates, as happened in the case of the *Alice and Francis*. Nor did this approach adversely affect their all-important personal reputations. When their associates asked why the costs were so large, the Livorno agents could place the blame on the Pisan *Consoli* who had issued the judgement: their hands were tied. The English factors in the port most likely disassociated themselves from the entire process, presenting the imposition as an arbitrary and unavoidable injustice on the part of the court. This undermined faith in the Tuscan authorities abroad.

---

[103] Antoine de Saint-Exupéry, *Le petit prince* (New York: Reynal & Hitchcock, 1943).

[104] Addobbati and Dyble, 'One hundred barrels', pp. 844–5.

[105] Trivellato, *The Familiarity of Strangers*, p. 106; Tazzara, *The Free Port of Livorno*, pp. 48–77; Filippini, *Il porto di Livorno*, vol. 1, pp. 87, 90–1.

[106] Addobbati, *Commercio, rischio, guerra*, pp. 52–6; Filippini, *Il porto di Livorno*, vol. 1, p. 45.

[107] Heywood, 'The English in the Mediterranean, 1600–1630', p. 36; Greene, 'Beyond the northern invasion', p. 47.

[108] Trivellato, *The Familiarity of Strangers*, p. 153.

A Multi-Centred Procedure meets a Port of Deposit

This alerts us to an important structural aspect of GA's international dimension, especially in the context of the Mediterranean where there was a particularly high concentration of competing jurisdictions. The fact that the procedure could take place across a number of different ports and jurisdictions meant that redress was difficult, and players effectively had to accept an adjustment made elsewhere even if they believed it to be unjust.[109] Once one set of merchants had made contributions it was almost impossible to undo the procedure, thanks to the number of parties involved and the distances which separated them. This is illustrated clearly in the case of *La Madonna di Monte Nero* in 1671, a GA which became the subject of a petition to the Grand Duke.[110] The original GA, made on account of a jettison, had been adjusted in Messina, but was later amended by the *Consoli* in Pisa when a few other items were discovered missing while unloading in Livorno. Called upon to justify this, the *Consoli* pointed out that they could hardly have done otherwise:

> since many receivers in Messina will have come up with and paid the said Average and [this] being not really their interest but that of their correspondents, they will have passed on the debt of the payment ... it would not be right if the receivers were held to account when they have acted in good faith and in execution of a judgement and calculation issed by that tribunal.[111]

If the multilateral nature of procedures could facilitate abuse, there was not much that could be done to alleviate this. For the system to work at all, decisions made in other centres had to be taken on trust. The petition against the Messinan GA does appear to have had a modicum of success, since the merchants succeeded in getting the case revised. Generally, however, the judgements of other centres were respected and enforced. In another 1670 case, a master asked that the *Consoli* ratify a GA adjusted in Marseille because he was having trouble extracting payment from merchants in Livorno, a request the *Consoli* were happy to oblige.[112] Once again, if the system was to work at all, there had to be a level of acceptance. This must sometimes have caused frustration, where some parties might have been inclined to think – not unreasonably, perhaps – that they were paying the price for a lax attitude on the part of some other authority. But as Ascanio Baldasseroni remarked a century later, 'the Genoese have complained many times on account of our [GA] regulations

---

[109] Jake Dyble, 'Lex mercatoria, private "order", and commercial "confusion": a view from seventeenth-century Livorno', *Quaderni Storici* 56 (2022), 673–700, at p. 694.

[110] ASP, CM, S, 985-333 (8 February 1671); Dyble 'Lex mercatoria', p. 687; Dyble, 'General average, human jettison', p. 1204.

[111] ASP, CM, S, 985-333 (8 February 1671), Information.

[112] ASP, CM, AC, 322-16 (19 November 1670).

when their port was the final destination. But when the case is the other way around, they too have practised exactly the same system'.[113]

The real problem for John Finch was that the English state's desire to see GA come under the jurisdiction of the English consul was not in the interests of the English merchants themselves. They were already enjoying a considerable level of autonomy and did not wish to see a consul interfering in their activities. As the seventeenth century progressed, national consuls increasingly became representatives of their states rather than representatives of merchant communities.[114] In these circumstances, the fact that the Tuscans defended their own jurisdiction against that of national consuls was attractive to foreign merchants.[115] It should be remembered that, when the French attempted to enforce their own consular jurisdiction in Livorno in 1713, it was the concerted resistance of the foreign merchants in the free port that ended the attempt.[116] Our case study is a case in point. We know that the *Alice and Francis* was heading to Izmir to defy the monopoly of the Levant Company.[117] In these circumstances, it was hardly in the merchants' interest to let a consul with close links to the state peruse their GA calculation.

It is likely this, rather than any pro-master attitude per se, which seems to have enticed several other ships in the same year to declare GA in Livorno rather than elsewhere. We have already seen how the *Alice and Francis* deliberately avoided declaring GA in Alicante. Two other ships in the year 1670, both Dutch, were similarly prevented from entering their scheduled destinations thanks to 'bad weather'. The *Speranza Incoronata* had arrived in Livorno in January, having endured an exceptionally long and eventful journey from Arkhangelsk the year before.[118] On its entry into the Mediterranean, the *Speranza* had also encountered six Algerian corsairs, probably the same fleet that would attack the *Alice and Francis*, and likewise claimed for damages and combat expenses. The *Speranza* had also been due to enter Alicante, but had, it was claimed, been unable to do so thanks to 'contrary weather'.[119] The

---

[113] Baldasseroni, *Delle assicurazioni marittime*, vol. 4, p. 228.

[114] Maria Fusaro, 'The invasion of northern litigants', pp. 38–40.

[115] Dyble, 'Divide and rule', pp. 385–6.

[116] Marcella Aglietti, *L'istituto consolare tra Sette e Ottocento. Funzioni istituzionali, profilo giuridico e percorsi professionali nella Toscana granducale* (Florence: Edizioni ETS, 2012), p. 43.

[117] *Calendar of State Papers, Domestic Series, of the Reign of Charles II*, vol. 10, p. 412, Levant Company to Consul Ricaut (1 September 1670). On the English consuls in this period in particular see Stefano Villani, 'I consoli della nazione inglese a Livorno tra il 1665 e il 1673: Joseph Kent, Thomas Clutterbuck e Ephraim Skinner', *Nuovi Studi Livornesi* 11 (2004), 11–34.

[118] ASP, CM, AC, 318-26 (22 January 1669).

[119] ASP, CM, AC, 318-26 (22 January 1669), *Testimoniale*.

Principe Enrico Casimiro meanwhile had recently departed Izmir when it was attacked by three corsairs off Sapientza in Greece.[120] After the battle, the ship made its *consolato* at Zante. Rather than declaring the GA at Messina, the first scheduled stop, it continued to Livorno: 'north-easterly winds' and a 'great sea' had forced it to turn away from Sicily, and it had then been 'forced' to continue with the Dutch convoy up to Livorno.[121]

It is impossible to establish if such explanations were genuine. There may have been a number of hidden factors involved, particularly in the case of the *Enrico Casimiro* which was part of a convoy. It does, however, seem suspicious that, in a single year, three ships which had all suffered combat damage should have all been 'forced' to enter Livorno in order to declare the GA. In the case of the *Enrico Casimiro*, a *curatore* was even appointed: the nominee was once again Michele Moneta, and his objections were identical to those he made in the case of the *Alice and Francis*.[122]

It seems probable that jurisdictional considerations were at the forefront of these decisions. On the trip down from North-Western Europe to the Ottoman Empire there were typically a number of major stops. On this clockface of Western Mediterranean ports – Cadiz, Alicante, Valencia, Marseille, Genoa, Livorno, Naples, Messina – only Livorno did not fall squarely under Spanish or French domination.[123] We have already seen that in Spanish territories the English consul had been awarded jurisdiction over cases between Englishmen thanks to the 1667 Treaty. The United Provinces likewise enjoyed the status of 'most favoured nation' in Spain thanks to the 1645 Treaty of Münster, meaning that they enjoyed the same rights.[124] By the late 1660s, a common arrangement in Spanish ports was that cases involving English, French, or Dutch merchants came before a *juez conservador*, a figure chosen from among the royal magistrates who enjoyed exclusive competence over the affairs of the *natio*. In some cases, they were chosen with the help of foreign ambassadors, and their loyalty could be ensured through the fact that the *natio* renumerated them.[125] It may be that masters preferred the more neutral setting of Livorno for declaring GA to declaring in a port under Spanish domination, where a figure more closely associated with the resident merchant community, or even the national state, enjoyed particular sway.

---

[120] ASP, CM, AC, 320-7 (28 May 1670).
[121] ASP, CM, AC, 320-7 (28 May 1670). *Testimoniale*.
[122] ASP, CM, AC, 320-7 (28 May 1670), Exceptions.
[123] Addobbati and Dyble, 'One hundred barrels of gunpowder', p. 844.
[124] Zaugg, *Stranieri di antico regime*, p. 60.
[125] It should be noted, however, that their exact jurisdiction was constantly renegotiated; they also faced opposition from local courts. See Zaugg, *Stranieri di antico regime*, pp. 59–71; Zaugg, 'Judging foreigners', pp. 175–6.

Conclusions

Overall, GA procedures should not be characterised as a strategic political-economic gambit, systematically utilised. They are better understood as an expression of the broader political economy of the port and the culture of license that characterised it. Access to justice was a means of promoting political-economic interests. Maria Fusaro shows how in the Venetian republic, English merchants and shipmasters were unable to access summary justice at the court of the *Cinque Savi alla Mercanzia* because of the risk they posed to Venice's own trade, instead being compelled to use the *Giudice del Forestier* until the end of the seventeenth century.[126] The Pisan court privileged the English and Dutch by waiving procedural niceties, though here they did informally and to the Northerner's benefit, since Tuscany had nothing to gain and everything to lose by alienating these important interest groups.

Though the case thus mirrors a political economy that was particular to Tuscany then, it also illustrates broader truths of relevance to the early modern maritime economy as a whole. The case of the *Alice and Francis* gives us a rare opportunity to prove the importance of private agreement and collusion, which are so often hidden from us, even when a court ostensibly handled the affair. It is clear that the court authorities exaggerated the structural advantages enjoyed by all masters: their willingness to couch *testimoniali* in the appropriate legal language and their propensity to give masters the benefit of the doubt in judgements is undeniable. If the Tuscan authorities were guilty as Finch charged them, it was as accomplices rather than as ringleaders, aiding and abetting rather than perpetrating.[127] Frauds and near-frauds, meanwhile, seem to have been ubiquitous, and were as common in England as anywhere else: Samuel Pepys's diary, in fact, relates an insurance case he heard before the King's Bench in which the shipmaster submitted a fraudulent report, which would in fact appear to have centred on a fraudulent GA claim:

> [the master] had given his men money to content them; and yet, for all this, he did bring some of them to swear that it was very stormy weather, and [they] did all they could to save her, and that she was seven feete deep water in hold, and were fain to cut her main and foremast.[128]

In defending their approach from accusations of malpractice, apologists for the court often made reference to the multilateral nature of the procedure and the requirement to respect judgements made in other centres. This was, however, a concrete and unavoidable reality. To a certain extent, judgements

---

[126] Fusaro, 'Politics of justice/politics of trade', pp. 145–7.

[127] Tazzara, *The Free Port of Livorno*, p. 127.

[128] Entry for 1 December 1663. Samuel Pepys, *Samuel Pepys's Diary*, ed. Phil Gyford <www.pepysdiary.com/diary/1663/12/01/> [accessed 18 August 2021].

made elsewhere simply had to be respected whether one liked it or not; if this were not the case, the system could not work. Acceptance, if sometimes begrudging and uneasy, characterised the system. Perhaps things would have been easier had actors been able to avail themselves of universally accepted laws regarding GA, of the type the mercatorists envisage. Yet on this evidence, there is no suggestion that they needed it. Instead – and this is crucial – a multijurisdictional system depended not on the uniformity of GA, nor even its broad similarity across jurisdictions, but rather recognition of the juridical and political authority inherent in other systems.[129] GA in fact functioned thanks to being embedded in what Lauren Benton calls an institutional regime: 'Institutional regimes (broadly defined as the repetition of structurally similar ways of organizing authority) make international regimes (narrowly defined as interstate agreements) possible by allowing political authorities to identify one another'.[130] If we instead define 'international regime' in broad terms, this then becomes an accurate description of the situation that prevailed in GA cases.

Finally, in light of the diplomatic disputes between England and Tuscany over GA, as well as the concurrent disputes over wage, we might tentatively begin to identify two different varieties of maritime capitalism at work in the last third of the seventeenth century. These two variants do not correspond to the central division of the New Institutionalist between the relative security of property rights in North-Western Europe when compared to the 'absolutist' Catholic states of the rest of the continent. Douglass North, as well as more recent economic historians such as Daron Acemoglu and James Robinson, have argued that a key reason for the divergent economic performance of Northern and Southern Europe was the far greater protection for property rights on offer in North-Western Europe. This in turn was the result of centralised but 'inclusive' political institutions, which put a bridle on arbitrary extraction by rulers and which allowed a larger section of the population to engage in a wide range of economic activities, leading to the emergence of a powerful merchant class.[131]

The court of the *Consoli*'s ability to adjudicate in GA cases did indeed have clear implications for entitlement to property, since it forced one set of property owners, unaffected by a *casus fortuitus*, to recognise the right of another party over their own possessions. It is also true that Tuscan authorities sometimes failed to adequately protect the property rights of the parties involved. Yet this was not the result of 'extractive' institutions, an over-mighty absolutist state which could not help but disrupt the activities of private individuals

---

[129] Dyble, 'Lex mercatoria', p. 694.

[130] Lauren Benton, *Law and Colonial Cultures: Legal Regimes in World History, 1400–1900* (Cambridge: Cambridge University Press, 2002), p. 24.

[131] Acemoglu and Robinson, *Why Nations Fail*, pp. 77–83, 102–3; North and Weingast, 'The evolution of institutions', pp. 803–32.

and help itself to the fruit of their labours. It was rather, as Stephan Epstein has suggested, the weakness of 'absolutist' states – or rather in this case, the weakness of the Tuscan commercial position – which was to blame.[132] The Tuscan authorities were afraid of driving away the English merchants on which the port's vitality depended. It was therefore the weakness of the Tuscan state vis-à-vis the English merchants in the port (or, at least, the fact that the Tuscans perceived their own position to be weak) which prompted them to waive their responsibility to adjudicate the case, and to properly represent the interests of the absent. It is thus impossible to form a judgement on the Tuscan institutional set up independent of the wider conditions in which these existed. To borrow the words of Alida Clemente and Roberto Zaugg, 'the regulative interventions of different states tend to overlap and produce complex configurations ... and the structural asymmetries in inter-regional relations play a crucial role with regard to the emergence ... of institutional mechanisms'.[133] In a similar vein, it was not primarily the Tuscan merchants, or those based in Tuscany, who suffered as a result of the *Consoli*'s decision not to intervene to protect the property rights of absent merchants. The merchants within the port presumably did well out of the fact that they were given free rein to negotiate the GA with the shipmaster. It was, as has been noted, the merchants outside of Tuscany who suffered. The Tuscan 'Northern GA policy' confirms, to again quote Clemente and Zaugg, that 'the institutional framework in which economic transactions take place cannot be reduced to the nation state: it is inherently transnational'.[134]

If there is a difference between the two jurisdictions as reflected in their treatment of GA, it is rather in the different weight they gave to economic interests of the different actors involved. The issue of mariners' compensation specifically, would seem to be an example of the English Parliament – even before the Glorious Revolution – seeking to promote the interests of the merchant class in a way which other maritime jurisdictions were not. Whereas other jurisdictions, including Tuscany, allowed the mariners some compensation through GA, in England, the matter had been placed solely in the hands of merchants, and a statutory limit placed on their generosity. English GA legislation, therefore, in as much as such a thing existed, was weighted towards the merchant at the expense of the seaman, just as laws over seamen's wages also favoured the interests of the merchant class by allowing them better control over

---

[132] Stephan Epstein, *Freedom and Growth. The Rise of States and Markets in Europe, 1300–1750* (London: Routledge, 2001), p. 8.

[133] Alida Clemente and Roberto Zaugg, 'Hermes, the Leviathan and the grand narrative of New Institutional Economics. The quest for development in the eighteenth-century Kingdom of Naples', *Journal of Modern European History* 15 (2017), 108–29, at p. 114.

[134] Clemente and Zaugg, 'The grand narrative of New Institutional Economics', p. 114.

the maritime labour force.[135] (This use of GA would also seem to be an English rather than a North-Western European phenomenon: Dutch GA provisions, as we have seen, guaranteed forms of compensation to mariners.)[136]

This difference over the approach to seamen's wages leads Maria Fusaro to posit two different 'varieties of capitalism' in England and in Southern Europe, in an interpretation which gives a negative rather than a positive valence to England's path.[137] In Fusaro's analysis, following the lead provided by Avner Offer and David Ormrod's analysis of the English agricultural economy, the English pre-modern maritime economy was characterised by the ease with which the risks of economic activity could be displaced by the propertied individuals onto the labour force.[138] This was not, in Fusaro's view, so much the result of England's particular political structures, but rather the result of a historically contingent economic and legal culture which conceived of the labour force through the prism of the master–servant relationship. Italian capitalism, by contrast, had emerged in an intellectual and political environment concerned with the dignity of work, and in a city-state context in which capitalism was 'based on a strong and articulated conception of community with jurisdictional and social implications'.[139] It thus retained a higher regard for security and protection in the workplace, or, in the case of GA, appraised the competing demands of the 'trade' and 'transport' sectors of the maritime economy differently. While we might not wish to exaggerate the role of the Pisan *Consoli* as protectors of seamen's interests, there was clearly no incentive to erode the security of their position in order to promote the interests of another class, as was the case in England.

It may be, in the final analysis, that an 'English variety of capitalism' did in fact result in a more productive economic environment and may have been a necessary step in birthing the industrial revolution: such speculations are clearly beyond the scope of the present investigation and at any rate concern issues much wider than maritime risk-sharing practices. Be that as it may, the findings on GA seem to better reflect the schema posited by Fusaro rather than that of Acemoglu and Robinson. The Tuscan 'failure' to protect merchants' property rights was not the result of the 'absolutist' or 'extractive' tendencies of their institutions; if the decisions of the *Consoli* were due to

---

[135] For the disputes over seamen's wages between England and Tuscany, see Addobbati, 'Until the very last nail'; Fusaro, 'The invasion of northern litigants'.

[136] The 1563 Ordonnance, for example, guaranteed compensation to seamen after a combat. See Ordonnance of Phillip II of 1563, Title IV, Article 2, quoted in Pardessus, *Collection de lois maritimes*, vol. 4, p. 79.

[137] Maria Fusaro, 'The burden of risk: early modern maritime enterprise and varieties of capitalism', *Business History Review* 94 (2020), 179–200.

[138] Fusaro, 'The burden of risk', pp. 190, 199.

[139] Fusaro, 'The burden of risk', p. 196.

anything beyond a structural favouritism built into GA itself, they were due to recognition of the fact that the transport sector, including mariners, did in fact form an indispensable part of the maritime economy, a part which had historically been in need of promotion and protection for the health of the sector as a whole.

Epilogue

After the discovery of the customs fraud on board the *Alice and Francis*, the incriminated parties were instructed to remain in the port. Dring, however, had other ideas.[140] Having no intention of brooking further delay, he boldly contacted the Governor's court and asked that they put out a final call for two unclaimed bales of silk belonging to one Ezechiel Lampsen, as he was 'ready for departure for Naples and Messina'.[141] This indemnifying action completed, he prepared for departure. News of this precautionary measure soon reached the ears of Girolamo Migliorotti at the customs house, who rushed to the *Auditore del Governo* to demand Dring's immediate arrest. But when his men arrived on the dockside, they were too late – the *Alice and Francis* had already taken to the open seas. Subsequent recriminatory efforts came to nothing. A master's freight money would usually be looked after by the merchant who was his principal contact in the port, but Robert Foot claimed to know nothing of the matter, adding that the English consul was likewise seeking Dring because he had left without paying his consular fees.[142] The swashbuckling Stephen Dring lived to fight another day.

---

[140] Addobbati and Dyble, 'One hundred barrels of gunpowder', pp. 842–3.
[141] ASL, *Capitano, poi Governatore Auditore Vicario*, 269, document 548.
[142] ASL, *Capitano, poi Governatore Auditore Vicario*, 269, document 559.

5

How Early Modern Shipping Managed Risk

Overview

We have considered the history of GA from several angles and constructed a fairly detailed picture of the institution itself. This chapter will now zoom out and consider how GA interacted with other risk-management instruments that shaped maritime trade in early modern Europe. Once established, GA became, in effect, a limited form of mutual insurance for certain types of damages, because it was known in advance that sacrifices would be shared between all players. GA was inherently limited, of course, because it could share risks only between those who were already financially implicated in the venture. Yet it was nonetheless an instrument which blunted the impact of mishaps by sharing costs, thus decreasing the risk of entry into a venture, especially when combined with other mechanisms for the distribution of costs and damages.

In order to assess GA's importance in this respect, as well as its overall impact on the structure of commerce more generally, it is necessary to contextualise it and to examine its interaction with the other instruments which dealt with risk and other institutions used by early modern actors. Only by sketching out GA's position and relative importance within this institutional topography can we hope to make pronouncements about its role and significance in structuring exchange. The most obvious question in this respect concerns GA's relationship with the best known and most ubiquitous tool for managing risk: premium insurance. Invented in the fourteenth century and in wide use by the seventeenth, premium insurance transfers sea risk to third parties, who are not necessarily interested in the venture, distributing risk beyond the trading community, and ultimately allowing anyone with spare capital to shoulder the burden.[1] Did GA still have a role to play after the widespread adoption of such an efficacious instrument?

---

[1] For the origins of insurance, see L.A. Boiteaux, *La fortune de mer: le besoin de sécurité et les débuts de l'assurance maritime* (Paris: S.E.V.P.E.N., 1968); Piccinno, 'Genoa, 1340–1620', pp. 46–77; Addobbati, *Commercio, rischio, guerra*, pp. 113–16. On the mingling of 'sharing' and 'shifting' in premodern insurance see Giovanni Ceccarelli, 'Risky narratives: framing general average into risk-management strategies

This chapter outlines the mechanics of the relationship between GA and premium insurance in Tuscany and other parts of Europe – a far from clear and straightforward issue, given the different provisions and practices that existed regarding the two instruments. It also examines the interactions between GA and sea loan, another 'archaic' risk-management instrument that has suffered from significant analytical neglect. A case from the archive allows us to uncover the way that these tools were used in concert: GA, a first line of defence, drew in the creditor of a sea loan, who in turn had insured the loan with the help of local underwriters. Some of the receiving merchants had offered security for the loan, some had then underwritten it, whilst some underwriters were from outside the circle of participants. The venture was thus undergirded by several security nets that bound participants and some outsiders into a tightly interconnected community of risk. Though a favoured recent analogy of business historians has been the risk-management 'toolbox', it is argued that this system might be seen more profitably as a water filtration system, with costs passing through several successive institutional layers to achieve maximum dispersal. With that being said, the findings once again demonstrate the extent to which early modern GA was above all the shipmaster's tool. Ships were very rarely insured in this period, and in some situations, GA was a master's only line of defence. Extraordinary expenses, moreover, would have proved ruinous had masters not been able to fall back on GA. Financial analysis of the case allows us to demonstrate in quantitative terms how ship interests could do very well out of GA, allowing serious operational costs to be defrayed.

The 'Evolutionary' Model of Institutional Development

We will engage head on with the question of whether premium insurance 'superseded' instruments like GA, but it should be noted that this question itself is, in part, founded upon teleological assumptions about the stadial evolution of commercial institutions which recent scholarship has sought to challenge: specifically, the assumption that insurance, more effective and, above all, more 'modern', axiomatically rendered older instruments obsolete.[2] Business historians have increasingly sought to criticise an older body of scholarship which posited an evolutionary series of ever more efficient or rational organisational 'technologies', where each new development quickly superseded its predecessors. Douglass North, in particular, has been criticised for insisting on the need to chart 'an evolutionary story of the institutionalisation of risk', which stretches 'from the *commenda* itself ... through its evolution at the

---

(13th–16th centuries)', in Maria Fusaro, Andrea Addobbati, and Luisa Piccinno (eds), *General Average and Risk Management in Medieval and Early Modern Maritime Business* (Cham: Springer, 2023), 61–91.

[2] See pp. 6–10.

hands of Italians, to the English joint-stock company'.[3] Recent archival work by early modern historians has found that those institutional innovations considered by North and others to be inherently more efficient did not in fact lead to the rapid eclipse of older instruments.[4] In some cases, the most 'modern' techniques did not even enjoy widespread use until after the end of the *ancien regime*, long after their initial emergence.[5] We must not risk falling into caricature here: North was well aware that the most efficient solution *in perfect conditions* (i.e. free from transaction costs) did not exist in historical reality.[6] What is problematic is the suggestion that actors always availed themselves of a single, superior institution, that newer innovations displaced older ones almost completely, or more likely failed to replace them, thus dooming a society to economic stagnation. Ron Harris's recent analysis of long-term institutional development, with particular emphasis on the importance of the emergence of the early modern joint-stock company, updates North's evolutionary framework and renders it more sophisticated, putting emphasis on the political-economic matrices in which institutions can exist – but his schema of 'endogenous', 'migratory', and 'embedded' institutions nevertheless relegates institutions like GA to a timeless 'proto' era.[7] It is perhaps telling that in an essay entitled 'General average and all the rest', Harris, having implicitly relegated GA to an also-ran from the outset, talks mainly about premium insurance.[8]

North made another, more straightforward mistake in his analysis, namely his assumption that premium insurance in its modern actuarial form leapt fully formed from the mind of the medieval merchant.[9] This misperception has been given additional impetus thanks to several other influential historiographical trends. In 1921, Frank Knight made a now-ubiquitous distinction between immeasurable and unquantifiable 'uncertainty' on the one hand, and quantifiable 'risk' which can be priced into economic decision making on the other, though it is perhaps less often remembered that Knight's ultimate aim in making this distinction was not a taxonomy of risk per se, but to explain profit creation in static markets.[10] In a historical context, this distinction can have the effect of suggesting that insurance was something radically 'modern', a watershed between one type of economic environment and another, an instrument of an altogether different nature from the risk-management

---

[3] Trivellato, 'Renaissance Florence', p. 243; North, *Institutions*, p. 127.
[4] Ceccarelli, 'Risky narratives', p. 10.
[5] Trivellato, 'Renaissance Florence', p. 246.
[6] North, 'Institutions', p. 98.
[7] Harris, *Going the Distance*.
[8] Harris, 'General average and all the rest'.
[9] North, *Institutions*, p. 125.
[10] Knight, *Risk, Uncertainty and Profit*, p. 17.

strategies which preceded it.[11] In reality, before the eighteenth-century advent of the insurance company, this ostensible instrument of risk transfer was still in many ways akin to a risk-sharing instrument whose animating spirit was not widely dissimilar to that of GA. Though a few outsiders with capital to spare did dabble in insuring, the overwhelming majority of underwriters were merchants themselves: there were no specialist underwriters and very few of the merchants who insured expected to reap large profits from their underwriting activities.[12] The chief aim of their engagement with insurance was to hedge risks, and the same individuals would sometimes enter the market as underwriters and sometimes as buyers of insurance. While underwriters appear to have been reasonably astute judges of risk for the purposes of premiums, in the seventeenth century there were no actuarial techniques adopted for calculating risk, and a paucity of relevant information would have prevented their effective use.[13] Given the reciprocal nature of the market, it has even been argued the premium is perhaps best viewed as 'compensation' to get round asymmetries of demand for risk coverage rather than a price, per se.[14] This is not to underplay the ultimate importance of insurance, or of the innovation it represented and its eventual role in the advent of a 'rationalistic' modernity, but rather to guard against the introduction of anachronisms which might skew our analysis of risk management in the seventeenth century.[15]

Archival evidence, moreover, is making it ever clearer that an institutional teleology is not an accurate guide to contemporary economic strategies. Early

---

[11] Stephen LeRoy and Larry Singell Jr, 'Knight on risk and uncertainty', *Journal of Political Economy* 95 (1987), 394–406, at p. 396; Ross Emmett, 'Reconsidering Frank Knight's Risk, Uncertainty and Profit', *Independent Review* 24 (2020), 522–41, at p. 538.

[12] Andrea Addobbati, 'Italy 1500–1800: cooperation and competition', in Adrian Leonard (ed.), *Marine Insurance: Origins and Institutions, 1300–1850* (Basingstoke: Palgrave Macmillan, 2016), 47–77, at p. 62; Addobbati, *Commercio, rischio, guerra*, p. 126; Sabine Go, 'Amsterdam 1585–1790: emergence, dominance, and decline', in Adrian Leonard (ed.), *Marine Insurance: Origins and Institutions, 1300–1850* (Basingstoke: Palgrave Macmillan, 2016), 106–29, at pp. 112, 120; Ceccarelli, 'Risky narratives', pp. 4–5; Giovanni Ceccarelli, *Risky Markets: Marine Insurance in Renaissance Florence* (Leiden: Brill, 2020), p. 206.

[13] See Lorraine Daston, *Classical Probability in the Enlightenment* (Princeton: Princeton University Press, 1988); Craig Turnbull, *A History of British Actuarial Thought* (Cham: Palgrave Macmillan, 2017); Ian Hacking, *The Emergence of Probability: A Philosophical Study of Early Ideas about Probability, Induction and Statistical Inference*, 2nd edn (Cambridge: Cambridge University Press, 2009). On the accuracy of early modern premium rates see Jeroen Puttevils and Marc Deloof, 'Marketing and pricing risk in marine insurance in sixteenth-century Antwerp', *Journal of Economic History* 77 (2017), 796–837.

[14] Addobbati, *Commercio, rischio, guerra*, pp. 9–10.

[15] Ceccarelli, *Risky Markets*, p. 61.

modern businesspeople used a range of institutional solutions concurrently, whether these were enforcement mechanisms to overcome agency problems or business partnership arrangements that determined their forms of commercial association.[16] This chapter demonstrates that those institutions directly pertaining to sea risks, including GA, were no different. In fact, the mixed approach was even more prevalent and important in maritime risk sharing, because the various institutions employed were often complementary. Each institution offered an additional layer of repartition, and, when working in concert, a cost would be redistributed several times through several different instruments to a wide range of players, even before other risk-management tactics, such as portfolio diversification and partial ownership of assets, are taken into account. In this sense, newer institutions were superimposed upon older ones rather than replacing them. This system of risk was not solely comprised of insurance and GA: the documentation in the archive of the *Consoli del Mare* amply testifies that the sea loan (a loan which involved the lender assuming not only the credit risk but sea risks as well) remained ubiquitous in seventeenth-century Livorno, though it has so far largely evaded scholarly attention outside of its medieval origins.[17] GA's relationship with this important institution, or rather the collection of slightly different practices which the Italians collected under the expression '*cambio marittimo*', will likewise be examined in detail in this chapter.[18] GA payments could be covered by premium insurance and *cambio marittimo*. Furthermore, GA played a role in its own right because it covered certain eventualities and situations which could not be covered by other risk-management institutions, a function of its non-contractual nature.

This chapter stops short of declaring that the resulting system of risk management was optimal, or even 'efficient'. Sheilagh Ogilvie has argued that the study of institutions by economic historians has all too often fallen into the trap of making such assertions, without pausing to consider how this might be definitively proved, or even what we mean by 'efficiency'.[19] What this documentary evidence can demonstrate is that actors, contrary to North's evolutionary model, did in fact avail themselves of a variety of risk-management institutions simultaneously, and that by using a variety of techniques which were complementary they achieved a far greater spread of risks than would otherwise have been possible. It also demonstrates that GA

---

[16] Trivellato, 'Renaissance Florence', pp. 242–7.

[17] See Zanini, 'Financing and risk'.

[18] Raymond De Roover, 'The *cambium maritimum* contract according to the Genoese notarial records of the twelfth and thirteenth centuries', *Explorations in Economic History* 7 (1969), 15–33, at p. 16.

[19] Sheilagh Ogilvie, 'Whatever is, is right? Economic institutions in pre-industrial Europe', *The Economic History Review* 60 (2007), 649–84, at pp. 656–8.

and sea loan were possessed of unique advantages and capabilities which responded to the context of seventeenth-century Mediterranean trade. This in turn suggests that their continued use was not the result of historical contingency, path dependency, or even high transaction costs, but was at least a sensible response to the conditions in which actors found themselves.

GA and Premium Insurance

A central feature of this interlocking risk-management structure was that GA payments were, unless specified otherwise by the policy, automatically covered by underwriters of marine insurance contracts.[20] The underwriter would pay proportionally, applying the GA contribution rate to the total amount they had underwritten. For example, if the GA contribution rate was 5 per cent, the underwriters' obligation would be expressed as '5 pieces for every 100 pieces insured'.[21] If the insured had purchased insurance for 100 per cent of their goods, then the underwriters would pay the entire GA contribution; if they had insured 80 per cent of the value, the underwriters would pay for 80 per cent of their GA contribution, and so on. The standard printed Tuscan insurance form, which provided the standard template for underwriters across Europe, states that the underwriter ran 'at all times the risk attached to the undermentioned merchandise, of every sea-related thing, of fire, of jettison into the sea, of reprisal, of theft by friends or enemies, of every event, danger, *fortuna*, disaster, impediment, or accident, even those that cannot be imagined'.[22] The form makes no explicit mention of 'Average' or 'General Average'. The standard version of the contract was given official backing in 1524 thanks to reforms passed by the Florentine *Ufficio di sicurtà*, though the wording had barely changed from the fourteenth century.[23] The absence of any mention of 'Average' is therefore in accordance with what we established in Chapter 2 about the early modern emergence of the word '[General] Average' as a catch-all term for common contribution.[24] It is nevertheless clear from the form that insurance covered all sea risks, and that GA contributions fell under this. This is consistent with contemporary understandings of the term 'risk', which, though it was to assume the meaning of '(the probability of) an undesired event or danger' in the modern period, in

---

[20] Casaregi, *Discursus legales*, vol. 1, p. 17; the exception was Venice where the standard insurance policy excluded Average: Karin Nehlsen-von Stryk, *L'assicurazione marittima a Venezia nel XV secolo* (Rome: Il Veltro Editrice, 1988), pp. 216–44.

[21] Rocco, *Responsorum*, p. 410.

[22] Quoted in Addobati, *Commercio, rischio, guerra*, p. 120.

[23] Ceccarelli, *Risky Markets*, pp. 15–16.

[24] See pp. 54–5.

its original form meant simply the concrete manifestation of any eventual profit or loss resulting from a venture.[25]

This coverage of GA by insurance assumes particular relevance for risk management in the seventeenth century because premium insurance was becoming ever more prevalent. It was already undergoing a long transformation from a deluxe product reserved only for those ventures presenting the highest risks and rewards to a quotidian instrument employed in the majority of voyages.[26] The increasing feasibility of insurance, as navigational technology and knowledge improved and violence was disciplined, is reflected in falling premium rates across the seventeenth and eighteenth centuries: while London to Livorno would attract a premium of around 8–9 per cent in 1620, by the end of the eighteenth century this would typically be less than 2 per cent.[27] It should be noted that this was a long-term trend: premium rates in the short and medium term could fluctuate enormously, not least thanks to endemic maritime warfare.[28] Nevertheless, the aggregate trend was downwards. Merchants in Livorno – perhaps the most developed European insurance market outside of London and Amsterdam – would have access to insurance at the most competitive prices and would have been at the forefront of this shift.[29] The seventeenth century is thus a period of particular interest for exploring the continued relevance of older instruments.

The eighteenth-century Livornese jurist Ascanio Baldasseroni wrote that underwriters should cover GA, notwithstanding the fact that these could emerge as the result of local rules which did not conform to those in place in the location in which the insurance contract was signed.[30] This practice seems to have prevailed operationally in our period, a thing which is to be expected given the Livorno market's particular dependence on foreign demand. Early modern merchants would frequently ask their correspondents in foreign centres to buy them insurance and re-insurance abroad, and the Livorno piazza, in particular, depended on this for its vitality.[31] Three connected cases

---

[25] Simona Morini, *Il rischio: da Pascal a Fukushima* (Bologna: Bollati Bolinghieri, 2014), p. 9; Addobbati, *Commercio, rischio, guerra*, p. 7.

[26] Addobbati, *Commercio, rischio, guerra*, p. 114.

[27] Addobbati, *Commercio, rischio, guerra*, p. 115.

[28] Ceccarelli, *Risky Markets*, pp. 103–8; Alberto Tenenti and Branislava Tenenti, *Il prezzo del rischio: l'assicurazione mediterranea vista da Ragusa: 1563–1591* (Rome: Jouvence, 1985), pp. 243–316; Christopher Kingston, 'America 1720–1820: war and organization', in Adrian Leonard (ed.), *Marine Insurance: Origins and Institutions: 1300–1850* (Basingstoke: Palgrave Macmillan, 2015), 205–26, at pp. 205–6.

[29] Addobbati, *Commercio, rischio, guerra*, p. 126.

[30] Baldasseroni, *Delle assicurazioni marittime*, vol. 1, pp. 208–9.

[31] Addobbati, *Commercio, rischio, guerra*, pp. 127–8. It should be noted, however, that this was officially prohibited in many centres. See Piccinno, 'Early development of marine insurance', p. 40.

preserved in the *Consoli* from the 1660s, concerning the insuring of cargo aboard the annual Dutch fleet coming from Izmir to Amsterdam, show that absorbing a GA emerging from a competent and recognised authority was a perfectly normal state of affairs, even when GA procedures differed from those employed in Tuscany.[32] The cases had been brought in 1669 by Mattus D'Attigian, whose insurers had been slow in paying out. In 1664, 'Chealam de Nourval' or 'Chealam de Norvilli' of Amsterdam had asked D'Attigian, his correspondent in Livorno, to insure some silk, mohair yarn, and 'other merchandise' for him worth a total of 3,500 pieces. The cargo had been loaded on three different ships and D'Attigian had taken out three insurance policies with the same six Livornese underwriters. The Dutch fleet had in fact already left Izmir at the time of drafting the insurance contract, which was to be valid from the moment the fleet left Livorno, a scheduled stop, until its safe arrival in Amsterdam. Norvilli was probably thus responding to the looming threat of the Second Anglo-Dutch War, either by buying himself emergency coverage which he had not originally envisaged needing or by insuring the section of the journey which he deemed far riskier. Perhaps rapidly rising premium rates on the Amsterdam piazza with the news of war had encouraged him to look elsewhere for his coverage.

His intuition was clearly not misplaced, for the fleet was trapped in the port of Cadiz for eight months by the English and was then forced to take a circuitous route home round the west of Ireland and northern Scotland, occasioning further misadventures. When the fleet finally arrived in Amsterdam, there were consequently several large GAs to be adjusted by the Dutch Chamber of Insurance and Averages.[33] These included expenses of wages and subsistence for the crews during the time in Cadiz and the extended journey, and expenses for the sending of messages to the States General. One of the ships, the *Giustizia*, had had to take refuge in the estuary of the Elbe, scraping its hull in the process and having to hire small boats in which to take its cargo the last stage of the journey to Amsterdam. The *Susanna* had had to cut its mast and anchor ropes in a storm, and also had to use small boats in order to transport the cargo on the final stretch.[34] The two ships, the *Susanna*'s mast and ropes aside, were thus claiming identical GAs. In the case of the *Giustizia*, however, the damages were repartitioned over cargo, ship, and freight; in the case of the *Susanna* the expenses incurred during the blockade were likewise partitioned over cargo, ship, and freight, but the expenses of the extended journey and the freighting of the small boats were partitioned over only cargo and freight,

[32] ASP, CM, AC, 314-14 (27 March 1669); ASP, CM, AC, 314-15 (27 March 1669); ASP, CM, AC, 314-16 (27 March 1669).

[33] On the chamber, see Go, 'The Amsterdam Chamber of Insurance and Average'.

[34] ASP, CM, AC, 314-16 (27 March 1669), Amsterdam report; ASP, CM, AC, 314-15 (27 March 1669), Amsterdam report.

with the freight standing 'in place of the ship'.[35] It was apparently the normal custom in Amsterdam that either ship or freight should contribute, but not both; and it is not explained in the documentation why this should only have been followed in one case and not adhered to in the other.[36] The difference was probably due to clauses written into the freight contracts themselves. Both customs were at variance with the one in Tuscany, where half of the ship and a third of the freight contributed in all cases. This presented no problem to the *Consoli*, however, who ratified D'Attigian's request for reimbursement in just two weeks. Such swift expedition was not carried out on faith: D'Attigian had to produce an attestation produced by the Dutch Chamber, detailing the voyage, judgement, and GA calculation, translated into Italian and further countersigned by three Amsterdam notaries, but it was nevertheless clearly an entirely unremarkable case from a juridical point of view.[37] The variance in GA procedure was never mentioned and the reluctant underwriters did not even bother to object.

It must be acknowledged that the example presented here concerns a very slight variant in GA procedures, which had little impact on the overall contribution rate: it was undeniable that these costs would have been accepted as GA in Livorno, and perhaps a more egregious departure from the GA principle would have occasioned objection. Nevertheless, the idea that GA costs were generally accepted unproblematically by underwriters is concordant both with what we have already seen regarding GA payments and with the findings of existing studies of pre-modern insurance markets. Giovanni Ceccarelli argues those pre-modern markets which managed to gain and maintain a position of international preeminence did so not so much through offering competitive premiums, but rather by increasing certainty for the purchasers of insurance, notably by increasing the certainty of a pay-out in the event of a disaster.[38] There was thus a strong incentive for authorities that sought to regulate that market, like the *Consoli*, to mandate the acceptance of GA claims adjusted abroad even if these followed slightly different rules. The position of the Livorno insurance market, more dependent than most on foreign demand, would have been seriously affected had underwriters objected to paying out for GA. This willingness to reimburse Average payments made under different rules was, moreover, a reflection of what was happening with GA itself, with the rules of the port where the adjustment was made determining

---

[35] ASP, *CM*, AC, 314-15 (27 March 1669), Amsterdam report.

[36] Go, 'GA adjustments in Amsterdam', p. 401. This was also apparently the case in England in the sixteenth century, with the rationale being that the freight was not earned until the end of the voyage; see Rossi, *Insurance in Elizabethan England*, p. 138.

[37] ASP, *CM*, AC, 314-15 (27 March 1669), Amsterdam report.

[38] Ceccarelli, *Risky Markets*, pp. 242–6. See also Addobbati, *Commercio, rischio, guerra*, p. 128.

the contribution to be made by the receivers in all subsequent destinations. As we saw in the previous chapter, an international system could only function if such discrepancies were accepted, and uniformity could certainly not be imposed unilaterally.

While the default position may have been that insurance contracts covered GA payments, this was not always the case. Stipulations could be inserted into the contracts which freed the underwriter from responsibility for Average, the so-called 'free from Average' clauses ('*franchi di avaria*'). This sometimes meant that a contract could be free from Average altogether ('*franchi di ogni avaria*'), making the underwriter liable only for total loss. Such clauses are sometimes found among eighteenth-century Tuscan contracts, and this form was the standard one adopted in Venice.[39] At other times, however, the clause could indicate that Averages were excluded only up to a certain low percentage: the rationale here was protecting underwriters against very small claims for everyday wear and tear.[40] As we have seen, '*avaria*' itself could mean a number of different things, so it is no surprise that the precise significance of the 'free from Average' clause could vary from jurisdiction to jurisdiction and from policy to policy depending on the precise contractual obligations outlined.[41] Interpreting the significance of these clauses and the weight of Averages upon the insurer is thus not straightforward.

The Impact of GA on Underwriters

Qualitative evidence suggests that Averages could present problems to the underwriter. We have already seen the Tuscan laywer, Ascanio Baldasseroni, complain heartily about the effect of master-friendly GA procedures on insurers. Such pressures could be even greater in times of war: Andrea Addobbati claims that many underwriters in Tuscany were ruined during the American Revolutionary Wars thanks to sky-high Averages.[42] Insurance

---

[39] Addobbati, *Commercio, rischio, guerra*, pp. 133–4; Maria Fusaro, 'Sharing risks, on averages and why they matter', in Maria Fusaro, Andrea Addobbati, and Luisa Piccinno (eds), *General Average and Risk Management in Medieval and Early Modern Maritime Business* (Cham: Springer, 2023), 3–31, at p. 12; Baldasseroni, *Delle assicurazioni marittime*, vol. 1, p. 207; Nehlsen-von Stryk, *L'assicurazione marittima a Venezia*, pp. 216–44.

[40] Targa, *Ponderationi*, p. 128.

[41] The confusion continued to generate problems even for contemporaries; see Baldasseroni, *Delle assicurazioni marittime*, vol. 1, pp. 179–90.

[42] Andrea Addobbati, 'Oltre gli intermediari. La Anton Francesco Salucci & figlio alla conquista dei mercati americani (1779–1788)', in Paolo Castignoli, Luigi Donolo, and Algerina Neri (eds), *Storia e attualità della presenza degli Stati Uniti a Livorno e in Toscana (Atti del Convegno 4-6 aprile 2002)* (Pisa: Plus, 2003), 145–83.

policies themselves, though preserved in large numbers, are of little use to us in assessing these claims and establishing the weight of GA on insurers, because they cannot tell us about eventual pay-outs by the underwriters and the various events which occasioned those pay-outs.

A sense of GA's relative importance and weight for an insurer can, however, be gleaned from merchant accounts books dealing with insurance, even if these have rarely survived and cannot generally provide us with serial figures over long periods.[43] The data presented in this analysis pertains to the final third of the century, and thus the part of our period in which the use of insurance was most extensive. The sources in question are two account books preserved in the Quaratesi collection in the Florentine state archive. These are the records left by this ancient Florentine family with a long history of commercial activity since the Middle Ages, with some family members living in both Pisa and Livorno.[44] The family were in fact responsible for one of the more famous artistic representations of a jettison at sea, 'St Nicholas saving a ship from the tempest', which formed part of the 'Quaratesi Polyptych'. This altarpiece was painted by Gentile da Fabriano, and was originally housed in the church of San Niccolò Oltrarno.[45]

The Quaratesi archive ranges from the fourteenth to the nineteenth century and is mostly comprised of documents related to the family's mercantile activities and the administration of their patrimony.[46] At least two of the seventeenth century account books contain accounts related to insurance. The first is a ledger maintained by one of the Quaratesi themselves though it is unclear who exactly: the author at one point makes reference to 'Girolamo Quaratesi, my brother' but his own name is never mentioned.[47] The account was made in Livorno, detailing underwriting carried out by this Quaratesi on his own account, and that carried out on behalf of his associate, Baccio del Beccuto, who likewise hailed from a prominent Florentine family active in trade across the

---

[43] Andrea Addobbati, 'War, risks, and speculation: the accounts of a small Livorno insurer (1743–1748)', in Phillip Hellwege and Guido Rossi (eds), *Maritime Risk Management: Essays on the History of Marine Insurance, General Average and Sea Loan* (Berlin: Duncker & Humblot, 2021), 161–88, at p. 165; Lewis Wade, *Privilege, Economy and State in Old Regime France: Marine Insurance, War and the Atlantic Empire under Louis XIV* (Woodbridge: The Boydell Press, 2023), p. 131.

[44] Giulia Camerani Marri, 'Archivio Quaratesi' in 'Notizie degli archivi Toscani', *Archivio Storico Italiano* 118 (1960), p. 368.

[45] See Lionel Cust and Herbert Horne, 'Notes on pictures in the royal collections. Article VII – The Quaratesi Altarpiece by Gentile da Fabriano', *The Burlington Magazine* 6 (1905), 470–5. See also Richard Goldthwaite, 'The practice and culture of accounting in renaissance Florence', *Enterprise & Society* 16 (2015), 611–47, at p. 631.

[46] Marri, 'Archivio Quaratesi', p. 368.

[47] ASF, *Quaratesi*, 357.

early modern period.[48] This first book covers the period 1670–85 with accounts for Beccuto for 1670–9. Beccuto appears to have been a passive partner in this first period, and the insurance policies signed in his name replicate exactly those underwritten by Quaratesi, though often for smaller amounts (usually half of that underwritten by the managing partner). The second book was maintained by Beccuto alone, began in 1691 and continued until 1695 when Beccuto 'passed on to a better life' in the early hours of a February morning.[49]

The first section of each account records insurances made. Each entry details the buyer of the insurance, the nature of the insured item, the port of origin, the port of destination, and the name of the relevant ship and its master. The value underwritten is recorded to the left of each entry, and the premium to the right: all premiums are slightly less than a round number, representing the fact that the amount received was reduced by the fee paid to the insurance broker. Journeys that finished successfully are marked with an 'A'; those where there was a pay-out are marked instead with a 'P'. In the second book, a total is made at the end of each year, detailing profit and loss: the premiums are totalled and set against the complete losses and the Averages (*sinistri e avarie*) which Beccuto paid out for, as well as another fee for his broker. The same calculation is performed in Quaratesi's book but at irregular and apparently arbitrary intervals. Quaratesi also transferred small sums out of his insurance account into other accounts on a regular basis, making his figures less straightforward to analyse.

The second part of Beccuto's book also provides a separate breakdown of these losses and Averages, as well as the *storni* – refunds of the premium when the voyage did not go ahead, or when it was discovered that the vessel or cargo had been over-insured. This breakdown allows us to analyse the relative weight of Averages as a proportion of overall outgoings. In line with the slightly more chaotic nature of Quaratesi's account, a similar breakdown is not always included in his book, meaning that only the years 1671–8 can be fully analysed. Quaratesi also employed a somewhat irregular accounting technique: rather than balancing his ingoings (premiums) and outgoings (losses, Averages, and *storni*) on a yearly basis, he simply interrupts his list of policies at random intervals to record the 'losses and Averages paid up to this date'.[50] So we are unable to analyse his account on a year-by-year basis, and instead are forced to divide the account up into three uneven periods: 23 June 1671 to 18 July 1672; 26 August 1672 to 7 September 1674; and 20

---

[48] Ricardo Court, '"Januensis ergo mercator": trust and enforcement in the business correspondence of the Brignole family', *The Sixteenth Century Journal* 35 (2004), 987–1003, at pp. 992–4.

[49] ASF, *Quaratesi*, 261.

[50] E.g. ASF, *Quaratesi*, 357, f. 16r.

September 1674 to 31 October 1678. Quaratesi, unlike Beccuto, did not note the amounts he underwrote when he accepted a premium.

In total, we can therefore analyse the frequency and relative weight of Average pay-outs for the years 1671–8 and 1691–5. It should be remembered at this point that there is no distinction made between GA and PA in the source, which considers only losses from 'Average' as a whole. Table 4 details a breakdown of the pair's outgoings in the period 1671–8 (Quaratesi recorded the losses for both partners as a single figure). Table 5 captures the whole of Beccuto's underwriting activities, showing the total premiums accepted and the losses broken down by type, including complete losses (perhaps sometimes mitigated by salvage), returned premiums, Averages (with no distinction made between PA and GA), and other small, miscellaneous outgoings such as payments to agents or attorneys.

Table 4. Quaratesi and Beccuto's underwriting activity, 1671–8 (pieces of eight). Archival References: ASF, *Quaratesi*, 357.

	1671–2	1672–4	1674–8	Total
Total Underwritten	-	-	-	-
Premiums Accepted	256.84	177.78	79.06	513.68
Total losses	343.76	196.71	1524.99	2065.46
Complete Losses	300.00	100.00	1417.49	1817.49
Returned premiums	13.25	21.59	47.48	82.32
Averages	4.50	75.12	60.02	139.64
Other	26.01	0.00	0.00	26.01
Averages as percentage of losses	1.31	38.19	3.94	14.48
0.5% Brokerage Fee	N/A	N/A	N/A	N/A
Earnings	-86.92	-18.93	-1445.93	-1551.78

Table 5. Beccuto's underwriting activity, 1691–5 (pieces of eight). Archival References: ASF, *Quaratesi*, 261.

	1692	1693	1694	1695	Total
Total Underwritten	23650	21072	15600	2950	63272
Premiums Accepted	1728.25	1596.77	1070.88	244.78	4640.68
Total Losses	95.01	2012.42	1728.13	1308.75	5144.31
Complete Losses	0	1878.8	1589.5	952.73	4421.03
Returned Premiums	77.24	63.39	37.5	43.5	221.63
Averages	17.77	53.18	98.13	305.74	474.82
Other Losses	0	17.05	3	6.78	26.83
Averages as percentage of losses	18.70	2.64	5.68	23.36	9.23
0.5% Brokerage Fee	118.25	105.36	78	14.75	316.36
Earnings	1514.99	-521.01	-735.25	-1078.72	-819.99

We can see that the underwriting directed by Quaratesi in the 1670s was not as extensive as that carried out by Beccuto in the later period. The overall weight of Average on the associates was modest, just under 15 per cent of total losses. Yet the percentage of losses deriving from Average in the 1670s account varies quite considerably: 1.31 per cent in the first period of just over a year, 38.19 per cent in the second period of around two years, and 3.94 per cent in the third period of around four years. There is no way for us to establish what the typical relative weighting of GA and PA might have been: while we can be fairly certain that most of the GAs left traces in the Consular archives, there are very few cases involving PA, and it seems likely that the majority were dealt with privately.[51] We can nevertheless be sure that the impact of GAs was even less pronounced than this figure suggests. The period in question was perhaps not the most turbulent faced by Livornese insurers, but nor can we say that this was a period of relative calm, in which Average contributions might have been lower than usual. The Franco-Dutch War (1672–8) was ongoing for most of the period, a conflict which included

---

[51] E.g. ASP, CM, AC, 319-6 (5 February 1669); see Dyble, 'Divide and rule', pp. 371–2.

the Third Anglo-Dutch War (1672–4), and both of these would have had an effect on Livornese underwriters, raising premiums but also increasing the rate of GAs and PAs.[52] It is thus unlikely that the figure of 15 per cent vastly understates the weight of Average losses generally sustained by underwriters.

The underwriting carried out by Beccuto in the 1690s was of a different level of magnitude. Quaratesi received a mean average of just under 130 pieces a year in premiums, with Beccuto generally insuring half that amount on each risk. From 12 June 1670 to 31 October 1678, Quaratesi accepted a total of 1,085 pieces in premiums. Beccuto accepted more in premiums each year in the 1690s than Quaratesi had in the entire period covered by his account book. We can also be fairly sure that Beccuto was re-entering the insurance market after a period of absence. The first year of activity recorded by the book details some refunded premiums, but no total losses or Averages. This reflects the delay that occurred between the underwriting of policies and the eventual insurance claims made upon them. Had this account book been a continuation of an existing account, we would expect to see losses and Averages from previous years carried over. Beccuto, like many investors, could have been persuaded to reengage more extensively in insurance by the intensification of the Nine Years War (1688–97), which, like most conflicts, increased premiums and tempted new and part-time investors into the market with the promise of large windfalls.[53] The war had a considerable impact on maritime trade, however, as the English and Dutch abandoned a traditional indulgence to neutral commerce and agreed to attack all vessels of whatever flag sailing to French ports or carrying the goods of French subjects.[54] English merchants were later to demand greater protection from the Royal Navy in 1690 on account of the number of ships they had lost in the Mediterranean.[55]

After an initial profit resulting from the aforementioned time lag, Beccuto consistently made a loss each year. Overall, he lost more than 800 pieces over this three-and-a-half-year period. This could conceivably be a result of extending his activities, as he took on more and more risks which would have been eschewed in the earlier, more cautious phase. Alternatively, he could simply have been unlucky. Either way, the Averages represent a slightly diminished though not altogether dissimilar proportion of losses: 9.23 per cent.

When we examine Beccuto's outgoings in more detail, however, another interesting qualification emerges. Beccuto was very rarely insuring ships,

[52] See Wade, *Privilege, Economy and State*, p. 132.
[53] Addobbati, *Commercio, rischio, guerra*, pp. 92, 116; Addobbati, 'War, risks, and speculation'; Ceccarelli, *Risky Markets*, pp. 103–20.
[54] George Clark, 'The Nine Years War, 1688–1697', in J.S. Bromley (ed.), *The New Cambridge Modern History. Volume 6: The Rise of Great Britain and Russia, 1688–1715/25* (Cambridge: Cambridge University Press, 1970), 223–53, at pp. 234–5.
[55] Clark, 'The Nine Years War', pp. 238, 244.

freight, or sea loans – the three ways in which he could have been covering risks run by the shipmaster and/or ship-owners. Of the 104 pay-outs recorded in his accounts, only three were the result of insurance made on a ship, and only two of insurance made on sea loans. Of these five pay-outs, none related to an Average. As Ralph Davis remarks in relation to seventeenth century England, and as Lewis Wade has found more recently in the case of seventeenth-century France, merchandise was insured far more often than ships were.[56]

GA was thus providing protection to ship-owners from risks which insurance was not yet covering: the insurance ledgers do not tell the whole story. Ship-owners were of course already hedged against such risks to a certain extent through the practice of shared ownership. Investors generally owned only a part of a ship in order to create a safer portfolio, but it should be noted that an ownership share of less than an eighth was extremely uncommon, at least in an Italian context.[57] GA thus provided a second line of defence. Once again, we find GA of particular importance for the transport side of the commercial sector. This risk-management dimension can be set alongside other bonuses for the transport sector, such as the opportunity to repartition routine costs, which we have already encountered when examining *consolati* and in the case of the *Alice and Francis*.

GA and Sea Loans

One case in particular allows us to state these two advantages in quantitative terms. A GA declared by the French ship, *Cavallo Marino*, in 1670 gave rise to a secondary dispute between insurers later down the line. We know that the master had taken out a sea loan prior to the voyage, because the lender subsequently had trouble extracting payment from his own insurers and took the case to court. The case thus sheds light on where GA costs flowed to next in this cascading waterfall of cost dispersal.[58] This allows us to observe the interaction of several risk-sharing instruments, which usually lie hidden. By breaking down this case in detail, we can fill in the blank analytical and operational space between those GA cases we have already examined, and the insurance accounts of Quaratesi and Beccuto, illustrating how a number of instruments were used as part of a complex and multifaceted risk strategy.

We have already encountered this particular case in Chapter 3, where it was used to illustrate how a number of costs might be entered into GA which we would not find mentioned in any jurisprudential description of GA. These

---

[56] Ralph Davis, *The Rise of the English Shipping Industry in the Seventeenth and Eighteenth Centuries*, 2nd edn (Newton Abbot: David & Charles Publishers, 1972), p. 87; Wade, *Privilege, Economy and State*, p. 133.

[57] Davis, *English Shipping Industry*, p. 83; Piccinno, 'Genoa, 1340–1620', p. 40.

[58] ASP, CM, AC, 321-26 (25 August 1670).

included wear and tear to the body of the ship itself, as well as some not-so-extraordinary expenses, such as anchorage and consular fees. The Provençal master of the *Cavallo Marino*, Antonio Garzille, managed to not only repartition some damage to his vessel by describing his actions as an 'evasive manoeuvre', but also, somewhat surreptitiously, entered two instances of the French *cottimo*, as well as anchorage charges and a number of small bribes to locals and officials, into his GA.[59] We can see from the GA documentation that the *Cavallo Marino* in fact paid two instances of the *cottimo*: '421.4 pieces … including the *cambium maritimum* paid in Alexandretta … to deputies of the French *natio*' and '525.4 pieces … paid as above'.[60] As evidence of these payments, Garzille produced two attestations (*relazioni*) authenticated by the French consuls. One opens by declaring 'that it was deliberated by the council of 26 February 1664 that to pay the debts of the *natio*, a tax and *cottimo* should [be levied] upon every sail … a thing which has been always carried out after the aforesaid time' for the 'ordinary and extraordinary expenses which the *natio* makes daily'.[61] The second attestation records that 'we make it known that, in light of the letters patent of his majesty given in Paris in the month of last month … that the sum of twelve hundred lire is levied upon all French ships that finish their voyages in Italy'.[62] In short, one levy was the regular *cottimo* which had been in place for at least six years. The other was the new imposition, the 'Navigation Act *alla francese*', as Guillaume Calafat terms it, designed to protect Marseille and penalise Livorno by incentivising French ships to miss out Livorno from their itineraries when returning from the eastern Mediterranean.[63]

At the outset of his voyage from Livorno to 'Cyprus and other parts of the Levant', Garzille had taken 4,000 pieces from Bartolomo Forno, a merchant based in Livorno, at '*cambio marittimo*' (literally, 'maritime exchange'). It is perhaps worth at this point briefly reviewing this concept, and clarifying the types of arrangement that could be covered by this capacious phrase. There have been very few studies of the family of risk-bearing loans (*cambium maritimum*, bottomry, respondentia) that were regularly used in pre-modern maritime commerce. Thanks no doubt in part to the widespread 'stadial' conception of institutional development already discussed, the early modern use of these instruments represents a region on our historiographical map which is almost entirely blank.[64] Andrea Zanini, one of the few scholars to have worked on these institutions, notes that 'despite its popularity in Genoese finance,

---

[59] ASP, *CM*, AC, 319-20 (18 March 1669).
[60] ASP, CM, AC, 319-20 (18 March 1669), Calculation.
[61] ASP, CM, AC, 319-20 (18 March 1669), First relation of the French consul.
[62] Ibid.
[63] Calafat, 'Livorno e la camera di commercio', pp. 238–9.
[64] Christopher Kingston, 'Governance and institutional change in marine insurance,

bottomry over the course of the early modern period has not yet been examined thoroughly'.[65] In particular, he remarks that 'the search should continue for documentation capable of shedding light, from a practical point of view, on the participation of bottomry creditors in General Average procedures'.[66]

Analysis, moreover, is beset by the range of terminology that was employed in different languages and local contexts, which raises further difficulties of comparison and translation.[67] All three of the contracts mentioned above were referred to, in the Italian context, using the term *cambio marittimo*. The origin of the term was the practice called *cambium maritimum*. This was sometimes called *cambio real* or 'royal exchange' in the work of contemporary English jurists, but the term seems to have dropped out of English commercial manuals in the eighteenth century.[68] The *cambium maritimum* was a loan disbursed for a maritime voyage in one currency and payable in another. It involved the lender shouldering sea risks as well as credit risk because repayment of the loan was dependent on the safe arrival of the ship. Raymond De Roover wrote that this was indicated by the phrase *ad risicum et fortunam dei maris et gentium* inserted into the medieval *cambium maritimum* contract, while Zanini reports that the phrase 'risk of sea, corsairs, and fire' conveyed this element within the early modern Genoese context.[69]

The *cambio marittimo* given by Forno to Garzille at the outset of the voyage, however, was in fact a straightforward sea loan – a *foenus nauticum* in Latin.[70] Here, there was no currency exchange involved, and the debtor provided security. In English, this instrument was further subdivided, with the term bottomry used when the security was the ship, and respondentia when

---

1350–1850', *European Review of Economic History* 18 (2014), 1–18, at p. 2; Harris, *Going the Distance*, pp. 110–18.

[65] Zanini, 'Financing and risk', p. 342, note 16.

[66] Ibid.

[67] Luca Lo Basso, 'Il finanziamento dell'armamento marittimo tra società e istituzioni: il caso ligure', *Archivio Storico Italiano* 174 (2016), 81–107; Luca Lo Basso, 'The maritime loan as a form of small shipping credit (17th–18th centuries): the case of Liguria', in Antonino Giuffrida, Roberto Rossi, and Gaetano Sabatini (eds), *Informal Credit in the Mediterranean Area (XVI-XIX Centuries)* (Palermo: New Digital Press, 2016), 145–73. On the medieval incarnations of these practices see C.B. Hoover, 'The sea loan in Genoa in the twelfth century', *The Quarterly Journal of Economics* 40 (1926), 495–529; De Roover, 'The organization of trade'; De Roover, 'The *cambium maritimum* contract'.

[68] Malynes, *Consuetudo vel lex mercatoria*, p. 379; Molloy, *De iure maritimo*, p. 309.

[69] De Roover, 'The *cambium maritimum* contract', p. 16; Zanini, 'Financing and risk', p. 349.

[70] Berti, 'I rischi nella circolazione marittima', p. 818; Davis, *English Shipping*, p. 85; Olivia Robinson, T.D. Fergus, and William M. Gordon, *An Introduction to European Legal History* (Abingdon: Professional Books, 1985), p. 156.

the security was cargo.[71] The use of the term *cambio marittimo* for sea loans in the Italian context without the element of currency exchange probably derives ultimately from the papal bull, *Naviganti* (1234), which had declared the sea loan usurious: merchants thus took to hiding what was effectively a sea loan under the guise of a simple exchange of currencies, the *cambium maritimum*, masking the payment of interest through a deliberately distorted valuation of the currencies involved.[72] Though the interest was once again in plain sight by the early modern period, the term *cambio marittimo* stuck.[73] A sea loan could be taken out by the shipmaster, and used to fund the cost of making the voyage, or could be taken by the merchants and used to fund the commercial part of the venture, or could even be taken on by merchants and shipmaster together.[74] The loan was again only repayable on the safe return of the ship, and thus it is said that the creditor assumed the sea risk. The creditor thus provided both capital and risk protection, and interest for the sea loan reflected this high degree of exposure.

It is, however, unclear in the existing literature what place GA occupied in all of this. Zanini notes that in Genoa, 'theoretically, losses related to Averages and jettison were borne by the creditor [of the sea loan]', but that this 'corresponds to a somewhat nebulous operational context', and that this might be affected by law, practice, or the agreements struck between parties.[75] This variation no doubt in part resulted from the fact that conventions surrounding the absorption of Averages by a sea loan creditor were vexed even at the time, thanks in part to the different norms adopted in different places. William Benecke, an English maritime jurist writing in the early nineteenth century, noted an

> astonishing variety in the laws respecting this subject, which are absolutely contradictory to each other ... the law of Hamburgh [sic] stipulates that the lender shall be free from General and Particular Average; the laws of Prussia ... charge the lender expressly with both kinds of Average. By the law of Holland, Particular Averages was the charge of the lender but not the General Average.[76]

---

[71] Francesca Trivellato, *The Promise and Peril of Credit: What a Forgotten Legend about Jews and Finance Tells Us about the Making of European Commercial Society* (Princeton: Princeton University Press, 2019), p. 299, note 7.

[72] On *Naviganti* and its effect on the sea loan, see De Roover, 'The *cambium maritimum* contract', pp. 17–18.

[73] Zanini, 'Financing and risk', p. 343.

[74] Zanini, 'Financing and risk', p. 346.

[75] Zanini, 'Financing and risk', p. 350.

[76] William Benecke, *A Treatise on the Principles Indemnity in Marine Insurance, Bottomry and Respondentia* (London: Baldwin, Cradock and Joy, 1824), p. 74; Zanini, 'Financing and risk', p. 12. See also John Weskett, *A Complete Digest of Theory, Laws and Practise of Insurance* (London: Frys, Couchman, & Collier, 1781), p. 46. This information

The French *Ordonnance de la Marine* (1681), meanwhile, established that the lender was not liable for PA, but should be responsible for all GA, and that this could not be altered even through agreement between the parties.[77] English jurisprudence was, typically, the least clear of all, the eighteenth-century John Weskett complaining that the English jurist Malynes and the Anglo-Irish Molloy (and 'all other books that have published since ... [which] are chiefly copied from them') were 'greatly defective, in not having cleared up one of the main points, viz. how lenders shall be dealt with in cases of Average'. He also states, using a refrain which is by now familiar to us, that there were 'no fixed laws, or rules universally known in England' on this matter.[78]

The case of the *Cavallo Marino* can shed some light on the operational context. The security in this case was both ship and cargo. The loan had been taken by the shipmaster Garzille along with the merchants Carlo Gilles and Federigo Dilman, two traders based in Livorno. Garzille had pledged the ship, with Gilles and Dilman pledging their cargo as security.[79] More than half of the cargo of the return journey (by value) was received by Gilles (12,205 pieces, 63.3 per cent of the total), who was presumably working in partnership or at least in tandem with Dilman. The remainder was received by merchants who took no part in the sea loan.[80] The loan was made at an interest rate of 24 per cent (960 pieces to be paid after the ship had been safely unloaded in Livorno).[81] Forno, having made the loan, then partially insured it. He bought 2,700 pieces worth of insurance on the Livorno market for a premium of 13 per cent, i.e. a fee of 351 pieces.[82] The principal underwriter of the insurance contract was Thomas Dethick, another Livorno-based merchant, who underwrote just below half the total amount (1,300 pieces). We learn from the GA calculation that Thomas Dethick already had a financial interest in the voyage, receiving a significant portion of the cargo on the return journey (1,980 pieces, 10.3 per cent of the total value of the cargo).[83] The remainder was shared between ten other underwriters insuring between 100 or 200 pieces each.[84] There were thus three levels of cost redistribution in play: the GA, activated *post hoc*; the sea loan, partially covering the GA; and the premium insurance, partially covering the sea loan.

---

seems ultimately to derive from the work of the London-based Hamburg merchant, Nicolas Magens; see *An Essay on Insurances*, pp. 19–20.

[77] René-Josué Valin, *Nouveau commentaire sur l'ordonnance de la marine, du mois d'août 1681* (Paris: Saurin, 1828), p. 436.

[78] Weskett, *A Complete Digest*, p. 46.

[79] ASP, CM, AC, 321-26 (25 August 1670), Copy of original contract.

[80] ASP, CM, AC, 319-20 (18 March 1669), Calculation.

[81] ASP, CM, AC, 321-26 (25 August 1670), Copy of original contract.

[82] ASP, CM, AC, 321-26 (25 August 1670), Insurance policies.

[83] ASP, CM, AC, 319-20 (18 March 1669), Calculation.

[84] ASP, CM, AC, 321-26 (25 August 1670), Insurance policies.

An Interlocking Community of Risk

After the master's GA declaration, Forno claimed that he had attempted to marshal his insurers to oppose the judgement, without any apparent success.[85] He notified the insurers of by means of a summons which was issued by the Governor's court in Livorno on 15 March. The summons called upon the insurers to join him in objecting to the GA, but no such opposition was forthcoming. The GA was awarded on 18 March, just a week after the original *testimoniale e domanda* had been submitted.[86] Once the GA had been awarded (1,532 pieces, at a rate of 7.2 per cent), he then had trouble extracting payment from the same underwriters who had not joined him in originally objecting (hence the existence of the case within the Consular archive).[87] As in the case of Norvilli, however, the *Consoli* straightforwardly awarded him the case, and the underwriters raised no objections: their refusal to pay does not seem to have resulted from any principled stand against the GA, but was simply a delaying tactic.

These subsequent events bring our attention to several important points. We might first of all note that, in Tuscany, the creditor of the sea loan did in fact cover GA payments – a thing we can hardly take for granted given the regional variation noted by the existing literature on sea loans.[88] Though the sea loan creditor and subsequently the underwriters were obliged to 'run the risk', they did not cover the GA losses in a blanket fashion. Instead, the creditor and the underwriters contributed to the GA in proportion, i.e. they were liable to pay 7.2 per cent of the amount they had underwritten.[89] Rather than picking up the tab for all 1,532 pieces then, Forno instead contributed 7.2 per cent of the total value of his sea loan of 4,000 pieces, thus contributing 288 pieces towards the GA.[90] As Zanini remarks of relationship between GA and sea loan in Genoa, 'the sharing of damages and charges deriving from general Average was the price that he was required to pay in order to avoid a total loss of the mortgaged objects'.[91]

With Forno's mode of contribution established, we are thus in a position to suggest an (almost) final answer to the fundamental question: who paid? The following tables and graphs show the origin of the various damages incurred during the voyage of the *Cavallo Marino*. This can then be compared with

---

[85] ASP, CM, AC, 321-26 (25 August 1670), Summons.

[86] ASP, CM, AC, 321-26 (25 August 1670), Summons; ASP, CM, AC, 319-20 (18 March 1669), Judgement.

[87] ASP, CM, AC, 321-26 (25 August 1670), *Testimoniale e domanda*.

[88] Other examples include ASP, CM, AC, 322-27 (9 December 1670); ASP, CM, AC, 419-9 (17 August 1700); ASP, CM, AC, 322-16 (9 November 1670).

[89] ASP, CM, AC, 321-26 (25 August 1670), *Testimoniale e domanda*.

[90] ASP, CM, AC, 419-9 (17 August 1700).

[91] Zanini, 'Financing and risk', p. 349.

the distribution of these expenses after they had passed through GA, a sea loan, and premium insurance on that loan. These charts take into account the fact that, in addition to the sea loan offered by Forno at the outset of the voyage, Garzille had been forced to accept two emergency sea loans in the Levant from merchants named Truillard and Costeau in order to finance the high upfront of the sums levied by the French consul in Aleppo.[92] These were repayable to two associates in Livorno at the high interest rate of 30 per cent. Since these contracts too 'ran the risk' of the voyage, a portion of the costs was presumably paid by these Tuscan associates. Two graphs are used to show who paid the damages: one shows how the damages would have hypothetically been split in an 'idealised' GA, with the ship and freight contributing their full values, while the second shows how they were actually distributed, using the ship-friendly custom in Tuscany of valuing the ship at half, and the freight at a third, of their real values.

Some caveats must be borne in mind here: firstly, that although we know how much Forno contributed to the damages, it is unclear in what proportion he covered the costs payable by the shipmaster, Garzille, and in what proportion his contribution covered those payable by the merchants, Gilles and Dilman, since the sea loan was in the name of both parties.[93] This information is not included in the original contract, and would presumably have been arranged privately between the parties themselves although we have no evidence about this. To overcome this, it has been assumed that Forno's contribution (and the subsequent contribution of the insurers) diminished Garzille's and Gilles's contributions proportionally, i.e. that Forno's contribution was first subtracted from the total damages, and then the remaining damages distributed according to each man's share in the venture. The second caveat is that, as shipmaster, Garzille would only have paid contribution for the ship-side in the first instance: he would only have been personally liable for a contribution based on a third-value of the freight, and only for the vessel if he happened to own shares in it. The final caveat is that the calculation only gives us the names of the receivers. These receivers may then have sought the payment from their principals – the actual owners of the goods. Alternatively, much of the cargo may have been insured in its own right. These graphs thus do not quite display the final resting place of these costs, which would have travelled further down the chain and been further distributed.

A comparison of the graphs lays bare the potentiality of GA for the shipmaster and ship-owners. Garzille and/or the ship-owners ended up paying just over 100 pieces of eight towards a GA of 1,532 pieces. Yet a full 28 per cent of the GA expenses were related to the refitting of the ship. We might therefore summarise this situation by saying that, effectively, Garzille and the ship-owners ended up paying just under 30 pieces of eight (28 per cent of their

[92] ASP, CM, AC, 319-20 (18 March 1669), Relation of the French consul.
[93] ASP, CM, AC, 321-26 (25 August 1670), Sea Loan Contract.

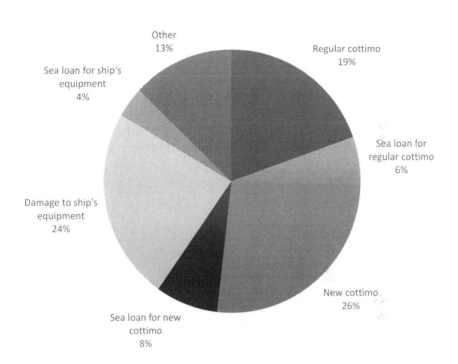

Figure 5. Breakdown of the GA costs in the case of the *Cavallo Marino*.

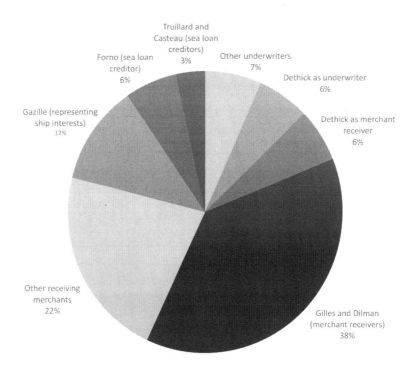

Figure 6. A hypothetical partition of GA costs in the case of the *Cavallo Marino* with ship and freight contributing their full value.

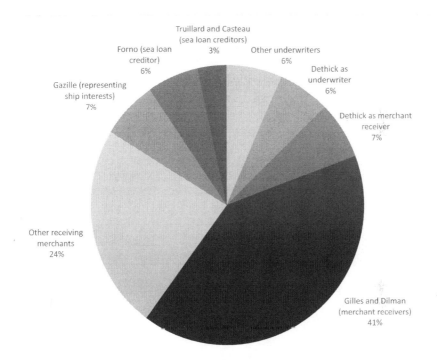

Figure 7. The actual distribution of GA costs in the case of the *Cavallo Marino* following Tuscan customs.

GA contribution) in return for a new mast (estimated by Garzille himself at 100 pieces), a new anchor rope (120 pieces), new caulking (65 pieces), and other general repairs ('*legnami per acomodar la nave*', 27.25 pieces): the Galley of Salamis indeed.[94] With savings like these, the existence of GA would also have reduced running costs and would surely be having an impact on freight rates (lower upfront costs for freighting the ship), as well as lowering the amount of cash which ship-owners would have to set aside for fitting out their vessels.

Beyond the particular advantage of GA for the shipmaster, we might also note that, despite the risk-sharing potentiality of the sea loan, the distribution through GA was still an important part of cost sharing. In the end, Forno and his insurers ended up assuming just under a fifth of the overall load. GA thus remained an important absorption mechanism even for cargo interests. We cannot necessarily say it was the foremost mechanism as it seems likely that the receivers, as noted above, would have insured their merchandise in turn, leading to further redistribution. Without this data we cannot assess the exact importance of GA within the overall picture. Nevertheless, we can see that through the use of GA and sea loan, Gilles and Dilman, receivers of 63.3 per cent of the cargo by value, had reduced their contribution to 43 per cent of the damages.

The sea loan, despite ultimately assuming quite a modest portion of costs, also demonstrated its advantages. By taking the sea loan at the beginning of the voyage, Garzille was already in possession of Forno's money at the time of the accident. This also meant that when it came to the GA, Garzille could simply repay a lesser amount to Forno, extracting his contribution before returning the loaned sum. He could then continue sailing, rather than keeping his ship in port while he awaited payment. If Garzille had availed himself of premium insurance rather than a sea loan, he would have risked one or more of the underwriters not paying up (as indeed happened when Forno tried to extract payment for the GA from his own insurers). Though enforcement via recourse to the court was, in the event, fairly straightforward, this would have been precious time wasted for Forno in which his asset was not making him any money. As Carlo Targa remarked in 1692:

> And why are there still those that take money [through *cambio marittimo*] in order to not run so much risk themselves? Because having considered the cost of insurance through premiums to shield themselves in anticipation of losses, having considered the risk of bad insurers, of wasting money, of taxes, and the rest, it turns out that, with the advantages that the good letters have in the *cambio* usages, *and the advantages of having the money in their power*, it is more useful to take capital under this heading and to insure themselves indirectly.[95]

---

[94] ASP, CM, AC, 319-20 (18 March 1669), Expenses; Baldasseroni, *Delle assicurazioni marittime*, vol. 3, p. 15.

[95] Targa, *Ponderationi*, pp. 72–3 [my italics].

The most efficient enforcement is, after all, no enforcement at all. And even in a situation where enforcement is entirely predictable and efficacious, there can still be a delay between a refusal to pay and the eventual enforcement of the payment. The use of the three instruments in conjunction – GA, sea loan, premium insurance – allowed not only for increased risk distribution but also more time-efficient enforcement, and allowed Garzille to keep his ship working in the meantime.

Other cases allow us to further clarify the practice concerning GA and sea loans. While sea loan creditors were eligible for GA payments, it appears they were not expected to contribute towards PA. The shipmaster Giovanni Lombardo declared GA after two corsair attacks and a storm on his way back from Biserta in North Africa.[96] The calculation explicitly calls upon Giuseppe Rossano, who had given Lombardo a sea loan, to answer for the GA pertaining to the cost of ransoming the ship from corsairs in Biserta, plates and glass broken in the attack, damage to the cargo during the attack and anything stolen by the corsairs, as well as all things jettisoned. Damage to the sail, iron fixtures, and wooden beams on the other hand, inflicted directly by the storm, were explicitly not assigned to Rossano.[97] While the partition of damages in this case is somewhat questionable – it is not clear, for example, why things stolen by the 'Turks' after boarding should have been considered GA – there is nevertheless a division made between Averages relating to the saving of the ship on the one hand (GA), and accidental damage on the other (PA), with the creditor of the sea loan clearly only responsible for the former. The Tuscan practice thus seems to be closest to that outlined in the French *Ordonnace de la marine* (1681), with the sea loan creditor taking responsibility for GA but not for PA.[98]

One further aspect of the relationship between GA and the sea loan emerges from the documentation but can only be briefly sketched here: the validity or otherwise of 'free from Average' clauses in sea loan contracts. The French *Ordonnance de la marine* (1681) decreed that such contractual clauses were not valid: they were, however, acceptable for premium insurance contracts, and may have been equally so for a sea loan in a Tuscan context. The issue is hinted at by a case which we have already had cause to examine in some detail in Chapter 3: the case of a ship also named *Madonna del Rosario*, part-owned by shipmaster Giuseppe Reali, whose ill-starred boat party had ended with his ship sinking in Livorno harbour. In that case too, Reali had taken a series of sea loans from Livorno merchants, Lorenzo Madasco being his largest creditor.[99] When Reali was trying to secure his GA from the *Consoli*, Madasco pointed

---

[96] ASP, CM, AC, 322-27 (9 December 1670).
[97] ASP, CM, AC, 322-27 (9 December 1670), Calculation.
[98] Valin, *Nouveau commentaire* (1828), p. 436.
[99] ASP, CM, AC, 321-14 (23 July 1670).

out that his contract specifically excluded the risk of Average, and therefore asked that he be absolved of the payment.[100] The *Consoli*, however, did not pronounce on this issue when they made their judgement, instead declaring that Madasco should bring a separate case against the relevant party: no such case was ever brought, and perhaps the issue was resolved privately.[101] It seems likely that, if such clauses were being inserted into contracts, then they were generally respected. However, it could equally be a novelty, or a point of confusion or contention. Further research could provide clarification on this point.

GA as Last Resort

So far, the case studies presented by this chapter have amply demonstrated the interplay of instruments designed to manage risk. In the case of the *Cavallo Marino*, as in most cases, the GA acted as the first line of defence offering a first round of partition, before other practices such as sea loan, premium insurance, and joint ownership of assets spread the risk further. In certain eventualities, however, GA would have been the only line of defence: namely in the exceptionally unlucky occasions when the value of the GA exceeded the value of the voyage. When there has been a physical sacrifice such as a jettison, of course, the costs to be repartitioned can logically never reach 100 per cent of the total value of the venture, because this would indicate the total loss of the ship and cargo. The same is not true, however, of expenses. In these cases, insurers and sea-loan creditors were only liable up to the value they had lent or insured, but interested parties were, apparently, considered liable for these 'overloaded' GA, as demonstrated by a case settled in 1670. This is further confirmation that the 'unit' of the GA procedure was not so much the ship and cargo themselves but rather the 'venture'. Those who had invested in the venture were liable for extraordinary costs, even when these exceeded their initial investment.

An 'overloaded' GA of this nature arose as a result of the misfortunes suffered by the ship, *La Madonna della Concettione*, and its shipmaster, Giacomo Addison.[102] Having set out from Livorno early in 1667, the ship was trapped in Tripoli for six months thanks to an uprising of inhabitants of the hinterland against the city. When the ship finally managed to leave Tripoli, it was recaptured by corsairs and taken back there: the ship had suffered damage, and once it was repaired they were forced to seek their freedom once more. This having been obtained (the report does not say how), the master put into Trapani on the return journey, where the ship and cargo were sequestered for

---

[100] ASP, CM, AC, 321-14 (23 July 1670), *Testimoniale e domanda*.
[101] ASP, CM, AC, 321-14 (23 July 1670), Judgement.
[102] ASP, CM, AC, 314-9 (16 March 1668).

ten months on suspicion that some of it belonged to Frenchmen (the War of Devolution between France and Spain was still in progress). The calculation mentions expense claims made in Palermo, the result of the extended litigation mentioned by the master. While the ship was sequestered, several items of cargo were stolen by Sicilians. Finally, when the ship eventually arrived at Livorno, the master was informed that quarantine times had increased in their absence from 20 to 40 days.[103] The GA thus consisted of: stolen cargo; damage to the boat and cargo from the corsair; six months of victuals for the crew of 14 men in Tripoli and 10.5 months of victuals in Sicily; 10.5 months of victuals for a Giovanni Zecchino, the receiving merchant in Livorno, who had assisted with the legal proceedings in Palermo; 'many payments' to the guards in Trapani (probably bribes); expenses for the legal proceedings, 'three months of prison and provisions, lawyers, and writings'; 'gifts' to the ministers of the 'royal court' (most certainly bribes); and expenses of victuals and wages for the mariners made for 20 days of the 40-day quarantine which 'had the said boat not been detained in Trapani, would have been only 20'.[104] This amounted to damages of 8,009 pieces, to be repartitioned over a voyage worth just 6,509 pieces: a GA contribution rate of 123 per cent.

In this particular case, the only interested parties were the shipmaster, who also had cargo on board the ship, and a single merchant, Giovanni Zecchino. Zecchino had arranged sea loans from various parties, the value of which totalled 7,020 pieces, more than the value of the security but still not enough to cover all expenses. Nine months later, two of those who had offered money through a sea loan, Iacob and Isack Comaccio, sued Zecchino and his guarantor, Giovanni Mestura, for the partial return of their pay-out.[105] Having given a loan of 1,000 pieces, the pair had been charged 1,232 pieces in respect to the GA. The two creditors claimed, however, that while 'the Average was justly owed, they were not held to the said Average other than at a rate of 100 per cent, while for the said judgement they were condemned only to contribute with the sums given at *cambio marittimo*'.[106] They demanded the return of 232 pieces, plus a penalty of 20 per cent.[107] The was a reference the doctrine of *solve et repete*, contained in the standard printed insurance form, which stipulated that the insurer should pay-out for a claim before contesting it in court. In return, the insured would be liable for a 20 per cent surcharge if the claim was later found to be unwarranted.[108] This prevented underwriters

---

[103] ASP, CM, AC, 314-9 (16 March 1668), *Testimoniale e domanda*.
[104] ASP, CM, AC, 314-9 (16 March 1668), Calculation.
[105] ASP, CM, AC, 319-8 (6 February 1669).
[106] ASP, CM, AC, 319-8 (6 February 1669), *Testimoniale e domanda*.
[107] ASP, CM, AC, 319-8 (6 February 1669).
[108] See a copy of the form contained in Pardessus, *Collection de lois maritimes*, vol. 4, p. 607.

from endlessly litigating to defer payment.[109] It seems that the same regulation was being applied to sea loans.

The judgement went in favour of the creditors, and the principle was upheld that the giver of a sea loan was liable only up to the sum he had actually lent. However, the fact that the *Consoli* had certified a GA claim worth 123 per cent of the voyages demonstrates that no such limit existed in cases of GA. For any expenses which exceeded the total value of the voyage, therefore, GA was therefore the only form of defence – for the master, at least, since he was generally paying such expenses up front. Such a principle was probably unwelcome for cargo interests, on the other hand, as it left them liable for costs over and above their interest in the venture which they were not even able to insure against. Despite the fact that the early modern master, in contrast to his medieval counterpart, was ever more likely to be a simple agent of the merchants rather than a co-adventurer, older notions of common venture still prevailed: the collective was still held responsible for the vicissitudes of the voyage even when the participants had received no benefit from the sacrifice.[110] In the Netherlands, merchants were by this point protected against such claims thanks to the principle that no one should 'pay to the sea more than he had entrusted to the same sea', a principle laid down for the first time by the jurist Taco van Glins in 1665 but which was probably in force even earlier.[111] Comparison with the Tuscan case not only lays bear the euphemistic quality of some of these whimsical juridical maxims (it was the master, not the sea, who was out of pocket), but once again demonstrates the variety of different approaches to GA and risk sharing, not only at the microscopic level of procedural niceties and fiscal hair-splitting, but at a conceptual level, with clear implications for competing sectoral interests.

Conclusions

The evidence presented here demonstrates that GA played a substantial role within a system of risk sharing that availed itself of a range of tools simultaneously. GA was most important for the ship interests, allowing shipmasters to transmit extraordinary, and even ordinary, costs to the merchants who hired them. Given the paucity of insurance for ships themselves, GA was particularly important for the management of risks in the transport sector, though one might equally draw the conclusion that there was less demand for insurance thanks to the protection which the sea loan and GA already offered. To the maritime community in general, GA provided a first line of defence, spreading a whole range of costs which are not generally considered by the normative

[109] Addobbati, 'Italy 1500–1800', p. 52.
[110] De ruyyscher, 'Maxims, principles, and legal change', pp. 274–5.
[111] Dreijer, *The Power and Pains*, p. 70.

literature. But it could also represent the only line of defence, in those unusual but not unheard-of situations in which certain risks, particularly those posed by conflict, resulted in excessive costs. Several technical aspects of GA's relationship with other risk instruments in Tuscany have been elucidated here: that the sea loan covered GA but not PA, that the creditor contributed to the damages according to the GA contribution rate, and that the sea loan was, in many if not all respects, taken to follow the same principles and legal provisions that premium insurance did with regard to risk transfer.

The picture that emerges from these sources is therefore not the linear institutional progression outlined by North and his followers. The importance of combining techniques is evident, with the extensive use of the sea loan being particularly revelatory. The mindset of the early modern businessperson was not that of the mathematician, arriving at elegant and accurate solutions, but that of the medieval stonemason, drawing on experience and intuition and distributing the weight with plenty of arches. The story of risk management may, in the long run, be one of progress, but it is not a story of stadial evolution.

Premium insurance did circumscribe GA in the end, but not straight away, and not because premium insurance represented a more sophisticated approach to risk that obviated earlier methods except in a few, well-defined situations. Here the chronology is key. Let us consider a question that has been hanging over the arguments of this book for some time now: why, if GA was so master-friendly – open to wide use and even abuse – did it go unchallenged for so long? Why did vociferous criticism and reform attempts emerge only in the 1780s? The answer lies not in any challenge posed by institution of insurance itself, but in the changes taking place in the way underwriting was organised. By the second half of eighteenth century, ever-increasing demand was incentivising the creation of profit-seeking, joint-stock insurance companies who could draw upon large reserves of capital.[112] Such a transition was not nearly complete by the 1780s, but was by this point affecting even those traditional markets like Livorno that favoured time-honoured practices.[113] The emergence of underwriters as a sectoral interest that did not overlap with merchants – for whom insurance was their main occupation rather than one of a number of maritime-business activities – accelerated the eventual 'disciplining' of GA, already presented for these purposes as 'anachronistic' in the way it operated if not yet in principle: a troublesome instrument that followed different rules everywhere and periodically upset the company's balance sheets. These dynamics will be considered further in the conclusion to this book.

---

[112] Addobbati, 'Italy 1500–1800', pp. 67–8.
[113] Addobbati, 'Italy 1500–1800', p. 71.

Conclusion

This book has provided an in-depth study of maritime risk sharing in the early modern Mediterranean and contextualised this within a broader sweep of history that stretches from the Roman Empire to the present day. The central protagonist in this story has been the institution now known as GA, a legal practice which crystalised out of earlier risk-sharing practices and continued to be refined and adapted over the period. Such a study is timely, with the question of risk sharing once again on the international agenda as humanity faces increasing levels of danger and uncertainty from both natural phenomena and growing international instability: the United Nations Inter-Agency Standing Committee, for instance, has recently established a risk-sharing platform to discuss ways in which international humanitarian organisations should share risk.[1] Even GA itself has been in the international spotlight, thanks in part to the well-publicised case of the ship *Ever Given*, its owners declaring a GA worth a reported half-a-billion dollars after it was finally dislodged from the Suez Canal in 2021.[2] The increased attention has led to renewed criticism of the institution from some quarters. After briefly summarising the historical findings of the study, therefore, this concluding section will turn to the implications for discussions around the present and future of GA.

This study examined normative and juridical sources from across Europe and the Mediterranean and compared these to GA records preserved in the Tuscan archives, finding significant differences between the two. This serves as another reminder to historians of the dangers of relying too heavily on normative juridical sources as evidence for how institutions worked on the ground. It even cautions against using these works as our departure points, allowing them to condition our thinking and our categories of analysis. The *Llibre del Consolat de Mar* was a very real source of normative authority throughout our period, but its provisions were in many ways an inadequate practical means of regulating GA, because the practices evidenced by the *Llibre* only distantly resembled the procedure that now existed on the ground. The *Llibre* and the *Lex Rhodia de Iactu* had a clear impact on the shape of the sea protests, as the continued importance of the consultation suggests, but their influence on the essence of the procedure was limited. By the very end of our

---

[1] 'Risk Sharing Framework' (9 June 2023), <https://interagencystandingcommittee.org/grand-bargain-official-website/risk-sharing-framework> [accessed 30 January 2024].

[2] Sarll, 'The "Ever Given"', p. 8.

period, jurists like Giuseppe Casaregi and Carlo Targa were wrestling with the tension between written norms and merchant usages, but resolution was a long way off: some civil law maxims, meanwhile, were indeed 'subtleties' that had little to do with operational practice.[3]

The fact that GA was subject to significant procedural variations across space and time has been amply demonstrated, confirming what Jolien Kruit has already proved with reference to the normative material.[4] But this study has also gone further, showing that ideas about how and when common contribution should work varied much more than has previously been claimed. Different situations involving common contribution would be crystalised under the rubric of GA only in the early modern period. In the Netherlands this was probably accomplished through a mixture of bottom-up change in operational practice and top-down interventions by jurists and states; in Tuscany, it seems that practice was in some ways ahead of the jurists.[5] Furthermore, there was not even the same agreement on GA in principle. Some merchants positioned GA closer to a strictly reciprocal form of mutual indemnity rather than as an equitable obligation arising on account of a sacrifice being made for the common benefit.[6] The idea that GA testifies to the existence of a lex mercatoria or lex maritima, or even can be used to stand for a common mercantile culture, simply does not stand up. The fundamental point with regard to the lex mercatoria is, as Emily Kadens and Albrecht Cordes point out, that merchants could get by very well without it.[7] As has been shown here, the stamp of approval from the court was often needed in order to 'export' the judgement to other centres, but these exported judgements were usually respected, if sometimes begrudgingly.[8]

GA's operation was not shaped by legal and economic considerations alone: it also clearly bore the imprint of political economy.[9] One of the most evident and consistent variations in Tuscan procedure was the practice of regularly allowing Northern masters to use a form of self-assessment for damages to the ship. The Tuscan authorities were willing to countenance procedural irregularities, and to allow Northerners to arrange proceedings in whatever way they saw fit, a thing which is consistent with the culture of the free port and Tuscany's broader maritime strategy. The importance of private agreement,

---

[3] See Rossi, 'Civilians and insurance'.
[4] See Kruit, 'General average'.
[5] De ruysscher, 'Maxims, principles and legal change', pp. 261–2; Dreijer, *The Power and Pains*, pp. 89–133.
[6] p. 185.
[7] Kadens, 'The myth', p. 1181; Cordes, 'Lex maritima?', p. 82.
[8] Dyble, 'Lex mercatoria', pp. 686–7.
[9] See Dyble, 'Divide and rule'.

cooperation, and even collusion in reaching outcomes is clear, even when resolution was ostensibly sought through an official channel.

GA's antiquity and supposed staticity are implicit assumptions baked into 'evolutionary' accounts of institutional development.[10] Rather than simply an archaic forefunner of 'modern' premium insurance, however, GA continued to be used in concert with other risk-management techniques, including premium insurance and sea loan. The GA that emerges from the archive of the *Consoli del Mare* was a capacious instrument and remained a useful part of the risk-sharing system, as one in a series of load-bearing arches which progressively distributed the weight of disasters through increasingly large communities of risk.[11] In this sense, the benefits of different risk-management instruments – GA, sea loan, premium insurance – were cumulative; one instrument did not replace the other. At the same time, these older risk instruments also responded individually to some particular demands of the seventeenth-century marketplace. A sea loan gave masters cash up front, preventing delays which the master might otherwise have incurred whilst seeking enforcement of insurance pay-outs via the courts.[12] On a more profound level, the historical and geographical variety within a single 'institution' offers an ontological challenge to those accounts of institutional development that tend to see institutions as discrete, well-defined entities existing largely independent of one another.[13]

Above all, GA remained an important cost- and risk-management instrument for the transport sector – an element sometimes overlooked in business history, which more readily takes the merchant as its protagonist. In Chapter 5, it was demonstrated in quantitative terms how GA could defray carriers' operating costs. The case of the *Cavallo Marino* is one of many concrete examples of Ascanio Baldasseroni's assertion that GA was the secret of the Galley of Salamis, whose parts were surreptitiously replaced over time.[14] This was a particular boon to a master who owned his vessel, or a share in it – the unsung foot soldier of maritime commerce who regularly endured the 'desperate perils, hard slogging, dogged grubbing for cargoes in ports from Livorno to Alexandria, ongoing disputes ... and small profit' which were the quotidian reality of trade in the Mediterranean.[15] More generally, it helped to keep costs low for the ship-owners. In this respect, a structural inevitability built into GA was exacerbated by the master's control over the evidence on which decisions were based. The advantage was then compounded by the court's willingness

---

[10] North, *Institutions*, p. 127; Harris, 'General average and all the rest'.
[11] p. 183.
[12] p. 178.
[13] Harris, *Going the Distance*.
[14] Baldasseroni, *Delle assicurazioni marittime*, vol. 3, p. 15; ASP, CM, AC, 319-20 (18 March 1669).
[15] Heywood, 'The English in the Mediterranean, 1600–1630', p. 34.

to aid them in making their accounts legally watertight, and in the readiness of the *Consoli* to give the master the benefit of the doubt in their judgements, even if the Pisan *Consoli* do not appear to have been particularly unusual in this respect. Unless one had chanced upon specific local information, it was very difficult to challenge a GA claim.

It is likely that this state of affairs was acceptable and perhaps even desirable at the beginning of our period. It cannot be that merchants were simply uninterested, as Pierallini suggested in the eighteenth century: the evidence examined here has shown a surprising level of merchant involvement in cases.[16] After all, unforeseen costs were part and parcel of seventeenth-century trade; allowing these to be borne by the carrier was simply unrealistic. Furthermore, despite the imbalance between ship and cargo interests – and in many ways because of it – seventeenth-century GA did in fact facilitate commerce, above and beyond its role as a risk-management tool: first of all, because of the benefits it provided to the ship, particularly the ability to partition some ordinary wear and tear, it helped to keep freight costs low. Had it not been possible to defray some of these expenses, shipmasters and ship-owners would have had to charge higher prices in order to make a profit on their voyages. This could have disincentivised investment by providing upfront costs. Secondly, by reducing upfront costs for ship-owners, GA helped out a sector of tight margins that quite literally kept the entire maritime economy afloat. Merchants were, at any rate, often shareholders in vessels in this period and were thus not repeatedly on the same side of the GA equation.[17]

The gradual disciplining of maritime violence was probably responsible in some measure for changes in attitude towards the end of the eighteenth century. The Mediterranean practice of corsairing was gradually halted, and violence between states became more restricted and better regulated whilst navigational technology improved.[18] In such circumstances, it may have seemed less obvious to merchants that the transport sector was worthy of such latitude in GA procedures. What is perhaps more important in this respect, however, were changes to the nature of the insurance market which saw insurance become an increasingly specialised sector in its own right. In particular, the final quarter of the eighteenth century saw a huge increase in demand for insurance with the onset of the American and French wars, and institutional change followed accordingly.[19] Underwriter was no longer one of many hats worn by the merchant; GA was a now a time-consuming and irritating expense item on the balance sheet of a specialised underwriter. Here we might once

---

[16] ASL, *Governo civile e militare*, 977, f. 29r.
[17] Davis, *English Shipping Industry*, pp. 81–7.
[18] Addobbati, *Commercio, rischio, guerra*, pp. 115–17.
[19] Doe and Pearson, 'Organizational choice in UK marine insurance', p. 53.

again repeat the words of Ascanio Baldasseroni, staunch opponent of spurious GA claims, and author of a treatise on insurance law published in 1786:

> the idea of facilitating commerce, very useful and necessary for the public good, together with the favour shown to shipmasters – who were, once upon a time, regarded as worthy subjects of the highest consideration for the courage that they demonstrated in confronting the risks of navigation (these days rendered so easy) – has undoubtedly opened the door to many abuses, especially in the regulation of Averages.[20]

Navigation was not and would never be 'easy', of course, but Baldasseroni would not be the last to lament the favour shown to shipmasters. GA was on its way to becoming the 'anachronistic' bugbear of marine insurers, who would follow Baldesseroni in depicting GA as an instrument much more appropriate to an unspecified point in the past.

The Present and Future of GA

Just as international organisations begin to show a renewed interest in the possibilities of risk sharing, GA itself is once again under renewed scrutiny in some quarters after the grounding of the ship *Ever Given* in the Suez Canal. Yet calls for reform and abolition of GA are nothing new, as we have seen. In the years leading up to the reforms to the York-Antwerp Rules agreed in Vancouver in 2004, the International Union of Marine Insurance (IUMI) called for limiting the scope of GA by restricting it to 'common safety' demands, i.e. that any expense admitted should be strictly related to saving the ship and cargo in a situation of immediate peril. The demand that GA be reigned in in this way has been periodically made for at least the last 300 years.[21] There were also calls to abolish GA in scholarly literature made over the same period, following in a tradition which is only somewhat younger.[22] For GA's most trenchant abolitionists, the institution is a remnant of a 'primitive era' which points to 'retardation rather than advancement'.[23] For the legal scholar Proshanto Mukherjee, it is an 'anachronism rooted in a romantic past'. For the Liverpool underwriter C.H. Johnson in 1925 it was 'an effete but time-honoured custom ... so opposed to modern ideals of economy and time,

---

[20] Baldasseroni, *Delle assicurazioni marittime*, vol. 1, p. 266.
[21] Cornah, 'The road to Vancouver', p. 156.
[22] Mukherjee, 'The anachronism in maritime law'; on this see also Knut Selmer, *The Survival of General Average: A Necessity or an Anachronism?* (Oslo: Oslo University Press, 1958); Musolino, 'A relic of the past'.
[23] Mukherjee, 'The anachronism in maritime law', pp. 196, 199.

labour and money'.[24] For the Lloyd's underwriter Douglas Owen in 1894, the system of GA was 'stupendous and compound-comminuted', sustained by 'Average adjusters and legal faddists'.[25] The 1877 Report of the Committee of Lloyd's on GA found it 'vast and complicated ... almost intolerable', and its representative at the Antwerp Conference that birthed the York-Antwerp Rules claimed it was 'a nest of fraud and abuses ... rendered obsolete by modern insurance'.[26]

Stripped of its more bombastic rhetoric and amorphous references to 'modernity', 'rationality', and 'progress', the practical argument against GA can be boiled down to the fact that it has become too complicated thanks to the number of interests involved. It therefore costs too much and takes too long to resolve, to everyone's eventual detriment.[27] In short, the transaction costs now outweigh the benefit. This central problem is exacerbated by the 'different laws' and 'divergent practices' regarding GA that have remained resistant to decades of attempts at systemisation.[28] An additional issue sometimes raised is that the majority of GAs were likely to have been caused by ship or crew fault, and that the procedure is thus also inequitable.[29] Critics maintain that insurance could fill any gap left by GA, with hull insurance policies covering extraordinary expenses incurred by the vessel, and insurance policies covering sacrificed property.[30] Absorption clauses – whereby the hull insurer absorbs GA-eligible expenses that are too small to warrant a GA declaration – presage how this might work in practice.[31] If this proves too big a step for the international maritime business community, many have hoped – as the IUMI did in the run up to 2004 – that GA can be returned to its 'original' focus on common safety rather than taking on an ever-increasing remit thanks to the common benefit approach.[32]

This criticism is not new, but more recents articulations of it threaten to introduce a geopolitical edge into discussions that were previously technical in nature and responded to sectoral interests. In 2022 in reaction to the *Ever Given*

---

[24] Quoted in Mukherjee, 'The anachronism in maritime law', p. 200.

[25] Ibid.

[26] International Union of Marine Insurers, 'Position paper of the International Union of Marine Insurers ("IUMI"): York-Antwerp Rules – CMI Questionaire' (2013), available at <https://comitemaritime.org/work/review-of-the-rules-on-general-average/> [accessed 31 January 2024], p. 3.

[27] Mukherjee, 'The anachronism in maritime law', p. 198.

[28] Ibid.

[29] International Union of Marine Insurers, 'Position paper', p. 3.

[30] Mukherjee, 'The anachronism in maritime law', p. 200.

[31] 'General Average Absorption Clause 2018', <www.bimco.org/contracts-and-clauses/bimco-clauses/current/general-average-absorption-clause-2018> [accessed 30 January 2024].

[32] Mukherjee, 'The anachronism in maritime law', p. 208.

case, Xie Ming argued that the *Ever Given* case may not qualify as a GA under Chinese law, since Article 193 of China's maritime law outlines a 'common safety' approach to GA and the vessel faced no immediate peril whilst lodged in the canal (there is no reference to the YAR in his article).[33] Since the majority of the half-a-billion-dollar claim is reported to be an undisclosed fee paid in compensation to the Suez Canal Authority, there would certainly be a case against the GA when defined in this way.[34] Xie then goes on to suggest that GA might be improved by allowing just 50 per cent damages to be made good through collective contribution when the property involved is not in immediate peril (i.e. a common-benefit situation). Though this is presented as an expansion of GA's remit (as indeed it is if we start from Article 193 of China's Maritime Law), when compared to the YAR it actually represents a diminuation of its scope. 'As China grows more powerful', Xie concludes, 'it is necessary to examine the impact of this incident on the country in order to safeguard China and the world's shipping interests'.[35]

Whatever the precise motivation behind connecting reform of GA to a broader recognition of China's power, the argument presents some curious parallels with a memorandum received by the Tuscan authorities in 1670. The English resident, John Finch, also expressed dissatisfaction with GA rules; he too claimed that his own national state's legislation could better protect merchants by providing an arbitrary limit on the 'pretensions' of shipmasters.[36] The seventeenth-century English state, finding itself in a new position of considerable naval and commercial power, was not so interested in the details of General Average law in the end, but did see in its difficulties an opportunity to obtain greater jurisdiction and sway over commerce.[37] It is possible that Xie's remark that to the effect that 'the revision ... of maritime legal systems ... will provide not only assurance ... but also proposals from China for the formulation of maritime legislation and regional rules by the countries along the routes' hints at a not wholly dissimilar agenda.

This book is not an analysis of contemporary maritime risk management so will not claim any special insight into GA's future. My own opinion, for what it is worth, is that any benefits derived by abolishing GA (which is, at any rate, dependent on a clause voluntarily inserted into freight contacts) would clearly be outweighed by the confusion, uncertainty, and delay resulting in the medium-term from its abolition. Furthermore, many of the contentious issues – master and crew liability for the accident, admissibility of certain expenses – would presumably

[33] Xie Ming, 'Legality, rationality of general average for MV Ever Given' (2022), <https://law.asia/legality-and-rationality-mv-ever-given/> [accessed 10 August 2023].
[34] Sarll, 'The "Ever Given"', p. 8.
[35] Ibid.
[36] p. 121.
[37] p. 129.

remain. Where a history of risk sharing can contribute to the debate more definitely regards the specifically historical claims that often accompany arguments about GA, which, interestingly, tend to be lent upon more by critics of the institution rather than defenders. The first point is that GA has always attracted a degree of controversy ever since the Late Middle Ages when merchants stopped travelling with their goods and masters tended to become agents rather than co-adventurers.[38] There is a long history of jurists, merchants, and above all professional underwriters complaining about GA, and, in the latter case, calling for its abolition. This observation is not a simple declaration of *plus ça change, plus c'est la même chose*: the fact that there have always been critics does not automatically imply that their complaints can thus be safely ignored. But it does mean that the suggestion, repeated for almost 200 years, that very recent developments have rendered GA unworkable and unacceptable should be taken with a grain of salt. It should certainly put paid to the lazy argument that GA should be abolished because it is inherently 'unmodern', 'anachronistic', or 'unsophisticated'.

GA has always by its very nature tended to be something of a shipmasters' tool. Even though shipmasters now have much less opportunity to defray running costs via GA, the structure of the instrument tends to arouse suspicion on the part of cargo interests (and their insurers) who are by the laws of mathematical average far more likely to be on the receiving end of GA declaration than its beneficiaries. Furthermore, voluntary actions on the part of the crew on the one hand and the influence of outside forces on the other are disentangled only with great difficulty, as even the ancient Greeks knew.[39] Furthermore, GA has never been a straightforward procedure to administrate. Early modern calculators may not have had to deal with modern container ships, but they still had to deal with tens or even hundreds of merchants in multiple jurisdictions and with multiple cargoes – all of this using significantly less information technology than we have at our disposal. An interesting statistical comparison can be offered in this regard. In an analysis of over 1,700 cases from the 1990s, fees for Average adjusters were estimated to represent 10 per cent of GA payments: in seventeenth-century Tuscany, the administrative and legal costs of processing cases represented 9 per cent of all payments.[40]

A related observation concerns the desire to return GA to its 'original' state by restricting its scope to the common safety of the vessel and excluding expenses made for the common benefit of the voyage.[41] This strand of criticism likewise has a long history:

---

[38] Addobbati, 'Principles and developments', p. 164; De ruysscher, 'Maxims, principles and legal change', p. 275.

[39] See pp. 93–4.

[40] International Union of Marine Insurers, 'Position paper', p. 3.

[41] Xie, 'Legality, rationality of general average'; Mukherjee, 'The anachronism in maritime law', p. 208. See Cornah, 'The road to Vancouver'.

> I am not able to approve it, because Average, or rather maritime contribution, does not have a proper place unless there should be a cut or a jettison in order to lighten a labouring ship ... I believe that these expenses ought not to be made good by the merchants or the owners of the merchandise, as they are more made for the fitting out and repairing of the ship than on account of saving the goods.[42]

Such sentiments were expressed as early as 1707 by Giuseppe Casaregi. Yet the apparently straightfoward continuity between the *Lex Rhodia de Iactu* and modern GA is quite illusory. In the many intervening centuries, there were lots of different rules regarding common contribution, which, in some cases, expanded the institution into a full-blown form of mutual insurance. The consolidation of these practices under the rubric of '(General) Average' in a form that we can broadly recognise only occurred in the early modern period.

For most of its history, moreover, GA has been a tool for the common benefit. Even the collection of Roman juridical opinions contained in the *Lex Rhodia* does not explicitly limit GA to instances of the common safety, and Roman laws concerneding contribution probably expanded in scope over time. For most of GA's history, it has been extraordinary expenses – not the straightforward cases of jettisoned cargo for common safety – that have occasioned the largest and most controversial GAs, not least because their 'voluntary' and sometimes 'extraordinary' aspects are often more difficult to prove. The 'original' GA restricted to preserving common safety in peril has more often than not been an exercise in wishful thinking. Ironically, for an instrument whose archetype was jettison during a storm, early modern GA was most useful when confronting the unpredictability of human affairs.

---

[42] Casaregi, *Discursus legales de commercio*, vol. 1, p. 281.

APPENDIX: ALL CASE STUDIES

Register	Case Number	Judgement Date	Ship Name	Voyage Details	GA Type	Amount Requested (Scudi)	Contribution Rate
25	3	28 June 1600	*Santa Caterina*	Cheese from Cagliari to Livorno	Jettison	428.00	9.20%
	8	30 May 1600	*Santa Maria Buonaventura*	Grain from Agrigento to Livorno/Viareggio	Jettison	280.00	5.54%
	21	16 May 1600	*Santa Maria Buonaventura*	Wine and feathers from Napoli to Livorno/Genoa	Jettison	342.00	17.13%
	22	5 May 1600	*Santa Maria Bona Ventura*	Wine from Napoli to Livorno	Jettison	56.50	5.95%
	23	4 May 1600	*Santa Maria Buona Ventura*	Wine, galls, windmill from Napoli to Livorno	Jettison	295.00	13.52%
	24	13 April 1600	*Corvo Volante*	Ivory from Olinda to Lisbon/Livorno	Jettison/ cut sail	1422.00	2.59%
	26	10 April 1600	*Santa Maria de Trinide*	Wool and specie from Cadis and Alicante to Livorno and Genoa	Jettison/cut rope/beaching	-	
	28	8 April 1600	*Francesca*	Leather from Barbary Coast to Livorno	Cut mast/ jettison of ship equipment	51.00	1.09%
27	26	1 September 1600	*Santa Maria della Nunziata*	Grain from Trapani to Livorno	Jettison	126.28	2.51%
	30	31 November 1600	*San Torpe*	Grain from Fellonica to Pisa	Jettison	148.23	28.12%

33	8 November 1600	*La Squarcia Bocca*	Cartagena and Alicante to Genova and Livorno	Cut boat/cut mast/jettison	1428.25	1.58%
28	15 December 1600	*Jonas*	Unknown cargo from Arkhangelsk to Livorno	Jettison	-	-
196	2 January 1639	*Nostra Signora del Carmine e San Francesco*	Grain from Porto Baudino to Genoa	Jettison/ cut mast	418.00	28.95%
	2 January 1639	*Santo Spirito e San Pietro Buena Ventura*	Beans from Porto Baudino to Genoa	Jettison/ cut mast	373.00	29.67%
197	14 February 1639	*Santa Maria*	Grain from Brindisi to Napoli	Jettison	1112.00	36.43%
	26 April 1640	*Tre Re*	Grain from Ancona to Livorno	Jettison	282.00	2.21%
	6 July 1640	*La Madonna di Monte Nero*	Cheese from Cagliari to Livorno	Jettison	842.00	30.41%
198	14 August 1640	*L'Annutiata Buona Ventura*	Silver, feathers, misc. from Algiers to Livorno	Jettison	1608.00	7.05%
199	15 November 1640	*San Domenico*	Unknown from Lisbon to Livorno	Expenses in warning ship	192.50 (pieces)	-
	20 November 1640	*Il Beato Felice Buona Ventura*	Cheese from Cagliari to Livorno and Genoa	Jettison/ broken mast	1743.00	23.70%

Register	Case Number	Date	Ship Name	Voyage	GA Type	Amount Requested (Pieces)	Contribution Rate
318	26	22 January 1669	*Speranza Incoronata*	Hides and caviar from Arkhangelsk to Livorno	Jettison/cut ropes/hired help/combat	11321.00	12.96%
319	3	30 January 1669	*La Madonna dei Poveri*	Fish and cheese from Messina to Livorno	Jettison/small boat cut away	989.00	41.10%
	13	28 February 1669	*San Giovanni*	Caviare and hides from Arkhangelsk to Livorno	Cut mast/ equipment cut away	1738.00	1.74%
	18	10 March 1669	*San Francisco di Paola*	Tuna and grain from Trapani to Livorno	Jettison	297.00	16.97%
	20	18 March 1669	*Cavallo Marino*	Various cargo from Alexandretta to Livorno	Cottimo/ avania/ broken masts/ unscheduled stops	1532.00	7.20%
	25	18 April 1670	*Madonna delle Grazie*	Grain from Lazio to Genoa	Jettison	351.50	14.70%
	28	28 April 1670	*Mercante Fiorentino*	Oils from Brindisi to London	Cut ropes/ beaching	784.80	4.55%
320	2	9 May 1670	*Madonna della Grazia*	Grain from Barletta to Genoa	Jettison/ cut masts	174.52	2.76%
	7	28 May 1670	*Principe Enrico Casimiro*	Leathers, wax and other cargo from Izmir to Amsterdam	Combat/ lost time	4832.00	3.51%

321	14	23 July 1670	Madonna del Rosario	Diverse merchandise from Livorno to Algiers	Recovery of sunken ship	393.00	6.79%
	25	25 August 1670	Madonna del Carmine	Grain from Croton to Livorno/Genoa	Broken mast (GA refused)	N/A	N/A
	30	30 August 1670	Alice and Francis	Diverse merchandise from London to Izmir	Combat	1935.64	2.28%
322	16	9 November 1670	La Madonna delle Gratie	Diverse merchandise from Constantinople to Marseille	Avania	1804.00	5.57%
	21	28 November 1670	Fonte Santo	Wool and leather from Izmir to Livorno	Avania and cottimo	453.00	5.55%
	27	9 December 1670	Madonna del Rosario	Diverse merchandise from Biserta to Livorno	Corsair attacks and captures	1046.64	27.02%
	30	15 December 1670	Santa Teresa	Salt from Salé to Livorno	Jettison	458.00	19.08%
	33	16 December 1670	Madonna del Carmine e S. Iacinto	Diverse merchandise from Izmir to Livorno	Broken mast/ avania/ cottimo/bribe	627.00	9.64%
	39	23 December 1670	La Madonna della Gratia	Diverse merchandise from Alexandria to Livorno	Avania / jettison	426.75	4.53%
417	1	9 January 1700	Galera Blosson	Leather from Salé to Livorno	Cut rope	111.25	4.28%
	5	19 January 1700	La Gran Pesca Olandese	Diverse merchandise Rotterdam to Livorno	Press of sail, rigging damage	479.50	2.41%

16	9 February 1700	Giacomo	Diverse merchandise Marseille to Alexandretta	Press of sail, rigging damage	309.50	15.37%
27	23 March 1700	La Madonna del Carmine	Wine, spice, fish from Lipari to Livorno	Jettison	416.50	9.35%
7	6 April 1700	La Venturiera	Beans from Tunis to Livorno	Jettison/ cut ropes	551.00	11.30%
11	14 May 1700	Sante Anime del Purgatorio	Diverse merchandise from Livorno to Tétuoan and back	Forced stop/ quarantine/ jettison	1222.00	16.95%
12	25 May 1700	N.a Signora delle Grazie e S. Niccola di Bari	Grain from Palermo to Livorno/Genoa	Jettison/ rigging damage	194.56	4.15%
20	1 July 1700	S. Anna e L'anime del purgatorio	Cheese and salt from Trapani to Livorno	Jettison/ rigging damage	694.56	41.90%
21	1 July 1700	S. Giuseppe	Diverse merchandise from Tunis to Livorno	Cut ropes/ jettisons	289.50	5.93%
9	17 August 1700	La Tunisina	Oils from Tunis to Livorno	Broken masts	110.00	1.48%
27	11 September 1700	S. Niccola	Grain from Talamone to Livorno	Jettison	197.00	29.31%
14	9 November 1700	L S.ma Annuntiata e S Fra. Xaviero	Grain from Licata to Livorno/Genoa	Small Boat/ jettison	669.13	12.39%

Bibliography

Primary Sources

Manuscript and Archival Collections

Archivio di Stato di Pisa

Consoli del Mare, Atti Civili, 23
Consoli del Mare, Atti Civili, 24
Consoli del Mare, Atti Civili, 25
Consoli del Mare, Atti Civili, 26
Consoli del Mare, Atti Civili, 27
Consoli del Mare, Atti Civili, 28
Consoli del Mare, Atti Civili, 196
Consoli del Mare, Atti Civili, 197
Consoli del Mare, Atti Civili, 198
Consoli del Mare, Atti Civili, 199
Consoli del Mare, Atti Civili, 230
Consoli del Mare, Atti Civili, 231
Consoli del Mare, Atti Civili, 232
Consoli del Mare, Atti Civili, 233
Consoli del Mare, Atti Civili, 234
Consoli del Mare, Atti Civili, 235
Consoli del Mare, Atti Civili, 236
Consoli del Mare, Atti Civili, 237
Consoli del Mare, Atti Civili, 238
Consoli del Mare, Atti Civili, 239
Consoli del Mare, Atti Civili, 240
Consoli del Mare, Atti Civili, 241
Consoli del Mare, Atti Civili, 242
Consoli del Mare, Atti Civili, 243
Consoli del Mare, Atti Civili, 244
Consoli del Mare, Atti Civili, 245
Consoli del Mare, Atti Civili, 246
Consoli del Mare, Atti Civili, 247
Consoli del Mare, Atti Civili, 248
Consoli del Mare, Atti Civili, 249
Consoli del Mare, Atti Civili, 250
Consoli del Mare, Atti Civili, 251
Consoli del Mare, Atti Civili, 252
Consoli del Mare, Atti Civili, 253

Consoli del Mare, Atti Civili, 314
Consoli del Mare, Atti Civili, 318
Consoli del Mare, Atti Civili, 319
Consoli del Mare, Atti Civili, 320
Consoli del Mare, Atti Civili, 321
Consoli del Mare, Atti Civili, 322
Consoli del Mare, Atti Civili, 358
Consoli del Mare, Atti Civili, 417
Consoli del Mare, Atti Civili, 418
Consoli del Mare, Atti Civili, 419
Consoli del Mare, Atti Civili, 420

Consoli del Mare, Miscellanea di Manoscritti, 112

Consoli del Mare, Suppliche, 967
Consoli del Mare, Suppliche, 978
Consoli del Mare, Suppliche, 985
Consoli del Mare, Suppliche, 989
Consoli del Mare, Suppliche, 1015
Consoli del Mare, Suppliche, 1016

Archivio di Stato di Livorno

Governo civile e militare, 977
Capitano, poi Governatore Auditore Vicario, 269
Magistrato poi Dipartimento di Sanità, 68

Archivio di Stato di Firenze

Auditore dei Benefici Ecclesiastici poi Segretaria del Regio Diritto, 5682
Auditore poi Segretario delle Riformagioni, 116
Inventario, N/484
Miscellanea Medicea, 358
Quaratesi, 261
Quaratesi, 357
Serristori, 483

The National Archives, UK

Accessed at State Papers Online: <www.gale.com/intl/primary-sources/state-papers-online> [accessed 18 August 2021].

Calendar of State Papers, Domestic Series, of the reign of Charles II, vol. 10.
Calendar of State Papers, Domestic Series, of the reign of Charles II, vol. 12.
Calendar of State Papers, Domestic Series, of the reign of Charles II, vol. 15.

High Court of the Admiralty, 13

State Papers Domestic: Supplementary, SP 46, vol. 137.
State Papers Foreign, Tuscany, 1582–1780, SP 98, vol. 11.
State Papers Foreign, Tuscany, 1582–1780, SP 98, vol. 12.

Printed Primary Sources

Contemporary books and articles

Code noir, *Le code noir, ou Recueil des reglemens rendus jusqu'à present* (L.F. Prault: Paris, 1788).
Degli statuti civili della Serenissima Repubblica di Genova (Genoa: Giuseppe Pavoni, 1613).
Aristotle (trans. Terence Irwin), *Nicomachean Ethics* (Cambridge, MA: Hackett Publishing Company, 2019).
Azuni, Domenico Alberto, *Dizionario universale ragionato della giurisprudenza mercantile*, 4 vols (Livorno: Glauco Masi, 1823).
Baldasseroni, Ascanio, *Delle assicurazioni marittime*, 5 vols (Florence: Bonducciana, 1786–1803).
Balderston, Marion, *James Claypoole's Letter Book: London and Philadelphia 1681–1684* (San Marino, CA: The Huntingdon Library, 1967).
Beawes, Wyndham, *Lex mercatoria rediviva* (Dublin: Williams, 1773).
Benecke, William, *A Treatise on the Principles Indemnity in Marine Insurance, Bottomry and Respondentia* (London: Baldwin, Cradock, and Joy, 1824).
Bolaño, Juan de Hevia, *Labyrinthus commercii terrestris et navalis* (Florence: Petrus Antonius Brigonci, 1702).
Casaregi, Giuseppe Lorenzo Maria, *Consolato del mare colla spiegazione di Giuseppe Maria Casaregi* (Venice: Silvestro Gnoato, 1802).
—*Discursus legales de commercio*, 2nd edn, 2 vols (Florence: Io. Cajetanum Tartinium, & Sanctem Franchium, 1719).
Cicero, Marcus Tullius (trans. Benjamin Patrick Newton), *On Duties* (Ithaca: Cornell University Press, 2016).
Coppi, Giovanni Vincenzo, *Annali memorie ed huomini illustri di Sangimignano* (Florence: Cesare e Francesco Bindi, 1695).
Costanzo, Giuseppe Buonfiglio, *Messina città nobilissima* (Venice: Chiaramonte, 1606).
Curicke, Reinhold, Franz Stypmann (ed.), *Resolutio questiorum illustrum ad ius maritimum pertinentium in scriptorum iure nautico et maritimo fasciculus* (Halle-Magdeburg: Sumtibus Orphanotrophei, 1740).
De Sérionne, Jacques Accarias, *Les intérêts des nations de l'Europe, dévélopés relativement au commerce* (Leiden: Elie Luzac, 1766).
Émérigon, Balthazard-Marie, *Traité des assurances et des contrats à la grosse*, 2 vols (Marseille: Jean Mossy, 1783).
Magens, Nicolas, *An Essay on Insurances* (London: J. Haberkorn, 1755).
Malynes, Gerard, *Consuetudo vel lex mercatoria*, 3rd edn (London: Redmayne, 1685).
Merchant, N.G., *The Compleat Tradesman, or The Exact Dealers Daily Companion* (London: John Dunton, 1684).
Michelot, Henri and Thomas Corbett, *The Mediterranean Pilot* (London: Richard and William Mount and Thomas Page, on Tower Hill, 1715).
Molloy, Charles, *De iure maritimo et navali or A Treatise of Affairs Maritime and of Commerce* (London: Walthoe, 1744).

Moniglia, Giovanni Andrea, 'La serva nobile' (1661), in *Delle poesie drammatiche*, 3 vols (Florence: Alla Condotta, 1689), vol. 3.

Morrison, Richard, 'General Average', *The Assurance Magazine, and Journal of the Institute of Actuaries* 12 (1866), 350–61.

Mun, Thomas, *England's Treasure by Forraign Trade* (London: J.G. for Thomas Clark, 1664).

Pardessus, Jean-Marie, *Collection de lois maritimes antérieures au 18. siècle*, 6 vols (Paris: L'Imprimerie Royale, 1837), vol. 4.

Park, James Allan, *A System of the Law of Marine Insurances* (London: T. Whieldon, 1787).

Peckius, Petrus, Arnold Vinnius, and Johannes Laurentius, *Ad rem nauticum pertinentes* (Amsterdam: Joannis Henrici Boom, 1708).

Pothier, Robert Joseph, *Traite du contrat d'assurance* (Marseille: Roux-Rambert, 1810).

Pufendorf, Samuel, *De jure naturae et gentium* (Frankfurt: Sumptibus Friderici Knochii, 1684).

Roberts, Lewes, *The Merchants Map of Commerce*, 3rd edn (London: R. Horn, 1677).

Rocco, Francesco, *Responsorum legalium cum decisionibus*, 2 vols (Naples: Luca Antonio Fusci, 1655), vol. 2.

Stracca, Benvenuto, *De mercatvra, sev mercatore tractatvs*, ed. Marco Cian (Turin: Giappichelli, 2024).

Targa, Carlo, *Ponderationi sopra la contrattazione marittima* (Genoa: Lampadi, 1750).

Townsend, William Charles, *The Lives of Twelve Eminent Judges of the Last and of the Present Century*, 2 vols (London: Longman, Brown, Green, and Longmans, 1846).

Valin, René-Josué, *Nouveau commentaire sur l'ordonnance de la marine, du mois d'août 1681*, 2 vols (La Rochelle: Legier & Mesnier, 1760).

—*Nouveau commentaire sur l'ordonnance de la marine, du mois d'août 1681*, new edn (Paris: Saurin, 1828).

Watson, Alan, *The Digest of Justinian*, 4 vols (Philadelphia: University of Pennsylvania Press, 2011).

Weytsen, Quintin and Mattheus De Vicq, *Tractatus de avariis* (Amsterdam: Henricus & Theodorus Boom, 1672).

Weskett, John, *A Complete Digest of Theory, Laws and Practise of Insurance* (London: Frys, Couchman, & Collier, 1781).

Official Documents and Publications

Records and Files of the Quarterly Courts of Essex County, Massachussets (1667–1671) (Salem: Essex Institute, 1914), vol. 4.

Cantini, Lorenzo, *Legislazione Toscana: Raccolta e illustrata dal dottore Lorenzo Cantini*, 32 vols (Florence: Pietro Fantosini e Figlio, 1802), vol. 4.

Hertslet, Edward (ed.), *Treatises and Tariffs regulating the Trade between Great Britain and Foreign Nations: Part V* (London: Butterworths, 1878).

Holt, Francis Ludlow, *Reports of Cases at Nisi Prius, at the Court of Common Pleas, and on the Northern Circuit* (London: Butterworth and Son, 1818).

Pyle Taunton, W. (ed.), *Reports of Cases Argued and Determined in the Court of Common Pleas and Other Courts* (Boston: Wells & Lilly, 1823), vol. 6.
Raithby, John (ed.), *Statutes of the Realm: Volume 5, 1628–80* (1819).
—*Statutes of the Realm: Volume 7, 1695–1701* (1819).

Newspapers

The London Gazette, n. 495 (11–15 August 1670).

Web-based primary sources

The Digest of Justinian (Latin original), <www.thelatinlibrary.com/justinian.html> [accessed 18 August 2021].
Gaius, *Commentaries* (Latin original), <www.thelatinlibrary.com/gaius.html> [accessed 18 August 2021].
Samuel Pepys, *Samuel Pepys's Diary*, ed. Phil Gyford, <www.pepysdiary.com/diary/1663/12/01/> [accessed 18 August 2021].

Secondary Sources

Printed works

Acemoglu, Daron and James Robinson, 'Unbundling institutions', *Journal of Political Economy* 113 (2005), 949–95.
—*Why Nations Fail: The Origins of Power, Prosperity, and Poverty* (London: Profile Books, 2013).
Addobbati, Andrea, *Commercio, rischio, guerra: il mercato delle assicurazioni marittime di Livorno, 1694–1795* (Rome: Edizioni di storia e letteratura, 2007).
—'Italy 1500–1800: cooperation and competition', in Adrian Leonard (ed.), *Marine Insurance: Origins and Institutions, 1300–1850* (Basingstoke: Palgrave Macmillan, 2016), 47–77.
—'La giurisdizione marittima e commerciale dei consoli del mare in età medicea', in Marco Tangheroni (ed.), *Pisa e il Mediterraneo: uomini, merci, idee dagli Etruschi ai Medici* (Milan: Skira, 2003), 311–15.
—'La neutralità del porto di Livorno in età medicea', in Adriano Prosperi (ed.), *Livorno 1606–1806: luogo di incontro tra popoli e culture* (Turin: Alimandi, 2009), 91–103.
—'Livorno: fronte del porto. Monelli, Carovane e Bergamaschi della Dogana (1602–1847)', in G. Petralia (ed.), *I sistemi portuali della Toscana mediterranea. Infrastrutture, scambi, economie dall'antichità a oggi* (Pisa: Pacini, 2011), 245–314.
—'Oltre gli intermediari. La Anton Francesco Salucci & figlio alla conquista dei mercati americani (1779–1788)', in Paolo Castignoli, Luigi Donolo, and Algerina Neri (eds), *Storia e attualità della presenza degli Stati Uniti a Livorno e in Toscana (Atti del Convegno 4–6 aprile 2002)* (Pisa: Plus, 2003), 145–83.
—'Principles and developments of general average: statutory and contractual loss allowances from the *Lex Rhodia* to the early modern Mediterranean', in Maria

Fusaro, Andrea Addobbati, and Luisa Piccinno (eds), *General Average and Risk Management in Medieval and Early Modern Maritime Business* (Cham: Springer, 2023), 145–66.

—'Until the very last nail: English seafaring and wage litigation in seventeenth-century Livorno', in Maria Fusaro, Bernard Allaire, Richard Blakemore, and Tijl Vanneste (eds), *Law, Labour and Empire: Comparative Perspectives on Seafarers, c. 1500–1800* (London: Palgrave Macmillan, 2015), 43–60.

—'War, risks, and speculation: the accounts of a small Livorno Insurer (1743–1748)', in Phillip Hellwege and Guido Rossi (eds), *Maritime Risk Management: Essays on the History of Marine Insurance, General Average and Sea Loan* (Berlin: Duncker & Humblot, 2021), 161–88.

—'When proof is lacking: a ship captain's oath and commercial justice in the second half of the seventeenth century', *Quaderni Storici* 153 (2016), 727–41.

Addobbati, Andrea and Jake Dyble, 'One hundred barrels of gunpowder. General average, maritime law, and international diplomacy between Tuscany and England in the second half of the 17th century', *Quaderni Storici* 168 (2021), 823–54.

Aglietti, Marcella, *I governatori di Livorno dai Medici all'unità d'Italia* (Pisa: Edizioni ETS, 2009).

—*L'istituto consolare tra Sette e Ottocento. Funzioni istituzionali, profilo giuridico e percorsi professionali nella Toscana granducale* (Florence: Edizioni ETS, 2012).

—'Patrizi, cavalieri e mercanti. Politiche di nobiltà tra Toscana e Spagna in età moderna', in Marcella Aglietti (ed.), *Istituzioni, potere e società. Le relazioni tra Spagna e Toscana per una storia mediterranea dell'Ordine dei Cavalieri di Santo Stefano* (Pisa: Edizioni ETS, 2007), 339–77.

Aglietti, Marcella and Andrea Addobbati, 'Premessa', in Andrea Addobbati and Marcella Aglietti (eds), *La città delle nazioni: Livorno e i limiti del cosmopolitismo (1566–1834)* (Pisa: Pisa University Press, 2016), 11–25.

Alfani, Guido and Vincent Gourdon, 'Entrepreneurs, formalization of social ties, and trustbuilding in Europe (fourteenth to twentieth centuries)', *The Economic History Review* 65 (2011), 1005–28.

Allaire, Bernard, 'Between Oléron and Colbert: the evolution of French maritime law until the seventeenth century', in Maria Fusaro, Bernard Allaire, Richard Blakemore, and Tijl Vanneste (eds), *Law, Labour and Empire: Comparative Perspectives on Seafarers, c. 1500–1800* (London: Palgrave Macmillan, 2015), 43–60.

Antunes, Cátia, 'Cross-cultural business cooperation in the Dutch trading world, 1580–1776: a view from Amsterdam's notarial contracts', in Francesco Trivellato, Leor Halevi, and Catia Antunes (eds), *Religion and Trade: Cross-Cultural Exchanges in World History* (Oxford: Oxford University Press, 2014), 150–68.

Antunes, Cátia and Amélia Polónia, *Beyond Empires: Global, Self-Organizing, Cross-Imperial Networks, 1500–1800* (Leiden: Brill, 2016).

Armstrong, Tim, 'Slavery, insurance, and sacrifice in the black Atlantic', in Bernhard Klein and Gesa Mackenthun (eds), *Sea Changes: Historicising the Ocean* (New York: Routledge, 2004), 167–85.

Armytage, Francis, *The Free Port System in the West Indies. A Study in Commercial Policy, 1766–1822* (London: Longmans, Green, & Co, 1953).

Arvind, T.T., '"Though it shocks one very much": formalism and pragmatism in the Zong and Bancoult', *Oxford Journal of Legal Studies* 32 (2012), 113–51.
Ascheri, Mario, 'Il processo civile tra diritto comune e diritto locale da questioni preliminari al caso della giustizia estense', *Quaderni Storici* 34 (1999), 355–87.
—*Introduzione storica al diritto moderno e contemporaneo* (Turin: Giappichelli, 2008).
—*The Laws of Late Medieval Italy (1000–1500): Foundations for a European Legal System* (Leiden: Brill, 2013).
Ashburner, Walter, Νόμος ροδίων ναυτικός. *The Rhodian Sea-Law* (Oxford: Clarendon Press, 1909).
Aubert, J.J., 'Dealing with the abyss: the nature and purpose of the Rhodian sea-law on jettison (Lex Rhodia de Iactu, D 14.2) and the making of Justinian's Digest', in J.W. Cairns and P.J. du Plessis (eds), *Beyond Dogmatics: Law and Society in the Roman World* (Edinburgh: Edinburgh University Press, 2007), 157–72.
Baggiani, Daniele, 'Tra crisi commerciali e interventi istituzionali. Le vicende del porto di Livorno in età tardo medicea (1714–1730)', *Rivista Storica Italiana* 104 (1992), 678–729.
Baruchello, Mario, *Livorno e il suo porto. Origini, caratteristiche e vicende dei traffici livornesi* (Livorno: Editrice Riviste Tecniche, 1932).
Basile, Mary Elizabeth, Jane Fair Bestor, Daniel R. Coquillette, and Charles Donahue, *Lex Mercatoria and Legal Pluralism: A Late Thirteenth-Century Treatise and its Afterlife* (Cambridge, MA: Ames Foundation, 1998).
Baucom, Ian, *Specters of the Atlantic: Finance Capital, Slavery, and the Philosophy of History* (Durham: Duke University Press, 2005).
Baud, Jean-Pierre (trans. Laura Colombo), *Il caso della mano rubata. Una storia giuridica del corpo* (Milan: Giuffrè, 2003).
Bayly, Chris, *The Birth of the Modern World, 1780–1914* (Malden: Blackwell Publishing, 2004).
Becker, Howard, *What about Mozart? What about Murder? Reasoning from Cases* (Chicago: The University of Chicago Press, 2014).
Belcher, Gerald, 'Spain and the Anglo-Portuguese alliance of 1661: a reassessment of Charles II's foreign policy at the Restoration', *Journal of British Studies* 15 (1975), 67–88
Belda Iniesta, Javier, 'The Clementines Dispendiosam and Saepe Contingit and the evolution of the medieval summary procedure', *Journal on European History of Law* 10 (2019), 46–67.
Bell, D.A., 'Questioning the global turn: the case of the French revolution', *French Historical Studies* 37 (2014), 1–24.
Bellomo, Manlio (trans. Lydia Cochrane), *The Common Legal Past of Europe, 1000–1800* (Washington, DC: Catholic University of America Press, 1995).
Bensa, Enrico, *Il diritto marittimo e le sue fonti* (Genoa: Cenni, 1889).
Benson, Bruce, *The Enterprise of Law: Justice without the State*, 2nd edn (Oakland: Independent Institute, 2011).
Benton, Lauren, *Law and Colonial Cultures: Legal Regimes in World History, 1400–1900* (Cambridge: Cambridge University Press, 2002).
Bernstein, Peter L., *Against the Gods: The Remarkable Story of Risk* (New York: John Wiley & Sons, 1996).

Berti, Marcello, 'I rischi nella circolazione marittima tra Europa nordica ed Europa Mediterranea nel primo trentennio del Seicento ed il caso della seconda guerra anglo-olandese (1665–67)', in Simonetta Cavaciocchi (ed.), *Ricchezza del mare, richezza dal mare, secc. XIII–XVIII* (Florence: Le Monnier, 2006), 809–25.

Blakemore, Richard, 'Pieces of eight, pieces of eight: seamen's earnings and the venture economy of early modern seafaring', *Economic History Review* 70 (2017), 1153–84.

Bitossi, Carlo, 'L'occhio di Genova. Livorno nella corrispondenza dei consoli genovesi nell'età moderna', in Adriano Prosperi (ed.), *Livorno 1606–1806: luogo di incontro tra popoli e culture* (Turin: Alimandi, 2009), 86–94.

Bogojevic-Gluscevic, Nevenka, 'The law and practice of average in medieval towns of the eastern Adriatic', *Journal of Maritime Law and Commerce* 26 (2005), 21–60.

Boiteaux, L.A., *La fortune de mer: le besoin de sécurité et les débuts de l'assurance maritime* (Paris: S.E.V.P.E.N., 1968).

Bono, Salvatore, *Corsari nel Mediterraneo: cristiani e musulmani fra guerra, schiavitù e commercio* (Milan: Mondadori, 2001).

—*Schiavi musulmani nell'Italia moderna: galeotti, vu' cumpra', domestici* (Naples: Edizioni scientifiche italiane, 1999).

—*Schiavi: una storia mediterranea (XVI–XIX secolo)* (Bologna: Mulino, 2016).

Bosco, Michele, 'Circolazioni "forzose" nel Mediterraneneo moderno. Norme giuridiche e pratiche di riscatto dei captivi attraverso le redenzioni mercedarie (secoli XVI–XVII)', *RiMe* 16 (2016), 165–96.

Braudel, Fernand (trans. Sian Reynolds), *The Mediterranean and the Mediterranean World in the Age of Phillip II*, 2 vols (New York: Harper and Row, 1972).

Braudel, Fernand and Ruggiero Romano, *Navires et marchandises à l'entrée du port de Livourne (1547–1611)* (Paris: Librairie Armand Colin, 1951).

Brooke, Geoffrey, 'Uncertainty, profit and entrepreneurial action: Frank Knight's contribution reconsidered', *Journal of the History of Economic Thought* 32 (2010), 221–35.

Brown, Richard, 'Microhistory and the post-modern challenge', *Journal of the Early Republic* 23 (2003), 1–20.

Buckland, William Warren, *The Roman Law of Slavery: The Condition of the Slave in Private Law from Augustus to Justinian* (Cambridge: Cambridge University Press, 1908).

Burr Litchfield, Robert, *The Emergence of a Bureaucracy: The Florentine Patricians, 1530–1790* (Princeton: Princeton University Press, 1986).

Burset, Christian, 'Merchant courts, arbitration, and the politics of commercial litigation in the eighteenth-century British empire', *Law and History Review* 34 (2016), 615–47.

Cadbury, Henry, 'Friends and the Inquisition at Venice, 1658', *The Journal of the Friends Historical Society* 52 (1968), 39–45.

Caferro, William, 'Premodern European capitalism, Christianity, and Florence', *Business History Review* 94 (2020), 39–72.

Calafat, Guillaume, 'Jurisdictional pluralism in a litigious sea (1590–1630): hard cases, multi-sited trials and legal enforcement between North Africa and Italy', *Past & Present* 242 (2019), 142–78.

—'Livorno e la camera di commercio di Marsiglia nel XVII secolo: consoli francesi, agenti e riscossione del cottimo', in Andrea Addobbati and Marcella Aglietti (eds), *La città delle nazioni: Livorno e i limiti del cosmopolitismo (1566–1834)* (Pisa: Pisa University Press, 2016), 237–76.
—'Ramadam Fatet vs. John Jucker. Trials and forgery in Egypt, Syria and Tuscany (1739–1740)', *Quaderni Storici* 48 (2013), 419–39.
—*Une mer jalousée: contribution à l'histoire de la souveraineté* (Paris: Éditions du Seuil, 2019).
Camerani Marri, Giulia, 'Archivio Quaratesi' in 'Notizie degli archivi Toscani', *Archivio Storico Italiano* 118 (1960), 368.
Carroll, Kenneth, 'Quakers in Venice, 1657–8', *Quaker History* 92 (2003), 22–31.
Castignoli, Paolo, 'Livorno da terra murata a città', in *Atti del convegno Livorno e il Mediterraneo nell'età medicea* (Livorno: Bastogi, 1978), 32–9.
Ceccarelli, Giovanni, 'Risky business: theological and canonical thought on insurance from the thirteenth to the seventeenth century', *Journal of Medieval and Early Modern Studies* 31 (2001), 607–58.
—*Risky Markets: Marine Insurance in Renaissance Florence* (Leiden: Brill, 2020).
—'Risky narratives: framing general average into risk-management strategies (13th–16th centuries)', in Maria Fusaro, Andrea Addobbati, and Luisa Piccinno (eds), *General Average and Risk Management in Medieval and Early Modern Maritime Business* (Cham: Springer, 2023), 61–91.
Cerutti, Simona, 'Fatti e fatti giudiziari: il consolato di commercio di Torino nel XVIII secolo', *Quaderni Storici* 34 (1999), 413–45.
—*Giustizia sommaria: pratiche e ideali di giustizia in una società di ancien régime* (Milan: Feltrinelli, 2003).
—'Normes et pratiques ou de la légitimité de leur opposition', in Bernard Lepetit (ed.), *Les formes de l'expérience. Une autre histoire sociale* (Paris: Albin Michel, 1995), 127–49.
Chowdharay-Best, George, 'Ancient maritime law', *Mariners Mirror* 62 (1976), 81–91.
Cifoletti, Guido, 'Lingua franca and migrations', in Stefania Gialdroni, Albrecht Cordes, Serge Dauchy, Dave De ruysscher, and Heikki Pihlajamäki (eds), *Migrating Words, Migrating Language, Migrating Law: Trading Routes and the Development of Commercial Law* (Leiden: Brill, 2020), 84–92.
Cipolla, Carlo, *Il burocrate e il marinaio: La "sanità" Toscana e le tribolazioni degli Inglesi a Livorno nel 17. secolo* (Bologna: Il Mulino, 2012).
Cipollone, Giulio, *Cristianità-Islam: cattività e liberazione in nome di Dio: il tempo di Innocenzo III dopo 'il 1187'* (Rome: Editrice pontificia università gregoriana, 1992).
Clarence-Smith, William, 'White servitude', in Keith Bradley and Paul Cartledge (eds), *The Cambridge World History of Slavery*, 4 vols (Cambridge: Cambridge University Press, 2011), vol. 3, 132–60.
Clark, George, 'The Nine Years War, 1688–1697', in J.S. Bromley (ed.), *The New Cambridge Modern History. Volume 6: The Rise of Great Britain and Russia, 1688–1715/25* (Cambridge: Cambridge University Press, 1970), 223–53.
Clemente, Alida and Roberto Zaugg, 'Hermes, the Leviathan and the grand

narrative of New Institutional Economics. The quest for development in the eighteenth-century Kingdom of Naples', *Journal of Modern European History* 15 (2017), 108–29.
Coase, Ronald, 'The nature of the firm', *Economica* 4 (1937), 386–405.
Coleman, D.C., 'An innovation and its diffusion: the "new draperies"', *The Economic History Review* 22 (1969), 417–29.
Colley, Linda, *Britons: Forging the Nation, 1707–1837* (New Haven: Yale University Press, 1992).
—*Captives: Britain, Empire and the World, 1600–1850* (New York: Anchor Books, 2004).
Colon, Germà and Arcadi García (eds), *Llibre del Consolat de Mar: edició del text de la Real de Mallorca, amb les variants de tots els manuscrits coneguts* (Barcelona: Fundació Noguera, 2001).
Coquillette, Daniel, 'Legal ideology and incorporation I: the English civilian writers, 1523–1607', *Boston University Law Review* 61 (1981), 1–89.
—'Legal ideology and incorporation II: Sir Thomas Ridley, Charles Molloy, and the literary battle for the law merchant, 1607–1676', *Boston University Law Review* 61 (1981), 315–71.
—'Legal ideology and incorporation III: reason regulated – the post-restoration English civilians, 1653–1735', *Boston University Law Review* 67 (1987), 289–361.
Cordes, Albrecht, 'Lex maritima? Local, regional and universal maritime law in the Middle Ages', in Wim Blockmans, Mikhail Krom, and Justyna Wubs-Mrozewicz (eds), *The Routledge Handbook of Maritime Trade around Europe 1300–1600* (London: Routledge, 2017), 69–85.
Cordes, Albrect and Stefania Gialdroni, 'Introduction', in Stefania Gialdroni, Albrecht Cordes, Serge Dauchy, Dave De ruysscher, and Heikki Pihlajamäki (eds), *Migrating Words, Migrating Language, Migrating Law: Trading Routes and the Development of Commercial Law* (Leiden: Brill, 2020), 1–9.
Cornah, Richard, *A Guide to General Average* (London: Richards Hogg Ltd, 1994).
—'The road to Vancouver: the development of the York-Antwerp Rules', *Journal of International Maritime Law* 10 (2004), 155–66.
Cornah, Richard, John Reeder, Richard Lowndes, and George R. Rudolf, *Lowndes and Rudolf: The Law of General Average and the York-Antwerp Rules* (London: Sweet & Maxwell, 2013).
Corrieri, Salvatore, *Il consolato del mare: la tradizione giuridico-marittima del Mediterraneo attraverso un'edizione italiana del 1584 del testo originale catalano del 1484* (Rome: Associazione nazionale del Consolato del mare, 2005).
Cortese, Ennio, *Le grandi linee della storia giuridica medievale* (Rome: Il Cigno, 2000).
Court, Ricardo, '"Januensis ergo mercator": trust and enforcement in the business correspondence of the Brignole family', *The Sixteenth Century Journal* 35 (2004), 987–1003.
Cozzi, Gaetano, *Repubblica di Venezia e stati Italiani: politica e giustizia dal secolo XVI al secolo XVIII* (Turin: UTET, 1999).
Curtin, Philip, *Cross-Cultural Trade in World History* (Cambridge: Cambridge University Press, 1984).
Cust, Lionel, and Herbert Horne, 'Notes on pictures in the royal collections. Article VII – The Quaratesi Altarpiece by Gentile da Fabriano', *The Burlington Magazine* 6 (1905), 470–5.

D'Angelo, Michela, 'Livorno 1421–1606: da villaggio a città-porto mediterranea', in S. Adorno, G. Cristina, and A. Rotondo (eds), *VisibileInvisibile – Economie urbane* (Syracuse: Tyche, 2013).
—*Mercanti inglesi a Livorno, 1573–1737: alle origini di una British factory* (Messina: Istituto di studi storici G. Salvemini, 2004).
Daston, Lorraine, *Classical Probability in the Enlightenment* (Princeton: Princeton University Press, 1988).
Davies, Jonathan, *Culture and Power: Tuscany and its Universities, 1537–1609* (Leiden: Brill, 2009).
Davis, Ralph, 'Earnings on capital in the English shipping industry', *The Journal of Economic History* 17 (1957), 409–25.
—*The Rise of the English Shipping Industry in the Seventeenth and Eighteenth Centuries*, 2nd edn (Newton Abbot: David & Charles Publishers, 1972).
Davis, Robert, *Christian Slaves, Muslim Masters: White Slavery in the Mediterranean, the Barbary Coast, and Italy, 1500–1800* (Basingstoke: Palgrave Macmillan, 2003).
Dedieu, J-P., Silvia Marzagalli, Pierrick Pourchasse, and Werner Scheltjens, 'Navigocorpus at work: a brief overview of the potential of a database', *International Journal of Maritime History* 24 (2012), 331–60.
Della Pina, Marco, 'La popolazione di Livorno nel Sei-Settecento: le componenti toscane', in Adriano Prosperi (ed.), *Livorno 1606–1806: luogo di incontro tra popoli e culture* (Turin: Alimandi, 2009), 149–57.
De Roover, Raymond, 'The *cambium maritimum* contract according to the Genoese notarial records of the twelfth and thirteenth centuries', *Explorations in Economic History* 7 (1969), 15–33.
—'The organization of trade', in M.M. Postan, E.E. Rich, and Edward Miller (eds), *The Cambridge History of Europe, Volume III: Economic Organization and Policies in the Middles Ages* (Cambridge: Cambridge University Press, 1963), 52–9.
De ruyssher, Dave, 'Antwerp 1490–1590: insurance and speculation', in Adrian Leonard (ed.), *Marine Insurance: Origins and Institutions, 1300–1850* (Basingstoke: Palgrave Macmillan, 2016), 79–105.
—'Maxims, principles and legal change: maritime law in merchant and legal culture (Low Countries, 16th Century)', *Zeitschrift der Savigny-Stiftung für Rechtsgeschichte. Germanistische Abteilung* 137 (2021), 260–75.
—'Peck, on maritime affairs', in Serge Dauchy, Georges Martyn, Anthony Musson, Heikki Pihlajamäki, and Alain Wijffels (eds), *The Formation and Transmission of Western Legal Culture: 150 Books that Made the Law in the Age of Printing* (Cham: Springer, 2016), 115–17.
De Vries, Jan and A.M. van der Woude, *The First Modern Economy: Success, Failure, and Perseverance of the Dutch Economy, 1500–1815* (Cambridge: Cambridge University Press, 1997).
Diaz, Furio, *Il Granducato di Toscana. I Medici* (Florence: UTET, 1976).
Doe, Helen, and Robin Pearson, 'Organizational choice in UK marine insurance', in Robin Pearson and Takau Yoneyama (eds), *Corporate Forms and Organizational Choice in International Insurance* (Oxford: Oxford University Press, 2015).
Donahue, Charles, 'Medieval and early modern lex mercatoria: an attempt at the probatio diabolica', *Chicago Journal of International Law* 5 (2004), 21–38.
—'Procedure in the courts of the *Ius Commune*', in Wilfried Hartmann and Kenneth

Pennington (eds), *The History of Courts and Procedure in Medieval Canon Law* (Washington, DC: Catholic University of America Press, 2017), 127–58.

Donati, Barbara, *Tra inquisizione e granducato: storie di Inglesi nella Livorno del primo seicento* (Rome: Edizioni di storia e letteratura, 2010).

Donlan, Sean, and Lukas Heckendorn Urscheler, 'Concepts of law: an introduction', in Sean Donlan and Lukas Heckendorn Urscheler (eds), *Concepts of Law: Comparative, Jurisprudential, and Social Science Perspectives*, new edn (Abingdon: Routledge, 2016), 1–19.

Dreijer, Gijs, *The Power and Pains of Polysemy: Maritime Trade, Averages, and Institutional Development in the Low Countries (15th–16th Centuries)* (Leiden: Brill, 2023).

Dreijer, Gijs and Otto Vervaart, 'Een tractaet van avarien – 1617', *Pro Memorie* 21 (2019), 38–41.

Dworkin, Ronald, *Taking Rights Seriously* (Cambridge, MA: Harvard University Press, 1978).

Dworkin, Steven, *A History of the Spanish Lexicon: A Linguistic Perspective* (Oxford: Oxford University Press, 2013).

Dyble, Jake, 'Divide and rule: risk sharing and political economy in the free port of Livorno', in Maria Fusaro, Andrea Addobbati, and Luisa Piccinno (eds), *General Average and Risk Management in Medieval and Early Modern Maritime Business* (Cham: Springer, 2023), 363–87.

—'Lex mercatoria, private "order", and commercial "confusion": a view from seventeenth-century Livorno', *Quaderni Storici* 56 (2022), 673–700.

—, Antonio Iodice, and Ian Wellaway, 'The technical challenges of measuring maritime trade in the early modern Mediterranean: Livorno and Genoa', *Histoire & mesure* 38 (2023), 135–62.

—'The threat of the "avania": financial risk in European–Ottoman trade and the growth of an Orientalist discourse, 1660–1710', in Jake Dyble, Alessandro Lo Bartolo, and Elia Morelli (eds), *Un mare connesso. Europa e mondo islamico nel Mediterraneo (secoli XV–XIX)* (Pisa: Carocci, 2024), 109–31.

Earle, Peter, *Corsairs of Malta and Barbary* (London: Sidgwick & Jackson, 1970).

Edigati, Daniele, 'Aspetti giuridici delle franchigie di Livorno: l'immunità personale *in criminalibus* ed il problema dell'estradizione (secoli XVI–XVIII)', *Nuovi Studi Livornesi* 17 (2010), 17–41.

Eltis, David, *The Rise of African Slavery in the Americas* (Cambridge: Cambridge University Press, 2012).

Eltis, David, and Stanley Engerman, 'Dependence, servility, and coerced labour in time and space', in Keith Bradley and Paul Cartledge (eds), *The Cambridge World History of Slavery*, 4 vols (Cambridge: Cambridge University Press, 2011), vol. 3, 1–24.

Emmett, Ross, 'Reconsidering Frank Knight's *Risk, Uncertainty and Profit*', *Independent Review* 24 (2020), 522–41.

Engels, Marie-Christine, *Merchants, Interlopers, Seamen and Corsairs: The 'Flemish' Community in Livorno and Genoa (1615–1635)* (Hilversum: Verloren, 1997).

Epstein, Stephan, *An Island for Itself: Economic Development and Social Change in Late Medieval Sicily* (Cambridge: Cambridge University Press, 2003).

—'Constitutions, liberties, and growth in pre-modern Europe', in Mark Casson

and Andrea Godley (eds), *Factors in Economic Growth* (Berlin: Springer, 2000), 158–81.
—*Freedom and Growth. The Rise of States and Markets in Europe, 1300–1750* (London: Routledge, 2001).
Epstein, Steven, *Speaking of Slavery: Color, Ethnicity, and Human Bondage in Italy* (Ithaca: Cornell University Press, 2001).
Fasano Guarini, Elena, 'La popolazione', in Adriano Betti Carboncini and Marco Bedini (eds), *Livorno e Pisa: due città e un territorio nella politica dei Medici* (Pisa: Nistri-Lischi & Pacini, 1980), 199–215.
—'Livorno nell'età moderna: mito e realtà', in Adriano Prosperi (ed.), *Livorno 1606–1806: luogo di incontro tra popoli e culture* (Turin: Alimandi, 2009), 19–30.
Febvre, Lucien, 'Pour l'histoire d'un sentiment: le besoin de sécurité', *Annales* 11 (1956), 244–7.
Felloni, Giuseppe, 'Una fonte inesplorata per la storia dell'economia marittima in età moderna', *Atti della Società Ligure di Storia Patria, nuova serie*, 38 (1998), 843–60.
Fenoaltea, Stefano, 'Spleen: the failures of the cliometric school', *Annals of the Fondazione Luigi Einaudi* 53 (2019), 5–24.
Fernandez Castro, Ana Belem, 'Handling conflicts in long-distance trade: a view of the Mediterranean through the experience of merchants operating in the Kingdom of Valencia in the late sixteenth century', in Louis Sicking (ed.), *Conflict Management in the Mediterranean and the Atlantic, 1000–1800* (Leiden: Brill, 2020), 237–59.
Fiaschi, Ranieri, *Le magistrature Pisane delle acque* (Pisa: Lischi e Figli, 1938).
Filippini, Jean-Pierre, *Il porto di Livorno e la Toscana (1676–1814)*, 3 vols (Naples: Edizioni Scientifiche Italiane, 1998).
Fisher, F.J., 'London's export trade in the early seventeenth century', *The Economic History Review* 3 (1950), 151–61.
Fiume, Giovanna, 'La schiavitù Mediterranea tra medioevo ed età moderna. Una proposta bibliografica', *Estudis. Revista de Historia Moderna* 41 (2015), 267–318.
—*Schiavitù mediterranee: corsari, rinnegati e santi di età moderna* (Milan: Mondadori, 2009).
Fodor, Pál, 'Maltese pirates, Ottoman captives and French traders in the early seventeenth century Mediterranean', in Géza Dávid and Pál Fodor (eds), *Ransom Slavery along the Ottoman Borders: Early Fifteenth–Early Eighteenth Centuries* (Leiden: Brill, 2007).
Fontenay, Michel, 'Esclaves et/ou captifs: preciser les concepts', in Wolfgang Kaiser (ed.), *Le commerce des captifs: les intermédiaires dans l'échange et le rachat des prisonniers en Méditeraneé, XVe–XVIIIe siècle* (Rome: École française de Rome, 2008), 15–24.
—*La Méditerranée entre la croix et le croissant: navigation, commerce, course et piraterie (XVIe–XIXe siècle)* (Paris: Classiques Garnier Numérique, 2011).
Fortunati, Maura, 'La lex mercatoria nella tradizione e nella recente ricostruzione storico giuridica', *Sociologia del diritto* 2–3 (2005), 29–41.
—'"Non potranno essere gettati". Assicurazione e schiavitù nella dottrina giuridica del XVIII secolo', *RiMe* 1 (2008), 51–66.

Foy, Charles, '"Unkle Sommerset's" freedom: liberty in England for black sailors', *Journal for Maritime Research* 13 (2011), 21–36.

Frankot, Edda, *Of Laws of Ships and Shipmen: Medieval Maritime Law and its Practice in Urban Northern Europe* (Edinburgh: Edinburgh University Press, 2012).

Frattarelli Fischer, Lucia, 'Ebrei a Pisa e Livorno nel sei e settecento tra inquisizione e garanzie granducali', in Aleksej Kalc and Elisabetta Navarra (eds), *Le popolazioni del mare: porti franchi, città, isole e villaggi costieri tra età moderna e contemporanea* (Udine: Forum, 2003), 253–95.

—'I bandi di Ferdinando I. La costruzione e il popolamento di Livorno dal 1590 al 1603', in Aleksej Kalc and Elizabetta Navarra (eds), *Le populazioni del mare: porti franchi, città, isole e villaggi costieri tra età moderna e contemporanea* (Udine: Forum, 2003), 87–98.

—'La Livornina. Alle origini della società livornese', in Adriano Prosperi (ed.), *Livorno 1606–1806: luogo di incontro tra popoli e culture* (Turin: Alimandi, 2009), 43–62.

—*L'arcano del mare: un porto nella prima età globale: Livorno* (Pisa: Pacini editore, 2018).

—'Livorno 1676. La città e il porto franco', in Franco Angiolini, Vieri Becagli and Marcello Verga (eds), *La Toscana nell'età di Cosimo III* (Florence: EDIFIR, 1993) 45–66.

—'Livorno città nuova: 1574–1609', *Società e storia* 11 (1989), 873–93.

—'Livorno. Dal pentagono di Buontalenti alla città di Ferdinando I', *Nuovi Studi Livornesi* 19 (2012), 23–48.

—'Lo sviluppo di una città portuale: Livorno, 1575–1720', in Marco Folin (ed.), *Sistole/Diastole: episodi di trasformazione urbana nell'Italia delle città* (Venice: Istituto veneto di scienze, lettere ed arti, 2006), 271–334.

—*Vivere fuori dal ghetto: Ebrei a Pisa e Livorno (secoli XVI–XVIII)* (Turin: Silvio Zamorani, 2008).

Fredona, Robert, and Sophus Reinert, 'Italy and the origins of capitalism', *Business History Review* 94 (2020), 5–38.

—'Political economy and the Medici', *Business History Review* 94 (2020), 125–77.

Fry, Danby P., 'On the phrase "Scot and Lot"', *Transactions of the Philological Society* 12 (1867), 167–97.

Fusaro, Maria, 'After Braudel: a reassessment of Mediterranean history between the Northern Invasion and the Caravane Maritime', in Maria Fusaro, Colin Heywood, and Mohamed-Salah Omri (eds), *Trade and Cultural Exchange in the Early Modern Mediterranean: Braudel's Maritime Legacy* (London: I.B. Tauris & Company, 2010), 1–22.

—'Cooperating mercantile networks in the early modern Mediterranean', *The Economic History Review* 65 (2012), 701–18.

—'Introduction. Risk management and jurisdictional boundaries in pre-modern Europe', *Quaderni Storici* 56 (2022), 587–94.

—*Political Economies of Empire in the Early Modern Mediterranean: The Decline of Venice and the Rise of England 1450–1700* (Cambridge: Cambridge University Press, 2015).

—'Politics of justice/politics of trade: foreign merchants and the administration of justice from the records of Venice's Giudici del Forestier', *Mélanges de l'Ecole Francaise de Rome* 126 (2014), 139–60.

—'Public service and private trade: northern seamen in seventeenth-century Venetian courts of justice', *International Journal of Maritime History* 27 (2015), 3–25.

—'The burden of risk: early modern maritime enterprise and varieties of capitalism', *Business History Review* 94 (2020), 179–200.

—'The global relevance of the legal history of the early modern Mediterranean', *Cromohs*, Current Debates (2023), <https://oajournals.fupress.net/index.php/cromohs/article/view/14575> [12 August 2023].

—'The invasion of northern litigants: English and Dutch seamen in Mediterranean courts of law', in Maria Fusaro, Bernard Allaire, Richard Blakemore, and Tijl Vanneste (eds), *Law, Labour and Empire: Comparative Perspectives on Seafarers, c. 1500–1800* (London: Palgrave Macmillan, 2015), 21–42.

Fusaro, Maria, and Andrea Addobbati, 'The grand tour of mercantilism: Lord Fauconberg and his Italian mission (1669–1671)', *English Historical Review* 137 (2022), 692–727.

Fusaro, Maria, Colin Heywood, and Mohamed-Salah Omri (eds), *Trade and Cultural Exchange in the Early Modern Mediterranean: Braudel's Maritime Legacy* (London: I.B. Tauris & Company, 2010).

Galgano, Francesco, *Lex mercatoria*, 5th edn (Bologna: Il Mulino, 2010).

Gardner, Jane, 'Slavery and Roman law', in Keith Bradley and Paul Cartledge (eds), *The Cambridge World History of Slavery*, 4 vols (Cambridge: Cambridge University Press, 2011), vol. 1, 414–37.

George, Rose, *Deep Sea and Foreign Going* (London: Portobello Books, 2013).

Ghezzi, Renato, 'Il porto di Livorno e il commercio mediterraneo nel Seicento', in Adriano Prosperi (ed.), *Livorno 1606–1806: luogo di incontro tra popoli e culture* (Turin: Alimandi, 2009), 324–40.

—*Livorno e il mondo Islamico nel XVII Secolo: naviglio e commercio di importazione* (Bari: Cacucci, 2007).

—'Livorno e i porti adriatici dalla fine del Seicento alla fine del periodo mediceo', *Nuovi Studi Livornesi* 11 (2004), 101–32.

—*Livorno e l'Atlantico: i commerci Olandesi nel Mediterraneo del Seicento* (Bari: Cacucci, 2011).

—'Mercanti armeni a Livorno nel XVII secolo', in *Gli Armeni lungo le strade d'Italia: atti del convegno internazionale: Torino, Genova, Livorno, 8–11 marzo 1997: giornata di studi a Livorno* (Pisa: Istituti editoriali e poligrafici internazionali, 1998), 43–53.

Ghobrial, John-Paul, 'Introduction: seeing the world like a microhistorian', *Past & Present* 242 (2019), 1–22.

—'Moving stories and what they tell us: early modern mobility between microhistory and global history', *Past & Present* 242 (2019), 243–80.

—*The whispers of cities: information flows in Istanbul, London, and Paris in the age of William Trumbull* (Oxford: Oxford University Press, 2013).

Gialdroni, Stefania 'Gerard Malynes e la questione della lex mercatoria', *Zeitschrift der Savigny-Stiftung für Rechtsgeschichte* 126 (2009), 38–69.

Ginzburg, Carlo (trans. John Tedeschi and Anne Tedeschi), 'Latitude, slaves, and the Bible: an experiment in microhistory', *Critical Inquiry* 31 (2005), 665–83.
—'Microhistory: two or three things that I know about it', *Critical Inquiry* 20 (1993), 10–35.
—'Our words, and theirs: a reflection on the historian's craft, today', *Cromohs* 18 (2013), 97–114.
Ginzburg, Carlo, and Carlo Poni, 'Il nome e il come: scambio ineguale e mercato storiografico', *Quaderni Storici* 40 (1979), 181–90.
Gluzman, Renard, 'What made a ship Venetian? (Thirteenth to sixteenth centuries)', in Georg Christ (ed.), *Cultures of Empire: Rethinking Venetian Rule, 1400–1700* (Leiden: Brill, 2020), 293–328.
Go, Sabine, 'Amsterdam 1585–1790: emergence, dominance, and decline' in Adrian Leonard (ed.), *Marine Insurance: Origins and Institutions, 1300–1850* (Basingstoke: Palgrave Macmillan, 2016), 106–29.
—'GA adjustments in Amsterdam: reinforcing authority through transparency and accountability (late sixteenth–early seventeenth century)', in Maria Fusaro, Andrea Addobbati, and Luisa Piccinno (eds), *General Average and Risk Management in Medieval and Early Modern Maritime Business* (Cham: Springer, 2023), 389–414.
—'Governance of general average in the Netherlands in the nineteenth century: a backward development?', in Phillip Hellwege and Guido Rossi (eds), *Maritime Risk Management: Essays on the History of Marine Insurance, General Average and Sea Loan* (Berlin: Duncker & Humblot, 2021), 247–63.
—'The Amsterdam Chamber of Insurance and Average: a new phase in formal contract enforcement (late sixteenth and seventeenth centuries)', *Enterprise & Society* 14 (2013), 511–43.
Godley, Andrew, and Mark Casson (eds), *Cultural Factors in Economic Growth* (Berlin: Springer, 2000).
Goldschmidt, Levin, 'Lex Rhodia und Agermanament der Shiffsrat: Studie zur Geschichte und Dogmatik des Europäischen Seerechts', *Zeitschrift für das gesammte Handelsrecht* 35 (1888), 37–90, 321–95.
Goldthwaite, Richard, 'The practice and culture of accounting in renaissance Florence', *Enterprise & Society* 16 (2015), 611–47.
Grafe, Regina, 'Was there a market for institutions in early modern European trade?', in Georg Christ, Stefan Burkhardt, Wolfgang Kaiser, Franz-Julius Morche, and Roberto Zaugg (eds), *Union in Separation – Diasporic Groups and Identities in the Eastern Mediterranean (1100–1800)* (Rome: Viella, 2015), 593–609.
Greene, Molly, 'Beyond the northern invasion: the Mediterranean in the seventeenth century' *Past & Present* 174 (2002), 42–71.
—*Catholic Pirates and Greek Merchants: A Maritime History of the Early Modern Mediterranean* (Princeton: Princeton University Press, 2010).
Greif, Avner, *Institutions and the Path to the Modern Economy: Lessons from Medieval Trade* (Cambridge: Cambridge University Press, 2006).
Grendi, Edoardo, 'Micro-analisi e storia sociale', *Quaderni Storici* 12 (1977), 506–20.
—'Ripensare la microstoria?', *Quaderni Storici* 86 (1994), 539–49.
Guarnieri, Giuseppe Gino, *Livorno medicea nel quadro delle sue attrezzature*

portuali e della funzione economica-marittima: dalla fondazione civica alla fine della dinastia medicea (1577–1737) (Livorno: Giardini, 1970).

Gustafson, Don F., 'Voluntary and involuntary', *Philosophy and Phenomenological Research* 24 (1964), 493–501.

Hacking, Ian, *The Emergence of Probability: A Philosophical Study of Early Ideas about Probability, Induction and Statistical Inference*, 2nd edn (Cambridge: Cambridge University Press, 2009).

Haggerty, Sheryllyne, 'Risk and risk management in the Liverpool slave trade', *Business History* 51 (2009), 817–34.

Harms, Robert, *The Diligent: A Voyage through the Worlds of the Slave Trade* (New York: Basic Books, 2002).

Harris, Ron, 'General Average and all the rest: the law and economics of early modern maritime risk mitigation', in Maria Fusaro, Andrea Addobbati, and Luisa Piccinno (eds), *General Average and Risk Management in Medieval and Early Modern Maritime Business* (Cham: Springer, 2023), 33–60.

—*Going the Distance: Eurasian Trade and the Rise of the Business Corporation, 1400–1700* (Princeton: Princeton University Press, 2020).

Hart, H.L.A., and Leslie Green, *The Concept of Law* (Oxford: Oxford University Press, 2015).

Hatzimihail, Nikitas, 'The many lives – and faces – of lex mercatoria: history as genealogy in international business law', *Law and Contemporary Problems* 71 (2008), 169–90.

Helmholz, R.H., *The Ius Commune in England: Four Studies* (Oxford: Oxford University Press, 2001).

Hershenzon, Daniel, *The Captive Sea: Slavery, Communication, and Commerce in Early Modern Spain and the Mediterranean* (Philadelphia: University of Pennsylvania Press, 2018).

—'Towards a connected history of bondage in the Mediterranean: recent trends in the field', *History Compass* 15 (2017), 1–13.

Herzog, Tamar, *A Short History of European Law: The Last Two and a Half Millennia* (Cambridge, MA: Harvard University Press, 2018).

Heywood, Colin, 'Microhistory/maritime history: aspects of British presence in the western Mediterranean in the early modern period', in Albrecht Fuess and Bernard Heyberger (eds), *La frontière méditerranéenne du XVe au XVIIe siècle* (Turnhout: Brepols Publishers, 2014), 83–111.

—'The English in the Mediterranean, 1600–1630: a post-Braudelian perspective on the northern invasion', in Maria Fusaro, Colin Heywood, and Mohamed-Salah Omri (eds), *Trade and Cultural Exchange in the Early Modern Mediterranean: Braudel's Maritime Legacy* (London: I.B. Tauris & Company, 2010), 23–44.

Hont, Istvan, *Jealousy of Trade: International Competition and the Nation-state in Historical Perspective* (Cambridge, MA: Harvard University Press, 2010).

Hoover, C.B., 'The sea loan in Genoa in the twelfth century', *The Quarterly Journal of Economics* 40 (1926), 495–529.

Horden, Peregrine and Nicholas Purcell, *The Boundless Sea: Writing Mediterranean History* (London: Routledge, 2019).

Hudson, Geoffrey, 'The York-Antwerp Rules: background to the changes of 1994', *Journal of Maritime Law and Commerce* 27 (1996), 469–78.

Hudson, Nicholas, 'From "nation" to "race": the origin of racial classification in eighteenth-century thought', *Eighteenth-Century Studies* 29 (1996), 247–64.

Hyman, John, 'Voluntariness and intention', *Jurisprudence* 7 (2016), 692–709.

Ibbetson, David, 'Comparative legal history: a methodology', in Anthony Musson and Chantal Stebbings (eds), *Making Legal History: Approaches and Methodology* (Cambridge: Cambridge University Press, 2012), 131–45.

Iodice, Antonio, 'General average in Genoa: between statutes and customs', in Maria Fusaro, Andrea Addobbati, and Luisa Piccinno (eds), *General Average and Risk Management in Medieval and Early Modern Maritime Business* (Cham: Springer, 2023), 259–96.

Iodice, Antonio, and Luisa Piccinno, 'Managing shipping risk: general average and marine insurance in early modern Genoa', in Phillip Hellwege and Guido Rossi (eds), *Maritime Risk Management: Essays on the History of Marine Insurance, General Average and Sea Loan* (Berlin: Duncker & Humblot, 2021), 83–110.

Jarzabkowski, Paula, Rebecca Bednarek, and Paul Spee, *Making a Market for Acts of God: The Practice of Risk-Trading in the Global Reinsurance Industry* (Oxford: Oxford University Press, 2015).

Kadens, Emily, 'The myth of the customary law merchant', *Texas Law Review* 90 (2012), 1153–206.

Kaiser, Wolfgang, *Le commerce des captifs: les intermédiaires dans l'échange et le rachat des prisonniers en Méditerraneé, XVe–XVIIIe siècle* (Rome: École Française de Rome, 2008).

Kaiser, Wolfgang, and Guillaume Calafat, 'The economy of ransoming in the early modern Mediterranean', in Francesco Trivellato, Leor Halevi, and Catia Antunes (eds), *Religion and Trade: Cross-Cultural Exchanges in World History* (Oxford: Oxford University Press, 2014), 108–30.

—'Violence, protection and commerce: corsairing and *ars piratica* in the early modern Mediterranean', in Stefan Eklöf Amirell and Leos Müller (eds), *Persistent Piracy: Maritime Violence and State-Formation in Global Historical Perspective* (London: Palgrave Macmillan, 2014), 69–92.

Khalilieh, Hassan, 'Human jettison, contribution for lives, and life salvage in Byzantine and early Islamic maritime laws in the Mediterranean', *Byzantion* 75 (2005), 225–35.

—*Islamic Maritime Law: An Introduction* (Leiden: Brill, 1998).

Kingston, Christopher, 'America 1720–1820: war and organization', in Adrian Leonard (eds), *Marine Insurance: Origins and Institutions: 1300–1850* (Basingstoke: Palgrave Macmillan, 2015), 205–26.

—'Governance and institutional change in marine insurance, 1350–1850', *European Review of Economic History* 18 (2014), 1–18.

Kirk, Thomas Allison, 'Genoa and Livorno: sixteenth and seventeenth-century commercial rivalry as a stimulus to policy development', *History* 86 (2002), 2–17.

—*Genoa and the Sea: Policy and Power in an Early Modern Maritime Republic 1559–1684* (Baltimore: John Hopkins University Press, 2013).

Knight, Frank, *Risk, Uncertainty and Profit* (Boston and New York: Houghton Mifflin, 1921).

Krikler, Jeremy, 'The Zong and the Lord Chief Justice', *History Workshop Journal* 64 (2007), 29–47.

Kruit, Jolien, *General Average, Legal Basis and Applicable Law: The Overrated Significance of the York-Antwerp Rules* (Zutphen: Paris Legal Publishers, 2017).
—'General average – general principle plus varying practical application equals uniformity?', *Journal of International Maritime Law* 21 (2015), 190–202.
Landes, David, *The Wealth and Poverty of Nations: Why Some Are so Rich and Some so Poor* (New York: W.W. Norton, 1998).
Lane, Frederic, *Profits from Power. Readings in Protection Rent and Violence Controlling Enterprise* (Albany: State University of New York Press, 1979).
Lefebvre D'Ovidio, Antonio, 'La contribuzione alle avarie dal diritto romano all'ordinanza del 1681', *Rivista del Diritto della Navigazione* 1 (1935), 36–140.
Leonard, Adrian, 'Introduction: the nature and study of marine insurance' in Adrian Leonard (ed.), *Marine Insurance: Origins and Institutions, 1300–1850* (Basingstoke: Palgrave Macmillan, 2016), 2–22.
—'London 1426–1601: marine insurance and the law merchant' in Adrian Leonard (ed.), *Marine Insurance: Origins and Institutions, 1300–1850* (Basingstoke: Palgrave Macmillan, 2016), 150–75.
—(ed.), *Marine Insurance: Origins and Institutions, 1300–1850* (Basingstoke: Palgrave Macmillan, 2016).
LeRoy, Stephen F., and Larry D. Singell, 'Knight on risk and uncertainty', *Journal of Political Economy* 95 (1987), 394–406.
Levi, Giovanni, 'Frail frontiers?', *Past & Present* 242 (2019), 37–49.
—'I pericoli del Geertzismo', *Quaderni Storici* 20 (1985), 269–77.
Lillie, Lisa, 'Commercio, cosmopolitismo e modelli della modernità: Livorno nell'immaginario inglese a stampa, 1590–1750', in Andrea Addobbati and Marcella Aglietti (eds), *La città delle nazioni: Livorno e i limiti del cosmopolitismo (1566–1834)* (Pisa: Pisa Univerity Press, 2016), 337–57.
Linebaugh, Peter, and Marcus Rediker, *The Many-headed Hydra: Sailors, Slaves, Commoners, and the Hidden History of the Revolutionary Atlantic* (London and New York: Verso, 2000).
Lo Bartolo, Alessandro, 'The *consoli del mare* of Pisa, 1550–1750: an institutional and social profile', in Jake Dyble, Alessandro Lo Bartolo, and Elia Morelli (eds), *Un mare connesso. Europa e mondo islamico nel Mediterraneo (secoli XV–XIX)* (Pisa: Carocci, 2024), 177–200.
Lo Basso, Luca, 'Il finanziamento dell'armamento marittimo tra società e istituzioni: il caso ligure', *Archivio Storico Italiano* 174 (2016), 81–107.
—'The maritime loan as a form of small shipping credit (17th–18th centuries): the case of Liguria', in Antonino Giuffrida, Roberto Rossi, and Gaetano Sabatini (eds), *Informal Credit in the Mediterranean Area (XVI–XIX Centuries)* (Palermo: New Digital Press, 2016), 145–73.
López Rodríguez, Ana, *Lex Mercatoria and Harmonisation of Contract Law in the EU* (Copenhagen: DJOF Publishing, 2003).
Lucas, Robert, 'On the mechanics of economic development', *Journal of Monetary Economics* 22 (1988), 3–22.
Luque Talaván, Miguel, 'La avería en el tráfico maritimo-mercantil indiano: notas para su estudio (siglos XVI–XVIII)', *Revista Complutense de Historia de América* (1998), 113–45.

Maccioni, Elena, *Il Consolato del Mare di Barcellona. Tribunale e corporazione di mercanti (1394–1462)* (Rome: Viella, 2019).

Magnusson, Lars, 'Mercantilism', in Samuels Warren, Jeff Biddle, and John Bryan Davis (eds), *A Companion to the History of Economic Thought* (Malden: Blackwell, 2003), 46–60.

Malanima, Paolo, 'When did England overtake Italy? Medieval and early modern divergence in prices and wages', *European Review of Economic History* 17 (2013), 45–70.

Mangiarotti, Anna, 'La politica economica di Ferdinando I de Medici', in Silvana Balbi de Caro (ed.), *Merci e monete a Livorno in età granducale* (Livorno: Cassa di Risparmio di Livorno, 1997), 17–36.

Mannini, Brunello, 'La riforma della Dogana di Livorno del 1566', *Studi livornesi* 7 (1992), 65–107.

Mannori, Luca, *Il sovrano tutore. Pluralismo istituzionale e accentramento amministrativo nel Principato dei Medici (secc. XVI–XVIII)* (Milan: Giuffrè, 1994).

—*Lo stato del granduca, 1530–1859: le istituzioni della Toscana moderna in un percorso di testi commentate* (Pisa: Pacini Editore, 2015).

Mannori, Luca, and Bernardo Sordi, *Storia del diritto amministrativo*, new edn (Rome: Laterza, 2013).

Marcocci, Giuseppe, 'I portoghesi a Livorno nei secoli dell'età moderna', in Adriano Prosperi (ed.), *Livorno 1606–1806: luogo di incontro tra popoli e culture* (Turin: Alimandi, 2009), 405–17.

Mauro, Frédéric, 'Merchant communities, 1350–1750', in James Tracy (ed.), *The Rise of Merchant Empires: Long Distance Trade in the Early Modern World, 1350–1750* (Cambridge: Cambridge University Press, 1990), 255–86.

McCord, Johnny, 'The Ever Given: one gut punch after another', *The Marine Insurer* 6 (2021), 48–9.

McIntyre, John, Ranjeesh Narula, and Len Trevino, 'The role of export processing zones for host countries and multinationals: a mutually beneficial relationship?' *International Trade Journal* 10 (1996), 435–66.

McLachlan, Jean, 'Documents illustrating Anglo-Spanish trade between the Commercial Treaty of 1667 and the Commercial Treaty and the Asiento Contract of 1713', *The Cambridge Historical Journal* 4 (1934), 299–311.

Melis, Federigo, *Origini e sviluppi delle assicurazioni in Italia (secoli 14–16), Volume 1: Le fonti* (Rome: Istituto Nazionale delle Assicurazioni, 1975).

Ménard, Claude, and Mary Shirley, 'The contribution of Douglass North to new institutional economics', in Sebastian Galiani and Itai Sened (eds), *Institutions, Property Rights, and Economic Growth* (Cambridge: Cambridge University Press, 2014), 11–29.

Minuti, Rolando, *Oriente barbarico e storiografia settecentesca: rappresentazioni della storia dei Tartari nella cultura francese del XVIII secolo* (Venice: Marsilio, 1994).

Morini, Simona, *Il rischio: da Pascal a Fukushima* (Bologna: Bollati Bolinghieri, 2014).

Mukherjee, Proshanto, 'The anachronism in maritime law that is general average', *WMU Journal of Maritime Affairs* 4 (2005), 195–209.

Musolino, Pino, 'A relic of the past or still an important instrument? A brief review of General Average in the 21st Century', *Il Diritto Marittimo – Quaderni I – New Challenges in Maritime Law: de lege lata e de lege ferenda* (2015), 257–88.

Nadalo, Stephanie, 'Negotiating slavery in a tolerant frontier: Livorno's Turkish bagno (1547–1747)', *Mediaevalia* 32 (2011), 275–324.

—'Populating a "nest of pirates, murtherers etc.": Tuscan immigration policy and "Ragion di Stato" in the free port of Livorno', in Timothy Fehler, Greta Kroeker, Charles Parker, and Jonathan Ray (eds), *Religious Diasporas in Early Modern Europe: Strategies of Exile* (London: Pickering and Chatto, 2014), 31–45.

Nehlsen-von Stryk, Karin, *L'assicurazione marittima a Venezia nel XV secolo* (Rome: Il Veltro Editrice, 1988).

Nielsen, Karen, 'Dirtying Aristotle's hands? Aristotle's analysis of "mixed acts" in the "Nicomachean Ethics"', *Phronesis* 52 (2007), 270–300.

North, Douglass, 'Beyond the New Economic History', *Journal of Economic History* 34 (1974), 1–7.

—'Institutions', *Journal of Economic Perspectives* 5 (1991), 97–112.

—*Institutions, Institutional Change, and Economic Performance* (Cambridge: Cambridge University Press, 1990).

—'Institutions, transaction costs, and the rise of merchant empires', in James Tracy (ed.), *The Political Economy of Merchant Empires* (Cambridge: Cambridge University Press, 1991), 22–40.

North, Douglass, and Robert Thomas, *The Rise of the Western World: A New Economic History* (Cambridge: Cambridge University Press, 1973).

North, Douglass and Barry Weingast, 'Constitutions and commitment: the evolution of institutions governing public choice in seventeenth-century England', *The Journal of Economic History* 49 (1989), 803–32.

Nussdorfer, Laurie, *Brokers of Public Trust: Notaries in Early Modern Rome* (Baltimore: John Hopkins University Press, 2009).

Ogilvie, Sheilagh, *Institutions and European Trade: Merchant Guilds, 1000–1800* (Cambridge: Cambridge University Press, 2012).

—'Whatever is, is right? Economic institutions in pre-industrial Europe', *The Economic History Review* 60 (2007), 649–84.

Oldham, James, 'Insurance litigation involving the *Zong* and other British slave ships, 1780–1807', *Journal of Legal History* 28 (2007), 299–318.

—'New light on Mansfield and slavery', *Journal of British Studies* 27 (1988), 45–68.

Olnon, Merlijn, 'Towards classifying Avanias: a study of two cases involving the English and Dutch nations of seventeenth century Izmir', in Alastair Hamilton, Alexander H. de Groot, and Maurits H. van den Boogert (eds), *Friends and Rivals in the East: Studies in Anglo-Dutch Relations in the Levant from the Seventeenth to the Early-Nineteenth Century* (Leiden: Brill, 2000), 159–86.

Ormrod, David, *The Rise of Commercial Empires: England and the Netherlands in the Age of Mercantilism, 1650–1770* (Cambridge: Cambridge University Press, 2009).

Pagano De Divitiis, Gigliola (trans. Stephen Parkin), *English Merchants in Seventeenth-Century Italy* (Cambridge: Cambridge University Press, 1998).

—'Livorno: porto della Toscana?', in Adriano Prosperi (ed.), *Livorno 1606–1806: luogo di incontro tra popoli e culture* (Turin: Alimandi, 2009), 341–9.

Pagratis, Gerassimos, 'Le fortune di mare. Incidenti della navigazione mercantile nei mari Ionio e Adriatico (1611–1795)', in Simonetta Cavaciocchi (ed.), *Ricchezza del mare, richezza dal mare, secc. XIII–XVIII* (Florence: Le Monnier, 2006), 841–61.

Panciera, Walter, 'Le "prove di fortuna" ovvero i testimoniali veneziani settecenteschi: una fonte per lo studio qualitativo e quantitativo della storia della navigazione', in Gerassimos D. Pagratis (ed.), *Le fonti della storia dell'Italia preunitaria: casi di studio per la loro analisi e 'valorizzazione'* (Athens: Papazissiz Publisher, 2019), 447–65.

Panessa, Giangiacomo, *Le comunità greche a Livorno. Tra integrazione e chiusura nazionale* (Livorno: Belforte, 1991).

Pansini, Giuseppe, 'La ruota Fiorentina nelle strutture giudiziarie del Granducato di Toscana sotto I Medici', in Bruno Paradisi (ed.), *La formazione storica del diritto moderno in Europa* (Florence: Società italiana di storia del diritto, 1977), 533–79.

Pardi, Giuseppe, 'Disegno della storia demografica di Livorno', *Archivio Storico Italiano* 76 (1918), 38–9.

Patterson, Orlando, *Slavery and Social Death: A Comparative Study: with a New Preface*, 2nd edn (Cambridge, MA: Harvard University Press, 2018).

Peabody, Sue, 'Slavery, freedom, and the law in the Atlantic world, 1420–1807', in Keith Bradley and Paul Cartledge (eds), *The Cambridge World History of Slavery*, 4 vols (Cambridge: Cambridge University Press, 2011), vol. 3, 594–630.

Pedemonte, Danilo, 'Deserters, mutineers and criminals: British sailors and problems of port jurisdiction in Genoa and Livorno during the eighteenth century', in Maria Fusaro, Bernard Allaire, Richard Blakemore, and Tijl Vanneste (eds), *Law, Labour and Empire: Comparative Perspectives on Seafarers, c. 1500–1800* (London: Palgrave Macmillan, 2015), 256–71.

Penna, Daphne, 'Finders keepers, losers weepers? Byzantine shipwreck and salvage in the eleventh and twelfth centuries', in Louis Sicking and Alain Wijffels (eds), *Conflict Management in the Mediterranean and the Atlantic, 1000–1800* (Leiden: Brill, 2020), 43–66.

—'General average in Byzantium', in Maria Fusaro, Andrea Addobbati, and Luisa Piccinno (eds), *General Average and Risk Management in Medieval and Early Modern Maritime Business* (Cham: Springer, 2023), 95–119.

Philip-Stéphan, Alexandra, 'Assurance de nègres. Mémoire de B.-M. Émérigon concernant l'affaire du brigantin Le Comte d'Estaing', *Revue historique de droit français et étranger* 86 (2008), 557–71.

Piccinno, Luisa, 'Genoa, 1340–1620: early development of marine insurance', in Adrian Leonard (ed.), *Marine Insurance: Origins and Institutions, 1300–1850* (Basingstoke: Palgrave Macmillan, 2016), 24–45.

—'Rischi di viaggio nel commercio marittimo del XVIII secolo', in Marco Cini (ed.), *Traffici commerciali, sicurezza marittima, guerra di corsa. Il Mediterraneo e l'Ordine di Santo Stefano* (Pisa: Edizioni ETS, 2011), 159–79.

Piergiovanni, Vito, *Diritto e giustizia mercantile a Genova nel XV secolo: i consolia di Bartolomeo Bosco* (Sigmaringen: Thorbecke, 1995).
—'Genoese civil rota and mercantile customary law', in Vito Piergiovanni (ed.), *From Lex Mercatoria to Commercial Law* (Berlin: Duncker & Humblot, 2005), 191–206.
—'Il mercante e il diritto canonico medievale: "mercatores in itinere dicuntur miserabiles personae"', *Atti della Società Ligure di Storia Patria, nuova serie* 52 (2012), 617–34.
—*Norme, scienza e pratica giuridica tra Genova e l'occidente medievale e moderno*, 2 vols (Genoa: Società Ligure di Storia Patria, 2012).
—'Statuti, diritto comune e processo mercantile', in Aquilino Iglesia Ferreirós and Fundació Noguera (eds), *El dret comù i Catalunya: actes del VII Simposi Internacional, Barcelona, 23–24 de maig de 1997* (Barcelona: Fundació Noguera, 1998), 137–51.
—'The rise of the Genoese civil rota in the XVIth century: the "decisiones de mercatura" concerning insurance', in Vito Piergiovanni (ed.), *The Courts and the Development of Commercial Law* (Berlin: Duncker & Humbolt, 1987), 24–39.
Pincus, Steve, *1688: The First Modern Revolution* (New Haven: Yale University Press, 2011).
Polanyi, Karl, *The Great Transformation: The Political and Economic Origins of Our Time*, new edn (Boston: Beacon Press, 2001).
Pomeranz, Kenneth, *The Great Divergence* (Princeton: Princeton University Press, 2000).
Pryor, John, *Geography, Technology, and War: Studies in the Maritime History of the Mediterranean, 649–1571* (Cambridge: Cambridge University Press, 1988).
Purpura, Gianfranco, 'La protezione dei giacimenti archeologici in acque internazionali e la Lex Rhodia del mare', in F. Maniscalo (ed.), *Mediterraneum. Tutela e valorizzazione dei beni culturali ed ambientali, III, Tutela del patrimonio subacqueo internazionale* (Naples: Massa, 2004).
Puttevils, Jeroen, and Marc Deloof, 'Marketing and pricing risk in marine insurance in sixteenth-century Antwerp', *The Journal of Economic History* 77 (2017), 796–837.
Ragin, Charles and Howard Saul Becker (eds), *What Is a Case? Exploring the Foundations of Social Inquiry* (Cambridge: Cambridge University Press, 1992).
Ravid, Benjamin, 'A tale of three cities and their raison d'etat. Ancona, Venice, Livorno and their competition for Jewish merchants in the sixteenth century', *Mediterranean Historical Review* 6 (1989), 138–62.
Rediker, Marcus, *The Slave Ship: A Human History* (New York: Viking, 2007).
Remie Constable, Olivia, 'The problem of jettison in medieval Mediterranean maritime law', *Journal of Medieval History* 20 (1994), 207–20.
Ressel, Magnus, 'La nazione Olandese-Alemanna di Livorno e il suo ruolo nel sistema mercantile europeo del XVIII secolo', in Andrea Addobbati and Marcella Aglietti (eds), *La città delle nazioni: Livorno e i limiti del cosmopolitismo (1566–1834)* (Pisa: Pisa University Press, 2016), 309–35.
Robinson, O.F., T.D. Fergus, and W.M. Gordon, *An Introduction to European Legal History* (Abingdon: Professional Books Ltd, 1985).

Romer, Paul, 'Increasing returns and long-run growth', *Journal of Political Economy* 94 (1986), 1002–38.
Rossi, Guido, 'Civilians and insurance: approximations of reality to the law', *The Legal History Review* 83 (2015), 323–64.
—'England 1523–1601: the beginnings of marine insurance', in Adrian Leonard (ed.), *Marine Insurance: Origins and Institutions, 1300–1850* (Basingstoke: Palgrave Macmillan, 2016), 130–48.
—*Insurance in Elizabethan England: The London Code* (Cambridge: Cambridge University Press, 2017).
—'The liability of the shipmaster in early modern law: comparative (and practice-orientated) remarks', *Historia et Ius* 12 (2017), 1–47.
Roth, Cecil, 'The inquisitional archives as a source of English history', *Transactions of the Royal Historical Society* 18 (1935), 107–22.
Rupprecht, Anita, 'A very uncommon case: representations of the *Zong* and the British campaign to abolish the slave trade', *The Journal of Legal History* 28 (2007), 329–46.
—'"Inherent vice": marine insurance, slave ship rebellion and the law', *Race & Class* 57 (2016), 31–44.
Sahlins, David Marshall, *Apologies to Thucydides: Understanding History as Culture and Vice Versa* (Chicago: University of Chicago Press, 2013).
Said, Edward, *Orientalism* (New York: Knopf Doubleday Publishing Group, 2014).
Saint-Exupéry, Antoine, *Le petit prince* (New York: Reynal & Hitchcock, 1943).
Sakai, Yasuhiro, *J.M. Keynes Versus F.H. Knight: Risk, Probability, and Uncertainty* (Singapore: Springer, 2019).
Sanacore, Massimo, 'Le fonti giurisdizionali Pisano-Livornesi e i conflitti di competenze nei secoli XVI–XVII', *Studi Livornesi* 4 (1989), 77–93.
Sanchez-Moreno, Carlos, 'Law of the sea, Rhodian', in Roger Bagnall, Kai Brodersen, Craige Champion, and Andrew Erskine (eds), *The Encyclopedia of Ancient History*, 12 vols (Chichester: Wiley-Blackwell, 2013), vol. 7, 1–2.
Santus, Cesare, 'Crimini, violenza e corruzione nel bagno di Livorno: gli schiavi "turchi" in alcuni processi del XVII secolo', in Andrea Addobbati and Marcella Aglietti (eds), *La città delle nazioni: Livorno e i limiti del cosmopolitismo (1566–1834)* (Pisa: Pisa University Press, 2016), 93–108.
—*Il 'Turco' a Livorno: incontri con l'Islam nella Toscana del seicento* (Milan: Officina Libraria, 2019).
Santus, Cesare, and Guillaume Calafat, 'Les avatars du "Turc". Esclaves et commerçants musulmans en Toscane (1600–1750)', in Jocelyne Dakhlia and Bernard Vincent (eds), *Les Musulmans dans l'histoire de l'Europe, tome 1. Une intégration invisible* (Paris: Albin Michel, 2011), 471–522.
Sarll, Richard, 'The "Ever Given": not your average dispute', *The Marine Insurer* 7 (2021), 8–9.
Savelli, Rodolfo, 'Modelli giuridici e cultura mercantile tra XVI e XVII secolo', in Franco Angiolini and Daniel Roche (eds), *Cultures et formations négociantes dans l'Europe moderne* (Paris: Editions de l'école des hautes études en sciences sociales, 1995), 403–20.
Schmitthoff, Clive (ed.), *The Sources of the Law of International Trade* (London: Stevens & Sons, 1964).

Selmer, Knut, *The Survival of General Average: A Necessity or an Anachronism?* (Oslo: Oslo University Press, 1958).
Senior, William, 'The history of maritime law', *The Mariner's Mirror* 38 (1952), 260–75.
Setton, Kenneth Meyer, *Venice, Austria, and the Turks in the Seventeenth Century* (Philadelphia: American Philosophical Society, 1991).
Shyllon, F.O., *Black Slaves in Britain* (London: Oxford University Press for the Institute of Race Relations, 1974).
Sicking, Louis, 'Naval warfare in Europe, c. 1330–c. 1680', in Frank Tallett and D.J.B. Trim (eds), *European Warfare, 1350–1750* (Cambridge: Cambridge University Press, 2010), 236–63.
Sicking, Louis, and Alain Wijffels (eds), *Conflict Management in the Mediterranean and the Atlantic, 1000–1800* (Leiden: Brill, 2020).
Siegler, Frederick Adrian, 'Voluntary and involuntary', *The Monist* 52 (1968), 268–87.
Shephard, James, 'The Rôles d'Oléron: a lex mercatoria of the sea?', in Vito Piergiovanni (ed.), *From Lex Mercatoria to Commercial Law* (Berlin: Duncker & Humblot, 2005), 207–53.
Speciale, Giuseppe, 'Diritto e mercato. Il "diritto che viene dalle cose". Dallo ius mercatorum al mercato in blockchain', in Aldo Andrea Cassi (ed.), *Le danze di Clio e Astrea. Fondamenti storici del diritto europeo* (Turin: Giappichelli, 2023), 459–512.
Spencer, Jonathan, 'Hull insurance and general average – some current issues', *Tulane Law Review* 83 (2009), 1227–88.
Steinfeld, Robert, *The Invention of Free Labour: The Employment Relation in English and American Law and Culture, 1350–1870* (Chapel Hill: University of North Carolina Press, 1991).
Stern, Philip, *The Company-State: Corporate Sovereignty and the Early Modern Foundations of the British Empire in India* (Oxford: Oxford University Press, 2011).
Tanzini, Lorenzo, 'Le prime edizioni a stampa in italiano del Libro del Consolato del Mare', in Rossana Martorelli (ed.), *Itinerando. Senza confini dalla preistoria ad oggi. Studi in ricordo di Roberto Coroneo* (Perugia: Morlacchi Editore, 2015), 965–78.
Taylor, Eric Robert, *If We Must Die: Shipboard Insurrections in the Era of the Atlantic Slave Trade* (Baton Rouge: Louisiana State University Press, 2009).
Tazzara, Corey, 'Managing free trade in early modern Europe: institutions, information and the free port of Livorno', *Journal of Modern History* 86 (2014), 493–529.
—'Port of trade or commodity market? Livorno and cross-cultural trade in the early modern Mediterranean', *Business History Review* 94 (2020), 201–28.
—*The Free Port of Livorno and the Transformation of the Mediterranean World* (Oxford: Oxford University Press, 2017).
Tetley, William, 'The general maritime law: the lex maritima (with brief reference to the *ius commune*) in arbitration law and the conflict of laws', *Syracuse Journal of International Law and Commerce* 20 (1994), 105–45.

Thompson, Norma, *The Ship of State: Statecraft and Politics from Ancient Greece to Democratic America* (New Haven and London: Yale University Press, 2001).

Toaff, Renzo, *La nazione ebrea a Livorno e Pisa* (Florence: Olschki, 1990).

Toledano, Ehud, 'Enslavement in the Ottoman empire in the early modern period', in Keith Bradley and Paul Cartledge (eds) *The Cambridge World History of Slavery*, 4 vols (Cambridge: Cambridge University Press, 2011), 25–46.

Toth, Orsolya, *The Lex Mercatoria in Theory and Practice* (Oxford: Oxford University Press, 2017).

Trakman, Leon, 'From the lex mercatoria to e-merchant law', *The University of Toronto Law Journal* 53 (2003), 265–304.

Trivellato, Francesca, 'Credito e tolleranza: i limiti del cosmopolitismo nella Livorno di età moderna', in Andrea Addobbati and Marcella Aglietti (eds), *La città delle nazioni: Livorno e i limiti del cosmopolitismo (1566–1834)* (Pisa: Pisa University Press, 2016), 39–50.

—'Economic and business history as cultural history: pitfalls and possibilities', *I Tatti Studies*, 22 (2019), 403–10.

—'Microstoria/microhistoire/microhistory', *French Politics, Culture & Society* 33 (2015), 122–34.

—'Renaissance Florence and the origins of capitalism: a business history perspective', *Business History Review* 94 (2020), 229–51.

—'Stati, diaspore e commerci mediterranei: mercanti ebrei tra Livorno, Marsiglia e Aleppo (1673–1747)', in Adriano Prosperi (ed.), *Livorno 1606–1806: luogo di incontro tra popoli e culture* (Turin: Alimandi, 2009), 361–74.

—*The Familiarity of Strangers: The Sephardic Diaspora, Livorno, and Cross-Cultural Trade in the Early-Modern Period* (New Haven: Yale University Press, 2009).

—*The Promise and Peril of Credit: What a Forgotten Legend about Jews and Finance Tells Us about the Making of European Commercial Society* (Princeton: Princeton University Press, 2019).

—'"Usages and Customs of the Sea": Étienne Cleirac and the making of maritime law in seventeenth century France', *The Legal History Review* (2016), 193–224.

Turley, David, *Slavery* (Oxford: Blackwell, 2003).

Turnbull, Craig, *A History of British Actuarial Thought* (Cham: Palgrave Macmillan, 2017).

Unger, Richard, 'Overview. Trades, ports and ships: the roots of difference in sailors' lives', in Maria Fusaro, Bernard Allaire, Richard Blakemore, and Tijl Vanneste (eds), *Law, Labour and Empire: Comparative Perspectives on Seafarers, c. 1500–1800* (London: Palgrave Macmillan, 2015), 1–17.

—'The technology and teaching of shipbuilding', in Stephan Epstein, Maarten Roy Prak, and Jan Luiten Van Zanden (eds), *Technology, Skills and the Pre-Modern Economy in the East and the West: Essays Dedicated to the Memory of S.R. Epstein* (Leiden: Brill, 2013), 161–204.

Van Cleve, George, '"Somerset's case" and its antecedents in imperial perspective', *Law and History Review* 24 (2006), 601–45.

Van Den Boogert, Maurits, *The Capitulations and the Ottoman Legal System: Qadis, Consuls, and Beratlıs in the 18th Century* (Leiden and Boston: Brill, 2005).

Van Meersbergen, Guido, 'Dutch and English approaches to cross-cultural trade in Mughal India and the problem of trust, 1600–1630', in Cátia Antunes and

Amélia Polónia (eds), *Beyond Empires: Global, Self-Organizing, Cross-Imperial Networks, 1500–1800* (Leiden: Brill, 2016), 69–87.

Van Zanden, Jan Luiten, 'Early modern economic growth. A survey of the European economy, 1500–1800', in Maarten Roy Prak (ed.), *Early Modern Capitalism: Economic and Social Change in Europe, 1400–1800* (London: Routledge, 2001).

—'The "revolt of the early modernists" and the "first modern economy": an assessment', *The Economic History Review* 55 (2002), 619–41.

Vanneste, Tijl, *Intra-European Litigation in Eighteenth-Century Izmir: The Role of the Merchants' Style* (Leiden: Brill, 2021).

Varisco, Daniel, *Reading Orientalism: Said and the Unsaid* (Seattle: University of Washington Press, 2017).

Vignoli, Paola, *I costituti della legge e dell'uso di Pisa (secolo XII). Edizione critica integrale del testo tràdito dal 'Codice Yale' (ms. Beinecke Library 415)* (Rome: Istituto storico italiano per il Medioevo, 2003).

Villani, Stefano, 'A "republican" Englishman in Leghorn: Charles Longland', in *European Contexts for English Republicanism* (Farnham: Ashgate, 2016), 163–77.

—'Between anatomy and politics: John Finch and Italy, 1649–71', in Gaby Mahlberg and Dirk Wiemann (eds), *The Practice of Reform in Health, Medicine, and Science, 1500–2000* (Aldershot: Ashgate, 2005), 151–66.

—'Dalla Gran Bretagna all'Italia: narrazioni di conversione nel Sant'Uffizio di Pisa e Livorno', in Andrea Addobbati and Marcella Aglietti (eds), *La città delle nazioni: Livorno e i limiti del cosmopolitismo (1566–1834)* (Pisa: Pisa University Press, 2016), 109–26.

—'I consoli della nazione inglese a Livorno tra il 1665 e il 1673: Joseph Kent, Thomas Clutterbuck e Ephraim Skinner', *Nuovi Studi Livornesi* 11 (2004), 11–34.

—'Livorno – diversis gentibus una', in Giovanni Tarantino and Paola Von Wyss-Giacosa (eds), *Twelve Cities – One Sea: Early Modern Mediterranean Port Cities and their Inhabitants* (Rome: Edizioni Scientifiche Italiane, 2023), 37–53.

—'Religione e politica: le comunità protestanti a Livorno nel XVII e XVIIII secolo', in Daniele Pesciatini (ed.), *Livorno dal medioevo all'età contemporanea. Ricerche e riflessioni* (Pisa and Livorno: Banco di Sardegna, 2003), 36–64.

—'Religious pluralism and the danger of tolerance: the English nation in Livorno in the seventeenth century', in Federico Barbierato and Alessandra Veronese (eds), *Late Medieval and Early Modern Religious Dissents: Conflicts and Plurality in Renaissance Europe* (Pisa: Edizioni il Campano Arnus University Books, 2012), 97–124.

—'Una finistra mediterranea sull'Europea: i "nordici" nella Livorno della prima età moderna', in Adriano Prosperi (ed.), *Livorno 1606–1806: luogo di incontro tra popoli e culture* (Turin: Alimandi, 2009), 158–77.

—'"Una piccola epitome di Inghilterra". La comunità inglese di Livorno negli anni di Ferdinandi II: questioni religiose e politiche', *Cromohs* 8 (2003), 1–23.

Villani, Stefano, and Lucia Frattarelli Fischer, '"People of every mixture". Immigration, tollerance, and religious conflicts in early modern Livorno', in Ann Katherine Isaacs (ed.), *Immigration and Emigration in Historical Perspective* (Pisa: Edizioni Plus, 2007), 93–107.

Von Wright, Georg Henrik, *The Varieties of Goodness* (London: Routledge, 1963).

Wade, Lewis, *Privilege, Economy and State in Old Regime France: Marine*

Insurance, War and the Atlantic Empire under Louis XIV (Woodbridge: The Boydell Press, 2023).

Wallerstein, Immanuel, *World-Systems Analysis: An Introduction* (Durham, NC: Duke University Press, 2004).

Walvin, James, *The Zong: A Massacre, the Law and the End of Slavery* (New Haven and London: Yale University Press, 2011).

Ware, Rudolph, 'Slavery in Islamic Africa, 1400–1800', in Keith Bradley and Paul Cartledge (eds), *The Cambridge World History of Slavery*, 4 vols (Cambridge: Cambridge University Press, 2011), 47–80.

Watson, Alan, 'Roman slave law: an Anglo-American perspective', *Cardozo Law Review* 18 (1996), 591–8.

Webster, Jane, 'The Zong in the context of the eighteenth-century slave trade', *The Journal of Legal History* 28 (2007), 285–98.

White, Joshua, *Piracy and Law in the Ottoman Mediterranean* (Redwood City: Stanford University Press, 2017).

Williamson, Oliver, *The Economic Institutions of Capitalism: Firms, Markets, Relational Contracting* (New York: Free Press, 2010).

Zamora Rodríguez, Francisco, 'Livorno al crocevia degli imperi iberici', in Andrea Addobbati and Marcella Aglietti (eds), *La città delle nazioni: Livorno e i limiti del cosmopolitismo (1566–1834)* (Pisa: Pisa University Press, 2016), 277–92.

Zanini, Andrea, 'Financing and risk in Genoese maritime trade during the eighteenth century: strategies and practices', in Maria Fusaro, Andrea Addobbati, and Luisa Piccinno (eds), *General Average and Risk Management in Medieval and Early Modern Maritime Business* (Cham: Springer, 2023), 335–59.

Zaugg, Roberto, 'Judging foreigners. Conflict strategies, consular interventions and institutional changes in eighteenth-century Naples', *Journal of Modern Italian Studies* 13 (2008), 171–95.

—'Mercanti stranieri e giudici Napoletani: la gestione dei conflitti in antico regime', *Quaderni Storici* 45 (2010), 139–70.

—'On the use of legal resources and the definition of group boundaries. A prosopographic analysis of the French nation and the British factory in eighteenth-century Naples', in Georg Christ, Stefan Burkhardt, Wolfgang Kaiser, Franz-Julius Morche, and Roberto Zaugg (eds), *Union in Separation – Diasporic Groups and Identities in the Eastern Mediterranean (1100–1800)* (Rome: Viella, 2015), 699–714.

—*Stranieri di antico regime. Mercanti, giudici e consoli nella Napoli del Settecento* (Rome: Viella, 2011).

Unpublished theses

Abela, Joan Angela, 'The impact of the arrival of the Knights of St John on the commercial economy of Malta, 1530–1565' (unpublished PhD thesis, University of Exeter, 2012).

Iodice, Antonio, 'Maritime average and seaborne trade in early modern Genoa, 1590–1700' (unpublished PhD thesis, University of Exeter/University of Genoa, 2021).

Sanacore, Massimo, 'I consoli del mare a Pisa, dall'età medicea alle riforme leopoldine' (unpublished MA thesis, University of Pisa, 1983).

Unpublished articles

Battistoni, Marta, 'Molina di Quosa e la casa di Michele'.

Web-based secondary sources

'Average', in T.F. Hoad (ed.), *The Concise Oxford Dictionary of English Etymology* (Oxford: Oxford University Press, 1996) <www.oxfordreference.com/display/10.1093/acref/9780192830982.001.0001/acref-9780192830982-e-1034> [23 February 2021].

'CMI: About Us', <https://comitemaritime.org/about-us/> [accessed 23 February 2020].

'General Average Absorption Clause 2018', <www.bimco.org/contracts-and-clauses/bimco-clauses/current/general-average-absorption-clause-2018> [accessed 30 January 2024].

'General Average: York-Antwerp Rules', <https://comitemaritime.org/work/york-antwerp-rules-yar/> [accessed 23 February 2020].

'Research Guide: The High Court of the Admiralty', <www.nationalarchives.gov.uk/help-with-your-research/research-guides/high-court-admiralty-records/> [2 Feburary 2024].

'Risk Sharing Framework' (9 June 2023), <https://interagencystandingcommittee.org/grand-bargain-official-website/risk-sharing-framework> [accessed 30 January 2024].

'Sailing into Modernity: Table of Roles', <www.exeter.ac.uk/research/centres/maritime/research/modernity/roles/> [accessed 1 February 2024].

'York-Antwerp Rules' (2016), <https://comitemaritime.org/work/york-antwerp-rules-yar/> [accessed 18 August 2021].

Allen, D.F., 'James II in pursuit of a pirate at Malta', *Electronic British Library Journal* (1990) <www.bl.uk/eblj/1990articles/pdf/article10.pdf> [accessed 18 August 2021].

Calafat, Guillaume, 'La somme des besoins: rescrits, informations et suppliques (Toscane, 1550–1750)', *L'Atelier du Centre de recherches historiques* 13 (2015), <https://journals.openedition.org/acrh/6558> [accessed 2 February 2024].

Catucci, Marco, 'MONIGLIA, Giovanni Andrea', in *Dizionario Biografico degli Italiani* (Rome: Istituto dell'Enciclopedia Italiana, 2011), vol. 75, <www.treccani.it/enciclopedia/giovanni-andrea-moniglia_(Dizionario-Biografico)/> [accessed 2 February 2024].

Cordes, Albrecht, 'Conflicts in 13th century maritime law: a comparison between five European ports', *Oxford University Comparative Law Forum 2* (2003), <https://ouclf.law.ox.ac.uk/conflicts-in-13th-century-maritime-law-a-comparison-between-five-european-ports/> [accessed 2 February 2024].

——'The search for a medieval lex mercatoria', *Oxford University Comparative Law Forum 5* (2003), <https://ouclf.law.ox.ac.uk/the-search-for-a-medieval-lex-mercatoria/> [accessed 2 February 2024].

Fortunati, Maura, 'Targa, Carlo', *Dizionario Biografico degli Italiani* (Rome: Instituto dell'Enciclopedia Italiana, 2019), vol. 95, <www.treccani.it/enciclopedia/carlo-targa_%28Dizionario-Biografico%29/> [accessed 18 December 2023].

George, Rose, 'Worse things still happen at sea: the shipping disasters we never hear about', *The Guardian* (10 January 2015) <www.theguardian.com/world/2015/jan/10/shipping-disasters-we-never-hear-about> [accessed 2 Februrary 2024].

Handley, Stuart, 'Molloy, Charles (1645/6–1690)' in *The Oxford Dictionary of National Biography* (2004), <www.oxforddnb.com/view/10.1093/ref:odnb/9780198614128.001.0001/odnb-9780198614128-e-18914> [accessed 2 Februrary 2024].

International Union of Marine Insurers, 'Position paper of the International Union of Marine Insurers ("IUMI"): York-Antwerp Rules – CMI Questionaire' (2013), available at <https://comitemaritime.org/work/review-of-the-rules-on-general-average/> [accessed 31 January 2024].

Lely, Peter, 'Finch, Sir John (1626–1682)', *Oxford Dictionary of National Biography* (2004), <www.oxforddnb.com/view/10.1093/ref:odnb/9780198614128.001.0001/odnb> [accessed 18 August 2021].

Lobban, Michael, 'Brougham, Henry Peter, first Baron Brougham and Vaux (1778–1868)', *Oxford Dictionary of National Biography* (2004), <https://doi.org/10.1093/ref:odnb/3581> [accessed 2 February 2024].

Melikan, R.A., 'Gibbs, Sir Vicary (1751–1820)', *Oxford Dictionary of National Biography* (2004), <https://doi.org/10.1093/ref:odnb/10608> [accessed 2 February 2024].

Piergiovanni, Vito, 'Casaregi, Giuseppe Lorenzo Maria', *Dizionario Biografico degli Italiani* (Rome: Instituto dell'Enciclopedia Italiana, 1978), vol. 21, <www.treccani.it/enciclopedia/giuseppe-lorenzo-maria-casaregi_(Dizionario-Biografico)> [accessed 2 February 2024].

The editors of *Encyclopedia Britannica*, 'The Gunpowder Plot', *Encyclopedia Brittanica*, <www.britannica.com/event/Gunpowder-Plot> [accessed 18 August 2021].

Xie Ming, 'Legality, rationality of general average for MV Ever Given' (2022), <https://law.asia/legality-and-rationality-mv-ever-given/> [accessed 10 August 2023].

Index

Accomandite 37
Act to prevent the Delivery
  up of Merchant Shipps
  (1664/1671) 125–7
Addison, Giacomo 182
Administration-as-justice 29, 78, 119
Alamanni, Lodovico 37
Aleppo 100, 174
Alessandro, Duke of Tuscany 31
Algiers 116, 117, 122
Alicante 88, 123, 132–3, 137–8, 140, 146, 147
Alice and Francis (ship) 120–7, 131–41, 148, 152, 162
American Revolutionary Wars 162, 187
Amsterdam
  Chamber of Insurance and
    Average 34, 37, 47, 125, 160–1
  GA practices 161
  Insurance market 159–60
  Ordonnantie 63
  Structural impact of role as final
    destination 144
Arbitration 78–9
Aristotle 68–9, 93–4
Arkhangelsk 146
Average
  Average of the English and Dutch
    Usage (so-called) 68, 69
  Average of the Indies 68, 69
  Averia (de Indias) 55
  Circumstances mandating common
    contribution *see under* General
    Average (GA)
  Common Average *see* Small Average
  Etymology 53–4, 72
  Finance of merchant *nationes* 55–6
  Free-from-Average clauses *see under*
    Insurance
  Many varieties 4, 55
  Origin of term 54–6, 158
  Particular Average (PA) 48, 49, 67, 69, 73, 91, 95, 119, 134, 166, 171–2
  Petty Average *see* Small Average
  Primage and Average 55, 67, 68, 72

Small Average 46, 55, 61, 63–4, 67, 73, 77, 101, 119
See also General Average (GA)

Baldasseroni, Ascanio
  Comparison of Genoese and Livornese
    GA 145–6
  Criticism of GA 106–7, 162, 188
  Definition of free port 28
  Definition of GA 46, 48
  Underwriters' responsibility for
    GA 159
Barcelona 56
Barcher, Giovanni 91
Basilica (Byzantine law collection) 53
Belasyse, Thomas, Lord Fauconberg 128
Benassai, Carlo 85, 140
Benecke, William 171
Biserta 179
Bolaño, Juan de Hevia 65
Borse di ricorso 38, 82–3
Bottomry *see* Sea loan
Bumpt, George 133
Buonaccorsi, Lorenzo 97
Burgos *Ordonnance* (1538) 55

Cabo de Gatt 111 n.154, 122, 133
Cadiz 96, 133, 147, 160
Callistratus (Roman jurist) 52
Cambio marittimo see Sea loan
Capponi, Andrea 139–40
Captain of Livorno *see* Governor of
  Livorno
Cardi, Paolo Maria 97
Casaregi, Giuseppe Maria
  Career 65, 72
  Edition of the *Llibre del Consolat de
    Mar* 56
  On Averages 15, 46, 65, 72–6, 101, 105, 185, 192
Catalonia 47
Cepparelli, Tommaso 39
Charles II, King of England and
  Scotland 122, 124, 128, 129
Chinese maritime law 190
Clutterbuck, Thomas 129, 136

Coase, Ronald   6–7
Collusion   107, 121, 148, 186
Comaccio, Iacob   181–2
Comaccio, Isack   181–2
Comité Maritime International   13
Commedia del Console   35–6, 119
Common Bench   127
Common safety vs common benefit *see under* General Average (GA)
Conservatori del Mare see under Genoa
Consiglio dei Quarantotto   36
Consolato see under Sea protest
Consoli del Mare di Pisa
   Appointment   31–2, 37
   Archive of   17, 157
   Reputation   35–6, 144
   Role in GA procedures   108, 110, 122
   see also Court of the *Consoli del Mare di Pisa*
Constitutum usus   47
Consuls of the Sea in Pisa *see Consoli del Mare di Pisa*
Cornah, Richard   49
Corpus Iuris Civilis   12, 45
Corsairs   33, 90, 111, 122, 133, 143, 146, 180
Corso   27, 187
Cosimo I, Grand Duke of Tuscany   31–2, 128
Cosimo III, Grand Duke of Tuscany   37, 93, 121, 128–9, 145
Cottimo   98, 169
Court of the *Consoli del Mare di Pisa*
   As meeting point of different legal regimes   15
   Attitude towards GA procedures   29, 119, 142
   GA Procedures   80–2
      Administrative fees   113–14, 191
      Calculations   82
      Capitoli   108–11, 117
      Discounted contribution of ship and freight   73, 82, 97, 107
      Exceptions   81, 107–11, 136
      Headings *see Capitoli*
      Interrogatories   81, 108–11, 117, 136
      Judgements   81, 136
      Ragioni   117
      Shipmasters' appearance   88
      Summons   81
      Valuation of goods   83–5
      Witnesses   81, 109–10, 117
   Origin and history   31–2

Personnel
   Assessor   39
   Attorneys   39, 40, 107
   Calculators   82–3, 107, 138–9, 191
   Chancellor   39, 107, 132
   Curatore   107, 136
   Experts   86–7, 136, 143
   Merchant deputies   85
   Notary   89
   Secretary *see* Chancellor
   Vice-chancellor   89, 136
Reforms
   of 1561   34, 83, 112–13
   of 1601   39
Customs fraud   139–41
Cyprus   174

D'Attigian, Mattus   160
Da Fabriano, Gentile   163
De' Medici, Alessandro *see* Alessandro, Duke of Tuscany
De' Medici, Cosimo I *see* Cosimo I, Grand Duke of Tuscany
De' Medici, Cosimo III *see* Cosimo III, Grand Duke of Tuscany
De' Medici, Ferdinando *see* Ferdinando I, Grand Duke of Tuscany
De' Medici, Ferdinando II *see* Ferdinando II, Grand Duke of Tuscany
De' Medici, Giancarlo, Cardinal   35
De Norvilli, Chealam   160, 173
De Satin-Exupéry, Antoine   143
De Vicq, Mattheus   15
Del Beccuto, Baccio   163–8
Del Beccuto, Ruberto   37
Del Frate, Tommaso   140
Dethick, Thomas   172, 175–7
Dickinfield, Carlos   133
Digest of Justinian   5, 12, 16, 47, 50–1, 65, for 14.2 *see Lex Rhodia de Iactu*
Dilman, Federigo   172, 174–8
Dring, Stephen
   Account of his voyage   133–5, 138
   Career   123
   Choice of Livorno to declare GA   137
   Collusion with Livorno-based merchants   139–40, 142
   Compensation paid to   126
   Disembarkation under sanitary regulations   88, 132, 139
   Escape from justice   152
Durkenfelds, Charles   136

INDEX

England
  Admiralty courts 13
  Antipathy between common and civil law courts 13
  Approach to GA in the 19th century 74
  Consul in Livorno 122, 123, 129, 146, 156, *see also* Clutterbuck, Thomas
  Consuls overseas 147
  English presence in the Mediterranean 21, 25, 26
  English presence in Venice 43, 148
  GA procedures 123, 124–7
  Natio (factory) in Livorno 122, 128
  Parliament 150
  State's desire to control mariners and merchants 121, 124, 146, 190
  Variety of maritime capitalism 121, 151
  See also London
Ever Given 9, 184, 188–9
Evolutionary story of risk 6–10, 17–18, 154–5, 169, 183, 186

Ferdinando I, Grand Duke of Tuscany 24, 27
Ferdinando II, Grand Duke of Tuscany 22–3, 128
Finch, Sir John 122, 126, 128–30, 146, 190
Florence 32, 33, 35, 36, 37, 128
Florentine patriciate 30, 31, 35–6, 40, 163
Foenus nauticum see Sea loan
Foot, Robert 139, 152
Forno, Bartolomo 169–70, 172–6, 178
Franco-Dutch War 166
Freight contract 55, 101, 141, 161, 190
Freight rates 178
French consuls 96, 99, 174
French *nationes* 99–101, 169
French Revolutionary Wars 187
Frosini, Alessandro 40
Frosini, Ambrosio 40
Frosini, Giovanni Vincenzo 40
Frosini, Michelangelo 40

GA *see* General Average (GA)
Gaeta 92
Galley of Salamis 107, 135, 178, 186
Garzille, Antonio 169–70, 172–8
General Average (GA)
  Administrative burden of 191
  Advantage for ship interests 174, 186–7, 191
  And precautionary acts 50, 74, 81, 98, 101
  And sea loan 154, 157, 168–80, 179, 183, 186
  And unseaworthiness 102
  Calls for abolition 5, 184, 188–9, 191
  Chinese law of 190
  Circumstances in which common contribution was used
    Assistants 97
    Avanias 99
    Beaching 57, 59, 60, 66, 89, 97, 98, 143
    Bribes 97, 100, 169
    Combat 97, 125–7, 131–4
    Compensation for crew 123, 126, 132, 136, 140, 150–1
    Compensation for Suez Canal Authority 190
    Cottimo 98, 100–1
    Divers' fees 97, 102–3
    Extraordinary expenses 89, 98, 169
    Gifts 100
    Mast cutting 50, 5, 63, 77, 93–4, 143
    Messengers 97, 160
    Ransom 50, 61, 68, 125
    Rope cutting 89, 98, 143, 160
    Seamen's wages 97, 128–30, 160
    Taxes 97
    Transshipment to small boats 50, 89, 160
    Victuals 160
    See also Jettison
  Common safety vs common benefit approach 5, 96, 191–2
  Consolidation out of previous practices 101, 192
  Contribution of freight towards 58, 63, 68, 72, 72, 84, 97, 160–8, 174–7
  Definition
    Modern-day 49
    Of Baldasseroni 48
    Of Casaregi 72
    Of Targa 68–9
    Of Weytsen 64
  English GA procedures *see under* England

INDEX

Genoese GA procedures *see under* Genoa
  Overloaded 180–2
  Principle 2, 46, 103
  Voluntary/Involuntary distinction 93–5
  York Antwerp Rules (YAR) 49–50, 52, 188–9, 190
  See also GA procedures *under* Court of the *Consoli del Mare*
Genoa
  Conservatori del Mare 34, 46, 66
  Consuls abroad 92
  Differences with Livorno 30
  Finance 169–70
  Free port 24, 142
  GA procedures 34, 91, 145–6
  Maritime law 47
  Political economy 142
  Reception of the *Llibre del Consolat de Mar* 56
  Rivalry with Livorno 29
  Rota (court) 41
Germinamento 60, 65–7, 119
Gherardini, Camillo 37
Ghibellini, Amadio 40
Gibraltar 96
Gilles, Carlo 172, 175–7
Goldman, Berthold 11
Goldschmidt, Levin, 59
Good faith 44
Governor of Livorno 32, 106, 117, 152
Grain 103, 141–2
Gravesend 132
Grendi, Edoardo 120

Hamburg 125, 171
Harris, Ron 8–9, 155
Hermogenian (Roman jurist) 52

Insurance
  Mutual Insurance 3, 53, 60–1, 105, 192
  Premium Insurance
    Absorption clauses 189
    And NIE 7, 9–10, 155, 186
    And the *ius commune* 118–19
    Authorities' desire to curb usage 63
    Companies 156, 183, 187
    Early modern insurance rates 159
    Free-from-Average clauses 162, 179–80
    Insurance ledgers as sources 163–6
    Interaction with GA 49, 64, 107–8, 154, 158–68
    Invention of 1–2, 153
    In Amsterdam 34, 37, 47, 125, 159–61
    In Livorno 160, 172
    In London 4, 159
    Present-day usage 9–10
    Prominence in histories of risk management 1
    Solve et repete 181
    Statuti di sicurtà 47
    Ufficio di sicurtà 158
    Use of actuarial methods 2, 156
    See also Lloyd's Coffee House
  Through sea loan 178
International Union of Marine Insurance (IUMI) 188–9
Israel, Aron di Samuel 138
Italy 1, 8, 17–18, 46, 56, 65, 151
Ius commune 185
  Alleged unsuitability for deciding mercantile cases 42, 102
  Court staff versed in the 15–16, 89
  Definition 12
  Jurists of the 16, 45–6
  Position vis-à-vis maritime-commercial law and practice 14, 41, 45, 118–19
  Presumptions regarding liability 90
  See also Corpus Iuris Civilis
Izmir 123, 136, 138, 147

Jettison
  And collective contribution 46, 53, 55
  And interrogatories 110, 117
  And sea loan 171
  Aristotle and 93–4
  As archetypal instance of GA 2, 5, 192
  Consultation before 53, 57–60, 91–3, 119
  Examples 90, 117, 145
  In sea protests 89–91
  In the *Llibre del Consolat de Mar* 57–62, 72, 89–90
  In the Tuscan insurance form 158

INDEX

In the work of Carlo Targa 66–7, 69, 71
In the work of Giuseppe Casaregi 73–6, 192
Low Countries legislation concerning 63
Of slaves 105, 105 n.123
Possible connection with etymology of Average 54
Roman law of *see* Lex Rhodia de Iactu
Tuscan legislation concerning 47
Juez conservador 147
Jurisdiction
   English attempts to expand consular jurisdiction 120–1, 123, 128–30, 146–7, 190
   GA as multi-jurisdictional process 80
   Over maritime-commercial cases in Tuscany 32–3, 143–4
   Tuscany's approach to 143–5
Justianian's *Digest see Digest* of Justinian

King's Bench 148
Knight, Frank 9, 155

Lampsen, Ezechiel 152
Lassels, Richard 47
Legal humanism 64–5
Leo X, Pope 56
Lestoch, Buiardi 133
Levant Company (English) 123
Lex Rhodia de Iactu
   Absence of word Average 54
   And ransom 125
   And sea protests 89–90, 184
   And slaves 105
   And the *Digest* 12, 47, 50
   As earliest expression of law of GA 12, 50
   Continuity with modern GA 192
   Contrast with GA as practised in Tuscany 16, 46, 118
   Italian jurists' use of 65–6, 72–6
   Rules on common contribution 50–4, 57
   Valuation of goods 83–5
Lex maritima 4, 185
Lex mercatoria
   Medieval 4, 11, 103, 119, 120, 149, 185
   New 12–13, 42
Lisbon 96
Livorno
   Attractive for declaring GA 147
   Foreign *nationes* 18, 22–7, 87
   Free port 20, 23–7
      Definition 23, 28–9
      Informal aspects 28–9, 124, 143
      Limitations 30–1
      Livornina 24–5, 28
      Reform of 1676 24, 28, 29, 86
   GA procedures *see under* Court of the Consoli del Mare
   Lack of native mercantile elite 16, 30
   Naval architecture 29–30
   Political economy 101, 119, 141–4, 148, 185–6
   Port-of-transit 79
   Tuscany's main international port 16
Llibre del Consolat de Mar
   And absence of merchants on board 62, 64
   And extraordinary expenses 63, 75, 101
   And sea protests 90
   And seamen's wages 128
   And Small Average 63, 75
   Casaregi's edition of 57, 74
   Constrast with GA as practised in Tuscany 16, 184
   Differences with *Lex Rhodia de Iactu* 48
   Goods stored on deck 104
   Origins 56
   Reception as *lex* 72
   Role in Tuscany 47–8
   Rules on contribution 56–62, 89
   Seamen's wages 128
   Use by Italian jurists 46, 65–6, 69, 72
   Valuation of goods 84–5
Lloyd's Coffee House 4
London
   London Gazette 122
   Insurance market 4, 159
   Merchants of 122
   Structural impact of role as final destination 144
Lombardo, Giovanni 179
Low Countries
   Biscayar and Castilian merchants resident in 55–6
   Early modern maritime law developments 62–4, 185
   First use of word Average 54–5

GA practices 46, 151, 171, 182
Legislation concerning Average
Een Tractaet van Avarien see
   Weytsen, Quentin
Hordenanzas 64
Ordonnance of 1551/53 55, 63–4, 126
Tracatus de Avariis see Weytsen, Quentin
See also Amsterdam
See also Netherlands
Luci, Emilio 39, 130, 138

Madasco, Lorenzo 179–80
Magens, Nicolas 125, 171 n.76
Magistrato di Sanità 88, 132
Malynes, Gerard 42, 102, 172
Marseille 24, 29, 84, 99, 101, 147
Mattei, Giovanni Pietro 97
Medina, Rafaello 87
Mediterranean (in historical analyses) 20–1
Meknes 96
Mercanzia (Florentine court) 32
Messina 123, 136, 138, 144, 147, 152
Mestura, Giovanni 181
Migliorotti, Girolamo 152
Mochi, Benedetto 39–40
Molloy, Charles 15, 172
Moneta, Michele 137, 147
Moniglia, Giovanni Andrea 35, 119
Mos gallicus and *mos italicus* 65
Mun, Thomas 91, 111
Muslims 27

Naples 136, 138, 147, 152
Nationes (definition) 26
Natural law 44
Naviganti (1234) (Papal bull) 171
Netherlands 46, 160, *see also* Low Countries
New Institutional Economics 4–5, 6–9, 121, 149–50
NIE *see* New Institutional Economics
Nine Years' War 167
Nomos Rhodion Nautikos (Byzantine maritime-legal collection) 52–3, 54, 57
North, Douglass 4, 6–7, 183

Ordonnance de la marine 126, 172, 179
Ottoman Empire 123, 147
Out-of-court discussion 118, 139–41

P&I clubs 10
Palermo 181
Paphos 95
Pasqual, Alexandro 132
Paul (Roman jurist) 51–2
Peck, Peter (the Elder) 15
Pepys, Samuel 148
Petitions to the Tuscan Grand Duke 28, 32
Pettinini, Niccolaio 138
Pierallini, Francesco Giuseppe 28, 106, 187
Pisa 31, 47, 56, 78–9, 106, 117
Political economy 30, 45, 120–1, 143–4, 148–52, 185–6
Poltri, Carlo 37
Portugal 132
Pratica segreta (Tuscan advisory council) 33 n.74
Premium Insurance *see under* Insurance
Private resolution 78–9, 103–4, 140
Prussia 171

Quarantine 128, 181
Quaratesi family 163
Quaratesi, Girolamo 163
Quaratesi Polyptych 163

Reale, Giuseppe 102, 112, 179–80
Respondentia *see* Sea loan
Ricorso 38, 82–3
Risk
   And uncertainty 9, 10, 155–6
   In the maritime environment 1
   Meanings 158–9
   See also Risk management
Risk management
   And enforcement of payments 179
   And the maritime economy 1–2
   And the maritime labour force 121, 125, 151
   Changes in late medieval period 62
   Community of risk 154, 173–4
   For the transport sector 10, 168, 174–8, 186–7
   In agriculture 151
   Multiple, simultaneous strategies 10, 19, 157, 182–3
   Partial ownership of assets 157, 168, 180
   Recent developments in global risk-management 184–5, 188
   See also Evolutionary story of risk

See also General Average (GA)
See also Insurance
See also P&I clubs
See also Sea loan
Rhodian Law of Jettison (Roman) *see Lex Rhodia de Iactu*
Rhodian Sea-Law (Byzantine) *see Nomos Rhodion Nautikos*
Rocco, Francesco   15, 65
Rome   56
Rossano, Giuseppe   179
Ruota (Florentine court)   32, 65, 72, 93

Sapientza   147
Schmitthoff, Clive   9
Sea loan
  As 'archaic' instrument   3
  As part of multi-faceted risk-management strategy   3, 154, 172, 179, 182, 186
  Attraction for ship-owners   10, 158, 178–9, 186
  Definition   3
  English terminology   170–1
  Extensive use in early modern Tuscany   157, 183
  In emergency   82, 100, 174
  In Genoa   171, 173
  Insuring of   168
  Interaction with GA   154, 157, 168–80, 179, 183, 186
  Italian terminology   170–1
Sea protest
  And bribes   100
  And the pre-jettison consultation   92–3
  And the shipmaster's liability   89 91, 94
  Between norms and practice   100, 102
  Consolato   80
  Definition   80
  Difficulty in falsifying   106, 110
  Fees   113
  In the case of the *Alice and Francis*   123, 132–5
  Mention of 'universal benefit'   98
  Testimoniale e domanda
    Creation   81, 88–9, 138–9
    Including valuation of property   88, 136
  Witnesses   81, 109
Seale, Gisberto   140
Second Anglo-Dutch War   160

Sephardic Jews   25, 27
Serristori, Antonio   129
Sgazzi, Virgilio Andrea   105
Shiltons, Isack   136
Ship of state   3
Shipwreck   47, 53, 58–61, *see also* And unseaworthiness *under* General Average (GA)
Sicily   147
Sidney, Humphrey   140
Slavery   27, 105, 116
Spain   55–6, 63, 129–30, 147, 181
Stracca, Benvenuto   41
Suez canal   9, 184, 188, 190
Summary procedure   42–4

Targa, Carlo   15, 65–8, 92–3, 102, 178, 185
Tétouan   96, 103
Third Anglo-Dutch War   167
Tiezzi, Ludovico   138
Titio, Agapito   39–40
Titio, Lorenzo   39
Toleration   22
Transaction costs   189, 191
Trapani   180
Tripoli (Libya)   180
Tuscany
  Economic strategy   124
  Lack of GA legislation or reform   34, 46
  Neutrality   27
  Suitability as site for study of historical risk management   17–18, 20
  Variety of maritime capitalism   121, 149
  See also Florence
  See also Livorno

Ulbaldini, Luigi   37
United Nations Inter-Agency Standing Committee   184

Valencia   147
Van Glins, Taco   182
Van Weltrusen, Guglielmo   86
Vancouver   188
Varieties of maritime capitalism   121, 149
Venice
  Differences with Livorno   16, 30, 148
  Political economy   16, 43, 148
  Statuta et Ordinamenta Super Navibus   54

Use of summary procedure   43, 148

War of Devolution   181
Weskett, John   172
Weytsen, Quentin   15, 64, 66, 72
Whincop, Thomas   136

Xie Ming   190

York-Antwerp Rules *see under* Average

Zante   93, 147
Zucchetti, Lorenzo   40

Printed in the United States
by Baker & Taylor Publisher Services